CLARENDON LATER ANCIENT PHILOSOPHERS

Series editors: Jonathan Barnes, University of Geneva
and A. A. Long, University of California, Berkeley

SEXTUS EMPIRICUS

AGAINST THE ETHICISTS

SEXTUS EMPIRICUS

AGAINST THE ETHICISTS

(ADVERSUS MATHEMATICOS XI)

Translation, Commentary,
and Introduction by

RICHARD BETT

CLARENDON PRESS · OXFORD

This book has been printed digitally and produced in a standard specification
in order to ensure its continuing availability

OXFORD
UNIVERSITY PRESS

Great Clarendon Street, Oxford OX2 6DP

Oxford University Press is a department of the University of Oxford.
It furthers the University's objective of excellence in research, scholarship,
and education by publishing worldwide in

Oxford New York

Auckland Cape Town Dar es Salaam Hong Kong Karachi
Kuala Lumpur Madrid Melbourne Mexico City Nairobi
New Delhi Shanghai Taipei Toronto
With offices in
Argentina Austria Brazil Chile Czech Republic France Greece
Guatemala Hungary Italy Japan South Korea Poland Portugal
Singapore Switzerland Thailand Turkey Ukraine Vietnam

Oxford is a registered trade mark of Oxford University Press
in the UK and in certain other countries

Published in the United States
by Oxford University Press Inc., New York

© Richard Bett 1997

The moral rights of the author have been asserted

Database right Oxford University Press (maker)

Reprinted 2007

ISBN 978-0-19-825097-5

PREFACE

Sextus Empiricus' *Against the Ethicists* has had a bad press—when it has been noticed at all. Ancient scepticism has in recent years become the subject of much scholarly energy; but *Against the Ethicists* has benefited very little from this pleasing development. My hope is that the present volume will alter this state of affairs. *Against the Ethicists* is of special, and previously unrecognized, significance for its place both within the totality of Sextus' work and in the history of Pyrrhonian scepticism as a whole. At any rate, that is what I attempt to demonstrate.

The bulk of the work for this volume was conducted while I held a Junior Fellowship at the Center for Hellenic Studies, Washington, DC, in the academic year 1994–5. It has rightly been said that eulogies of the Center have become 'a literary *topos* in prefaces to books written by former Fellows' (Glucker 1978: 9). I have no intention of trying to improve on the genre; I will simply say, much as many others have said before, that the working conditions at the Center are fabulous, and that I will undoubtedly always remember the nine months there as a high point in my life, both professionally and personally. I thank the directors, Deborah Boedeker and Kurt Raaflaub, together with the Senior Fellows, for electing me, and I hope this volume will reassure them that my time as a Fellow was well spent. I also thank my colleagues during that year for discussions, on topics both large and small, from which the book has benefited; especially helpful were Istvan Bodnar, Don Morrison, Doug Olson, Ineke Sluiter, and above all Juha Sihvola, who read the Introduction at an early stage and subjected it to searching criticisms which importantly altered my approach for the better. In addition, I thank Steve White and Gail Fine for advice on points of detail; and my wife, Geraldine Henchy, for reading the translation at several stages, thus helping to ensure that it read, as much as possible, as English rather than as 'translationese'—and also for spotting the relevance of the painting mentioned in the Commentary on section 159. Finally, I thank the editors of the Clarendon Later Ancient Philosophers series, Tony Long and Jonathan Barnes, whose detailed comments saved me from a great many mistakes and pigheadednesses. I am not sure, and I should not be taken to imply, that any of these people agrees that *Against the Ethicists* should be read in the distinctive fashion I propose.

Two books bearing upon the subjects treated here appeared too late for me to take proper account of them. The first is the Italian translation of and commentary on *Against the Ethicists* by Emidio Spinelli (cited in the Bibliography as Spinelli 1995). Spinelli's interpretation of the work is in many ways very different from mine; his approach is also more heavily weighted towards the philological. For both reasons it seems to me that the two volumes will usefully complement one another. The temptation for me to engage in a sustained dialogue with Spinelli was strong, but the result would have been intolerable for almost any reader; I have contented myself with noting a very few of the detailed points that he includes and that I had missed. The other work is R. J. Hankinson's *The Sceptics* (London/New York, 1995). This too contains a great deal of material relevant to my concerns, and it would have been desirable to make mention of it in various places. However, this omission is mitigated by the fact that the single most relevant chapter, the one on Sextus' ethical scepticism, is based on an earlier article, to which I do refer numerous times (Hankinson 1994).

R.B.

Baltimore, December 1995

CONTENTS

LIST OF ABBREVIATIONS

DK   H. Diels and W. Kranz, *Die Fragmente der Vorsokratiker* (Berlin, 6th edn., 1951)

LS   A. Long and D. Sedley (eds.), *The Hellenistic Philosophers* (Cambridge, 1987). Citations are by volume and page number (when the reference is to the editors' discussion of a specific point), by section number (when the reference is to a general topic), or by section number plus letter, e.g. 68G (when the reference is to a specific ancient text).

LSJ   Liddell, Scott, and Jones, *Greek-English Lexicon* (Oxford, 9th edn., 1968)

SVF   H. von Arnim, *Stoicorum Veterum Fragmenta* (Leipzig, 1903–5). Citations are by fragment number in vols. I–II, by page number in vol. III.

Abbreviations for ancient authors, and the titles of ancient works, are given in the *index locorum*.

INTRODUCTION

I. Sextus Empiricus and the Pyrrhonist Tradition

Sextus Empiricus is the only Greek sceptic of whom we have complete books surviving. He was a doctor (*PH* II. 238, *M* I. 260), and probably, as his title suggests, a member of the Empiric school of medicine, as were several other Pyrrhonists.[1] In one troublesome passage (*PH* I. 236–41), he appears to argue that the views of the Methodic school are closer to his own brand of scepticism than are the views of the Empiric school. But we do not have to suppose that he is distancing himself from all forms of Empiricism; it may be a particular form of Empiricism, not shared by himself, which he is anxious to dissociate from scepticism.[2] Though he probably lived in the second century AD, his dates are not certain.[3] He refers to no contemporary events; and the latest definitely datable person he refers to is the emperor Tiberius (*PH* I. 84). His major philosophical opponents are the Stoics of the Hellenistic period; these philosophers lived centuries before his own time (whenever exactly that was), but one could not tell this from the way he writes about them.[4] He apparently views philosophical dogmatism (i.e. the advancing of positive theses) as needing to be combated regardless of the period in which it was expressed—hence the peculiar sense of isolation from time and place which one has in reading his works. Nothing else is known of his life; he may have lived and written in Rome, but this too is uncertain.[5]

Three of Sextus' works have survived entire or in part.[6] *Outlines of*

---

[1] DL IX. 116; [Galen], *Isagōgē* XIV. 683; and see the other texts in Deichgräber 1965: 40–1.

[2] On this, see Frede 1987a.

[3] See House 1980: 227–31, who argues that he could have lived anywhere 'from A.D. 100 to the first part of the third century' (231). A more precise dating—*fl.* 150–70—is argued for by Caizzi 1993: 328–30.

[4] Throughout the volume, therefore, 'the Stoics' will refer, unless otherwise specified, to the Hellenistic Greek Stoics rather than to the Roman Stoics (some of whom may have been his contemporaries).

[5] See House 1980: 231–4.

[6] He also refers to works called *Medical Treatises* (*M* VII. 202; cf. *M* I. 61) and *On the Soul* (*M* VI. 55, X. 284); neither has survived.

Pyrrhonism (hereafter referred to by the initials of the title in Greek, *PH*) is in three books; the first expounds the sceptical outlook in general terms, while the other two address the views of non-sceptical philosophers in the three areas of philosophy standard in the Hellenistic period—logic, physics, and ethics. The section on ethics occupies the final portion of Book III (168–279). Covering much the same material as *PH* II–III, but at greater length, are two books *Against the Logicians*, two books *Against the Physicists*, and one book *Against the Ethicists*.[7] It is clear that the work to which these five books originally belonged is incomplete; the beginning of the first book of *Against the Logicians* refers back to a just-completed general treatment of scepticism (i.e. the analogue of *PH* I) which has not survived.[8] A strong case has been made that this work was ten books long—that is, that the lost, general portion of the work occupied five books;[9] if so, the size of the general portion, relative to the corresponding part of *PH*, must have been considerably greater than in the case of the five books which have survived (unless each of the general books was much shorter). In any case, Sextus refers to this entire work by the title *Sceptical Treatises* (*Skeptika Hupomnēmata*—*M* I. 29 (26), II. 106, VI. 52; cf. DL IX. 116).[10] We also have a third work, which has survived complete in six books, each of them attacking some specialized field; in order, the fields are grammar, rhetoric, geometry, arithmetic, astrology, and music. The subject-matter of this work is thus quite distinct from that of the other two, and it contains relatively few passages having close parallels with sections of the other works. In the manuscripts this work and the incomplete work are erroneously grouped together as a single work, at the head of which appears the title *Against the Learned* (*Pros Mathēmatikous*). This title was clearly intended to apply only to the six books on specialized fields—this is clear from the first sentence of the first book and the final sentence of the sixth—but the practice has persisted of referring to *Against the Logicians* by the abbreviated title *M* VII–VIII, to *Against the Physicists* by *M* IX–X, and to *Against the Ethicists* by *M* XI; though potentially misleading, this traditional nomenclature is convenient, and I shall follow it.

It has usually been supposed that *PH* is the earliest of the three works, followed by *M* VII–XI and then *M* I–VI. We know from back-references that *M* VII–XI preceded *M* I–VI (*M* I. 35, III. 116); but the position of

---

[7] These are the titles now standardly given to these books; they do not appear in the manuscripts. See the note on the title at the beginning of the Commentary.

[8] See Janáček 1963.   [9] See Blomqvist 1974.

[10] That this is the work referred to in these passages is shown by Blomqvist 1974.

PH cannot be determined so straightforwardly. I shall argue that close comparison of the parallel passages in *PH* III and *M* XI supports the view that *PH* is *later* than *M* VII–XI (see sect. IV below; Comm., *passim*; and Appendix A); I shall also suggest—though here the evidence is not so compelling—that *PH* is later than *M* I–VI (see Comm., ch. VII, with Appendix A).

Sextus stands near the end of a long tradition of thought which he calls 'Pyrrhonian' (*PH* I. 7). As he says, the name derives from Pyrrho of Elis, a shadowy figure who lived probably around 360–270 BC. Pyrrho wrote nothing, and most of what we know about him comes directly or indirectly from his biographer and disciple Timon of Phlius, whose work itself survives only in fragments.[11] It is debatable to what extent Pyrrho's outlook resembled any which is expressed in Sextus' works, and Sextus himself seems to be unsure on this question; *PH* I. 7 is very non-committal about the appropriateness of the term 'Pyrrhonian'. But Pyrrho does seem to have arrived at some form of mistrust of the way the world is presented to us both in ordinary experience and in philosophical or scientific theory; and he appears, as a result of this attitude, to have achieved an extraordinary level of tranquillity and indifference to circumstances. Both points—and, just as significantly, the nature of the connection between them—can reasonably be understood as anticipating the outlook of the later movement that took its name from him.[12]

Pyrrho did not found a school; after Timon and a few other immediate followers, his outlook ceased to have any adherents.[13] It is, however, possible that Pyrrho had some influence on the sceptical movement begun in the Academy by Arcesilaus (*c*.315–240 BC).[14] But in the first century BC a certain Aenesidemus of Cnossos started a new philosophical movement which explicitly claimed Pyrrho as its inspiration. It has standardly been assumed, on the basis of the passage of Photius which is our most detailed source of information about Aenesidemus (*Bibl.* 169b18– 170b35), that he started as a member of the Academy, founding his new movement as a reaction against his own former colleagues; but serious

[11] On Timon and the centrality of his evidence concerning Pyrrho, see Long 1978c.

[12] I argue in Bett 1994a that Pyrrho's outlook was substantially different from that of Sextus—yet not so different as to make incomprehensible his adoption as a figure-head by the later Pyrrhonists. (See also Bett 1994d: sect. IV.) For a different view, see Annas 1993: 203–5, Annas and Barnes 1994: pp. ix–x.

[13] The unbroken succession of Pyrrhonists listed by DL at IX. 115–16 is suspect; see Glucker 1978: 351–4, Caizzi 1992a: 177–9.

[14] For contrasting views on this, see Sedley 1983, Caizzi 1986.

doubt has recently been cast on this interpretation of the passage.[15] Nevertheless, the passage does make clear that Aenesidemus compared the Academy, and especially its representatives in his own day, unfavourably with his own Pyrrhonist outlook; unlike the Academy, he claimed to be really consistent in his radical policy of 'determining nothing', and to have achieved happiness as a result. We shall consider the character of his views later on (sect. III). It is doubtful whether Aenesidemus, any more than Pyrrho himself, can be said to have founded a Pyrrhonist 'school' in any formal sense. But we know the names of numerous later Pyrrhonists besides Sextus; for our purposes, the most important is Agrippa (DL IX. 88; cf. 106), the compiler of the Five Modes, which present in schematic form a style of arguing very prominent in Sextus' writings. We do not hear of any Pyrrhonists later than Sextus' pupil Saturninus (DL IX. 116). That was not, however, the end of Pyrrhonism's influence on the history of philosophy; for the rediscovery of Sextus' writings in the sixteenth century greatly affected the direction taken by philosophy in the early modern period and beyond. But that is another story.[16]

II. The Distinctive Character of *Against the Ethicists*

Against the Ethicists (*M* XI) consists of two rather different parts. The first part (1–167, or chs. I–V—I shall label this part A) begins with a good deal of preliminary discussion about the fundamental concepts in ethics—the good, the bad, and, to a lesser extent, the indifferent[17] (1–41, chs. I–II). There follows an extended argument to the effect that nothing is good or bad (42–109, ch. III), then a discussion (by far the longest on this topic in Sextus) of how and why the sceptic is better off than the non-sceptic (110–67, chs. IV–V). Part A clearly forms a single, continuous argument. Following this is a discussion of whether there is any such thing as a 'skill relating to life' (*technē peri ton bion*), and whether, if there is, it can be taught (168–256, chs. VI–VII—this I shall label part B). There is little in common between the subject-matters of part B and part A, and there are virtually no cross-references between the two parts.

[15] See Caizzi 1992*a*.

[16] For preliminary orientation on this vast topic, see Schmitt 1983, Popkin 1979. On the obscurity of Sextus in the medieval period (despite the existence of a Latin translation), see Porro 1994.

[17] We shall see that *M* XI vacillates as to whether to include the indifferent in the discussion; for a possible explanation of this, see Comm. on 90–5, end.

These points, coupled with the ungainly manner in which part B is
attached to part A (see 168 with Comm.), as well as the abrupt manner
in which part B, and then the book as a whole, conclude (see 257 with
Comm.), suggest that the two parts did not originally belong together—
that Sextus has brought together materials from two disparate sources.[18]
(We shall return to the matter of Sextus' heavy reliance on earlier sources.)
This is perhaps confirmed—though here the matter is more speculative
—by the fact that part B employs certain forms of argument which are
quite distinct from those employed in part A, and which may be associated with a different phase in the history of Pyrrhonism. It is even
arguable that part A and part B are on a significant point inconsistent
with one another (see Comm. on 216–18). Because part A occupies the
majority of the book, and is philosophically more significant than part B,
the general discussion of *M* XI in this section will focus largely on part
A; we shall return in the next section to ask whether the interpretation
I am about to offer can be said to apply to part B as well.

M XI has received relatively little attention (and that little attention
has been devoted almost exclusively to part A). Those few who have
written about it have tended either to ignore or to dismiss as a bad
confusion the distinctive character of the view it promotes. Either it has
been claimed or assumed that *M* XI's position is essentially no different
from that of the better-known *PH* (though perhaps expressed more
obscurely or ineptly);[19] or *M* XI has been regarded as deviating from *PH*,
but misguidedly and in contravention of the basic attitudes of Pyrrhonian
scepticism.[20] Both interpretations, I shall argue, are mistaken. *M* XI is
indeed expressing a different view from *PH* (and particularly the ethical
section of *PH* III), but this is not in itself grounds for criticism; there is
no reason why *M* XI should be obliged to conform to the canons of *PH*.[21]
M XI's distinctive view is consistent in its own terms, and can be legitimately understood as a variety of scepticism. This is not to deny that
M XI contains a large number of bad arguments. But the interest and
the coherence of its basic outlook are not thereby fatally flawed. These
verdicts will, of course, be argued for in the Commentary; but it is worth
sketching in advance the interpretation which will be pursued.

[18] My language here assumes that each of part A and part B are drawing, at any rate for
the most part, on a *single* source. On the plausibility of this, see second paragraph of
Appendix B.
[19] See McPherran 1990, Hankinson 1994, Annas 1993: ch. 17, Nussbaum 1994: ch. 8.
[20] See Striker 1983, Annas and Barnes 1985: ch. 13, Annas 1986, Striker 1990a.
[21] For this reason it is hazardous to use *PH* as evidence for the character of the views
expressed in *M* XI, and I have avoided this practice wherever possible.

The crucial difference between the two works has to do with their reactions to the claim, to which any constructive ethical theorist in antiquity would have been committed, that certain things are good by nature and certain other things bad by nature. The policy of *PH* III is to suspend judgement about whether anything is by nature good or by nature bad (see esp. 235). This is just what one would expect from the programmatic remarks at the beginning of *PH* I (8–10; cf. 28); quite generally, the sceptic is said to suspend judgement about the real nature of things, because of the 'equal force' (*isostheneia*) of the opposing considerations bearing upon any given topic. By contrast, *M* XI argues for the conclusion that *nothing* is by nature either good or bad (see 68–95 with Comm.). The sceptic is portrayed as someone who *accepts* this conclusion, not (as *PH* and standard accounts of ancient scepticism as a whole would suggest) as someone who balances this conclusion with the positive conclusions of the non-sceptics, or 'dogmatists', in order to produce suspension of judgement about the topic. The sceptic is also said to be willing to assert claims to the effect that things are good or bad *relatively speaking*—good or bad *for certain persons*, or *in certain circumstances*; these, then, apparently do not qualify as claims about the natures of the things in question. Both the denial that anything is good or bad by nature and the relativizing of all assertions to the effect that things are good or bad are taken to be vital to the attainment of the sceptic's tranquil attitude (see 118, 130, 140 with Comm.); the dogmatists are in trouble on both counts, and so are perpetually tormented.

Why do relativized assertions about the goodness or badness of things not count as assertions about the natures of those things? The answer is that, in order for anything to be *by nature* good or bad, it must be good or bad *for everyone*, not just good for some people and not for others; and it must be good or bad *in all circumstances*, not just in some circumstances. The first part of this is stated at 69–71; the second part is a relatively easy extension of the first, and is clearly presupposed when the relativized assertions are mentioned (see Comm. on 118, point 2).[22] The central idea is that for something to be *by nature* F is for it to be *intrinsically*, and hence *invariably*, F—i.e. F regardless of its relations to any particular persons or events; so anything which is good or bad only sometimes or for some people is *thereby* not good or bad by nature. I refer to this as 'the Universality Requirement'. Now, as stated so far, this

---

[22] The second part is also presupposed in the arguments to the effect that nothing is by nature good or bad (68–95)—at least, if my discussion of the workings of the more controversial Recognition Requirement is on the right lines; I shall return to this issue shortly.

requirement would have been widely accepted in ancient philosophy. A partial exception is Aristotle; for him, things which are true by nature are true not invariably, but 'always or for the most part'.[23] But the Universality Requirement (again, strictly in the form just stated) is accepted without question by, for example, Polystratus, an Epicurean of the third century BC, whose view is in other ways diametrically opposed to that of Sextus (*De Contemptu* 23, 26–25, 15 = LS 7D1–3).

What is more controversial (and this is the main point of contention with a view like Polystratus') is that Sextus equates what is the case *by nature* with what is *really* the case.[24] That is, in order for something to qualify as *in reality* good or bad, on Sextus' understanding, it must be good or bad intrinsically (and hence, again, invariably). Thus the relativized assertions mentioned above not only fall outside the category of assertions about the nature of things; they also fall outside the category of assertions about how things really are. For Polystratus, the fact that something is, for example, good only in certain circumstances does not at all disqualify it from *really being* good in those circumstances; for Sextus, this fact does disqualify it from really being good in any circumstances— indeed, the very phrase 'really being good in circumstances C' is for him a *contradictio in adjecto*. It has sometimes been alleged that Polystratus clearly exhibits the fact that a view like the one expressed here by Sextus is mistaken. This is not so; the two simply have *different* conceptions of what it is for something to be *really* good (or really F, for any F), and Polystratus makes no attempt to address Sextus' conception. Moreover, Sextus' conception, though not uncontroversial (and though certainly unfamiliar to us today), is by no means without other adherents in the ancient world; the most celebrated is Plato, but the Stoics would also agree with Sextus at least as regards good and bad.[25]

Nothing is really, or by nature, either good or bad, then, in that nothing is invariably either good or bad. But how does Sextus think he is entitled to conclude that nothing is invariably either good or bad? The

---

[23] Aristotle actually denies the requirement in the context of the question as to what, if anything, is by nature just (*NE* V. 7); however, the denial is said to hold only up to a point (1134b27–8), and precisely how, or when, something may be naturally just while also admitting of variation is not explained. On this passage, see Gauthier and Jolif 1958–9: ii. 391–6, esp. 394–5.

[24] For Sextus' use of 'by nature' (*phusei*) interchangeably in this context with 'in reality' (*tais alētheiais*) or 'really' (*ontōs, tōi onti*), see 68–78 with Comm.

[25] On the relations between the views of Sextus and Polystratus, and on the agreement between Sextus, Plato, and the Stoics, see Bett 1994c: sect. III, also Comm., point 2 on 118.

principal argument for this conclusion (68–78) exploits the prevalence of disagreement about ethical matters. But the way in which the fact of disagreement is used is again different from what one would expect from *PH*. The argument does not turn, as standardly in *PH*, on the claim that this disagreement is unresolvable (in fact, *no* argument in part A of *M* XI turns on this claim); instead, the mere *existence* of disagreement about the goodness of something is taken to be sufficient to show that that thing is not in reality good. How can this be so?

This move depends on another assumption, which I shall call the Recognition Requirement. This is the assumption that, in order for something really to be good (or bad) for a certain person, that thing must be *recognized as* good (or bad) by that person; there can be no such thing as a good which is not regarded as such by the person for whom it is a good. In this context, as typically in Greek ethics, 'good' is understood as equivalent to 'beneficial' (see 69–71 with Comm.); the Recognition Requirement thus amounts to saying that only those things which the beneficiary recognizes as benefits really are benefits. This requirement is not actually stated in the argument at 68–78, or anywhere else. But it is clearly presupposed in another argument (see 90–5 with Comm.), and the main argument becomes much more comprehensible if it is operating there as well (see 68–78 with Comm.).

What exactly does the Recognition Requirement consist in? Since it is never stated explicitly, this is not entirely obvious. The most promising version of such a requirement would seem to be something of the following kind: in order for one truly to be benefited (or harmed) at time *t*, one must recognize at some time—not necessarily at *t* itself, but perhaps only later, with hindsight or after careful reflection—that one is or was benefited (or harmed) at *t*. This does not imply that whatever one regards as a benefit thereby automatically is a benefit; recognizing that one has been benefited is here said to be a *necessary* condition of having been benefited, not a sufficient condition. The requirement, stated thus, relies merely on the idea that a purported benefit of which one has no cognizance whatever (i.e. no awareness whatever of its being a benefit) cannot really be a benefit. This idea is certainly not beyond question; but its intuitive appeal (to many people, at least) seems hard to deny.[26]

It might be objected that the 'benefits' (or 'harms') to which Sextus actually refers are not individual instances of benefit, as assumed in the

[26] For more on these points, including some possible counter-examples to the requirement, see Bett 1994c: 134–6.

previous paragraph's formulation, but generic goods or benefits such as virtue, pleasure, and health (and generic harms such as folly). In view of this, it might be held, the Recognition Requirement, if it really was operating behind the scenes in Sextus' arguments, would need a different formulation along the following lines: a purported generic good, G, cannot genuinely be such as to benefit unless it is recognized as being such as to benefit. But this is much less plausible; one would need considerably more than the intuitively appealing idea referred to just above in order to make it convincing. In fact, however, the previous paragraph's formulation of the Recognition Requirement is sufficient for Sextus' needs. In order for some purported generic good—pleasure, for example—to be beneficial by nature, it must, according to the Universality Requirement, be *invariably* beneficial; that is, it must be beneficial for everyone who experiences it, and on every instance of its occurrence.[27] But now, if people disagree about whether pleasure is beneficial, that shows, at minimum, that there are some instances of pleasure which are not regarded as beneficial by those who experience them. And, by the Recognition Requirement as formulated in the previous paragraph, that means that there are at least some instances of pleasure which *are not* beneficial. Hence pleasure will fail to qualify as good or beneficial by nature. The Recognition Requirement, in its weaker and more plausible formulation, does therefore yield Sextus' general conclusion that nothing is by nature good, given the two main points which figure explicitly in the argument at 68–78: (1) the Universality Requirement and (2) the premiss concerning the existence of disagreement—namely, that there is *nothing* which everyone in fact agrees in regarding as good. It is not clear that Sextus has provided adequate support for this latter premiss (see Comm. on 68–78); but he certainly thinks that he has done so (71, 78).

It is natural enough for a sceptic to have been drawn to the Recognition Requirement. What it denies, as we have seen, is that there can be benefits (or harms) to oneself of which one remains entirely unaware; only someone with a full-fledged theory of the real natures of things, underlying our experience of them, could, Sextus might say, be attracted to such a notion. Of course, the dogmatists who hold such theories are, by the same token, unlikely to be immediately swayed by arguments which depend on the Recognition Requirement. But it is not clear that making converts of the dogmatists is high on Sextus' list of priorities in

---

[27] See above, n. 22 and accompanying text.

this work;[28] laying out a satisfying and defensible position of his own may be all he is really concerned to do.

Sextus argues, then, that nothing is by nature either good or bad, but that things may be good or bad relatively to persons and/or to circumstances; he also argues that acceptance of these conclusions makes the sceptic's life greatly preferable to that of the dogmatist. Anyone familiar with the scepticism of *PH* may well react that this position is not (at least in the ancient sense) a form of *scepticism* at all; instead of suspension of judgement, it may be said, we have Sextus committing himself to numerous weighty assertions. Yet *M* XI also says repeatedly that the sceptic—i.e. the person who accepts the assertions just mentioned— 'suspends judgement about everything' (144, 160, 168; cf. 111, 150, 152). Unless Sextus is very confused indeed, it follows that the notion of suspension of judgement is also to be understood in *M* XI in a different, weaker sense than that in which it occurs in *PH*. And such a sense is not too difficult to discern. The sceptic of *M* XI suspends judgement in the sense that he neither issues nor commits himself to any assertions claiming to specify the nature of things. The denial that anything is by nature good or bad does not violate suspension of judgement in this sense (to deny that X is by nature good is not to assert that X is by nature *other than* good); nor do the assertions of relativized claims about good and bad (because, given the Universality Requirement, relativized claims are not claims about the nature of things).[29] (For more on this matter, see Comm. on 118, point 4.) Whether Sextus succeeds in maintaining even this weaker form of suspension of judgement throughout the book is not so clear; we shall see a number of cases where he at least appears to violate it. But the danger of violating one's suspension of judgement is ever present for ancient sceptics in general; it is certainly not peculiar to *M* XI, and there is nothing about *M* XI's distinctive position which makes it especially liable to violate its own distinctive form of suspension of judgement.

If I am right, the vexed question of the *scope* of Sextus' scepticism— whether it applies merely to philosophical doctrines, or to ordinary,

---

[28] *PH* III. 280–1 paints the sceptics as benefactors of humanity (including the misguided dogmatists). But there is nothing in *M* VII–XI corresponding to this; nor is there anything in the sceptical outlook in general that would require it.

[29] Nor do the Universality Requirement and the Recognition Requirement themselves. Meta-level claims about what it is for something to be by nature good, or about necessary conditions for a thing's being good, are not themselves statements to the effect that some particular object or set of objects is by nature good, or by nature of any other character.

everyday beliefs and assertions as well[30]—can be answered for *M* XI as
follows. The sceptic refrains from any attempt to specify the nature of
things. This allows him to make some assertions which would normally
be considered philosophical, such as 'Nothing is by nature good'; and it
allows him to make any kinds of ordinary assertions *except* those which
purport to specify (or which presuppose statements purporting to specify)
the nature of things. There is room for discussion about exactly which
types of assertions this would allow and which types it would exclude.
But it would allow all assertions that are relativized to persons or to
circumstances (potentially a huge class); and it would exclude assertions
such as that pain is by nature bad. According to Sextus at *PH* I. 30,
ordinary people, no less than philosophers, hold certain beliefs of this
latter kind, and this seems plausible enough. *M* XI, like *PH*, is committed to avoiding such beliefs—and the fact that ordinary people as well as
philosophers hold them makes no difference to this. Sextus is not, however, as clear about the last point as one might have liked (see 163–6 with
Comm.) In any case, it looks as if *M* XI allows us to retain at least
substantial portions of our normal habits of thought and speech. The
question whether it is possible to live and act as a sceptic—again, a
serious one for many ancient sceptics, including perhaps Sextus himself
in other works—is therefore not especially pressing for the scepticism of
M XI. (On these points, see further Comm. on 118, point 5.)

III. Relations with Aenesidemus and Relations between Part A and Part B

This reading of *M* XI may be considered suspect, because it places *M* XI
so far outside the mainstream of Pyrrhonist thinking. But this reaction
assumes that there was a single outlook to which Pyrrhonists of all
periods—beginning with Aenesidemus, or perhaps even with Pyrrho
himself—subscribed, and that that outlook is represented by *PH*. Such
an assumption is perhaps understandable; *PH* I purports to tell us in
general terms how the Pyrrhonian sceptic proceeds, and it is the only
text by a Pyrrhonian sceptic to do so. But there is in fact no reason to
assume that *PH* I speaks for the entire Pyrrhonist tradition; it may
simply tell us Sextus' own version of Pyrrhonism, as adhered to at the

---

[30] This has received much discussion in recent years, though without special attention
to *M* XI. See Burnyeat 1983, 1984, Barnes 1982*a*, Frede 1984, 1987*b*, Brennan 1994.

time of writing. Moreover, some of the (admittedly scarce) evidence on
Pyrrhonism from sources independent of Sextus suggests that M XI, as
I propose to interpret it, was not so anomalous after all.

A passage from Photius, the ninth-century Patriarch of Constantin-
ople, offers a brief summary of the contents of Aenesidemus' *Purrōniōn
Logoi*, '*Pyrrhonist Discourses*' (169b18–170b35 = LS 71C, 72L). In this
passage we are told that Aenesidemus argued for the non-existence of
several kinds of things; according to Aenesidemus, Photius says, there
are *no such things as* signs (i.e. reliable indicators of the character of
things that are not currently, or not ever, apparent in experience) (170b12–
14), no such things as causes (170b17–20), and no such thing as the
ethical 'end' (*telos*) (170b31–5). Immediately after the second of these
three points, Photius says that Aenesidemus launched the *same* kind of
attack on good and bad (170b22–5). Then again, we are told that
Aenesidemus avoided stating anything 'unambiguously' (*anamphibolōs*,
169b40, 170a29), and criticized the Academics for doing so. What this
turns out to mean is that he refused to make *unqualified* assertions, but
instead would say of a thing that it is sometimes F, sometimes not-F, or
F for this person, but not-F for that person (170a2–3, 5–6, 9–11).[31] We
know very little of the details of Aenesidemus' arguments on these matters;[32] but the similarities between this position and Sextus' position in
M XI, as I have claimed it to be, should be clear. Like Sextus in M XI,
Aenesidemus is represented as arguing for negative existential conclusions, not as promoting suspension of judgement about the existence or
the nature of the things under discussion; like Sextus in M XI, he is
apparently prepared to issue certain assertions—viz. those which are
subject to relativizing qualifications.[33]

There is a complication regarding the topic of the good and the bad.
Though Photius does say that Aenesidemus subjected the good and the
bad to the same kind of critique as was applied to other items—and this
statement is immediately preceded by a mention of an argument against
the *existence* of a certain type of entity—he also says that Aenesidemus

[31] Also 'no more F than not-F'. This is not relevant to our present concerns, but it will
be of some interest later; see 118 with Comm., point 3.

[32] However, Sextus does tell us something about Aenesidemus' arguments against the
existence of signs (M VIII. 215, 234). The first of these references is to the fourth book of
Aenesidemus' *Pyrrhonist Discourses*; this accords with Photius' account of the contents of
the books (*Bibl.* 170b12–17). Sextus also tells us that, according to Aenesidemus, appearances which are not uniform for everyone are false (M VIII. 8), which looks like an
application of the Universality Requirement.

[33] For a much more detailed discussion of Aenesidemus, with which my account is in
general agreement, see Woodruff 1988. But Woodruff does not mention any correspondence with M XI.

'clos[ed] these things [i.e. the good and the bad] off from our apprehension and knowledge' (170b25–6). More generally, too, Photius' report alternates between attributing to Aenesidemus views of the form 'X cannot be known' and views of the form 'X does not exist', and appears to feel no difficulty in doing so. *M* XI's conclusion, as I portrayed it above, was not epistemological; it was that *nothing is* in reality good or bad, not that good and bad cannot be known. However, Photius is not the only source for Pyrrhonist views to alternate between claims of these types. The summary of Pyrrhonism by Diogenes Laertius in his life of Pyrrho (IX. 74–101) exhibits precisely the same kind of alternation. He frequently says that the Pyrrhonists 'did away with' (*anēiroun*) certain items, or argued that certain items do not exist (IX. 90, 94, 96, 97, 98, 99, 100, 101); but he also sometimes says that they argued that certain items (even the very *same* items) cannot be known (IX. 95, 101).[34] And this is true, in particular, of good and bad. Diogenes introduces a Pyrrhonist argument about good and bad by saying that it shows that there is nothing by nature good or bad, and this is clearly borne out by the following sentences; but he concludes the same argument by saying that that which is good by nature cannot be known (IX. 101). In addition, as we shall see, the main argument in *M* XI itself shifts unexpectedly from talk of our *grasping*, or failing to grasp, that which is really good to talk of the *non-existence* of anything really good (see 68–78 with Comm.).

So although Photius does not specifically tell us that Aenesidemus argued that there are no such things as good or bad, it is entirely possible that he did so; for other evidence, including *M* XI itself, suggests that there was at least some version of Pyrrhonism in which the conclusion Photius does attribute to Aenesidemus—the conclusion that good and bad cannot be apprehended by us—would be understood as closely connected with the conclusion that nothing is in reality good or bad. The two conclusions are not incompatible,[35] and it is not too hard to see a

---

[34] I am here revising the view expressed in Bett 1994c, n. 54, that claims of the latter type are a sign of Diogenes' confusion. Though neither Photius nor Diogenes can be considered among the most desirable witnesses to have to rely on concerning questions of philosophical detail, on the current issue each provides some confirmation for the other (since they are certainly independent of one another).

[35] As is implied by Barnes 1992: 4255 in connection with this issue in DL. Note that the epistemological claim is not that it cannot be known, of any given object, whether or not it is by nature good; that certainly *would* be incompatible with the claim that there is nothing by nature good. The negative epistemological claims in both the Photius passage and the DL passage are all of the form 'X cannot be known' or 'X is closed off from our apprehension and knowledge', rather than of the form 'It cannot be known whether or not X exists' (or '. . . whether or not X is F' or '. . . whether or not X is a Y'). See also the following note.

connection between them. If a thing does not exist, it certainly cannot be known about; if Aenesidemus argued successfully that nothing is in reality good or bad, he would have succeeded in 'closing these things off from our apprehension and knowledge'.[36] A similar connection seems to be implicitly drawn in *M* XI (see Comm. on 68–78).

There is evidence, then, of a Pyrrhonist outlook, associated in the first instance with Aenesidemus, which seems to have been much closer to *M* XI as I will be interpreting it than is the outlook represented (officially, at least[37]) by *PH*. This is true even if attributing to Aenesidemus an argument that nothing is by nature good or bad, on the basis of Photius, is over-bold. At any rate, assertions of various types of relative state-ments are attributed to Aenesidemus, as well as arguments for the non-existence of various other items; there is also an argument that nothing is by nature good or bad belonging to a summary, that of Diogenes Laertius, which overlaps considerably with Photius' summary of Aenesidemus' book, and which is associated with the Pyrrhonist school in general. Moreover, Diogenes' summary of this argument has a great deal in common with Sextus' main argument to the same conclusion (see Appendix A on *M* XI. 68–78, *PH* III. 179–82, DL IX. 101); so much in common, indeed, that they must be drawing on the same source. So if, as I wish to argue, *M* XI is offering a form of Pyrrhonism significantly different from that of *PH*, it does not follow that it is an anomaly in the Pyrrhonist tradition. On the contrary, there are strands of that tradition, about which we know only indirectly and to a limited degree, with which *M* XI, as so interpreted, appears to fit quite happily. And those strands, since they originate with Aenesidemus, would seem to be earlier than the scepticism of *PH*. We shall come back to this point in the next section.

The above remarks are intended to apply primarily to part A of *M* XI. As noted above, there are reasons for thinking that part B originally came

---

[36] Suppose that some dogmatist claims to know, of certain things, that they are in reality good, and of certain other things that they are in reality bad. It would be an entirely reasonable rebuttal to say, 'No, you do not have any such knowledge, and nor does anyone else; for *there is nothing* in reality good or bad which could be the object of such knowledge'. I leave aside the standard problems of reference which arise in connection with non-existent items; I am relying on the intuitive and unanalysed thought, which would surely have been available to Aenesidemus or any other Pyrrhonist, that things which do not exist cannot be the objects of knowledge. In these terms, 'That which is by nature good cannot be known' can easily be seen as following from 'Nothing is by nature good'.

[37] This qualification is necessary because, as we shall see, *PH* III does not entirely succeed in maintaining consistency with this outlook; see sect. IV below.

from a different source. But does part B also propose a type of Pyrrhonism distinct from *PH* and closer to the type associated with Aenesidemus?

This question is not easy to answer, because part B is singularly reticent about the form of scepticism to which it belongs. It consists of a large number of arguments against the existence of a 'skill relating to life', such as the Stoics claimed to possess, and against its teachability even if it does exist; but it says nothing about suspension of judgement, or about what exactly a sceptic is entitled to say or think. (On this, see further Comm., introductory remarks to ch. VI.) There is one explicit back-reference to part A's arguments that nothing is by nature good; but this can readily be understood as an insertion by Sextus into a context in which such matters did not originally belong (see 185 with Comm.). Part B appears to be generally consistent with the Pyrrhonism of part A (216–18, the passage mentioned at the beginning of sect. II, is the only probable exception) (see Comm. on 171–3). However, it does not give the impression of having been designed so as to be uniquely suited to the Pyrrhonism of part A.

Besides, there is at least one feature of part B which, while not necessarily inconsistent with anything in part A, is plausibly associated with the Pyrrhonism not of Aenesidemus, but of the later sceptic Agrippa.[38] Unlike part A, part B does contain arguments from *unresolvable* disagreement, rather than from the mere existence of disagreement (see 173–7, 229, 230 with Comm.); and the Mode of Disagreement—where the kind of disagreement referred to clearly is unresolvable (*PH* I. 165, 170)—is one of Agrippa's Five Modes. There is also a circularity argument (183), and the Mode of Circularity was another of the Five Modes (however, this may have been imported from elsewhere in Sextus' own works—see Comm. ad loc.—rather than reproduced from the main source for part B). There is, then, some reason to think that Sextus' source for part B belonged to a different, and later, phase in the history of Pyrrhonism than his source for part A.[39] Still, given our ignorance of the detailed development of Pyrrhonism, this suggestion cannot be pushed very hard.

---

[38] While Diogenes gives the Five Modes under the name of Agrippa (IX. 88), Sextus says that they were developed by 'the later sceptics' (*PH* I. 164). In this context 'later' must at least mean 'later than the authors of the Ten Modes', which have just been covered; *PH* I. 36 says that the Ten Modes come from 'the older sceptics', but *M* VII. 345 calls them 'the Ten Modes of Aenesidemus', and DL IX. 87 and Aristocles in Eusebius, *Praep. evang.* XIV. 18. 11–12 make clear that Aenesidemus was at least among those who employed them. (The scepticism of Hankinson 1994, n. 2, on this point seems to me unjustified.)

[39] Why should we not say that Aenesidemus *is* the source for part A? For an apparent difficulty with this, see Comm. on 42.

IV. The Order of Composition of Sextus' Works

The similarity between the position adopted in *M* XI and views which appear to have been held by Aenesidemus is one of several reasons for thinking that *M* XI (and presumably the entire work of which it forms a part[40]) was composed before *PH*. For, as already suggested, the outlook of the ethical portion of *PH* is rather different from that of *M* XI. Instead of *denying* that anything is by nature good or bad, as does *M* XI, the ethical part of *PH* III does what the work as a whole, and the standard picture of Pyrrhonian scepticism, would lead one to expect: it *suspends judgement* on the question as to whether anything is by nature good or bad (*PH* III. 235; cf. 182). Again, there is no hint in *PH* III that the sceptic is willing to endorse statements about what is good or bad provided they are qualified by suitable relativities. Furthermore, *PH* III (182) does make use of an argument related to one of the Five Modes of Agrippa—an argument based on unresolvable disagreement about what is good—in the part corresponding to part A of *M* XI; as we saw, such arguments appear in *M* XI only in the possibly later part B. (In fact, the argument at *PH* III. 182 is closely related to an argument that appears in part B of *M* XI; see Appendix A on *M* XI. 173–7, *PH* III. 182, 239.) *PH* III, then, does not show the same links with Aenesidemus as are shown by *M* XI; rather, it fits comfortably into a version of Pyrrhonism which is different and, since Aenesidemus was the *initiator* of the revived Pyrrhonist tradition, presumably later. Other things being equal, it is reasonable to suppose that the order of Sextus' own works reflects the order of the versions of Pyrrhonism with which each conforms.

The picture just outlined is a slight oversimplification. *PH* III (179–90) does include versions of the same arguments to the effect that nothing is by nature good or bad as appear in *M* XI (68–95). However, in *PH* III Sextus attempts, not wholly successfully, to integrate these arguments into the distinct version of Pyrrhonism officially adopted in that book (see Appendix A on *M* XI. 68–78, *PH* III. 179–82, and on *M* XI. 79–89, *PH* III. 183–90). That he should attempt to do so is only to be expected if these arguments were a central part of his original ethical treatise, *M* XI; and that he should not entirely succeed is only to be expected if, by the time of composing *PH*, he was no longer willing to subscribe to the variety of Pyrrhonism, associated with Aenesidemus, in

---

[40] We shall return to the question of the relations between *M* XI and *M* VII–X in sect. V.

which those arguments were originally embedded. The presence of these arguments in *PH* III therefore in no way undermines the supposition that *M* XI preceded it; the arguments, in fact, are most easily understood as an awkward relic of the attitude towards ethics to which Sextus first adhered, but which he then gave up in favour of something more modern.

The connection between *M* XI and Aenesidemus, together with the lack of connection (other than the 'awkward relic' just mentioned) between the ethical portion of *PH* III and Aenesidemus, is not the only reason for thinking that *M* XI is the earlier of the two. There are two other reasons. One has to do with further differences of detail between the two books; the other has to do with the degree of resemblance between *M* XI and certain passages of DL, compared with the degree of resemblance between the corresponding passages of *PH* III and the same passages of DL.

As already observed, the ethical portion of *PH* III covers much of the same ground as *M* XI. While *PH* III is of course generally briefer, it includes many of the same arguments; even though, as just noted, the eventual use to which these arguments are put differs significantly in the two works, the arguments themselves are often stated in very similar terms, sometimes in almost identical language. Quite clearly, one of them is a revised version of the other (as is true in general for *PH* II–III and *M* VII–XI); the later work adds some material, subtracts some material, and makes numerous alterations in the material which they both share. The differences in the shared material have to do with the character of the reasoning, the language, and the organization; they are sometimes slight, sometimes substantial. Now, on these points it is *PH* III which again and again seems to be the superior version—by standards which, it is fair to assume, Sextus would have shared with ourselves (and which are independent of the broader philosophical differences between the two works). Very often, *PH* III expresses itself clearly and aptly where *M* XI is obscure or clumsy;[41] very often, *PH* III omits dubious argumentation or replaces it with something more cogent;[42] and very often the order of the topics in *PH* III is smoother or more appropriate than it is

---

[41] This fact has itself been obscured in certain cases, where editors have altered the text of *M* XI on the basis of parallels with *PH* III. The text is thereby in some sense improved— that is, it reads more easily. But it is question-begging to assume that the 'improved' text is a more *authentic* text of *M* XI. With two partial exceptions (see Comm., textual point (c) on 188–96), I have avoided all textual changes of this type; cf. n. 21.

[42] Hence the many bad arguments in *M* XI, though philosophically frustrating, are of considerable interest with respect to the order of composition of Sextus' works—and thus, in broader terms, with respect to the history of Pyrrhonism.

in *M* XI. Collectively, these comparisons suggest very strongly that *PH* III is the improved, revised version. The indications are not, of course, all equally strong. But sometimes the support for the hypothesis that *PH* III is the later work is extremely powerful; that is, it is sometimes extremely difficult to believe that Sextus would have *first* composed a certain passage in *PH* III and *then* altered it to the version that appears in *M* XI—the reverse hypothesis is overwhelmingly more plausible. At present, of course, my argument has the status of bare assertion; it will be developed piecemeal in the Commentary and in Appendix A. But the general picture that will emerge is as I have described.

There are admittedly a few cases where *PH* III clearly suffers from problems from which *M* XI is exempt. I have already mentioned the arguments that nothing is by nature good or bad; there is one other case besides these (62–6; cf. *PH* III. 191–2). But now, all these cases involve *entire* extended passages which do not fit quite properly into their contexts in *PH* III, but which clearly do fit where they are situated in *M* XI. And this phenomenon is perfectly consistent with the hypothesis that *M* XI came first. Indeed, it supports that hypothesis; as suggested above, the awkwardnesses of the *PH* III versions are best explained by supposing that these passages originally belonged in *M* XI, and are being used in contexts in *PH* III for which they were *not* originally designed, and to which they are not entirely suited. The ways in which *PH* III is superior to *M* XI have to do, on the other hand, with the *details* of the arguments in question—the organization of the steps, the clarity with which they are presented, and so on; the work that is superior in *these* respects would be expected to be the later one.

The final argument for the priority of *M* XI is based on a comparison between Sextus and Diogenes. As has been suggested a number of times, Sextus' writings rely heavily on earlier sources. The main reason for believing this is the very close correspondences which can often be observed between Sextus and other authors, particularly Diogenes. Sometimes the language is identical or extremely similar, sometimes only the argumentative structure; but the extent of the correspondences compels us to suppose either that one author is drawing on the other or that both are drawing on earlier sources now lost to us. Diogenes postdates Sextus by at least a generation (IX. 116), so if one is copying the other, it would have to be Diogenes who is copying Sextus. Yet this seems to be ruled out by the equally noticeable differences between the two. There is a great deal in Diogenes' summary of Pyrrhonism (IX. 74–101) which he did not get from Sextus. But he could hardly have invented this material;

and in any case, Diogenes, unlike Sextus, is quite explicit that he is
following earlier sources, and his life of Pyrrho is no exception. It follows
that Diogenes and Sextus must both be following earlier sources.[43] And
since the passages in Sextus with which there is some parallel in DL
range across every book in *PH* and *M* VII–XI,[44] we may assume that his
heavy indebtedness to earlier sources was more or less uniform throughout his writings.[45]

Now, there are just two passages in Diogenes' life of Pyrrho which
have parallels in *M* XI and the ethical portion of *PH* III; DL IX. 101
parallels *M* XI. 69–78 and *PH* III. 179–82, and a portion of DL IX. 100
parallels *M* XI. 219–23 and *PH* III. 256–8 (and also *M* I. 10–14).[46] In
both cases, it is the passage of *M* XI which is much closer to the DL
passage; the passage of *PH* III is clearly related to both the other two, but
there are far fewer detailed similarities between it and the DL passage.
Clearly, then, *M* XI is sticking closer to the common source or sources[47]
than is *PH* III.[48] And the obvious explanation—indeed, as far as I can
see, the only reasonable one—is that Sextus composed *M* XI *first*, with
the common source or sources in front of him, and *then* revised (and
contracted) *M* XI, without further direct consultation of the common

[43] This argument is indebted to Barnes 1992, which also supplies the details to support
it. In this connection, Barnes considers the work of Karel Janáček, which I discuss in
Appendix C; however, his case does not *depend* on Janáček's studies, about which he has
some reservations.
[44] See the list of parallels in Appendix II of Barnes 1992; and note that 'M VIII 263–
446' (under 'Against Criteria') should read 'M VII 263–446'.
[45] I have not mentioned *M* I–VI in this connection. But Janáček has conducted a similar
comparison between *M* V and Hippolytus' *Refutation of all Heresies*, arguing that these
texts are also based on a lost earlier source. See Janáček 1964 (and note that the appearance
of Marcovich 1986, a text of Hippolytus substantially different from the one used by
Janáček, does not seem to affect his arguments in this article). There is no reason to doubt
that Sextus' dependence on sources was just as great in the rest of *M* I–VI.
[46] There is also DL IX. 108, which parallels *M* XI. 162–6 but nothing in *PH* (see
Comm. on 162–7). Though not exactly comparable with the two other cases just mentioned, this arguably points in the same direction as they do. (The passage just before this
has a remoter parallel in *PH* I, but this affords no basis for comparison; on parallels
between DL and *PH* I, see n. 48 below.)
[47] 'Common source or sources' is vague; for an attempt at greater precision, see
Appendix B.
[48] I think this pattern applies to the whole of *M* VII–XI versus *PH*: i.e. there is no case
where a passage of DL is paralleled both by a passage from *M* VII–XI and by one from *PH*
and where the similarity between *PH* and DL is clearly stronger than that between *M* VII–
XI and DL; there are some cases where the parallels are more or less equally strong, and
several others where the parallels between *M* VII–XI and DL are clearly stronger. And the
only cases where a passage from DL is paralleled by a passage from *PH*, but not by any
passage from *M* VII–XI, are those where the *PH* passage is from Book I—i.e. where the
corresponding portion of the longer work is lost. (Again, see Appendix II of Barnes 1992.)

source or sources, so as to produce the ethical portion of *PH* III. (For the details, see Appendix A on *M* XI. 68–78, etc. and on *M* XI. 219–23, etc.)

M XI, then, belongs to Sextus' earliest work, and *PH* III revises it. This is of interest not just as the solution to a philological puzzle; it should also affect our opinions about Sextus' development and about the history of Pyrrhonism as a whole. As noted in section I, the standard view runs counter to the one just proposed; on the supposed stylistic basis for this standard view, see further Appendix C.

V. *M* VII–X and their Relation to *M* XI

If we assume that *M* VII–XI and *PH* were each composed in their entirety at separate periods of Sextus' life—and stylistic analysis makes this, at least, highly plausible (see Appendix C)—then it follows from my arguments that *M* VII–XI as a whole precedes *PH* as a whole. Now, it looks as if this picture may be supported by considerations bearing upon the parts of *M* VII–XI other than *M* XI itself. However, the relation between *M* XI and *M* VII–X is itself far from straightforward.

I have already recorded my impression that *M* VII–XI is always at least as close as, and often much closer than, *PH* is to the parallel passages of DL. If this is correct, then the reasoning presented in section IV supports the conclusion that *M* VII–XI is the earlier work.[49] Then again, several scholars have recently noted cases where the treatment of a certain issue or the organization of a certain discussion in *PH* seems superior to its counterpart in *M* VII–X.[50] The possible consequences for the order of Sextus' works have not generally been followed up;[51] but if these judgements are well founded, they may be taken as pointing in the same direction as my comparisons between *M* XI and the ethical section of *PH* III. Finally, *M* VII–XI in general conveys a greater initial impression of what is usually called 'negative dogmatism' than does *PH*;[52] that

---

[49] Just one example: DL IX. 97–9 (on causes) has a number of close parallels in *M* IX. 207–17, but none in *PH*—even though *PH* contains a discussion of causes (III. 13–29).

[50] See Long 1978*a*: 38 (cf. Long 1978*b*: 298), Barnes 1990*a*: 2677, Brunschwig 1988: 151–2, 157–8, Ebert 1987, *passim* (and, in more detail, Ebert 1991).

[51] Brunschwig 1988, n. 9, is an exception. Ebert 1987 argues that, on the subject of signs, the *source* for *PH* is later than the source for *M*, and is revising the material that served as the source for *M*. It seems much simpler to suppose that *PH* itself is a revised version of *M*; the only thing preventing Ebert from drawing this conclusion seems to be his assumption that Sextus, throughout his career, was *nothing but* a 'compiler' (100).

[52] See Janáček 1972: 54–60, 132.

is, whereas *PH* is generally careful to emphasize that the sceptic suspends judgement about the reality of the items under consideration, it
often looks in *M* VII–XI as if the sceptic is arguing for their unreality.
Among other things, the word *anairein*, 'do away with'—that is, 'argue
for the non-existence of'—is used in *M* VII–XI to refer to the sceptic's
activity with regard to these items; compare DL, where, as noted in
section III above, the same word is used in the same type of context. In
PH, by contrast, the word is never used in this context. Now, 'doing
away with' the things believed in by the dogmatists seemed to be central
to the version of Pyrrhonism associated with Aenesidemus, to which *M*
XI seemed to owe a great deal; if *M* VII–XI in general speaks of the
sceptics 'doing away with' such things, whereas *PH* never does, then *M*
VII–XI in general would appear to be closer than *PH* to Aenesidemus'
version of Pyrrhonism.[53] Obviously, these matters deserve detailed examination of a kind which I am in a position to conduct only on *M* XI
and the ethical section of *PH* III. My purpose is merely to suggest that,
corresponding to each one of the three types of reasons I have offered for
accepting the priority of *M* XI, there is some promising line of thought
applying to *M* VII–XI as a whole.

Even in advance of detailed examination, however, this account is
subject to difficulties. For though it is true that *M* VII–X talks of the
sceptic 'doing away with' things, it is also true that Sextus frequently
tells us in *M* VII–X that the result of his arguments is that one is forced
to *suspend judgement about* the existence of the things being discussed (*M*
VII. 443, VIII. 298, 476–7, IX. 137, 191–2, X. 168); and this, of course,
is the same result as is standard in *PH*. In view of these repeated remind-
ers, it is reasonable to assume that, even when he sounds as if he is
asserting negative conclusions—for example, 'Body is nothing' (*M* IX.
439), 'Motion is nothing' (*M* X. 168), 'Number is nothing' (*M* X. 309),
'Nothing either comes into being or perishes' (*M* X. 350)—he really
means these conclusions to be juxtaposed with the positive arguments of
the dogmatists, so as to yield suspension of judgement on whether the
things in question really exist. This does not mean that my sketch of an
argument, based on the greater appearance of negative dogmatism in *M*
VII–X than in *PH*, was simply mistaken. The mention of the sceptic's
'doing away with' things in *M* VII–X, but not in *PH*, and other differences of the same type, may be accounted for by supposing that the

[53] Note again that Sextus cites Aenesidemus in the course of his arguments against the
existence of signs (*M* VIII. 215, 234)—cf. n. 32 above.

adaptation of arguments which had their origin in the phase of Pyrrhonism dominated by Aenesidemus to a later and different form of Pyrrhonism is less complete, and is conducted more clumsily, in *M* VII–X than it is in *PH*; and this surely speaks in favour of the priority of *M* VII–X. But the use of the notion of suspension of judgement in *M* VII–X does make the relation between *M* VII–X and *M* XI problematic. In *M* XI, as we have seen, Sextus does *not* suspend judgement about the existence of anything by nature good and bad, but *denies* its existence. We can tell this not just because he repeatedly *says* 'There is nothing by nature good or bad' (as *M* VII–X show, that by itself would be inconclusive), but because this is central to his whole argument; the *acceptance* of this conclusion is argued to be crucial to the sceptic's attainment of happiness.

How are we to account for this apparent inconsistency between the approaches of two parts of the same work? One possibility is simply that Sextus was working with sources from different periods in the logical and physical parts of his treatise, on the one hand, and in the ethical part, on the other; perhaps the adaptation of material originally at home in Aenesidemus' form of Pyrrhonism to a later form had already begun in the sources for *M* VII–X, but not in the sources for *M* XI (or at any rate, in the source for part A of *M* XI). This cannot be definitively ruled out—although it attributes to Sextus a depressingly low level of autonomy over, or comprehension of, what he was doing in this work. After all, we have seen that something like this may be true *within* *M* XI (but here the practice is much more defensible, since there are very few actual incompatibilities between the two parts). However, there is a more interesting possibility.

In section II above I suggested that, with respect to good and bad, Sextus accepted what I called the Recognition Requirement: nothing can *really be* good or bad unless it is *recognized* as good or bad by the person or persons for whom it is good or bad. I also suggested (and this is not peculiar to good and bad or to Sextus) that *M* XI is not prepared to count anything as being really, or by nature, a certain way unless it is that way universally, or without qualification (the Universality Requirement). It follows from these two requirements that there is a conclusive test for something's not being by nature good or bad—a test which requires no hazardous speculation about the character of some true reality underlying the appearances of things. Provided there is not universal recognition that a certain type of thing—for example, pleasure—is good or bad, that type of thing *cannot* be *by nature* good or bad. So that if one has, as Sextus thinks he has, reason to believe that there is *nothing* universally agreed to be good or bad, one has reason to believe that nothing is by nature good or bad; again, although this is a conclusion having to do with the natures of things, it is a conclusion which does not require our having access to some underlying reality, but merely access to people's stated opinions. It is therefore a conclusion about which there is no need for a sceptic to suspend judgement.[54] The situation is arguably very different for the subject-matter of logic (in which is included prominently what we would call epistemology) and physics; one is in no position to make definite judgements for or against the existence of the entities with which these subjects deal (such as criteria of truth, signs, gods, or causes) *unless* one is prepared to commit oneself to assertions about the 'non-evident' properties of things.[55] This, at least, is how Sextus himself appears to regard the matter in *M* VII–X; there is no hint of anything resembling the Recognition Requirement in these books. It follows that, for the sceptic, there is no room for anything other than suspension of judgement in the areas of logic and physics. If all this is correct—and again, I propose it as no more than a tentative suggestion—there is no conflict between the seemingly very different strategies of *M* VII–X and *M* XI; the difference is due to the fact that, according to Sextus at this time (perhaps according to his immediate source or sources as well), certain questions about good and bad admit of far more definite answers than any questions in the areas of logic and physics. In the case of good and bad, therefore, the negative conclusions, stemming probably from Aenesidemus, do not need to be modified; in the case of other parts of philosophy, they do.

VI. Concluding Remarks

It may seem perverse to have spent so much time in this introduction dealing with the order of composition of Sextus' works and the relations

---

[54] Unless, of course, the Recognition Requirement itself is something about which a fully consistent sceptic will suspend judgement. I suggested earlier (see n. 29) that this need not be true for the scepticism of *M* XI. But it is probably true for the scepticism of *PH*. This may have been one factor helping to produce the rather different approach in the ethical portion of *PH* III, where the existence of anything by nature good or bad is treated in the same way as the existence of the entities treated in logic and physics.

[55] Here, too, it makes good sense for a sceptic to regard the disagreements among the dogmatists as *unresolvable* (because their resolution would require access to the 'non-evident'), rather than (as in the ethical case) as admitting of the definite judgement that all the disagreeing parties are wrong.

between different works and between different parts of the same work. But if my interpretation of *M* XI is correct, its place among Sextus' writings is intimately connected with much of what is interesting about it. If I am right, *M* XI is, to a greater extent than any other book of Sextus, a relic of a phase in the history of Pyrrhonism far earlier than Sextus himself; if so, this gives it a historical interest that exceeds the interest of many of the specific arguments it contains (many of which are, as I have already suggested, very faulty). But the question of whether this is so cannot be separated from questions about how *M* XI is related to the rest of Sextus' output, both chronologically and in terms of philosophical stance.

Besides representing a distinctive variety of Pyrrhonism, *M* XI is of interest, like most of Sextus' writings, because it preserves important information about the dogmatic philosophies to which he was opposed. Here it is Stoic ethics on which Sextus is most informative, though there are data to be gleaned on numerous other philosophers and schools as well. In the case of Stoic ethics, we frequently have reports from Diogenes and/or from Stobaeus on the same topics; but even where this is so, Sextus' reports are sometimes fuller than those of the other two, and sometimes give the impression of being more precise or more accurate.

However, *M* XI contains less of such doxographical material than many other books of Sextus, and especially than *M* VII–X; and this has led to a further complaint about Sextus' attitude towards ethics, and about this book in particular. Sextus, it has recently been said, 'was clearly something of a philistine about ethics'; rather than offering detailed expositions of the dogmatic ethical theories to which he was opposed, 'he relies on a few very general arguments purporting to show that ethics, as a discipline, is in bad shape', and the assumption that this is all that is needed is 'condescending' and 'misguided'.[56]

But this accusation does not take into account the special character of *M* XI's argument. If Sextus' aim were to induce suspension of judgement about what is, or whether anything is, really good or bad, then it would indeed be necessary for him to assemble, as comprehensively as possible, the various theories about this topic, and to show that they are all equally convincing or unconvincing. But again, this is not what Sextus is trying to do in *M* XI. Instead, he is arguing for the conclusion that *nothing is* by nature good or bad; and his argument does not depend on the equipollence of competing views, but merely on the *fact* of disagreement. If he is right that nothing is by nature good or bad, and if the belief that

---

[56] Annas 1993: 356–7; cf. Annas 1992*b*: 206–7.

this is so is what the sceptic needs for the attainment of happiness, Sextus simply has no reason to go into great detail about the theories based on the false belief that there *are* things by nature good or bad.[57]

All of this is not to deny that Sextus may at times be over-hasty, foolish, or even intellectually dishonest. It would be pointless to pretend that his is a philosophical mind on a par with Plato's or Aristotle's. But for all its shortcomings, *M* XI should not be dismissed as frivolous or as fundamentally misguided. Relative to the evidence at our disposal, the form of Pyrrhonism which it offers is unusual; but for that very reason, its historical and philosophical interest is substantial. It deserves to be approached on its own terms, and it deserves more serious consideration than it has usually received.

VII. A Note on the Translation and Commentary

The translation follows the text of Mutschmann (1914), except where indicated in the Commentary. In general, philosophically significant terms have been translated with the same English terms throughout; my decisions on these matters, including on when to deviate from strict consistency, are explained in the Commentary, as are other difficult points of translation. Ancient Greek texts did not employ paragraphs, so the division into paragraphs is a matter for decision by modern editors. My divisions correspond in most cases to those of Mutschmann, and this is no surprise; the breaks in the train of thought in Sextus are usually well marked and obvious. The division into chapters is present in the ancient manuscripts, and is generally assumed to be the work of Sextus himself. Quotations from the translation in the Commentary sometimes contain emphasis which is not present in the translation itself; this is for the purpose of pin-pointing the specific issue under discussion.

The Commentary is divided into sections, each covering a stage of the discussion that can conveniently be taken in as a unity; in most cases the sections cover single paragraphs in the translation, in some cases two or more paragraphs. Each section is preceded by a heading; collectively the headings provide a somewhat more detailed guide to the structure of the book than is offered by the ancient chapter titles. The Commentary addresses four main types of issues: (a) matters of text and translation and other points of philological detail, such as the origins of the numerous quotations from Homer, tragedy, and comedy; (b) the doctrines of

---

[57] See also Comm., introductory remarks to ch. VI, on Sextus' preference for general arguments.

other philosophers summarized by Sextus—their significance and Sextus' reliability in reporting them; (c) Sextus' own arguments—their precise character, their connections with other ideas of Sextus or other sceptically inclined philosophers, and their cogency; and (d) the similarities and differences between passages of *M* XI and corresponding passages of *PH* III (as well as, in ch. VII, passages of *M* I), and their significance for the order of composition of Sextus' works. Usually issues of type (a) (if any—occasionally there are none) are addressed separately at the beginning of each section; sometimes, however, questions of translation cannot be considered in isolation from the arguments in which the terms in question occur. Those philological points of type (a) which will, in my judgement, be of interest only to those with knowledge of the Greek language and/or training in Classics are enclosed within square brackets. Discussion of issues of types (b) and (c), which occupies most of the space in each section, follows the order in which the issues themselves occur in the text. Issues of type (d) are included in the Commentary only when they contribute, in my judgement, to the elucidation of the passage of *M* XI under discussion. Further discussion of issues of type (d), in cases where there is no such direct contribution, occurs in Appendix A (where occasionally passages of DL, as well as of Sextus, are considered).

The amount of attention devoted to textual matters, under issues of type (a), may seem rather large, given the main orientation of this volume and this series. There are two reasons for this focus. First, though the edition I am following is the last critical edition of the text (with few exceptions, Bury 1936 follows the text of Bekker 1842), it is by no means a recent edition. Second, I suspect that the majority of English-speaking students of Sextus will be primarily acquainted with the Greek text of Sextus as it appears in the Loeb edition of Bury; I have therefore noted not only deviations from the text of Mutschmann, but also (at least where the effect on the sense is significant) differences between Mutschmann and Bury. My textual proposals are based on considerations of sense, rather than on inspection of the manuscripts; it is worth noting, however, that many of my changes are in the direction of greater fidelity to the manuscripts, as Mutschmann reports them, than is exhibited by Mutschmann's own text. Few of my changes consist in a choice of one manuscript reading over another, and few of the textual points in the Commentary centre around disagreements among the manuscripts. Where this is true, however, I do not identify the manuscripts individually, but speak simply of 'most MSS', 'some MSS', etc.; the interested reader is referred for the details to Mutschmann's apparatus criticus.

TRANSLATION

AGAINST THE ETHICISTS

(1) We have previously gone over the difficulties brought by the sceptics against the logical and physical parts of philosophy; it is left for us to append in addition those which can be brought against the ethical part. For in this way each of us, by taking on the perfect—that is, sceptical—disposition, will live, as Timon says

> With the greatest ease and tranquillity
> Always heedless and uniformly unmoved
> Paying no attention to the whirls of sweet-voiced wisdom.

(2) Now, since almost all have agreed in supposing that ethical enquiry is about the differentiation of good things and bad things (as indeed Socrates, the man who seems first to have initiated it, declared as most in need of investigation 'Whatever bad and good is wrought within the halls'), we too will need right at the start to examine the distinction in these things.

I. What is the Principal Distinction among Matters concerning Life

(3) All those philosophers who seem to proceed by methodical exposition of basic principles—and most conspicuously of all, those of the Old Academy and the Peripatetics, and also the Stoics—are accustomed to make a division, saying that, of existing things, some are good, some bad, and some between these, which they also call indifferent. (4) Xenocrates, however, somewhat unusually compared with the others, and using the singular forms, said, 'All that exists either is good or is bad or neither is good nor is bad.' (5) And while the rest of the philosophers accepted such a division without proof, he thought it proper also to include a proof, as follows. If there is anything which is distinct from good things and from bad things and from things which are neither good nor bad, that thing either is good or it is not good. And if it is good, it will be one of the three; but if it is not good, either it is bad or it neither is bad nor

is good. But if it is bad, it will be one of the three, while if it neither is good nor is bad, it will again be one of the three. Thus everything that exists either is good or is bad or neither is good nor is bad. (6) But in effect he too accepted the division without proof, since the argument employed to construct it is none other than the division itself; hence, if the proof contains its warrant within itself, the division, being no different from the proof, will also be warranted by itself.

(7) But still, although it seems to be agreed upon by everyone that the distinction among existing things is threefold, some people none the less think up specious arguments, agreeing that the distinction among existing things is something like this, but sophistically pressing objections against the division laid out. And we will be clear about this if we start again from a little further back.

(8) The technical writers say that a definition differs from a universal merely in its syntax, and is the same in meaning. And reasonably so; for the person who says 'A human being is a rational mortal animal' says the same thing as far as meaning is concerned—though it is verbally different—as one who says 'If something is a human being, that thing is a rational mortal animal'. (9) And that this is the case is clear from the fact that not only does the universal encompass the particulars, but the definition also extends to all the specific instances of the object being defined—for example, the definition of a human being to all specific human beings, and that of a horse to all horses. Besides, if a single false instance is subsumed under it, each one becomes unsound—both the universal and the definition. (10) But now, just as these two are verbally different but identical in meaning, so too the perfect division, they say, differs from the universal in syntax while having a universal meaning. For one who divides in this way—'Of human beings some are Greeks, some barbarians'—says something equivalent to 'If some are human beings, those are either Greeks or barbarians'. For if any human being is found who is neither Greek nor barbarian, necessarily the division is unsound and the universal is false. (11) Hence, too, the statement 'Of existing things, some are good, some bad, some between these' is in meaning, according to Chrysippus, a universal of the following kind: 'If some things are existents, those things either are good or are bad or are indifferent.' Such a universal, however, is false, since a false instance is subsumed under it. (12) For they say that when two things exist, one good, the other bad, or one good, the other indifferent, or bad and indifferent, then 'This one among existing things is good' is true, but 'These are good' is false; for *they* are not good, but one is good, the other bad. (13)

And 'These things are bad' is again false; for *they* are not bad, but one of them is. Similarly in the case of indifferents; for 'These things are indifferent' is false, just as is 'These things are good' (or '. . . bad'). (14) The objection, then, is something like this; but it does not seem to touch Xenocrates, because he does not use the plural forms, and thereby have his division falsified in the case of reference to things of different kinds.

(15) Others have objected in the following way. Every sound division, they say, is a cutting of a genus into its proximate species, and for this reason a division like this is unsound: 'Of human beings some are Greeks, some Egyptians, some Persians, and some Indians.' For one of the proximate species does not have the corresponding proximate species paired with it, but the subspecies of this; it should say this: 'Of human beings some are Greeks, some barbarians,' and then, by subdivision, 'Of barbarians some are Egyptians, some Persians, and some Indians.' (16) Therefore, in the case of the division of existing things, too, since whichever things are good and bad make a difference to us, while whichever are between the good and bad are indifferent to us, the division should not have been as it is, but rather as follows: 'Of existing things some are indifferent, others make a difference, and of the things which make a difference some are good, others bad.' (17) For such a division is like the one which says 'Of human beings some are Greeks, some barbarians, and of the barbarians some are Egyptians, some Persians, and some Indians.' But the one which has been set out was like one of this type: 'Of human beings some are Greeks, some Egyptians, some Persians, and some Indians.'

But it is not necessary now to prolong discussion of these objections; (18) however, it will perhaps be fitting to clarify the following point in advance. The word 'is' means two things; one is 'actually is'—as when we say at present 'It is day' instead of 'It actually is day'—and the other is 'appears'—as when some mathematicians often tend to say that the distance between two stars *is* a cubit, meaning something equivalent to 'appears so but is not necessarily actually so' (for perhaps it is actually 100 stades, but it appears to be a cubit on account of the height, i.e. on account of the distance from the eye). (19) Since, then, the component 'is' is ambiguous, when we say in sceptical fashion 'Of existing things some are good, some bad, and some between these', we insert the 'are' as indicative not of what is actually the case but of appearance. For we have plenty of disputes with the dogmatists about the nature and existence of the things which are good and bad and neither; (20) but we have the habit of calling each of these things good or bad or indifferent according to their appearance—as Timon too seems to indicate in his *Images*, when he says

> For indeed I shall tell, as it appears to me to be,
> A word of truth, having a correct standard,
> That the nature of the divine and the good is everlasting,
> From which arises a most even-tempered life for a man.

So, now that the division mentioned above is in place in the manner indicated, let us see what we ought to think about the items within it, beginning our argument with the conception of them.

II. What are the Good, the Bad, and the Indifferent

(21) Since the controversy in which we are engaged with the dogmatists on this topic has as its most important element the distinguishing of good things and bad things, it will be fitting before all else to fix the conception of these things; for, according to the wise Epicurus, it is not possible either to investigate or to raise difficulties without a preconception. (22) Well then, the Stoics, holding on to the 'common conceptions' (so to speak), define the good in this way: 'Good is benefit or not other than benefit,' by 'benefit' meaning virtue and excellent action, and by 'not other than benefit' the excellent human being and the friend. (23) For virtue, being the ruling part in a certain state, and excellent action, being a certain activity in accordance with virtue, are, precisely, benefit; while the excellent human being and the friend, also being themselves among the good things, could not be said to be either benefit or other than benefit, for the following reason. (24) Parts, say the sons of the Stoics, are neither the same as wholes nor of a different kind from wholes; for example, the hand is not the same as the whole human being (for the hand is not a whole human being), nor is it other than the whole (for it is *together with* the hand that the whole human being is conceived as a human being). Since virtue, then, is a part of both the excellent human being and the friend, and parts are neither the same as wholes nor other than wholes, the excellent human being and the friend are called 'not other than benefit'. So that every good is encompassed by the definition, whether it is simply a benefit, or whether it is not other than benefit. (25) Then, as a consequence, they say that good is spoken of in three ways, and they indicate each of the significations, in turn, in accordance with its own application. In one way, they say, that by which or

from which one may be benefited is called good—which is the most primary good, namely virtue; for from this, as from a spring, all benefit naturally arises. (26) In another way, it is that in connection with which it results that one is benefited; in this way not only the virtues will be called goods, but also the actions in accordance with them, since in connection with these, too, it results that one is benefited. (27) In the third and final way, that which is able to be of benefit is called good, this definition encompassing the virtues and virtuous actions and friends and excellent human beings, gods, and good daimons. (28) For this reason, the claim that 'good' is used in multiple ways is not meant equivalently both by Plato and Xenocrates and by the Stoics. For the former, when they say that the Form is called good in one way and that which partakes of the Form in another way, put forward significations which are widely divergent from one another, and indeed have nothing in common, as we observe in the case of the word 'dog'. (29) For just as by this is signified a 'case' under which falls the barking animal, and also one under which falls the aquatic animal, and besides these the philosopher, as well as the star, and such 'cases' have nothing in common, nor is the first contained in the second, nor the second in the third, so in calling good the Form and that which partakes of the Form there is an exposition of significations, but of ones which are separate and exhibit no inclusion of one in the other. (30) The older philosophers, then, as I said earlier, held some such position. But the Stoics maintain that, in the case of the term 'good', the second signification contains the first, and the third contains the first two. There have also been those who say that good is that which is to be chosen for its own sake. And others hold the following: 'Good is that which contributes to happiness', while others say 'that which is capable of making happiness complete'. And happiness, as Zeno and Cleanthes and Chrysippus defined it, is a good flow of life.

Anyhow, in general terms the definition of the good is like this. (31) But while good is spoken of in three ways, some are in the habit of directing further attention straight to the definition of the first signification (according to which it was stated 'Good is that by which or from which one may be benefited'), on the grounds that if good truly is that from which one may be benefited, one must say that only generic virtue is good (for from this alone does being benefited result), and that each of the specific virtues, such as practical wisdom, moderation, and the rest, falls outside the definition. (32) For from none of these does being of benefit, pure and simple, result; rather, from practical wisdom comes being wise, not being of benefit more generally (for if being of benefit, pure and simple, should result, it will not be, determinately, practical wisdom, but generic virtue), and from moderation the predicate corresponding to it, being moderate, not the general one, being of benefit, and similarly in the remaining cases. (33) But those who are faced with this charge say this: When we say 'Good is that from which being benefited results', we are saying something equivalent to 'Good is that from which it results that one is benefited in respect of one of the things in one's life'. For in this way each of the specific virtues, too, will be a good, not as conferring being of benefit in general, but as providing that one is benefited in respect of one of the things in one's life; for example, being wise, in the case of practical wisdom, or being moderate, in the case of moderation. (34) But these people, wishing to defend themselves and escape the previous charge, have become involved in another one. For if the statement is as follows: 'Good is that from which it results that one is benefited in respect of one of the things in one's life', generic virtue, though it is a good, will not fall under the definition; for from this it does *not* result that one is benefited in respect of one of the things in one's life (since in that case it will become one of the specific virtues), but simply that one is benefited.

(35) And other things, connected with the dogmatists' pedantry, tend to be said against such definitions. But for us it is sufficient to show that one who says that the good is that which is of benefit, or that which is to be chosen for its own sake, or that which contributes to happiness, or gives some such definition, does not inform us what good is but states its property. But one who states the property of the good does not show us the good itself. At any rate, everyone agrees without hesitation that the good is of benefit, and that it is to be chosen (which is why it is called 'good' (*agathon*)—that is, wonderful (*agaston*)), and that it is productive of happiness. (36) But if one asks the further question *what is* this thing which is of benefit and to be chosen for its own sake and productive of happiness, they will no longer be of the same mind, even though they previously agreed in calling it that which is of benefit and that which is to be chosen, but will be carried off into an interminable war, one person saying that it is virtue, another pleasure, another freedom from pain, another something different again. (37) But if it had indeed been shown, by means of the definitions stated above, what the good is, they would not be in conflict, as if the nature of the good was unknown. Therefore the definitions which have been laid out do not teach us what the good is, but the property of the good. Hence they are unsound not only in this respect, but also in so far as they aim for something impossible;

(38) for one who does not know some existing thing cannot recognize that thing's property either. For instance, if one says to a person who does not know what a horse is, 'A horse is an animal inclined to neigh', one does not teach that person what a horse is; for to the person who does not recognize the horse, neighing, which is a property of the horse, is also unknown. And if one puts forward, to a person who has not apprehended what an ox is, the statement 'An ox is an animal inclined to bellow', one does not exhibit the ox; for the person who does not know the latter likewise does not apprehend bellowing, which is a property of the ox. (39) Thus it is also idle and profitless to say to the person who is without a conception of the good that good is that which is to be chosen or that which benefits. For it is necessary first to learn the nature of the good itself, and then after that to understand that it benefits and that it is to be chosen and is productive of happiness. In the case where this nature is not known, definitions like these also do not teach us the thing which is being sought.

(40) For the sake of example, then, it will suffice to have said this about the notion of the good. And from this, I think, the technical points made about the bad by those who hold varying opinions are also clear. For bad is the opposite of the good; it is harm or not other than harm—harm when it takes the form of vice and the inferior action, not other than harm when it takes the form of the inferior human being and the enemy. (41) And between these—I mean, between the good and the bad—is that which is in neither state (which is also called indifferent). What is the force of these definitions, and what should be said against the definitions, can be learned from what has been said about the good. But now, with these things established at the outset, let us move on and enquire whether good and bad also really exist by nature in the way in which they are conceived.

III. Whether there are Good and Bad by Nature

(42) We argued above, then, that the dogmatists did not outline the conception of good and bad in a convincing fashion; but for the purpose of becoming more readily conversant with the arguments about its existence it is sufficient to say—as Aenesidemus, for one, used to say—that while all people think good that which attracts them, whatever it may be, the specific judgements which they have about it are in conflict. (43) And just as people agree (to take a random case) about the existence of

shapeliness of body, but are in dispute about the shapely and beautiful woman—the Ethiopian preferring the most snub-nosed and blackest, the Persian favouring the most aquiline and whitest, while someone else says that the woman who is intermediate with respect to both features and colouring is the most beautiful of all—(44) in the same way both ordinary people and philosophers think, in line with a common preconception, that there is such a thing as good and bad, and take good to be what attracts and benefits them, and bad what is in opposition to that, yet are at war with one another as far as specifics are concerned: 'For different men delight in different things', and, as Archilochus put it, 'One man's heart is warmed at one thing, one at another', given that one cherishes glory, another wealth, another well-being, and someone else pleasure. And it is the same story in the case of the philosophers. (45) For the Academics and the Peripatetics say that there are three types of goods, and that some have to do with the soul, some have to do with the body, and some are external to both soul and body; having to do with the soul are the virtues, having to do with the body are health and well-being and keenness of sensation and beauty and everything which is of a similar kind, and external to soul and body are wealth, country, parents, children, friends, and things like that. (46) The Stoics, on the other hand, also said that there are three types of goods, but not in the same way; for they said that some of them have to do with the soul, some are external, and some neither have to do with the soul nor are external, excluding, as not being goods, the type of goods having to do with the body. And they say that having to do with the soul are the virtues and excellent actions, external are the friend and the excellent human being and excellent children and parents and the like, and neither having to do with the soul nor external is the excellent human being in relation to himself. For it is not possible for him either to be external to himself or to belong to the soul; for he consists of soul and body. (47) But there are some who are so far from excluding the type of goods having to do with the body that they actually let the most primary good reside in them; those who are fond of the pleasures of the flesh are of this kind. And so that we may not seem to be dragging out the argument excessively, in presenting the case that people's judgement about good and bad is in disharmony and conflict, we will base our treatment on a single example, namely health, since we are rather well accustomed to discussion about this.

(48) Some, then, think that health is a good, others that it is not a good; and of those who suppose it to be a good, some have said that this is the greatest good, some that it is not the greatest good; and of those

who have said that it is not a good, some have said that it is a preferred
indifferent, others that it is an indifferent but not preferred. (49) So
then, that health is a good, indeed the primary good, no small number of
poets and authors, and generally all ordinary people, have maintained.
Simonides the lyric poet says that not even fine wisdom brings delight,
if one does not have glorious health; and Licymnius, after beginning with
these words:

> Bright-eyed mother, longed-for queen
> Of the most exalted holy throne of Apollo,
> Soft-smiling Health,

assigns to her what sort of exalted feature?

> What joy can come from wealth or children
> Or from the royal rule of a godlike man?
> Apart from you no one is happy.

(50) And Herophilus in his *Regimen* says that wisdom cannot manifest
itself and skill is non-evident and strength cannot compete and wealth is
useless and reason is powerless if health is missing. (51) This, then, is
what these people thought; but the Academics and the Peripatetics said
that it is a good, but not the primary good. For they supposed that each
of the goods must be assigned its own rank and value. Hence Crantor,
wishing to give us a clear picture of the matter being discussed, employed a most elegant parable. (52) If we conceive, he says, a theatre
common to all the Greeks, and that each of the goods is present at this
place, and is coming forward and competing for the first prize, we will be
led straight away to a conception of the difference among the goods. (53)
For first wealth will leap up and say, 'I, men of all Greece, providing
ornament to all people and clothes and shoes and every other enjoyment,
am needed by the sick and the healthy, and in peace I provide delights,
while in war I become the sinews of action.' (54) Then of course all the
Greeks, hearing these words, will unanimously order that the first prize
be given to wealth. But if, while wealth is already being proclaimed the
winner, pleasure appears,

> In whom is love, is desire, is intimacy,
> Allurement, which steals the sense even of shrewd thinkers,

(55) and taking a position in the middle says that it is just to declare *her*
the winner—

> For wealth is not steady, but lasts just a day;
> It blooms a short time and then flies away,

and it is pursued by people not for its own sake, but for the sake of the enjoyment and pleasure which result from it—then surely all the Greeks, supposing that this is exactly how the matter stands, will shout that pleasure must be crowned. (56) But as she too is about to carry off the prize, once health enters with her companion gods, and teaches that pleasure and wealth are no use in her absence—

> For what benefit is wealth to me when I am sick?
> I would rather live a painless life, from day to day and having little
> Than to be wealthy but diseased—

(57) then again all the Greeks, having heard her and having been informed that it is not possible for happiness to exist when bedridden and sick, will say that health wins. But though health is already victorious, once courage enters, with a great throng of warriors and heroes around her, and taking her position says (58) 'If I am not present, men of Greece, the possession of your goods passes to others, and your enemies would pray for you to have abundant supplies of all goods, presuming that they are going to conquer you'; then, having heard this, the Greeks will award the first prize to virtue, the second to health, the third to pleasure, and they will rank wealth last.

(59) So then, Crantor placed health in the second position, staying in line with the philosophers mentioned above; but the Stoics said that it is not a good but an indifferent. They think that the indifferent is spoken of in three ways: in one way it is that towards which there occurs neither impulse nor repulsion—for example, the fact that the number of stars or hairs on one's head is odd or even; (60) in another way it is that towards which impulse and repulsion do occur, but not more towards one thing than another, as in the case of two drachmas indistinguishable both in markings and in brightness, when one has to choose one of them; for there does occur an impulse towards choosing one of them, but not more towards one than the other. (61) They call indifferent in the third and final way that which contributes neither to happiness nor to unhappiness; in this signification they say that health and disease and all bodily things and most external things are indifferent, because they are conducive neither to happiness nor to unhappiness. For that which it is possible to use well and badly will be indifferent; virtue can always be used well, and vice badly, but health and things concerned with the body can

be used sometimes well and sometimes badly, hence they will be indifferent. (62) Now, of indifferents they say that some are preferred, some dispreferred, and some neither preferred nor dispreferred; and that preferred are things which have sufficient value, dispreferred are those which have sufficient disvalue, and neither preferred nor dispreferred is a thing such as extending or bending one's finger, and everything like that. (63) And among the preferred belong health and strength and beauty, wealth and glory and similar things, while among the dispreferred are disease and poverty and pain and things resembling them. (64) This is the Stoics' position; but Aristo of Chios said that health, and everything like it, is *not* a preferred indifferent. For to call it a preferred indifferent is equivalent to deeming it a good—the difference is almost solely in name. (65) For quite generally the indifferent things between virtue and vice have nothing to differentiate them, nor are some of them by nature preferred and some dispreferred, but in keeping with the circumstances, which differ with the times, neither do the things which are said to be preferred turn out to be invariably preferred, nor are the things which are said to be dispreferred necessarily dispreferred. (66) At any rate, if healthy people have to serve the tyrant and for this reason be destroyed, while the sick are exempted from this service and thereby also exempted from destruction, the sage will choose being sick on this occasion rather than being healthy. And thus neither is health invariably a thing preferred nor sickness a thing dispreferred. (67) As, then, in writing names we sometimes place some letters first and at other times others, suiting them to the different circumstances (D when we are writing the name of Dion, I when it is Ion, O when it is Orion), not because some letters are given precedence over others by nature, but because the situations require us to do this, so too in the things between virtue and vice there is no natural precedence of some over others, but rather a precedence according to circumstances.

(68) But now that from these remarks, and largely by way of examples, the preconception about good things and bad things, and indifferent things besides, has been shown to be in disharmony, it will next be necessary to get to grips with the things which have been said by the sceptics on the subject under discussion. (69) Well now, if there is anything by nature good, and there is anything by nature bad, this thing ought to be common to all and to be good or bad for everyone. For just as fire, being by nature warming, warms everyone and does not warm some but chill others, and in the same way as snow, which chills, does not chill some people but warm others, but chills everyone equally, so

that which is by nature good ought to be good for everyone, and not good for some but not good for others. (70) For this reason Plato too, in establishing that god is by nature good, argued from similar cases. For, he says, as it is a distinctive feature of hot to heat and it is a distinctive feature of cold to chill, so too it is a distinctive feature of good to do good; but the good, surely, is god; it is therefore a distinctive feature of god to do good. (71) So that if there is anything by nature good, this is good in relation to everyone, and if there is anything by nature bad, this is bad in relation to everyone. But nothing is good or bad in a way which is common to all, as we will establish; therefore there is nothing by nature good or bad. (72) For either everything which is thought good by someone is to be described as good in reality, or not everything. And everything is *not* to be so described; for if we call good everything which is thought good by anyone, then since the same thing is thought bad by one person and good by another, and by a different person is thought indifferent, we will be granting that the same thing is simultaneously good and bad and indifferent. (73) For example, Epicurus says that pleasure is a good thing, whereas the person who said 'I would rather be mad than feel pleasure' takes it as a bad thing, and the Stoics say it is an indifferent thing and not preferred—Cleanthes saying that it neither is natural nor has value in life, just as a cosmetic is not natural; Archedemus that it is natural like the hairs in the armpit, but does not have value; and Panaetius that some of it is natural and some of it contrary to nature. (74) Accordingly, if everything which seems good to someone is good absolutely, then since pleasure seems good to Epicurus, bad to one of the Cynics, and indifferent to the Stoic, pleasure will be simultaneously good and bad and indifferent. But the same thing cannot be by nature opposite things—simultaneously good and bad and indifferent; therefore not everything which seems good or bad to someone should be said to be good or bad. (75) But if that which seems good to someone is also good for everyone, we ought to be in a position to apprehend this, and to be capable of discerning the difference among the things which are thought good, so that we can say that one thing, which seems to this person good, is in reality good, while another thing seems good to that person, but is *not* by nature good. (76) This difference, then, is grasped either through plain experience or through some reasoning. But it is not feasible that it should be through plain experience. For it is in the nature of everything which strikes us through plain experience to be grasped in a common and concordant fashion by those who have no interference in their perceptions, as can be observed in the case of nearly all appearances. But the same thing is *not* called good concordantly by everyone, but by some virtue is called good, and what shares in virtue, by others pleasure, by others freedom from pain, and by some something else. The really good does not therefore strike everyone through plain experience. (77) But if it is grasped by reasoning, then since each one of all those who belong to the different schools has a private method of reasoning—Zeno one, by means of which he thought that virtue is good; Epicurus another, by means of which he thought pleasure is good; and Aristotle a different one, by means of which he thought health is good—each will in turn introduce a private good, which is not by nature good nor common to all. (78) Therefore nothing is by nature good. For if the private good of each person is not the good of all nor good by nature, and beyond the private good of each person there is nothing which is by common accord good, there is nothing good.

(79) Besides, if there is some good, this ought to be by its very definition a thing to be chosen, since every person chooses to get this, just as he chooses to avoid the bad. But nothing is to be chosen by its very definition as 'thing to be chosen', as we shall show; therefore there is not anything good. (80) For if anything is by its very definition a thing to be chosen, either choosing itself is to be chosen or something else besides this; for example, either choosing wealth is to be chosen or wealth itself is to be chosen. (81) And choosing itself could not be a thing to be chosen. For if choosing is by its very definition to be chosen, we ought not to be eager to get what we are choosing, so that we may not be deprived of continuing to choose. For just as ⟨we put off⟩ drinking or eating, so that we may not, once having drunk or eaten, be deprived of wanting any longer to drink or eat, so if choosing wealth or health is to be chosen, we should not pursue wealth or health, so that we may not, once having got them, be deprived of continuing to choose. (82) But we *do* pursue the getting of them; so choosing is not to be chosen, but rather to be avoided. And in the same way as the lover is eager to get the woman whom he loves, so that he may escape the distress involved in being in love, and as the person who is thirsty hastens to drink, so that he may escape the torment involved in being thirsty, so too the person who is troubled in his choosing of wealth hastens, in virtue of his choosing, to get wealth, so that he may be released from continuing to choose. (83) But if that which is to be chosen is something other than choosing itself, either it is among the things separate from us or among the things relating to us. And if it is separate from us and external, either something happens to us because of it or nothing happens; from the friend, for

example, or the excellent human being or child or any other of the so-called external goods—either a motion and a welcome condition and a wonderful experience happens to us because of it, or no such thing happens and we are not in any different state of motion when we regard the friend or the child as something to be chosen. (84) And if absolutely nothing of this kind happens to us, that which is external will not be something to be chosen at all. For how is it possible that we should make a choice of that towards which we are unmoved? (85) And furthermore, if the delightful is so conceived from our delighting in it, and the painful from our experiencing pain, and the good (*agathon*) from our experiencing wonder (*agasthai*), it will follow that a thing from which neither delight is produced in us, nor a wonderful state, nor any pleasing motion, implants in us no choice. (86) But if a certain tranquil condition and pleasing experience occurs in us from the external thing, such as the friend or the child, the friend or the child will not be to be chosen for his own sake, but for the sake of the tranquil condition and pleasing experience. But such a condition is not external but relating to us. None of the external things, then, is to be chosen for its own sake or good. (87) Nor, however, is that which is to be chosen and good among the things relating to us. For this either belongs solely to the body or it belongs to the soul. But it could not belong solely to the body; for if in reality it belongs solely to the body, and is no longer also an experience of the soul, it will escape our awareness (for all awareness is on the part of the soul), and will be equivalent to things which exist externally and have no affinity with us. (88) But if the pleasing effect which it has extends to the soul, it will be something to be chosen and good as far as that is concerned, but not in so far as it is a movement merely of the body. For everything which is to be chosen is judged to be so by way of sensation or thought, not by way of an unreasoning body. But the sense or intelligence which grasps that which is to be chosen belongs by its very definition to the soul; so none of the things which happen to the body is to be chosen for its own sake and good, but if any, those which happen to the soul, (89) which again sends us headlong into the original difficulty. For since each person's intelligence contains judgements discordant with that of his neighbour, it is necessary that each person should hold good that which appears so to himself. But that which appears good to each person is not good by nature. Neither in this way, therefore, is anything good.

(90) The same argument applies also to bad. Indeed, it has in effect been presented by the investigation of the good, first, since when one is

done away with, the other is also done away with at the same time—for each of the two is conceived in virtue of its holding in relation to the other; and then, since it is possible again to rest such a point directly on a single example, namely folly, which the Stoics say is the only thing which is bad. (91) For if folly is by nature a bad thing, then in the same way as the hot is known to be hot by nature from the fact that those who come near it are heated, and the cold from the fact that they are chilled, folly too will have to be known as being by nature a bad thing from the fact that they are harmed. Either, then, it is those who are called foolish who are harmed by folly, or the wise. (92) But the wise are not harmed; for they are remote from folly, and they could not be harmed by a bad thing which is not present to them but separate. But if folly harms fools, it harms them either being evident to them or non-evident. (93) And there is no way it could do so being non-evident; for if it is non-evident to them, it is neither a bad thing nor a thing to be avoided by them, but just as no one avoids or is disturbed at grief which is non-apparent and pain which is unfelt, so no one will shun as a bad thing folly which is unsuspected and not evidenced. (94) But if it is recognized by them in an evident fashion and is by nature a bad thing, fools ought to avoid it as by nature a bad thing. But fools do *not* avoid, as evidently a bad thing, that which is called 'being a fool' by those who are remote from it, but each person accepts his own judgement and deems bad that of the person who thinks the opposite. (95) So neither is folly evident to fools as by nature a bad thing. Hence, if neither are the wise harmed in any way by folly, nor is folly a thing to be avoided by fools, it must be affirmed that folly is not by nature a bad thing. But if this is not, neither is any other of the things called bad.

(96) But some members of the Epicurean school, in confronting such difficulties, tend to say that the animal avoids pain and pursues pleasure naturally and without being taught; at any rate, when it is born and is not yet a slave to opinions, it cries and shrieks as soon as it is struck by the unfamiliar chill of the air. But if it naturally strives towards pleasure and turns away from pain, then by nature pain is a thing to be avoided by it and pleasure a thing to be chosen. (97) But the people who say this have not observed, first, that they are giving a share of the good even to the most despised animals (for even they participate abundantly in pleasure), and then that not even pain is absolutely a thing to be avoided; indeed, pain is relieved by pain, and health and also physical strength and growth come about through pain, and men do not pick up the most exact skills and sciences without pain, so that pain is not by nature entirely a thing

to be avoided. (98) Furthermore, not even what seems pleasant is by nature entirely to be chosen; at any rate, often things which affect us pleasurably on the first encounter are thought unpleasant the second time, even though they are the same—which accords with the pleasant's not being such by nature, but moving us sometimes in this way, sometimes in that way, depending on the different circumstances.

(99) Yes, but even those who believe that only the fine is good think that it is shown by the non-rational animals, too, that this is by nature to be chosen. For, they say, we see how certain noble animals, such as bulls and cocks, fight to the death even though no delight or pleasure is in store for them. (100) And those human beings who have given themselves up to destruction for their country or parents or children would never have done this, when no pleasure after death was hoped for on their part, if the fine and good had not naturally drawn them, as well as every noble animal, towards choosing it. (101) But these people, too, are not aware that it is the height of stupidity to think that the above-mentioned animals are driven to fight to their last breath by a conception of the good. For one can hear them saying themselves that the wise disposition alone perceives the fine and good, while as far as the recognition of this is concerned, folly is blind; hence the cock and the bull, not sharing in the wise disposition, could not perceive the fine and good. (102) (And besides, if there is anything over which these animals fight to the death, this is none other than winning and being the leader. But there are times when being defeated and being a subject is finer, seeing that either one is indifferent. Therefore winning and being the leader is not by nature good but indifferent.) (103) So that if they were to say that the cock or the bull or any other of the brave animals pursues the fine, how is it that humanity also aims at the same thing? For in showing that those animals concern themselves about this, it has not been shown that humanity is also this way, (104) since surely, if humanity too is said to concern itself with the fine because certain animals are brave and apt to despise pleasure as well as to resist pains, then, since most animals are gluttonous and ruled by their stomachs, we shall say, on the contrary, that humanity strives more after pleasure. (105) But if they should say that some animals are lovers of pleasure, but that humanity is not entirely of this kind, we too will reverse ourselves and say that it is not immediately the case that if some animals, in accordance with natural reason, pursue the fine, humanity too aims for the same end. (106) And someone else will say that winning and being the leader is fought over by animals for its own sake, but by humanity not for its own sake, but on

account of the delight and joy in the soul which accompanies it, this being a welcome condition. And this may be supposed all the more in the case of human beings, for whom glory and praise and gifts and honours are sufficient to please and relax the mind and in this very process to make it apt to resist troubles. (107) Hence, too, it is perhaps for this reason that those who engage in heroic combat to the end, and give themselves up to destruction for their country, fight and die in manly fashion; for even if they die and pass on from life, yet they are doubtless pleased and feel joy at the praise while they are alive. (108) And it is even probable that some of them choose a death which was foreseen, thinking that similar praise also awaits them after death. Nor is it unlikely that others suffer this fate because they perceive that the circumstances of their lives will be even more difficult to bear, when they observe

> Sons being destroyed and daughters dragged off
> Bedchambers being plundered and infant children
> Thrown to the ground in dreadful battle.

(109) There are many reasons, then, why some people choose death with good repute; it is not because they think that the fine, which certain of the dogmatists go on about, is eagerly to be pursued. But let this much suffice on the difficulties concerning these matters.

IV. Whether it is Possible to Live Happily if one Postulates Things Good and Bad by Nature

(110) We have, then, enquired sufficiently about nothing's being good or bad by nature; let us now look into whether, even if these are admitted, it is possible to live 'with a good flow' and happily. The dogmatic philosophers, then, claim that this is precisely how things are; for according to them, the person who achieves the good and avoids the bad is happy; hence they also say that practical wisdom is a science relating to life, which is able to distinguish good things and bad things and able to produce happiness. (111) The sceptics, on the other hand, neither affirming nor denying anything casually but bringing everything under examination, teach that for those who suppose that there are good and bad by nature an unhappy life is in store, while for those who make no determinations and suspend judgement 'Is the easiest human life'. (112) And we can learn this if we start again from a little further back.

Now, all unhappiness comes about because of some disturbance. But,

in addition, every disturbance besets people either because of their intensely pursuing certain things or because of their intensely avoiding
certain things. (113) But all people intensely pursue what is thought by
them good and avoid what is supposed bad. All unhappiness, therefore,
comes about by way of the pursuit of good things as good and the
avoidance of bad things as bad. So, since the dogmatist is confident that
this is by nature good and that is by nature bad, always pursuing the one
and avoiding the other, and being disturbed for this reason, he will never
be happy. (114) For either everything which anyone pursues is immediately also good by nature, and everything which anyone avoids as a thing
to be avoided is such in reality; or a certain one of the things pursued is
to be chosen, and not all, and a certain one of the things avoided is to be
avoided; or these things depend on being in a certain state in relation to
something, and in relation to this person this thing is to be chosen or to
be avoided, but in relation to the nature of things it is neither to be
chosen nor to be avoided, but at one time to be chosen and at another
time to be avoided. (115) If, then, someone should reckon that everything which is in any way pursued by anyone is by nature good, and
everything which is avoided is by nature to be avoided, he will have a life
which is unlivable, being compelled simultaneously to pursue and avoid
the same thing—to pursue it in so far as it has been supposed by some
people a thing to be chosen, but to avoid it in so far as it has been
considered by others a thing to be avoided. (116) But if one should say
not that everything which is pursued or avoided is to be chosen and to
be avoided, but that a certain one of them is to be chosen and a certain
one avoided, he will live, but he will not live without disturbance; for by
forever pursuing what is considered by him to be by nature good, and
evading what is supposed bad, he will never be released from disturbance, but when he has not yet got hold of the good, he will be violently
disturbed because of his desire to get it, and in addition, when he has got
it, he will never be at peace, because of his excess of joy or because of his
vigilance over what he has acquired. (117) And the same argument applies also to bad; for neither is the person who is untouched by it free
from care, being persecuted in plenty both by the disturbance which
comes with avoiding it and by that which comes with guarding against it;
nor does the person who is in the midst of it have any rest from his trials,
as he considers 'How he might escape sheer destruction'. (118) But if
someone should say that a certain thing is not more by nature to be
chosen than to be avoided, nor more to be avoided than to be chosen,
every event being in a certain state in relation to something and, in

accordance with differing states of affairs and circumstances, turning out as at one time to be chosen and at another time to be avoided, he will live happily and without disturbance, being neither uplifted at good as good nor dejected at bad, nobly accepting what happens by necessity, but freed from the trouble associated with the opinion that something bad or good is present. Indeed, this will come to him from his thinking nothing good or bad by nature. Therefore it is not possible to live happily if one conceives certain things to be good or bad.

(119) Besides, that which is productive of something bad is surely to be avoided as also bad. For example, if pain is a bad thing, that which is productive of pain will surely also be classed together with pain as being a thing to be avoided; and if death is among the things which are bad, that which causes death will also be among the things which are bad as well as to be avoided. So in general, too, if the bad is to be avoided, necessarily that which is productive of the bad will also be to be avoided and bad. (120) But the things said by some people to be by nature good are also productive of bad things, as we will explain. In effect, then, the things which are said by some people to be good are bad, and for this reason are responsible for unhappiness. For it is actually because of such goods that everything bad exists, love of money and love of glory and love of victory and love of pleasure and whatever other things are like these. (121) For each person, in pursuing intensely and with excessive confidence what he thinks is good and to be chosen, falls without realizing it into the neighbouring vice. For example (for what is being said will be clear when examples are supplied which are familiar to us), (122) the person who has a preconception that wealth is good should eagerly take all steps towards getting wealth, and on every occasion should rehearse to himself the comic precept, 'Make money, friend, winter and summer', and accept the tragic one, 'Gold, finest thing received by mortals'. But taking all steps towards getting wealth is none other than being a lover of money. Therefore the person who imagines wealth to be the greatest good, in his eagerness for this, becomes a lover of money. (123) Again, the person who reckons that glory is to be chosen aims intensely for glory, but to aim intensely for glory is to be a lover of glory; therefore reckoning glory a thing to be chosen and by nature good is liable to produce something very bad, love of glory. (124) And we will find the same thing in the case of pleasure; for certain wretched consequences— namely, the love of pleasure—necessarily attend those who strive to- wards getting it. So that if that which is productive of bad things is bad, and it has been shown that the things thought good by some of the

philosophers are productive of all the bad things, it must be said that the things which are thought good by some are in effect bad.

(125) Nor, however, is it possible for those on the opposite side to say that, in connection with the pursuit of them and the impulse towards them, something bad comes to those who are impelled and in pursuit—such as love of money to the person going after wealth, and love of glory to the person going after glory, and some other disturbance to the person going after something else—but that, in connection with the getting of them, there occurs a release from disturbances and a rest from the previous trouble; (126) for the person who has got wealth no longer intensely seeks wealth, and the person who has taken hold of pleasure will relax the intensity of his eagerness for it. So just as the animals which live on the precipices are driven for the sake of drinking through pain to pleasure, and once satisfied, are immediately relieved from their prior hardships, so too humanity is necessarily troubled during its striving towards the good, but having got what it desired is also released from trouble. (127) We say that it is just not possible to maintain this, nor is this how the matter stands. For even if they get the things which are thought by them to be good, they are afflicted and grieved all the more, because they are not the only ones who have them; for it is on this condition, that they be alone in possessing them, that they consider the goods valuable and worth fighting for, and so jealousy is implanted in them towards their neighbours and malevolence and envy. The result is both that the pursuit of the things said to be goods is not without sorrow, and that the acquisition of them is the gathering of bad things in larger number. (128) And again, the same argument applies also to the bad things themselves. For someone who has a preconception that certain things are by nature bad, such as a bad reputation, poverty, lameness, pain, disease, and in general folly, is not troubled only by these things, but also by the vast number of other bad things caused by them. (129) For when they are present, he is storm-tossed not only by them, but also by his belief about them, on account of which he feels sure that he is in the presence of a bad thing, and he is ravaged by such a preconception as if by a bad thing of greater proportions. But when they are not present, he equally has no rest, but since he is either guarding against the future or is in fear, he has care as an intimate companion. (130) But when reason has established that none of these things is by nature good or by nature bad, there will be a release from disturbance and a peaceful life will await us.

But indeed it is evident from what has been said that because of the things thought by some to be goods, masses of bad things happen, and because of the bad things other bad things come into being, so that thanks to them happiness becomes unattainable. (131) But following this it must be pointed out that neither is it possible to get help by making our way through dogmatic philosophy. For if anything by nature good or by nature bad is assumed, one who is consoling the person disturbed at the intense pursuit of the good as good or the excessive avoidance of the bad as bad reduces the disturbance either by saying this—that it is proper neither to pursue the good nor to avoid the bad; (132) or by establishing this—that while this thing which is being pursued by him has very little value, and it is not appropriate to pursue it, this other thing has greater value, and it is fitting to go after it (e.g. wealth has less value, virtue greater value, and one should pursue not the former but the latter); or that while this thing which has little use brings many troubles, this other thing which turns out to be very useful brings few troubles. (133) But to say that it is not appropriate either to pursue the good intensely or to avoid the bad runs counter to the point of view of the dogmatists, who are always going on about the selection and rejection of these things, and about choices and avoidances. (134) And to say that one should not pursue this thing, since it is worthless, but should strive towards this other thing, since it is more splendid, is characteristic of men who are not removing disturbance but rearranging it; for just as someone pursuing the first thing was troubled, so he will also be troubled pursuing the second thing, (135) so that the philosopher's reasoning produces one disease in place of another, since in turning away the person who is striving for wealth or glory or health as something good towards pursuing not these things but the fine, perhaps, and virtue, he does not free him from pursuit, but transfers him to another pursuit. (136) Just as the doctor, then, if he removes pleurisy but produces inflammation of the lungs, or gets rid of inflammation of the brain but brings on lethargy instead, does not put an end to the danger but alters it; so too the philosopher, in introducing one disturbance instead of another, does not help the disturbed person. (137) For it is not possible to say that the disturbance which is brought on instead is moderate, while the one which is removed is more violent. For the same kind of opinion which the disturbed person had about the thing previously pursued, he has also about the second thing; but his opinion about the first thing, after all, was that it was good, and that was why he eagerly sought it; (138) therefore in thinking also that the second thing is good, and seeking it with equal eagerness, he will have equal disturbance, or maybe

even more violent disturbance, to the extent that he has been converted
to thinking that the thing now being pursued by him is of greater value.
If the philosopher should contrive, then, that the person who is troubled
pursues one thing instead of another, he will not release him from trouble. (139) But if he simply teaches that this thing has little use, but brings
many troubles, while this other thing which turns out to be very useful
brings few troubles, he will be producing a comparison between one
choice and avoidance and another choice and avoidance, and not a removal of disturbance—which is absurd. For the person who is troubled
does not want to find out what is more troublesome and what less
troublesome, but desires to be released from trouble. (140) It will only be
possible to avoid this, then, if we show to the person who is disturbed on
account of his avoidance of the bad or his pursuit of the good, that there
is not anything either good or bad by nature, 'But these things are judged
by mind on the part of humans,' to quote Timon. But such a teaching is
certainly peculiar to scepticism; it is scepticism's achievement, therefore,
to procure the happy life.

V. Whether the Person who Suspends Judgement about the Nature of Good and Bad Things is in All Respects Happy

(141) That person is happy who conducts himself without disturbance
and, as Timon said, is in a state of peace and calm—'For calm extended
everywhere', and 'When I perceived him, then, in windless calm'. Of the
things which are said to be good and bad, on the other hand, some are
introduced by opinion, some by necessity. (142) By opinion are introduced whatever things people pursue or avoid in virtue of a judgement;
for example, among external things, wealth and glory and noble birth
and friendship and everything like that are called 'to be chosen' and
'good', among those having to do with the body, beauty, strength, and
good condition, and among those having to do with the soul, courage,
justice, practical wisdom, and virtue in general; and the opposites of
these things are called 'to be avoided'. (143) But by necessity come
whatever things happen to us in virtue of a non-rational sense experience, and whatever some natural necessity produces ('But no one would
choose them willingly' or avoid them), such as pain or pleasure. (144)
Hence, such being the difference in the objects, we have already established the fact that the only person who conducts himself without disturbance in the matter of the things which according to opinion are good

and bad is he who suspends judgement about everything—both earlier, when we discussed the sceptical end, and at present, when we showed that it is not possible to be happy while supposing that anything is by nature good or bad. (145) For the person who does this is swept around accompanied by never-ending disturbances, avoiding some things and pursuing others, and drawing on himself, because of the good things, many bad things, but being pounded, because of his opinion about the bad things, by many times more bad things. (146) For example, the person who says that wealth, perhaps, is good and poverty bad, if he does not have wealth is disturbed in two ways, both because he does not have the good, and because he busies himself over the acquisition of it; but when he has acquired it, he is punished in three ways, because he is elated beyond measure, because he busies himself with a view to the wealth's remaining with him, and because he agonizes and is afraid of its loss. (147) But the person who ranks wealth neither among the things by nature good nor among the things by nature bad, but utters the expression 'not more', is neither disturbed at the absence of this nor elated at its presence, but in either case remains undisturbed. So that as regards the things thought by opinion to be good and bad, and the choices and avoidances of these things, he is perfectly happy, (148) while as regards sensory and non-rational movements he gives way. For things which take place not because of a distortion of reason and worthless opinion, but by way of an involuntary sense experience, are impossible to get rid of by the sceptic's method of reasoning; (149) for in the person who is troubled on account of hunger or thirst, it is not possible through the sceptic's method of reasoning to engender an assurance that he is not troubled, and in the person who is soothed by relief from these things it is not possible to engender a persuasion about the fact that he is not soothed.

(150) What help towards happiness, then, say the dogmatists, do you derive from suspension of judgement, if you are bound to be disturbed in any case, and to be unhappy through being disturbed? Great help, we will say. For even if the person who suspends judgement about everything is disturbed at the presence of that which gives pain, he still bears the distress more easily compared with the dogmatist, (151) first because it is not the same thing to be persecuted, when one is pursuing good things and shunning bad things (which are infinite in number), by the disturbances associated with these pursuits and avoidances, as if by Furies—or not to suffer this, but to busy oneself with avoiding and guarding against one single bad thing detached from all the others. (152) And second, even this thing which the suspenders of judgement avoid as bad

is not excessively disturbing. For the affliction is either somewhat small,
such as the hunger or thirst or cold or heat, or something similar, which
happens to us every day; (153) or on the contrary it is very violent and
extreme, as in the case of those who are gripped by incurable agonies, in
the course of which doctors often provide pain-killing medicines so that
the person can get a brief respite, and so be helped; or it is middling and
prolonged, as in certain diseases. (154) And of these, that which presents
itself every day disturbs us the least, since it has remedies which are easy
to provide—food and drink and shelter; while the most extreme, even if
it is the most highly disturbing, none the less frightens us, after all, in the
momentary manner of a lightning flash, and then either destroys us or is
destroyed. (155) And that which is middling and prolonged neither
persists through one's whole life nor is continuous in its nature, but has
many periods of rest and easing off; for if it was continuous, it would not
have extended over a long time. The disturbance which happens to the
sceptic, then, is moderate and not so fearful. (156) Nevertheless, even if
it is very great, we should hold responsible not those who are suffering
involuntarily and by necessity, but nature, 'Who cares nothing for laws',
and the person who by forming opinions and in virtue of a judgement
draws the bad thing upon himself. For just as one ought not to hold
responsible the person who has a fever because he has a fever (for he has
a fever involuntarily), while one ought to hold responsible the person
who does not abstain from things which are disadvantageous (for it lay in
his power to abstain from disadvantageous things), so one ought not to
hold responsible the person who is disturbed at the presence of painful
things; (157) for it is not through him that the disturbance due to the
affliction comes about, but it is bound to come about whether he wishes
it or not; but the person who through his own suppositions fashions for
himself a mass of objects to be chosen and to be avoided ought to be held
responsible; for he stirs up for himself a flood of bad things. And this can
be seen in the case of the things called bad themselves. (158) For the
person who has no further opinion about the affliction's being bad is
possessed by the inevitable movement of the affliction; but the person
who in addition invents the idea that the affliction is solely an alien thing,
that it is solely a bad thing, doubles with this opinion the trouble which
occurs in virtue of its presence. (159) For do we not observe that even in
the case of people undergoing surgery, often the actual patient who is
being cut endures in manly fashion the torment of the cutting, neither

> Turning pale over his fine complexion, nor
> Wiping tears from his cheeks

because he is undergoing only the movement associated with the cutting; while the person standing beside him, as soon as he sees a small flow of blood, goes pale, trembles, sweats all over, feels faint, and finally collapses speechless, not because of the pain (for it is not present in him), but because of the opinion about the pain's being a bad thing? (160) Thus the disturbance due to the opinion about something bad as bad is sometimes worse than that which occurs on account of the actual thing said to be bad. Therefore the person who suspends judgement about all matters of opinion enjoys the most complete happiness, (161) and during involuntary and non-rational movements is indeed disturbed—

> For he is not born from an oak of ancient legend, nor from a rock
> But was of the race of men—

but is in a state of moderate feeling.

(162) Hence one also needs to look down on those who think that he is reduced to inactivity or to inconsistency—(163) to inactivity, because, since the whole of life is bound up with choices and avoidances, the person who neither chooses nor avoids anything in effect renounces life and stays fixed like some vegetable, (164) and to inconsistency, because if he comes under the power of a tyrant and is compelled to do some unspeakable deed, either he will not endure what has been commanded, but will choose a voluntary death, or to avoid torture he will do what has been ordered, and thus no longer 'Will be empty of avoidance and choice', to quote Timon, but will choose one thing and shrink from the other, which is characteristic of those who have apprehended with confidence that there is something to be avoided and to be chosen. (165) In saying this, of course, they do not understand that the sceptic does not live in accordance with philosophical reasoning (for as far as this is concerned he is inactive), but that in accordance with non-philosophical practice he is able to choose some things and avoid others. (166) And if compelled by a tyrant to perform some forbidden act, he will choose one thing, perhaps, and avoid the other by the preconception which accords with his ancestral laws and customs; and in fact he will bear the harsh situation more easily compared with the dogmatist, because he does not, like the latter, have any further opinion over and above these conditions. (167) But these topics have been spoken of more precisely in the lectures on the sceptical end, and it is not necessary 'Once again to relate things clearly said'. Hence, having expounded on good and bad things, whose difficulties stretch over almost the entire subject of ethics, let us go on to consider next whether there is any skill relating to life.

VI. Whether there is any Skill Relating to Life

(168) We have shown well enough that it is possible for people who adopt suspension of judgement about everything to live acceptably; but there is nothing to prevent us from also scrutinizing in a parallel way the stance of the dogmatists, even though it has been scrutinized in part already. For they promise to impart a certain skill relating to life, (169) and for this reason Epicurus said that philosophy is an activity which procures the happy life by arguments and debates, (170) while the Stoics say straight out that practical wisdom, which is the science of things which are good and bad and neither, is a skill relating to life, and that those who have gained this are the only ones who are beautiful, the only ones who are rich, the only ones who are sages. For the person who possesses things of great value is rich, but virtue is of great value, and the sage alone possesses this; therefore the sage alone is rich. And the person who is worthy of love is beautiful, but only the sage is worthy of love; therefore only the sage is beautiful. (171) Well, such promises snare the young with vain hopes, but they are in no way true. Hence Timon too at one point makes fun of those who promise to deliver these things, saying 'Ravagers with many wild voices, givers of hope', (172) and at another point he introduces the people who pay attention to them, regretting the pointless hardships they experienced, in these words:

> Someone said lamenting, as mortals do lament,
> 'Alas, what am I to suffer? What wisdom is to be born in me now?
> As to my mind I am a beggar, there is not a grain of sense in me.
> In vain I expect to escape sheer destruction.
> Three and four times blessed, though, are those who have nothing
> And who have not eaten up at leisure what they grew to ripeness.
> Now I am fated to be overcome by wretched strife
> And poverty and whatever else chases mortal drones.'

(173) And that these things are so, we can learn if we pay attention to the following.

The skill which is deemed to relate to life, and in virtue of which they suppose that one is happy, is not one skill but many discordant ones, such as the one according to Epicurus, and the one according to the Stoics, and one belonging to the Peripatetics. Either, then, one is to follow all of them equally or just one or none. (174) And to follow them all is not feasible because of the conflict among them; for what this one commands as a thing to be chosen, this other one forbids as a thing to be

avoided, and it is not possible to pursue and avoid the same thing simultaneously. (175) But if one is to follow one, either it should be any one
whatsoever; which is impossible. For it is equally a consequence that one
is willing to follow all of them; for if one is to give one's attention to this
one, why to this one rather than to that one, and vice versa? It remains,
therefore, to say that one must follow the one which has been preferred.
(176) Either, then, we will follow that which has been preferred by
another skill, or that which has been preferred by itself. And if it is that
which has been preferred by itself, it will be untrustworthy—or we will
have to regard them all as trustworthy; for if this one is trustworthy in
so far as it has been judged by itself, the rest will also become trustworthy; for each of them has been judged by itself. (177) But if it has been
judged by another skill, it must again, even in this case, be distrusted; for
just as it, in so far as it disagrees with the others, was in need of a
judgement, so also the skill which judges it, in so far as it disagrees with
the remaining methods, will need one judging it, and for this very reason
will not be a trustworthy criterion of the first one. If, therefore, it is not
possible to follow either all the skills relating to life or one, it remains
that one follow none.

(178) And besides: as I said before, since there are many skills relating to life, the person who relies on one of these must of necessity be
unhappy, not only because of the reasons mentioned before but also
because of the one which will be stated as the argument moves forward.
For every person is in the grip of a certain passion; either he is a lover
of wealth or a lover of pleasure or a lover of glory; and being of such a
character he cannot be calmed down by any of the dogmatists' methods,
(179) but the lover of wealth or the lover of glory has his desire kindled
all the more by the Peripatetic philosophy, according to which wealth
and glory are among the goods, while the lover of pleasure is further
inflamed by Epicurus' method (for in his way of thinking pleasure is
represented as the completion of happiness), and the lover of glory is also
thrown headlong into this very passion by the Stoic arguments, according to which virtue is the only thing that is good, and that which derives
from virtue. (180) So every one of what the dogmatic philosophers call a
science relating to life is a fortification of the bad things which afflict
humanity, not a cure for them.

But even if we concede that there is one skill relating to life, and this
one is agreed upon—for example, the Stoic one—not even in this case
will we accept it, because of the many and varied disasters which are
brought with it. (181) For if the skill relating to life, being practical

wisdom, is a virtue, and only the sage has virtue, the Stoics, not being sages, will not have practical wisdom nor any skill relating to life, and not having this, neither will they teach it to others. And if in fact, according to them, no skill can be put together, neither will the one relating to life be put together; but the first point is indeed true, therefore the second is true. (182) For a skill is a system made up of apprehensions, and an apprehension is an assent to an apprehensive impression. But there is no apprehensive impression on account of the fact that neither is every impression apprehensive (for they are in conflict), nor is any one of them, because of the impossibility of discriminating among them. But if there is not an apprehensive impression, neither will there be any assent to it, and thus neither will there be an apprehension. But if there is not an apprehension, neither will there be a system made up of apprehensions—that is, a skill. From which it follows that neither is there any skill relating to life.

(183) In addition to this, the apprehensive impression is judged, according to the Stoics, to be apprehensive by the fact that it comes from an existing thing and corresponds with the existing thing itself in the manner of a stamp and a seal; and the existing thing is proved to be existing from the fact that it sets in motion an apprehensive impression. But if, in order that the apprehensive impression may be judged, the existing thing needs to be recognized, and in order that this may be apprehended, the apprehensive impression needs to be confirmed, and each one is untrustworthy on account of the other, then since the apprehensive impression is unknown, skill too is destroyed, since it is a system of apprehensions.

(184) And if the science relating to life—that is, practical wisdom—is capable of contemplating things which are good and bad and neither, either it turns out to be other than the goods of which it is said to be the science, or it is itself the good, as indeed some of them say in defining it: 'Good is virtue or what shares in virtue.' (185) And if it is other than the goods of which it is said to be the science, it will not be a science at all; for every science is the knowledge of certain existing things, but we earlier showed good and bad things to be non-existent, so that neither will there be any science of good and bad things. (186) But if it is itself a good thing and is deemed to be a science of good things, it will be a science of itself; which is again absurd. For the things of which there is a science are conceived prior to the science. For example, medicine is said to be the science of things which are healthy and unhealthy and neither; but the things which are healthy and unhealthy exist before

medicine and precede it. And again, music is the science of things which are in tune and out of tune, rhythmic and unrhythmic; but music does not exist prior to these. (187) And they themselves said that dialectic is the science of things which are true and false and neither; accordingly, the things which are true and false and neither exist before dialectic. If, then, practical wisdom is the science of itself, it ought to exist before itself; but nothing can exist before itself; therefore, neither in this way can it be said that there is any science relating to life.

(188) Moreover, every existing skill and science is apprehended from the skilful and scientific actions which it gives rise to—medicine, for example, from medical procedures, lyre-playing from the activities of the lyre-player, and also painting and sculpture and all similar skills. But the skill which is deemed to be occupied with life has no action resulting from it, as we will establish; therefore there is not any skill relating to life. (189) For example, since many things are said by the Stoics about the guidance of children and about honouring one's parents and also piety towards the departed, we will select a few cases from each category for the sake of example and put them forward with a view to constructing our argument.

(190) Well then, about the guidance of children, Zeno, the founder of the school, covers some such points as these in his *Discourses*: 'Have intercourse with one's boy-friend no more and no less than with one who is not one's boy-friend, nor with females than with males; for it is not different things, but the same things, that suit and are suited to boy-friend and non-boy-friend, and to females and males.' And again: 'Have you had intercourse with your beloved? I have not. Did you not desire to have intercourse with him? Yes indeed. But though desiring to get him for yourself, were you afraid to ask him? God, no! But you did ask him? Yes indeed. But he didn't submit to you? No, he didn't.' (191) And about honouring one's parents, one could cite their blather about sex with one's mother. At any rate Zeno, having put down the things which are recorded about Jocasta and Oedipus, says that it was not an awful thing for him to rub his mother. 'If he had helped her by rubbing her body with his hands when she was sick, there would have been nothing shameful; if, then, he stopped her suffering and cheered her up by rubbing her with another part, and creating children that were noble on their mother's side, what was shameful in that?' (192) And Chrysippus in his *Republic* says this, word for word: 'It seems good to me to organize these matters, too—as is the custom even now among many peoples, to no bad effect—so that the mother has children with the son and the

father with the daughter and the brother with the sister born of the same mother.' And an example of their piety towards the departed would be their recommendations about cannibalism; for they think it right to eat not only the dead, but also their own flesh, if some part of their body should ever happen to be cut off. (193) And the following is said by Chrysippus in his *On Justice*: 'And if some part of our limbs is cut off which is useful for food, do not bury it or otherwise dispose of it, but consume it, so that from our own parts another part may come into being.' (194) And in his *On What Is Proper*, in discussing the burial of one's parents, he says explicitly:

When one's parents have passed away, one should employ the simplest mode of burial, consistently with the body's being nothing to us, like nails or hair, and with our not needing to give it any such care and attention. Hence, too, if their flesh is useful as food, people will use it, like their own parts as well—for example, when a foot is cut off, it is incumbent on one to use it, and similar things; but if they are of no use, people will either bury them and place the monument upon them, or cremate them and scatter the ashes, or dispose of them in a more distant spot and pay no attention to them, like nails or hair.

(195) Thus say the Stoics; but we should bring against them the next point in our argument. Either they recommend doing these things on the assumption that young people are going to put them into practice, or that they will not put them into practice. And it is certainly not on the assumption that they will put them into practice; for the laws forbid them, unless one has to live with the Laestrygonians and Cyclopses, among whom it is lawful 'To eat human flesh and then to drink pure milk'. (196) But if it is on the assumption that they will not put them into practice, the skill relating to life becomes redundant, since the practice of it is impossible. For just as painting is useless in a population of blind people (for the skill is for people who have sight), and in the same way as lyre-playing has no rewards in a city of deaf people (for it gives delight to those who have hearing), so too the skill relating to life is worth nothing to people who cannot use it.

(197) Besides, every skill, whether it is theoretical, like geometry and astronomy, or practical, like fighting with heavy arms, or productive, like painting and sculpture, has an action peculiar to itself by which it differs from other dispositions; but there is no action peculiar to practical wisdom, as I will establish; therefore practical wisdom is not a skill relating to life. (198) For just as the action which is common to the musical and the unmusical person is not musical, and that which is common to the grammatical and ungrammatical person is not grammatical, so quite

generally the action which is common to the skilled and unskilled person is not skilled. Hence, too, that which is common to the wise and the foolish person could not be an action peculiar to practical wisdom. (199) But *every* action which seems to be brought about by the wise person is found to be an action common also to the person who is not wise; for example, if we regard honouring parents as an action of the wise person, or returning money deposited with us to those who entrusted it, or any other such thing, we will also find those who are not excellent doing any one of these things. So that there is no action peculiar to the sage by which he will differ from those who are not sages. And if this is so, neither will practical wisdom be a skill relating to life, since no skilful action is peculiar to it.

(200) But in meeting this point, they say that while all the actions are common to all people, they are nevertheless distinguished by coming about from a skilful disposition or an unskilful one. For caring for one's parents and otherwise honouring one's parents is not the action of the excellent person; characteristic of the excellent person is doing so from practical wisdom. (201) And just as giving health is common to both the doctor and the ordinary person, but giving health in a medical fashion is peculiar to the skilled person, so too, honouring one's parents is common to both the excellent and the non-excellent person, but honouring one's parents from practical wisdom is peculiar to the sage—so that he *does* have a skill relating to life, the distinctive action of which is the perform-ance from the best disposition of each of the things performed. (202) But those who employ this counter-argument seem to be wilfully deaf, and to be saying anything at all rather than something relevant to the question under examination. For while we were straightforwardly showing that there is no action peculiar to the wise person by which he differs from those who are not wise, but that everything which is brought about by him is also brought about by those who are not excellent, they did not have the power to refute this; but they say that the action common to both of them comes about sometimes from a wise disposition, sometimes from an inferior one—which is beside the point. (203) This is not a demonstration that there is not an action common to both the wise and those who are not such, but it is in need of a demonstration, since someone could ask how we are to distinguish when these things come about from the wise disposition and when they do not; for the common actions themselves do not reveal this, in so far as they are common. (204) Hence even the example introduced from medicine is found rather to count against them. For when they say that giving health, being common to both the doctor and the non-doctor, is peculiar to the skilled person

when it is accomplished in a medical fashion, then either they know the difference in the way it is done by the doctor compared with the ordinary person—for example, that it is done quickly and painlessly and in an orderly manner and with quality—or they do not know this, but suppose that all these things are also common to ordinary people. (205) And if they know it, they have admitted right away that there is some action apparent which is peculiar to the doctor, and that it follows that they should move on from this and teach that there is also some action peculiar to the sage, by which he differs from the one who is not a sage. But if they do not know it, but will say that everything which is brought about by the doctor is also brought about by the ordinary person, they will be depriving the doctor of the action peculiar to him, and—since, as far as the appearance is concerned, there is no difference in the actions which are brought about—they will not be distinguishing between the skilled and the unskilled person, nor between that which is effected by a skilled disposition and by an unskilled one, on account of the fact that the individual non-apparent disposition cannot be identified on its own, since it is non-apparent. (206) Therefore it is no help to them to agree that the actions brought about by the sage and by the non-sage are common to both, but that they differ in coming about on one occasion from a wise disposition, on another occasion from a foolish one.

But there are others who think that these actions are distinguished by consistency and order. (207) For just as, in the case of the intermediate skills, doing a certain thing in an orderly manner and being consistent in his results is peculiar to the skilled person (for the ordinary person might also sometimes perform the skilled action, but rarely and not all the time, nor uniformly and in the same way), so too they say that the action of the wise person is being consistent in his right deeds, while that of the fool is the opposite. (208) But these people, too, are plainly not oriented in accordance with the nature of things, with respect to the investigation at hand. For that there is some order of life which has been articulated in a determinate manner by way of skilled reasoning seems rather like a pious wish. For everyone, in preparing himself for the different and varied circumstances which arise, is always unable to maintain the same order, and especially the person of good sense, who is conscious of the instability of fortune and the insecurity of circumstances. (209) Besides, if the wise person had a single and determinate order of life, he would have been plainly apprehended even from this by those who are not wise; but he is *not* apprehended by these people; therefore the wise person is not to be grasped from the order of his actions. Hence if every skill is apparent from the actions peculiar to it, but there is no action peculiar to practical wisdom from which it is apparent, practical wisdom cannot be any skill relating to life.

(210) Furthermore, if practical wisdom is a skill relating to life, it would not have benefited anyone else more than the sage who possesses it, affording him self-control in his impulses towards the good and in his repulsions from the bad. But practical wisdom does *not* benefit the sage, as we will establish; therefore it is not any skill relating to life. (211) For the sage, who is called self-controlled, is called self-controlled either in so far as he engages in no impulse towards the bad or repulsion from the good, or in so far as he has inferior impulses, but masters them by reason. But he could not be said to be self-controlled on account of his not engaging in inferior judgements; for he will not control what he does not have. (212) And just as no one would call the eunuch self-controlled about sexual intercourse, or the person with a bad stomach self-controlled about the enjoyment of food (for no desire for these things arises in them at all, to make them struggle, with self-control, against the desire), in the same way the sage should not be described as self-controlled, because that over which he is to be self-controlled does not arise in him. (213) And if they will claim that he is self-controlled in so far as he does engage in inferior judgements but rises above them by reason, they will be conceding, first, that practical wisdom was of no benefit to him right when he was in a state of disturbance and in need of help, and then, that he is found to be even more unhappy than inferior people. (214) For in that he has an impulse towards something, he is certainly disturbed, and in that he masters it by reason, he holds on to the bad thing within himself, and for this reason is more disturbed than the inferior person who no longer suffers this (for whereas he is disturbed, in that he has an impulse, he retains his disturbance in a weakened form, in that he gets the things which are desired). (215) Therefore the sage is not self-controlled as far as his practical wisdom is concerned; or if he is, he is more unhappy than all human beings. But if each skill benefits above all the person who possesses it, and it has been shown that what is deemed to be the skill relating to life does not even benefit its possessor, it must be affirmed that there is not any skill relating to life.

VII. Whether the Skill Relating to Life is Teachable

(216) It has in effect been shown, then, along with there not being any skill relating to life, that it is not teachable either; for of things which do not exist no learning takes place. Nevertheless, for good measure, let us

allow its existence, and teach that it is unteachable. (217) Well then, the arguments about learning, among the philosophers, are many and varied; but we will select and present the most important points, of which some are arguments directed more generally on the part of the sceptics towards the conclusion that learning is nothing, while others speak more specifically about practical wisdom itself. But first in order let us look at the more general attacks.

(218) In every case of learning, then, the subject being taught and the teacher and the learner and the means of learning have to be agreed upon; but none of these things is agreed upon, as we will show; therefore there is not any learning. And since we first mentioned the subject being taught, we should first raise difficulties about it.

(219) If in fact any subject is taught, either what exists is taught or what does not exist. But neither is what exists taught, as we will show, nor what does not exist, as we will explain; therefore no subject is taught. Now what does not exist is not taught; for it has no attribute, and hence not that of being taught. (220) And besides, if what does not exist is taught, what does not exist will be true; for learning is of things which are true. But if what does not exist is true, it will immediately also be real; at any rate the Stoics say that 'True is what is real and is in opposition to something'. But it is absurd that what does not exist should be real; therefore what does not exist is not taught. And surely, what is taught is taught by setting in motion an impression, but what does not exist cannot set in motion an impression; therefore what does not exist is not teachable. (221) In addition to this, if what does not exist is taught, nothing true is taught; for the true belongs among the things which exist and are real. But if nothing true is taught, everything which is taught is false. But it is indeed absurd that everything which is taught should be false; therefore what does not exist is not taught. Since in fact, if what does not exist is taught, it is taught either in virtue of being non-existent or in virtue of something else. Well, it is not taught in virtue of being non-existent; for if what is taught is taught in virtue of being non-existent, nothing which exists will be taught—which is absurd. Nor, however, is it in virtue of something else; for the 'something else' exists, but the non-existent does not exist. So that what does not exist could not be taught. (222) It is left to us, then, to say that what exists is taught; and this too we will show to be something impossible. For if what exists is taught, it is either in virtue of being existent or in virtue of something else. And if it is taught in virtue of being existent, nothing will be untaught; but if none of the things which exist is untaught, neither will

there be anything taught; for it is necessary that there be something untaught, in order that from this learning may come about. So that what exists could not be taught in virtue of being existent. (223) Nor, however, in virtue of some other attribute of it which is non-existent, but every attribute of it is existent. So that if what exists is not taught in virtue of being existent, neither will it be taught in virtue of anything else; for that other attribute of it, whatever it is, is existent. If, then, neither what exists is taught nor what does not exist, and there is nothing beyond these, none of the things which exist is taught.

(224) Besides, since of the 'somethings' some are bodies, and others are incorporeal, if anything is taught, either body is taught or the incorporeal; but neither is body taught nor the incorporeal; therefore nothing is taught. Now body is not taught, especially according to the Stoics; for the things which are taught are 'sayables', and 'sayables' are not body. (225) Besides, if body neither is sensible nor is intelligible, body is not taught. For that which is taught must be either sensible or intelligible, and if it is neither, it is not taught. And that body is neither sensible nor intelligible we have established in *Against the Physicists*. (226) For whether body is, as Epicurus says, a certain aggregation of size and shape and resistance, or whether it is that which has the three dimensions together with resistance, since it is not characteristic of non-rational sensation, but of a certain rational capacity, to grasp everything which is grasped by way of a conjunction of several things, body will not be among sensible things. (227) And even if it were sensible, it will again be untaught; for of sensible things nothing is taught—for example, no one learns to see white, nor to taste sweetness, nor to perceive the fragrance from something, or be chilled or heated by something, but the grasp of all these things is untaught. Therefore neither is body sensible, nor, even if it were sensible, will it be teachable in virtue of this. (228) Nor, however, as an intelligible thing can it be taught. For if neither length, taken separately, is body, nor breadth nor depth, but the compound of all these, then since they are all incorporeal, we will also have to conceive of the aggregation of them as incorporeal and not body; and for this reason body must also be unteachable. (229) Further, of bodies some are sensible, others intelligible. So if body is taught, either the sensible is taught or the intelligible. But neither is the sensible taught, because it appears and is evident by itself to everyone, nor is the intelligible, because of its non-evidentness and the as yet unresolved disagreement about it, some saying that it is indivisible, others that it is divisible, and some saying that it is without parts and smallest, others that it is composed of parts

and can be divided to infinity. Therefore body is not teachable. (230) But yet neither is the incorporeal. For it is either some Platonic Form or the Stoics' 'sayable' or void or place or time or some other such thing. But whichever of these it is, its subsistence is still under investigation and is the subject of unresolved disagreement; (231) but to say that things which are still disputed are taught, as if they were undisputed, is completely absurd. But if some of the things which exist are bodies and others are incorporeal, and it has been shown that none of these is taught, then what is taught is nothing.

(232) Besides, if anything is taught, it is either true or false. And it is not false, as is immediately apparent; and if it is true it is intractable, as we showed in *On the Criterion*, and about intractable things there is no learning; therefore what is taught does not exist. (233) In addition to this, what is taught is either skilled or unskilled. But it is not unskilled, since then it will not need learning. But if it is skilled, either it is immediately apparent, or it is non-evident. And if it is immediately apparent, it is both unskilled and untaught; but if it is non-evident, it is not teachable precisely because of its being non-evident.

(234) From these points, then, the subject being taught is established as intractable; and together with it are eliminated both the teacher, because of having nothing to teach, and the learner, because of having nothing to learn. None the less, it will be possible to raise similar difficulties in their case as well. (235) For if there is any teacher and there is any learner, either the skilled person will teach the skilled person, or the unskilled the unskilled, or alternatively the skilled person will teach the unskilled, or the unskilled the skilled. But neither can the unskilled teach the unskilled—just as the blind cannot lead the blind—nor the skilled the skilled; for he has nothing at all to teach him. Nor, however, can the unskilled teach the skilled, just as the blind cannot ever lead the sighted; for the ordinary person is defective as regards the principles of the skill, and for this reason is not suited for teaching. (236) It is left to us to say, then, that the skilled person teaches the ordinary person, which again is something not feasible; for we have subjected the skilled person to difficulties along with the principles of the skill, (237) and in addition, the unskilled person, if he is taught and becomes a skilled person, becomes a skilled person either when he is unskilled or when he is a skilled person; but neither can he become a skilled person when he is unskilled, nor when he is a skilled person is he still *becoming* a skilled person, but he *is* one. (238) And with reason; for the unskilled person is like the person who is blind or deaf from birth, and in the same way as neither

the person blind from birth comes to a conception of colours, nor does the person deaf from birth come to a conception of sounds, so too the unskilled person, in so far as he is unskilled, being defective as regards the grasp of skilled principles, cannot have knowledge of these things. But the skilled person is no longer being taught, but has been taught.

(239) Furthermore, just as these things are intractable, so too the means of learning is intractable. For it comes about either by plain experience or by discourse; but it comes about neither by plain experience nor by discourse, as we will establish, so that neither is the means of learning easy to deal with. (240) Well then, learning does not come about by plain experience, since plain experience is of things which are revealed. But what is capable of being revealed is apparent; and the apparent, in so far as it is apparent, can be grasped by everyone in common, but what can be grasped by everyone in common is unteachable. Therefore what is capable of being shown by plain experience is not teachable. (241) Nor, however, is anything taught by discourse. For either the discourse signifies something, or it does not signify a single thing. But if it does not signify a single thing, it will not be a teacher of anything. But if it does signify something, it signifies either by nature or by convention. And it does not signify by nature, because it is not the case that everyone understands everyone—Greeks understanding barbarians and barbarians Greeks. (242) But if it signifies by convention, it is clear that those who have previously apprehended the things with which the words are correlated will grasp these things not through being taught by them what they did not know, but through recalling and renewing in their minds those things which they did know; while those who are in need of learning the things which are unknown, and who do not know the things with which the words are correlated, will not have a grasp of anything. (243) Hence if neither the subject being taught exists, nor the teacher nor the learner nor the means of learning, learning is nothing.

This, then, is how the sceptics direct their argument more generally towards the conclusion that learning does not exist; but it will also be possible to transfer the difficulties to the so-called skill relating to life. (244) For either the wise person will teach this to the wise person, or the fool to the fool, or the fool to the wise person, or the wise person to the fool. But neither could the wise person be said to teach this to the wise person (for both of them are perfect with respect to virtue and neither of them needs learning), nor the fool to the fool (for both have need of learning and neither of them is wise, so that he can teach the other).

(245) Nor, however, will the fool teach the wise person; for neither is the blind person capable of indicating colours to the sighted person. It remains, then, that the wise person is capable of teaching the fool; which is itself, too, something intractable. (246) For if practical wisdom is a science of things which are good and bad and neither, then the fool, who does not have any practical wisdom, but has ignorance about all these things, will only hear what is said when the wise person is teaching the things which are good and bad and neither, and will not know the things themselves. For if he should grasp them while in a state of folly, folly will be capable of knowing the things which are good and bad and neither. But folly is *not*, according to them, capable of perceiving these things; therefore the fool will not grasp the things which are said or done by the wise person in accordance with the rationale of practical wisdom. (247) And in the same way as the person blind from birth, as long as he is blind, does not have a conception of colours, and the person deaf from birth, as long as he is deaf, does not grasp sounds, so too the fool, in so far as he is a fool, does not grasp things which are wisely said and done. Neither, then, can the wise person instruct the fool in the skill relating to life.

(248) Furthermore, if the wise person teaches the fool, practical wisdom ought to be capable of perceiving folly, just as skill is capable of perceiving lack of skill; but practical wisdom is *not* capable of perceiving folly; therefore the wise person is not capable of teaching the fool. For the person who has become wise as a result of some training and practice (for no one is this way by nature) either has folly underlying in him, and acquired practical wisdom in addition, or became wise by way of the loss of the former and the acquisition of the latter. (249) And if folly is underlying in him and he acquired practical wisdom in addition, the same person will be simultaneously wise and foolish; which is impossible. But if he acquired the one by the loss of the other, he will not be able to gain knowledge of the disposition which was there before, but which is now not present, by means of the disposition which came into being later. (250) And reasonably so; at any rate, the apprehension of every object, sensible or intelligible, comes about either empirically by way of plain experience or by way of analogical transition from the things which have appeared empirically; and this transition is either by resemblance, as when Socrates, who is not present, is identified from the image of Socrates, (251) or by composition, as when we conceive the non-existent centaur by way of combination from a human being and a horse, or by way of analogy, as when by enlargement from the normal human being

the Cyclops is grasped, who is not like 'A bread-eating man, but a wooded mountain peak', and by diminution the pygmy. (252) Hence, if folly is grasped by practical wisdom—and the fool by the wise person as well—it will be perceived either by way of experience or by way of transition from experience. But it is perceived neither by way of experience—for no one knows folly by way of experience, in the same way as white and black and sweet and bitter—nor by way of transition from experience—for none of the things which exist is like folly. But if the wise person makes the transition from this, it is either by resemblance or by composition or by analogy, so that practical wisdom will never grasp folly. (253) Yes, but perhaps someone will say that the wise person can understand the folly belonging to someone else by the practical wisdom in himself—which is silly. For folly is a disposition which is productive of certain actions. (254) If, therefore, the wise person perceives and apprehends it in another, either he will apprehend the disposition itself, on its own, or he will give attention to its actions and from them will also recognize the disposition itself, (255) just as one recognizes the medical disposition from medical procedures, and that of the painter from painterly procedures. But neither can he grasp the disposition itself, on its own— for it is non-apparent and not to be perceived, and it is not possible to inspect it through the body's form—nor can he grasp it from the actions which are produced by it—for all the apparent actions, as we showed earlier, are common to practical wisdom and folly. (256) But if, in order that the wise person may teach the fool the skill relating to life, he has to be capable of perceiving folly, just as the skilled person is capable of perceiving lack of skill, and it has been shown that folly cannot be grasped by him, the wise person must not be able to teach the fool the skill relating to life.

(257) Having raised difficulties, then, about the most essential of the issues investigated in the area of ethics, at this point we round off our entire exposition of the sceptical method.

COMMENTARY

Title

The title *Against the Ethicists* does not appear in the MSS; it has been added in editions since Bekker, together with the now standard titles for the rest of *M* VII–XI, by analogy with the titles which precede in *M* I–VI (with a minor exception in the case of *M* II, where the MSS read *Peri Rhētorikēs*, 'On Rhetoric'). *M* XI has no heading in the MSS; however, at the *end* of the book the MSS give it the label 'the tenth of Sextus Empiricus' treatises'; analogous labels appear at the beginning and/or the end of *M* VIII–X. (*M* VII is preceded by the words *Against the Logicians* (*Pros tous Logikous*), but as part of a longer title.) The number 'tenth' may be plausibly explained by the hypothesis that *Against the Logicians*, *Against the Physicists*, and *Against the Ethicists* were originally preceded by five books of a more general character, making a complete work of ten books. DL IX. 116 refers to ten books of *Skeptika* by Sextus; and *Skeptika Hupomnēmata* (Sceptical Treatises) is the title by which Sextus himself refers to the composite work to which *Against the Ethicists* belongs. (On this see Blomqvist 1974, also Introduction, sect. I.) A list of the chapter titles, with numbers, appears at the beginning in the MSS of *M* XI (*M* VII–XI is not entirely consistent in this regard); I follow the practice of most other translators in omitting these.

1–2: Transition and Introduction

[There is a textual difficulty in the third line of the quotation from Timon; I follow Nauck's conjecture, *dinois*, also followed by Mutschmann, for the unintelligible *deilois* which appears in all MSS. Brunschwig (1994*c*: 213) defends *deilois*; but his translation 'wretchedness' seems strained.]

The 'logical and physical parts of philosophy' have been treated in *M* VII–VIII and *M* IX–X respectively. The divisions of philosophy are discussed at the beginning of *M* VII (1–26); the tripartite division into logic, physics, and ethics is said to be preferable to others on grounds of completeness—*entelesteron* (16). (*PH* II. 13 proposes to adopt the same division, but here Sextus avoids suggesting its superiority. This accords with the generally stricter sceptical attitude maintained by *PH* as against *M* VII–XI; see Introduction, sect. V.) This division is there said to have been adopted 'most explicitly' (*rētotata*) by Xenocrates, the Peripatetics, and the Stoics—though Plato is also said to have been 'in effect' (*dunamei*) its originator. (A similar but earlier suggestion about Plato occurs in Arius *apud* Stob. II. 49, 18–23; cf. DL III. 56(50), which appears to be drawing on the Platonist Thrasyllus, Tiberius' court philosopher.) The Stoics' use of the division is widely attested elsewhere (see e.g. the texts in LS 26). Xenocrates is not elsewhere recorded as proposing it, but Sextus' report is generally accepted, as conforming to the systematic character of Xenocrates' works (see e.g. Heinze 1892: 1, Dörrie 1967: 1519, Dillon 1977: 23, LS I. 160). The attribution of the division to the Peripatetics is more doubtful. A tripartite distinction among ethical, logical, and physical propositions and problems is alluded to by Aristotle at *Topics* 105b19–26; but this does not conform to Aristotle's usual views, nor apparently the views of any Peripatetics, about the relations among the sciences. The standard order of Aristotle's works, established by Andronicus of Rhodes in the first century BC, looks as if it conforms to the plan logic, physics, ethics; but it is difficult to know what significance to read into this. Sextus' statement may be due to the influence of Antiochus (and possibly the same is true of Andronicus' ordering); on this, see below on 3–6, and cf. Cic. *Fin.* V. 9, in the Antiochean part of the work, which ascribes the threefold division to the Peripatetic system 'like most of the others'.

The order in which Sextus treats the three divisions of philosophy conforms to that of Zeno, Chrysippus, and certain other Stoics, as reported by DL VII. 40. Plut. *Sto. rep.* 1035A, on the other hand, says that Chrysippus proceeded in the order logic, ethics, physics; but the passage goes on to say that Chrysippus *also* repeatedly claimed that physics should precede ethics. Sextus does not fully justify his proceeding in this way, though *M* VII. 24 argues that logic should come first, since methods for discovering the truth, which belong under logic, are necessary in all fields whatever (cf. *PH* II. 13, which makes the same point, but again more non-committally). *M* VII. 20–3 neutrally reviews various different ordering schemes, but does not mention the one Sextus actually goes on to employ.

The second sentence of 1 might be thought to imply that it is specifically the ethical part of philosophy which enables us to live the tranquil life characteristic of scepticism. But the point is, rather, that it is by completing a *comprehensive* survey of philosophy (which we will have done by surveying the one remaining part, ethics), and by adopting the appropriate attitude towards it, that we will be able to achieve the 'perfect—that is, sceptical—disposition'. Suspension of judgement (*epochē*) in all areas of philosophy, based on an examination of theories proposed in those areas, is necessary for the achievement of tranquillity; this is the position suggested at the beginning of *PH* (I. 1–34), and there is no reason to think that the present work differs in this respect. None the less, the examination of ethics does turn out to have a special relevance to the attainment of tranquillity; on this, see on 110–11, and see 110–67 generally (cf. *PH* I. 25–30, III. 235–8).

The quotation from Timon is part of a passage in which a speaker, presumably Timon himself, asks Pyrrho how he achieves his extraordinary (and even godlike) tranquillity; a continuous fragment of seven lines can be assembled from the present text together with *M* I. 305 and DL IX. 65 (see LS 2D, Caizzi 1981*a*: T. 61, Lloyd-Jones and Parsons 1983: 392–3). According to DL, the passage comes from Timon's poem *Images* (*Indalmoi*). It is usually supposed that the lines quoted by Sextus at *M* XI. 20 give Pyrrho's reply to this question; on this, see below ad loc. Quotations from Timon are more frequent in *M* XI than in any other book of Sextus (eight separate quotations: no other book contains more than three), and all of them have to do, in one way or another, with appropriate or inappropriate ways of living, or attitudes to life. This was clearly a prominent theme throughout Timon's work—most of what we know about Pyrrho has to do with these matters, and most of this information comes directly or indirectly through Timon—and the subject-matter of *M* XI makes quotations on this theme especially apposite. (By contrast, the ethical portion of *PH* III contains no words of Timon. But, except for the very brief discussion at 235–8, *PH* III contains nothing equivalent to *M* XI's long section on the relative happiness or unhappiness of the dogmatist and the sceptic (110–67), in which four of *M* XI's eight quotations occur; and in any case, *PH* is generally sparing of quotation compared with the more expansive *M* VII–XI.) I see no reason not to suppose that Sextus was personally acquainted with Timon's works, despite the cautions of Caizzi (1992*b*: 315). It is noteworthy that the present quotation does not specifically name Pyrrho (it is DL which preserves the line in which Pyrrho is addressed); Timon is cited simply for his useful description of the attitude the sceptic should aim for. This accords with Sextus' general reticence about the figure of Pyrrho, which may well reflect an uncertainty about what the supposed founder of scepticism really thought; see, in particular, the extremely cautious explanation at *PH* I. 7 of why scepticism is sometimes called Pyrrhonism, and for discussion, see Caizzi 1981*b*: esp. 125–8.

Sextus' remark about Socrates derives at least in part from the biographical tradition; the line from the *Odyssey* (IV. 392) also appears in DL in the context of Socrates' concentration on ethics (II. 21), and DL cites as his authority Demetrius of Byzantium (a Peripatetic probably no later than mid-first century BC; see DL V. 83, Martini 1901). But Sextus is asserting something slightly different from DL (and from what he himself asserts, again quoting the same line, at *M* VII. 21). DL (and Sextus at *M* VII. 21) says that Socrates rejected physics and confined himself to ethics, a claim which is ancient and widespread—which might indeed be said to have begun with Plato himself (*Ph.* 96a–99d). (Sextus elsewhere (*M* VII. 8) cites Xenophon and Timon on this point; see, however, DeFilippo and Mitsis 1994, which argues that such interpretations of Xenophon's portrait of Socrates are exaggerated.) Sextus here (a) says that Socrates appears to have been the *first* to practise ethical enquiry, and (b) cites Socrates in support of the allegedly universal view that ethical enquiry is *about* the good and the bad, and the difference between them. Sextus' caution about the first point is appropriate. It also enjoyed some traditional support—Cicero endorses it explicitly (*Tusc.* V. 10–11, *Acad.* I. 15, *Fin.* V. 88); but it is not explicit in the earliest writers about Socrates, though it may be inferred from such passages as Xen. *Mem.* I. 1. 11–16 and Ar. *Met.* I. 3–6, which present philosophy prior to Socrates as primarily concerned with physical matters, and Socrates as concentrating on ethics instead. It is not quite clear how to square point (a) with the well-known ethical interests of Socrates' contemporary Democritus; for awareness of these interests in the Hellenistic period, see e.g. Arius *apud* Stob. II. 52, 13–53, 20, Cic. *Fin.* V. 23, 87–8. The last of these texts says that Democritus' ethical ideas are 'not yet fully polished' (*nondum . . . perpolita*), and goes on to describe Socrates instead as the pioneer of genuine ethical enquiry. The evidence does not permit a definitive judgement on this verdict; but it is true that Democritus' ethical fragments (even allowing for the fact that many of those ascribed to him may not be genuine) do not suggest a particularly systematic approach to the subject.

Point (b) need not be seen as anachronistically attributing to Socrates the *articulated view* that the good and the bad are the primary subject-matter of ethics; rather, Sextus is reporting that Socrates characterized his own activity as that of investigating the good and the bad (a claim which he presumably got from Demetrius or someone else drawing on the same materials; this is precisely the point of the Odyssey quotation in DL), and is claiming that this *in fact* constitutes a vote for the view that

that is the subject-matter of ethics—since Socrates was the first practitioner of ethics.

It is interesting that there is no mention here of the intermediate category of the indifferent, even though the first chapter, which immediately follows, declares Sextus' willingness to make use of the threefold, and according to him standard, division good/bad/indifferent. This is the first example of *M* XI's intermittent silence concerning the category of the indifferent; contrast *PH* III. 168, which uncomplicatedly assumes the threefold division.

CHAPTER I (3–20)

The first chapter is purely programmatic. Its central purpose is simply to declare the intent to proceed in accordance with the threefold division referred to at the outset, and to insist that this procedure does not involve Sextus in any objectionable dogmatic commitments. The division is said to be generally agreed upon (3, 7), despite the possibility of minor variations in its formulation (Xenocrates, 4), and despite the lack of any adequate proof of its correctness (5–6). Two objections to the division are summarized (8–17); Sextus makes no attempt to answer them, but he regards them as quibbles constituting no serious problem, and even claims (7) that their proponents in any case accept more or less the same position as everyone else. But though the threefold division is thus to be adopted in the discussion to follow—by the end of the chapter (20), the division is said to be 'in place' (*keimenēs*)—Sextus emphasizes (18–20) that this is not to be understood as committing him to the belief that anything is, in its real nature, good, bad, or indifferent; rather, things *appear* to us as good, bad, or indifferent, and the threefold division is simply the most convenient way to classify these appearances (and also to engage in debate with the dogmatists about whether things do have these qualities in reality).

This chapter has been described as containing 'a rather stupid critique of [the threefold] division considered solely qua division', which 'is irrelevant to ethics' (see Annas 1986: n. 8). But though Xenocrates' variant formulation and the 'sophistical' (7) objections are indeed arcane and technical, their inclusion serves to vindicate Sextus' general claim as to the naturalness of the division; the suggestion is that if the most that has been achieved by way of objection or reformulation is of this quibbling

nature, the division must be basically a sensible one. The passage is not
'an indication that Sextus . . . was more interested in logic than in ethics
proper' (ibid.); on the contrary, it implies precisely that those who wish
to enquire seriously into ethics will keep such logical niceties to a minimum (cf. 35 on the 'dogmatists' pedantry').

3–6: The threefold division, and Xenocrates' variant formulation

Point of translation: *henikais ptōsesi*, 'singular forms' (4; cf. *plēthuntikais
ptōsesi*, 'plural forms', 14). *Ptōsis* is usually rendered 'case', and is so
rendered here in Bury. But 'case' in English is used to mark the distinction between nominative, accusative, etc., whereas *ptōsis* refers to words
in any of their grammatical modifications—including, as here, that of
number (see LSJ). At least, this is the most common usage of *ptōsis* in
linguistic contexts; it is argued in Frede 1994*a* (also Frede 1994*b*) that in
Stoicism *ptōsis* did not refer to word-forms at all. See also linguistic point
(f) on 22–30.

The claim that *all* systematic philosophers employ the threefold division
seems at first sight greatly exaggerated. But with the exception of the
phrase 'which they also call indifferent'—for the term *adiaphoron*, in this
ethical usage, does seem to have originated with the Stoics—Sextus'
assertion is not without plausibility. Ancient ethics in general is centred
around the goal of specifying the highest good in human life (for a recent
general discussion of this, see Annas 1993: ch. 1). But this way of proceeding will naturally devote much attention to those things which contribute to, or are components of, this highest good (the good things), as
well as to those things which actively thwart its attainment (the bad
things). It is also natural to conclude that many things are neither helpful
nor harmful to the attainment of the highest good, and to think of these
things as being 'between' those which are good and those which are bad.
Very schematically, ancient ethical theories as a group may be said to
conform in effect to this pattern. However, Sextus' claim that the Old
Academy, the Peripatetics, and the Stoics are united in making the
division 'most conspicuously' (*epiphanestata*) is somewhat misleading.
The description clearly fits the Stoics, who had a general methodological
concern for correct, precise, and explicit divisions, and whose employment of this division in ethics is well attested elsewhere (e.g. DL VII. 61,
101, Stob. II. 57, 19–20, Epictetus, *Diss.* II. 19. 13). But there is little
evidence of a self-conscious emphasis on the threefold division in the

early Academy, other than Sextus' own citation of Xenocrates just below, or in the Peripatetic school for at least two centuries following Aristotle's death; indeed, by no means all these Peripatetics had any interest in ethics, and the approach of those who did was often quite untheoretical (for the evidence, see Wehrli 1967–78). Aristotle makes use of the division good/bad/neither at *NE* 1173a5–13—and so does his opponent in this passage, someone who holds that pleasure is not a good. It has regularly been supposed that this opponent is Speusippus, Plato's nephew and successor as head of the Academy (see e.g. Gauthier and Jolif 1958–9: ii. 822); for doubts about this, see Gosling and Taylor 1982: ch. 12. But in any case, the use of the division in one specialized context does not show that the division was generally adopted as a basic organizing principle for ethical discussion, either by Peripatetics or by Academics. The same may be said of the occasional references to the threefold division in Plato; see esp. *Gorgias* 467e and *Lysis* 220b–c.

Whatever the immediate source for Sextus' claim, it is probably the result of two related developments: (1) the influence of Antiochus, who, in addition to working out a syncretistic philosophy of his own, advanced the *historical* view that the philosophy of the Old Academy, the Peripatetics, and the Stoics was in all essentials the same (see e.g. Cic. *Acad.* I. 43, *Nat. D.* I. 16, *Fin.* V. 7, and for discussion, Barnes 1989: esp. 78–81; for Sextus' acknowledgement of Antiochus as a source, see *M* VII. 162, 202); and (2) the apparent adoption of Stoic elements in later Peripatetic ethics, as revealed especially by Arius Didymus' summary of Peripatetic ethics, preserved in Stobaeus (II. 116–52). (On this work, see Annas 1990a, 1993, Moraux 1973: 259–443.) Arius does include an explicit reference to the threefold division (131. 8–12, and see Moraux 1973: 363)—at least, if the usually accepted restoration of the text is correct.

That Sextus should be concerned to emphasize, and even exaggerate, the extent of agreement on a question may seem surprising, given the importance which he accords throughout his works to disagreement among philosophers. But the kind of agreement on fundamental categories that he is concerned to establish here is clearly compatible with a great deal of substantive disagreement. Later in the book (42–68) he will stress the disagreements among philosophers about what things are in fact good, bad, or indifferent; but such disagreements actually presuppose broad agreement about the terminology and concepts by means of which the debate is to be conducted, and to insist upon such broad agreement is the function of this chapter and, at least according to its opening statement of intent (21), the next. For another example of this type of procedure,

52 COMMENTARY

see *M* VIII. 300–36, which discusses the 'conception' (*epinoian*, 300) of proof; at the close of this discussion Sextus says 'Let this be laid down' (*touto . . . hupokeisthō*, 336) as a basis for the assembling of opposing arguments about whether there is in fact any such thing as proof. For discussion of this strategy, including Sextus' difficulties in maintaining it consistently, see Brunschwig 1988; on the difficulties, see also on ch. II below.

The sentence from Xenocrates in 4 must be regarded as a verbatim quotation, or something very close to it, since Sextus refers specifically to Xenocrates' unusual linguistic formulation. (It is not entirely clear whether he is pointing merely to Xenocrates' use of the singular rather than the plural, or also to his use of 'neither good nor bad' rather than 'indifferent'; but the latter is more likely, since both features play a role in the subsequent discussion (5, 14).) The proof in 5 may or may not be an exact reproduction of Xenocrates' words, but there is no reason to doubt its faithfulness as a summary of his argument. (Again, the whole passage suggests a systematizing cast to Xenocrates' thought; see above on 1.) While Xenocrates wrote numerous ethical works (see the list of titles in DL IV. 11–14), this material is perhaps most likely to have been taken from his book *On the Good*. Xenocrates' proof is directed to showing that nothing can be *other* than (a) good, (b) bad, or (c) neither good nor bad. Since this is a simple and obvious tautology, it is not surprising that, as Sextus says (6), the attempted proof is circular. More interesting would be an argument to the effect that all three categories must have items instantiating them (or an argument in favour of some positive characterization of the third category, such as the Stoic notion of the indifferent— DL VII. 98–103 in effect contains such an argument). It is not clear *why* Xenocrates 'thought it proper' to add the attempted proof, or whether his preference for the singular forms had any particular rationale. (On the latter point, Dillon 1977: 35 suggests that it may have been motivated by the need to escape objections like that laid out in 8–14; but chronology seems to rule this out, since the authors of that objection, whoever they are, rely on a Stoic conception of definition—see below.)

As noted above, Sextus does not regard the absence of a proof as an objection to the *use* of the threefold division. But this does not mean that he is himself sympathetic to the idea of a division or anything else being 'warranted by itself'; his point in 6 is to establish the uselessness of the attempted proof. Elsewhere Sextus is highly critical of the suggestion that certain statements might be in some way self-justifying (see e.g. *PH*

I. 178-9, the Two Modes, and the various treatments of 'hypothesis' at *M* VIII. 367-78, *PH* I. 173-4, *M* III. 1-17). Here too, Sextus would no doubt say, the lack of a proof of the threefold division prevents us from claiming that it is 'warranted' in the sense of capturing the real nature of things; but this is no problem for him, since that is not the spirit in which he himself proposes to employ the division (see 18-20). *PH* II. 213-27 argues against the idea of a 'science of division' (*epistēmē diairetikē*, 213), but there is no corresponding discussion in *M* VII-VIII.

7-17: Objections to the threefold division

Points of text and translation:

(a) *Heuresilogousin*, 'think up specious arguments', 7. This word—literally 'invent words', 'be verbally inventive'—is not always used with a pejorative connotation (see e.g. Polybius 26. 1. 2, Philodemus, *Rhet.* I. 207S). But frequently there is the implication that the verbal or argumentative inventiveness displayed is pointless, deceptive, or otherwise suspect; see e.g. Strabo 13. 1. 69, Plut. *Aud. po.* 31E, and *PH* I. 63, the only other occurrence of the word in Sextus (cf. *PH* II. 9, 84 for the noun *heuresilogia*). It is clear from *sophistikōs*, 'sophistically', that such an implication is intended here; hence the word 'specious' in my translation.

[(b) *Proseiloumenoi*, 'pressing objections against', 7, is an extremely rare word. Active forms occur at *Il.* X. 347 and Eur. *Hel.* 445, in the sense 'press forward' or 'press against' (in both cases, the context is one of physical hostility); the middle form occurs at one other place in Sextus (*M* IX. 3), and elsewhere only once in Hesychius, in a context which is unhelpful in elucidating the present case (s.v. *aproseilos*). LSJ cites the Sextus usages as passive, and translates 'be confined, cooped up'; this would make sense at *M* IX. 3, but is clearly impossible here. This must be the middle voice, with the sense 'press one's attack against', or something close to it—which fits *M* IX. 3 better as well.

(c) In 16 I adopt the emendation of Blomqvist (1968: 96-7), changing the MSS reading *hoper* to *dioper*, and changing the editors' period before *echrēn* to a comma. The lack of a verb with *hoper* is problematic, and the changes also make the logic of the passage a little better; the omission of ⟨di⟩ immediately following *Indoi* is easy. For a parallel case of a clause with *dioper* followed by a main clause with *oun*, Blomqvist refers us to *M* I. 194, and for similar uses of *oun*, to *M* III. 76, IX. 401.]

The objection in 8–14 is not stated in the most perspicuous way, but may be summarized as follows: If one accepts that a definition of the form 'An A is a B' is equivalent to a conditional statement of the form 'If something is an A, that thing is a B', one should accept something similar in the case of division; thus a division of the form 'Of A's, some are B's, some C's, etc.' is equivalent to 'If some things are A's, those things are either B's or C's, etc.' Hence the division 'Of existing things, some are good, some bad, some indifferent' is equivalent to 'If some things are existents, those things are either good or bad or indifferent'. But this amounts to saying, absurdly, that *everything* belongs to just *one* of these three classes—which is falsified by any case of two things which are not both good or both bad or both indifferent. Since Xenocrates formulates his version of the division in the singular, he is not liable to this supposed difficulty; his version of the division would be equivalent to 'If something is an A, that thing is either a B or a C, etc.', which leads to no such absurd consequence.

In 12–13 Sextus lists each of the three possible pairings of two objects: (1) good/bad, (2) good/indifferent, (3) bad/indifferent. He then asserts that (a) 'These things are good', (b) 'These things are bad', and (c) 'These things are indifferent' are all false, since only *one* of the objects, not both of them, is good, bad, or indifferent respectively. As it stands, this is somewhat confusing. He should either have said that *at most* one item would be good, bad, or indifferent respectively; or he should have made explicit that (a) is to be taken in conjunction with (1) and (2) only, (b) in conjunction with (1) and (3) only, and (c) in conjunction with (2) and (3) only. Still, the general idea is straightforward enough.

The initial idea that definitions are equivalent to a certain form of conditionals is pretty certainly Stoic. First, a conditional serving as a definition appears in Cic. *Acad.* II. 21, in the course of a summary of Stoic epistemology. Then the reference to Chrysippus in 11 shows that at least the starting-point of the objection is a piece of Stoic doctrine (though it does not show that Chrysippus subscribed to the specific view here attributed to him; see below). In addition, the philosophical usage of the term *katholikon*, 'universal', seems to be Stoic in origin; the word appears nowhere in Aristotle (even though *katholou* is of course common), but Zeno wrote a book entitled *katholika* (DL VII. 4). Sextus makes it sound as if *katholikon* is a name for conditionals of the type discussed. But the *meaning* of *katholikon* is presumably just 'universal [proposition]'; the impression conveyed by Sextus is no doubt due to the Stoics' having *analysed* such propositions as conditionals. The universal form of these conditionals is indicated by the formulation of the antecedent (8), *ei ti estin*, 'If something is'; the 'something' is the highest genus in Stoic ontology (on this, see LS 27, Brunschwig 1994*b*, and on 224 below), so this formulation signals that *all* items falling under the description which follows are within the scope of the conditional. (In modern symbolism the logical form would be indicated with a universal quantifier.)

If the equivalence of definitions and 'universals' is Stoic, then the 'technical writers' (*technographoi*) mentioned in 8 must be either Stoics or writers who summarized aspects of Stoic logic. *M* VIII. 428 perhaps favours the former alternative; it uses the word *technologia*, 'technical discussion', in the context of a reference to introductory logical works by Stoics. (The word *technographoi* is frequently used to refer to the writers of technical treatises in rhetoric—e.g. DL II. 17, IX. 23, [Longinus] 12. 1; cf. Dionysius of Halicarnassus, *Isaeus* 20 (= DK 85A13)—but could presumably refer to writers of technical handbooks in a variety of fields.) But in either case, the authors of the objection—the 'some people' of 7— must be *different* from the 'technical writers'; for what is being objected to—the threefold division good/bad/indifferent—is itself pre-eminently Stoic. The objectors must therefore be using one Stoic position, the position summarized by the 'technical writers', to make a point against another Stoic position (a strategy employed frequently by Sextus himself, as well as by the sceptical Academy).

This raises the question at what point the summary of Stoic views stops and the polemical use of them begins. The answer, I think, must be the beginning of 10; I therefore suppose that 'they say' (10, 12) refers back to the 'some people' of 7, *not* to the 'technical writers' (whose contribution is thus restricted to 8–9). 8–9 discusses the equivalence of definitions and 'universals'; 10 then asserts that, by parity of reasoning, divisions too are equivalent to a certain form of universally quantified conditionals, and it is *this* supposed equivalence which creates trouble for the division good/bad/indifferent. Nowhere else is there any indication that the Stoics held that divisions as well as definitions were equivalent to a certain form of conditionals—least of all those bearing the absurd implication alleged in 12–13; and if Long and Sedley (LS 30) are right to suppose that the motivation for a conditional analysis of definitions is to avoid the appearance of treating concepts (*ennoēmata*) such as 'the human being' or 'the horse' as entities—which in Stoic ontology they are not—no analogous motivation obtains in the case of divisions, which convey no such impression. ('Of human beings, some are Greeks, some barbarians' refers to human beings, not to 'the human being'.) Besides, if the Stoics had actually said that divisions were equivalent to a certain form of conditionals, there would be no reason for Sextus even to introduce the issue of the equivalence of *definitions* and a certain form of conditionals; the topic of definitions is relevant only if it can be used to extract a *concession* having to do with the main subject, divisions. The conditional analysis of divisions, then, is better understood as an implication which the objectors think—or choose to claim—that the Stoics are obliged to accept. (The particle *alla gar*, 'but now', at the opening of 10, is regularly used to mark objections.) It is true that 11 says that 'according to Chrysippus' a certain division-statement is equivalent to a certain conditional. But this may be taken as referring to what, in the *objectors'* view, Chrysippus is committed to, rather than to anything he actually said; compare *M* VII. 155, where a report of an argument by Arcesilaus concludes by saying that 'according to the Stoics too' the wise person will suspend judgement in all cases. (I therefore take issue with LS I. 181–2 and Crivelli 1994, which attribute all the views summarized in 8–11 to the Stoics.)

Who were the objectors? It is conceivable that what we have recorded here is a dispute internal to the Stoic school, about the correct formulation of the threefold division. But in that case, since Sextus mentions that Xenocrates is not subject to the objection, one would expect that he would also say something to the effect that certain Stoics altered the formulation so as to escape this difficulty. Besides, the objection is so unsympathetic to the spirit of Stoic divisions that a source hostile to Stoicism seems far more likely. The objectors may perhaps have been sceptics; Sextus himself regards the objection as 'sophistical' and unimportant, but the sceptics need not always speak with one voice.

Sextus is right not to feel any need to respond to the objection (17). There is really no reason why any Stoic should agree that 'Of A's, some are B's, some C's, etc.' is equivalent to 'If some things are A's, those things are *all* either B's or C's, etc.' If the Stoics had employed a conditional analysis of divisions—and, as noted above, there is no good reason to assume that they did—nothing would prevent them from analysing 'Of A's, some are B's, some C's, etc.' as equivalent to 'If some things are A's, those things are either B's or C's, etc.', but construing this, in turn, as allowing, for *each* of the things that are A's, that it is either a B or a C, etc. Indeed, Crivelli (1994) has argued that utterances of plural sentences could be understood, according to the Stoics, either in a 'collective' or in a 'distributive' fashion, depending on the context.

If this is correct, the Stoics are in an excellent position to respond to the objection; the objectors are assuming that the 'collective' understanding of the conditional is the only possible one, but it is obviously the 'distributive' understanding that is meant here. (Crivelli himself, however, seems to misinterpret the present passage (497–8). He oddly takes Chrysippus to be the author of the objection, and he takes him to be admitting—for unspecified reasons—only the 'collective' understanding of the conditional in this context.)

The second objection, 15–17, also turns Stoic material against the three-fold division as so far formulated. The assertion that 'Every sound division . . . is the cutting of a genus into its proximate species' is repeated almost word for word in DL's summary of Stoic logic (VII. 61), which also refers just below to subdivision. (On the DL passage and its sources, see Mansfeld 1986: 351–73.) In this case the hypothesis of an internal Stoic dispute is more plausible; this objection, unlike the first one, is really a sympathetic attempt to improve on the formulation of the division, rather than an attempt to make fun of it. It is clear, in any case, that variant formulations of the division were current within Stoicism; the same passage of DL offers as an example of division 'Of existing things, some are good, some not good', and then as an example of subdivision, 'And of those which are not good, some are bad, some indifferent'. Some Stoics may well have considered that the true 'proximate species' of 'existing things' are (a) things which 'make a difference to us' (*diapheronta estin hēmin*, 16) and (b) things which are indifferent—and that the distinction between good and bad represents a subdivision of the former. Again, Sextus is right to treat this reformulation as unimportant for his purposes.

18–20: The status of the division in what follows

Issues of translation and text:
    [(a) *Ou pantōs* (18), which is relatively common in Sextus, is occasionally to be translated 'not at all', 'by no means' (*M* I. 197, probably *M* V. 43, perhaps *PH* II. 187). But it much more commonly means 'not entirely' or 'not necessarily' (e.g. *PH* I. 146, 202, II. 83, 148, *M* VII. 42, 197, 357, X. 17, 151, XI. 97), and this fits the present context much better; the parenthetical 'perhaps' clause that follows indicates that what is at issue here is a lack of definiteness (not the emphatic assertion that

things are *not* the way they appear). For *ou pantōs* answered by *tacha* (or vice versa), cf. *M* I. 281, VII. 197.]

(b) *Huparchei* is translated 'actually is' (or 'is actually') throughout this section. Both Bury and Russo render it 'exists', at least where this is grammatically possible. But it is clearly impossible in the final sentence of 18 ('is actually 100 stades'), and is ill-advised elsewhere as well. The uses of *esti* under discussion are predicative uses; *huparchei* should therefore be translated so as to correspond with this. *Huparchei* can certainly mean 'exists', and is sometimes so rendered below (183; cf. 41, 42, 185); but the operative contrast here is between *how* things appear and *how* they are in fact. On the choice of 'actually is', rather than 'really is', see below. (*Huparchei* is translated 'is real' at 220; but there the potential confusion to be discussed immediately below is not at issue.)

(c) The words translated 'in his *Images*' (20) do not actually appear in the MSS; they are the plausible, and as far as I know universally accepted, emendation of Fabricius. (The MSS contain several variants, none of which makes any sense.)

(d) On the translation of the fragment from Timon (20), see below.

The claim that 'is' can sometimes mean 'appears' also occurs at *PH* I. 135. There Sextus seems to imply that this is a specifically sceptical usage, whereas here the example of the mathematicians shows that he takes himself to be adopting a usage which enjoys some broader currency. It is important to note that this passage does *not* say that, *whenever* Sextus uses 'is', he is to be understood as meaning 'appears'. In fact, the opposite is implied; Sextus says that 'It is day' means 'It actually is day' (18), and he says that this is something that 'we say', without any hint that he, as a sceptic, might want to distance himself from this usage. It is only in the statement 'Of existing things, some are good, some bad, and some between these' (19) that Sextus states that 'are' is to be understood as meaning 'appear'; as noted earlier, he thereby adopts a useful and standard ethical classification, but without asserting that anything is, in its real nature, good or bad. This is said to be a case of speaking 'in sceptical fashion' (*skeptikōs*); but that does not mean that the sceptic must *always* use 'is' in the sense 'appears'. To speak 'in sceptical fashion' is to speak consistently with the sceptical outlook, and to say 'Some things are good, some bad, etc.' is inconsistent with that outlook *unless* 'is' means 'appears'; but in *M* XI, as we shall see, Sextus thinks that it is quite possible sometimes to make assertions (consistent with the sceptical outlook) in which 'is' does *not* need to be understood in the restricted sense

'appears' (see esp. 68–78, 112–18 with Comm.). (*PH* I. 135 is sometimes
read as licensing us to read 'appears' whenever Sextus, in his own person, says 'is'. But the text does not justify this; Sextus says that by 'is' he
means 'appears' 'here as in other places' (*entautha hōsper kai en allois*),
not 'here as in all other places'. In any case, *M* XI's stance on this issue
should not be assumed to be the same as that of *PH*—see Introduction,
n. 21, with accompanying text.)

The reason why he takes this to be possible, I shall suggest, is that, in
using 'is' in the sense 'actually is', one is not necessarily committing
oneself to a claim about the way things are *by nature*. For something to
have a certain property by nature, it must have that property *invariably*
(see esp. on 69–71, also Introduction, sect. II). Hence statements which
are relativized to specific persons or circumstances do not count as statements about the nature of things, even though they may use 'is' in the
sense 'actually is' rather than in the sense 'appears'; the sceptic is entitled
to make such statements, because suspension of judgement, in *M* XI,
consists purely in refraining from all attempts to specify the nature of
things (see on 118, esp. point 4). It is thus only *unqualified* claims against
which the sceptic must be on guard. If the sceptic says, 'Of existing
things, some are good, some bad, and some between these', then 'are'
must be used in the sense 'appear', because the claim otherwise *would* be
a claim about the nature of things; with 'It is day', on the other hand,
which refers only to the present moment ('as when we say *at present* "it
is day"'), there is no such danger.

I translate *huparchei* by 'actually is' rather than by 'really is' because
Sextus later sometimes uses 'really' or 'in reality' (*tais alētheiais, ontōs, tōi
onti*) interchangeably with 'by nature' (68–78, 114). As the case of 'It is
day' makes clear, the use of 'is' (*esti*) in the sense *huparchei* is precisely
not such as to commit one, by itself, to any claim about how things are
by nature. The translation 'actually is' is intended to be non-committal
in this respect; *huparchei* here simply means 'is in the full sense, rather
than in the restricted sense "appears"'—with no implication that the *real
nature* of things is necessarily at issue. Of course, *some* sentences containing 'is' in the sense 'actually is' do commit one to a view about the nature
of things; to say 'Of existing things, some are good, some bad, and some
between these', with 'are' meaning 'actually are', would involve one, as
Sextus suggests, in a view 'about the *nature and existence* (*phusin hupostaseōs*)
of the things which are good and bad and neither' (19). But this depends
on the character of the claim in question, not just on the use of *esti* in the
sense *huparchei*.

Sextus' use of the notion of appearance has recently been discussed by Brennan (1994). Much of Brennan's treatment is thoroughly compatible with my own, at least as regards the present passage (see esp. 165–8). One significant point of disagreement is this: Brennan takes Sextus' use of the words 'Of existing things, some are good, some bad, and some between these' to be merely a recitation of the view of the dogmatists, whereas I take Sextus to be *accepting* at least the principle of classification contained in these words. Brennan's reading requires us to attribute a confusion to Sextus which my reading avoids; if Sextus is merely *quoting* the dogmatists, he has no need to insist, in the interests of sceptical caution, that 'are' means 'appear'; in fact, if the quotation is to be accurate, he ought *not* to do so (see Brennan 1994: 168 n. 26).

The quotation from Timon is included as corroborating Sextus' 'habit' of referring to things as 'good or bad or indifferent according to their appearance' (20). Sextus understands Timon to be speaking about the good 'in sceptical fashion', like himself, making what might look like a dogmatic claim about 'the nature of the divine and the good', but in fact intending this as a claim about appearances.

These lines of Timon have usually been taken as central in the reconstruction of the views of Pyrrho, and for that reason have generated much controversy. I have discussed them at length in Bett 1994*d*; here a very brief summary of the issues must suffice. Previously the lines have always been thought to have been spoken by Pyrrho, and to represent Pyrrho's answer to the question posed to him in the fragment of which the quotation in 1 above is a part—that is, the question of how he achieves his superhuman tranquillity. The main topic of disagreement in recent years has been whether the view Pyrrho here expresses is recognizable—as Sextus thinks it is—as an instance of scepticism. I argue that the view expressed cannot be understood otherwise than as strongly dogmatic; that this view is incompatible with the rest of what we know of Pyrrho's thought—even though his thought did differ in important ways from that of Sextus and other later Pyrrhonists (this is discussed in more detail in Bett 1994*a*); and that we should therefore drop the assumption that Pyrrho is the speaker of these lines. This is, after all, an assumption; no ancient author besides Sextus quotes or refers to this fragment, and Sextus does not mention Pyrrho. Of course, if this fragment does represent Pyrrho's answer to the question posed to him in the other fragment, Pyrrho must be the speaker; but this, too, is an assumption, with no strong evidence to recommend it. I offer the suggestion that the speaker of the present fragment may be Timon himself, prior to his full initiation into Pyrrho's outlook; but the speaker and the context are bound to remain highly speculative.

A few remarks need to be made about the translation of the fragment:

(1) It makes a considerable difference whether or not one places a comma at the end of the third line (as traditionally); I have retained the comma. Burnyeat (1980) (followed by LS 2E) proposed to eliminate the traditional comma, and hence to translate the second couplet

> Namely, that the nature of the divine and the good is at any time [*aiei*]
> That from which life becomes most equable for a man.

This eliminates any reference to eternally existing natures, and this, it is suggested, greatly reduces the level of troublesome dogmatism in the fragment. I argue against this proposal in Bett 1994*d*: sect. II.

(2) I have translated *kataphainetai* in the first line by 'appears'; Sextus clearly thinks that that is what it means, and his point in the context depends on his understanding it that way (see above). It is another question whether this is how the word was originally intended by Timon; in Bett 1994*d*: sect. III I argue that Sextus has misunderstood Timon, and that, as Timon meant it, the first couplet should be translated

> For indeed I shall tell, as it *is evident* to me that it is,
> A word of truth, having a correct standard,

(i.e. 'I shall tell what to me evidently is a word of truth, etc.'). It would not be surprising for Sextus to have misunderstood the sense of *kataphainetai*. The word never appears in Sextus' own writings, nor do the related words *kataphanēs* and *kataphaneia*; *kataphainomai* seems to be relatively common in the fifth and fourth centuries BC, and rare after that. (See Bett 1994*d*: 319.) The word may well have been for Sextus an archaic one, whose nuances he was not well attuned to. As several scholars have noticed (e.g. Burnyeat 1980: 88, Caizzi 1981*a*: 256), Sextus does not seem confident about his reading of the fragment; the words 'seems to indicate' (*eoike dēloun*) suggest hesitation or uncertainty. The obscurity, from his perspective, of the word *kataphainetai* may very well have been the reason, or one reason, for this.

(3) It is possible that 'of truth', in the second line, should be read with 'standard' rather than with 'a word'; or, again, it may be deliberately intended to be ambiguous.

Other significant treatments of the fragment, or of parts of it, not already referred to are Long 1978*c*: 84-5, Reale 1981: 306-15, Ferrari

1981: 356–61, Stopper 1983: 270–1, Ausland 1989: 429–34, Brunschwig 1994*c*.

On 'conception', *ennoia*, 20, see comments on ch. II.

CHAPTER II (21–41)

This chapter, like the previous one, is presented as being introductory. Its announced purpose is to arrive at a clear 'conception' of the objects being discussed. As Sextus says, citing Epicurus, such clarity is just as necessary when criticizing the theories of others as when attempting to construct theories oneself (21); and in the final sentence of the chapter, the 'conceptions' of good, bad, and indifferent are said to be 'established at the outset' (41)—the next question being whether anything really answers to these 'conceptions'. Roughly half the chapter attempts to follow through on this promise; Sextus begins by offering a relatively detailed summary of Stoic definitions of the good (22–30), and ends by pointing out that the bad and the indifferent can be dealt with analogously (40–1). But the chapter also has another, competing aim: to mount *objections* to the dogmatists' definitions of the good (and also, by implication, the bad and the indifferent—cf. 'what should be said against the definitions', 41). Two objections are proposed. The first (31–4) applies to just one of the Stoics' numerous definitions, is attributed to an unnamed 'some', and is implicitly dismissed by Sextus as pedantic (35). This by itself, then, might well be understood along the same lines as the objections in the previous chapter—that is, as designed to bolster the definitions by exhibiting the feebleness of the points which have been raised against them. But the second objection (35–9), with which Sextus identifies, is more serious, and is apparently directed against all the definitions offered above and more; and at the beginning of the following chapter (42) Sextus is willing to say, on the basis of this objection, that 'the dogmatists did not outline the conception of good and bad in a convincing fashion'.

The chapter as a whole, then, has a somewhat schizophrenic character. Inasmuch as the offering of definitions is a theoretically committed activity—or was, at any rate, in ancient philosophy, where definitions were intended to specify the nature of the things being defined, not simply to stipulate the way a certain word is to be used—it is understandable that

Sextus would want to find arguments against the definitions offered by the Stoics and others; indeed, since such definitions at least imply the *reality* of their objects, a sceptic could hardly avoid being suspicious of them. But if definitions are to be used as a way to 'fix the conception' (21) of the objects to be discussed, it is plainly counter-productive also to *undermine* the definitions outlined for this purpose.

In contrast, the parallel chapter of *PH* III (169–78) is consistently critical of dogmatic attempts to specify the 'conceptions' of good, bad, and indifferent. The chapter is introduced as 'setting out beforehand' (*proekthemenoi*, 168) these three 'conceptions'. But with this minor exception, there is no ambivalence about the purpose of the chapter; when Sextus says in conclusion (178), 'Thus it is clear that they did not bring us to the conception of each of the things previously mentioned', he is accurately and comprehensively summing up what has just been argued. He adds that the dogmatists' failure in this regard is not surprising, given that the objects whose 'conceptions' were sought may not even exist; this then leads directly into the topic of the next chapter. The chapter in *PH* III, then, is superior to the one in *M* XI in the clarity of its aims. It is superior in certain other respects as well (see below).

This difference is one example of a more general difference between *PH* and *M* VII–XI regarding the topic of 'conception'. Sextus says several other times in *M* VII–XI that it is necessary at the beginning of the discussion of a topic to get clear on the 'conception' of the object under discussion; see *M* VIII. 300, IX. 12, X. 6 (and cf. *M* II. 1). But he also derives *objections* from the 'conceptions' which he has outlined (VIII. 332a, IX. 29); and in at least one of these passages, as in the present chapter, the objections actually undermine his stated purpose of reaching a settled understanding of what is to be discussed. As mentioned above (see on 3–6), Sextus opens the discussion of proof in *M* VIII by presenting what is supposedly a single 'conception' of proof (300–36); but almost immediately afterwards he says that since there are many competing 'conceptions' of proof, none of them is trustworthy (332a). For discussion of this passage and of this general difficulty, see Brunschwig 1988. In *PH*, on the other hand, Sextus *never* opens a topic with a neutral review of the relevant 'conceptions'; the words *ennoia* and *epinoia*, which I have translated 'conception' (see on 21 below), are always used to refer to conceptions exclusive to the dogmatists, and in such contexts, as in the cases of the good, the bad, and the indifferent, the conceptions in question are commonly attacked (see e.g. II. 22 (29), 70–1, 135–43, III. 13 (23)). (In *M* VII–XI, as well, this is frequently the spirit in which 'conceptions' are introduced—e.g. *M* VII. 263-4, IX. 366, X. 50, 215; my point is that *M* VII–XI is not consistent in this regard.) *PH* also has a chapter explicitly attacking definitions as such (II. 205-12). Nothing in *M* VII–XI corresponds to this—not surprisingly, since in *M* VII–XI, despite Sextus' frequent exposure of difficulties in the dogmatists' 'conceptions' of various types of entities, he is not willing to reject the practice of definition altogether. Sextus introduces the 'special' section of *PH* (II–III; for the term, see I. 5-6) by arguing that the sceptic may very well have a 'notion' (*noēsis*, II. 10) of any of the objects treated by the dogmatists, without thereby being in any way committed to the existence of those objects; such 'notions' occur to us 'passively' (*pathēmatikōs*), without requiring any theorizing on our part. Dogmatic definitions, by contrast, are liable to land us with theoretical commitments (see above). *PH* consistently avoids this liability, whereas *M* VII–XI does not.

We shall see comparable differences in clarity and organization between the two works at many points in later chapters; this is one of three main reasons for thinking, contrary to the generally prevailing view, that *M* XI precedes *PH* III (see Introduction, sect. IV).

21: Transition and introduction

As already noted, 'conception' is used as the translation of both *epinoia* (21, 42) and *ennoia* (20, 22). *Ennoia* is Stoic terminology for generic impressions whose contents are universal concepts (*ennoēmata*), such as man, horse, or white (Aetius 4. 11. 1-4 (= LS 39E), Plut. *Comm. not.* 1084F-1085B). The Stoics define a 'preconception' (*prolēpsis*) as a 'conception' which is acquired naturally, rather than by training (Aetius, loc. cit.); the acquisition of this class of 'conceptions' is a key part of the normal development of the human mind. Though the Epicureans do not use *ennoia* in the same technical way, their usage of *prolēpsis* is the same—indeed, Epicurus was the originator of this usage (DL X. 31, 33, 37). Sextus regularly uses *epinoia* interchangeably with *ennoia* (e.g. *M* VIII. 332a-336a), and this usage, too, may be Stoic in origin; *epinoia* is defined by [Galen], in a context containing many Stoic echoes (*Def. med.* 19. 381K (= *SVF* II. 89)), as a 'stored notion' (*enapokeimenē noēsis*), which is also the definition Plutarch (loc. cit.) attributes to the Stoics for *ennoia* (cf. DL X. 33 for the same phrase in connection with *prolēpsis*). For the connection between *ennoiai* and definitions in Stoic thought, see below; on *prolēpsis*, see also linguistic point (a) on 68-78. For further discussion of these terms and the associated doctrines, see Sandbach 1971, Todd 1973*b*, LS I. 241, II. 241.

By Sextus' time all three terms were part of the common philosophical vocabulary. Sextus himself clearly would not want to be committed to the epistemological and psychological theories in which these terms were originally embedded; his point, as we have seen, is simply that before discussing any topic, it is important to have a clear picture of what it is we are talking about. However, the difficulties he experiences here and elsewhere in *M* VII–XI suggest that he has not fully succeeded in extricating himself from the theoretical connotations of these terms; see below on 22–30. (*PH* does better, in part because it is much more cautious in their use; in addition to the points above, note that *prolēpsis* is used in *PH* exclusively to refer to universally shared non-theoretical attitudes—I. 211, 225, II. 246.)

The claim attributed to Epicurus recurs with almost identical wording at *M* I. 57; the repetition does not prove that Sextus is *quoting* Epicurus, but the point fits squarely within Epicurean epistemology (see LS 17).

Despite the title of the chapter, only the good and the bad are mentioned in 21; cf. on 1–2, 40–1, 90–5.

22–30: Stoic definitions of the good

Points of language, translation, and text:

(a) I translate *ho philos* in 22–4 by 'the friend'. This perhaps reads oddly, since it is not specified *whose* friend is at issue. But the lack of specification has a point in Stoic doctrine. On the Stoics' view, only the virtuous can truly be or have friends (DL VII. 124, Stob. II. 108, 15–25); so *anyone* who is genuinely X's friend, no matter who X may be, is possessed of virtue, and hence is a good.

(b) 'The sons of the Stoics' (24) may refer, as LS (II. 368) suggests, to later Stoics. But elsewhere (*M* IX. 336, *PH* III. 170) Sextus attributes the same point about parts and wholes to 'the Stoics' without restriction. And in the present passage, the point is used to explain or justify a definition which is itself attributed generically to the Stoics. I therefore prefer to read this as simply a periphrasis for 'the Stoics' (cf. e.g. *M* VI. 19, 30).

[(c) Blomqvist (1968: 97) proposes altering *heteroia*, 'of a different kind', in the first sentence of 24, to *hetera*, 'other'. This may be correct; *hetera* would suit the argument better. But it is also possible that *heteroia* is a piece of mild inaccuracy on the part of Sextus or his source. I therefore retain the MSS reading.]

(d) 'Significations' (*sēmainomenōn*) and 'application' (*epibolēn*), 25. Sextus' expression here is needlessly convoluted, and his terminology has caused translators some difficulty. (*PH* III. 171 has nothing corresponding to this passage; Sextus simply says, 'They say that the good is spoken of in three ways'.) The three 'significations' are the three meanings of the word 'good' which were implicitly just referred to; the word has a different 'application'—i.e. a different pattern of usage—corresponding to each of these three meanings. The Stoics, then, explain each of the three meanings, as they occur (needless to say) in the usages specific to them. For *epibolē* as the 'application' of a word, cf. *M* III. 4, X. 2. It is doubtful whether, in the Stoics' own terminology, 'signification' would be used to refer to the meaning of an individual word such as 'good'; on this see LS 33. But outside the Stoics' distinctive theory of language the term is used, from Aristotle onwards (e.g. *Rhet.* III. 1405b8, *Top.* 102a2), to refer to the meaning of any stretch of language, including individual words.

(e) 'Plato and Xenocrates', 28. The Greek literally reads '*those around* [*tois peri*] Plato and Xenocrates'. But in doxographical accounts, 'those around X' is often used as a periphrasis for 'X' (e.g. DL II. 62, 105, 134, IX. 62), and this usage seems most probable here.

(f) *Ptōsis*, 29, is rendered, as standardly, by 'case'. I have placed quotation marks around 'case' in the translation because this is not the normal use of the English word; the translation seems legitimate, however, because we do not appear to have the normal usage of *ptōsis* here, either. As noted earlier (see on 3–6 above), the word most commonly refers to the grammatical inflections of words; though not restricted to the cases of nouns, it is, in this usage, at least closely related to our use of 'case' (and is in fact more typically applied to the cases of nouns than to other grammatical inflections—see *Scholia in Dionys. Thrac.* 382, 36–383, 2, and the title 'on the five cases' ascribed to Chrysippus at DL VII. 192). But here *ptōsis* instead refers to what is *signified* by a word; Sextus seems, indeed, to be using the term interchangeably with *sēmainomenon*, 'signification' (see point (d) above), from which he has momentarily switched. Different types of objects 'fall under' the different 'cases'—i.e. the different significations—of the the same word 'dog'. The notion that *ptōsis* refers—or should refer—to the *sēmainomenon* is also argued for in *Scholia in Dionys. Thrac.* 523, 9–27. Long (1971: 105–6) suggests that this non-standard usage of *ptōsis* is connected with Stoicism; but there is nothing in either the present passage or the Scholia passage which requires us to understand them as drawing on Stoic ideas. The Stoic concept of *ptōsis* is itself far from clear. But if the Stoics did use the term to refer to linguistic entities, it does not look as if they used it to refer to what is signified by words. Nor do they seem to have used it, as commonly, to refer to the *inflections of* words, but rather to the inflected words themselves (in the point of translation on 3–6 above this latter distinction was passed over as not relevant); for this interpretation see LS 33, Atherton 1993: 279–86. For a very different view, according to which the Stoic concept of *ptōsis* is the *metaphysical* concept of an individual quality, see Frede 1994*a*. Atherton and Frede agree, however, that the present passage does not accurately portray the Stoic view—whether or not it is attempting to do so.

[(g) The text at the end of 29 ('so in calling good', etc.) has been questioned by Heintz 1932: 248–9. But though the language is indeed awkward—and this is reflected in my translation—it is no more so, I think, than some other sentences in *M* XI. (Cf. linguistic point (i) on 48–67, point (c) on 150–61, point (f) on 197–209.) At any rate, Sextus' general meaning is clear whether or not the text is altered as Heintz suggests.]

Sextus does not explain why the following discussion is devoted almost exclusively to Stoic definitions. But one obvious explanation is that, as he suggests (22), the Stoics themselves saw definitions as articulations of the 'conceptions' present in any ordinary mature human being. Indeed, among their several definitions of definition itself, the Stoics define it as 'bringing us through a brief reminder to a conception of the things underlying the words' ([Galen], *Def. med.* 19. 349, 2–4 (= LS 32D); and Cic. *Tusc.* 4. 53). The technical nature of much of this section may seem to count against this claim. But it is in no way contrary to the spirit of Stoic philosophy to suggest that our 'conceptions' are much more elaborate, and more far-reaching in their implications, than we ourselves generally realize; for according to the Stoics, the rationality in every human being, though perverted in most actual cases, is akin to the divine reason which pervades and governs the universe.

It is, however, somewhat less clear how the lengthy and detailed exposition of Stoic views is supposed to contribute to Sextus' own purposes. For *he* does not—or at any rate, should not—hold this ambitious and controversial view about definitions, conceptions, and rationality; so one would expect him simply to conduct an introductory clarification of his subject-matter, using as little jargon or other theoretical baggage as possible. The fact that he does not do so suggests that *ennoia, epinoia,* and *prolēpsis* are still, for him, theoretically loaded terms; to use them at all carries the danger that one will be drawn into a Stoic-style quest for correct definitions, and Sextus does not entirely succeed in resisting the temptation. The resulting tension with his own aspirations as a sceptic then leads him into his secondary project, at odds with the alleged purpose of the chapter, of exhibiting the dogmatists' definitions as pointless and inadequate. This tension is perhaps reflected at the very beginning, in the phrase 'holding on to the "common conceptions" (so to speak)' (22). The qualification 'so to speak' is curious, since the term 'common conceptions' is not only present in Stoic texts (Alexander of Aphrodisias, *De Mixtione* 217. 3, summarizing Chrysippus, Cic. *Tusc.* 4. 53, and cf. the title of Plutarch's *Comm. not.*), but is also not unusual in Sextus' own writings (e.g. *M* IX. 61, 66, 124, III. 56, and cf. 44 below, 'common preconception'). Sextus is not, then, drawing attention to the oddity of the term itself. He must instead be suggesting that its applicability in *this* context is in some way dubious; and the point may be that, though the Stoics purport to be in line with ordinary ideas about the good, their multiple abstruse definitions show that this is mere pretence.

The Stoic definition of good as 'benefit or not other than benefit' also occurs at DL VII. 94. DL does not explain the definition, proceeding immediately to the material discussed by Sextus at 25–7. But Sextus' explanation receives indirect support from DL VII. 104, which defines benefiting as 'setting in motion or being in a state according to virtue' (*kinein ē ischein kat'aretēn*). In this definition 'setting in motion' refers to virtuous actions, and 'being in a state' to the virtues themselves (on this, see Tsekourakis 1974: 68–72), which accords with Sextus' report that under the heading of 'benefit' come 'virtue and excellent action'; the remaining goods therefore belong, as Sextus says, under the heading 'not other than benefit'. The point of this curious term seems to be to justify applying the label 'good' to friends and excellent persons—which it would seem perverse to refuse—even though there is an essential connection between goodness and benefit (on this, see DL VII. 103), and friends and excellent persons cannot themselves be described as species of benefit. The term 'not other than benefit' concedes this last point, but emphasizes that these things are none the less intimately and non-accidentally *connected* with benefit, in the manner explained in 24. They are connected in that virtue, which is itself a species of benefit, 'is a part of both the excellent human being and the friend', and parts are intimately connected with—specifically, neither identical with nor 'other than'—the wholes of which they are parts. (The general point about parts and wholes, with the example of the hand, also occurs at *M* IX. 336.) As Tsekourakis (1974: 70) remarks, Sextus should strictly have reversed this last point, saying that *wholes* are neither identical with nor other than the parts which comprise them; for the excellent human being and the friend, which are 'not other than benefit', are the wholes of which virtue, a benefit, is a part. The parallel passage of *PH* III, in keeping with its frequently superior clarity, does express the point in this way (170).

For the Stoics, virtue is a part of the virtuous person in a quite literal sense; as Sextus says (23), it is 'the ruling part in a certain state'. The 'ruling part' (*hēgemonikon*) is the soul's central faculty, in which all mental states reside (Aetius 4. 21 (= *SVF* II. 836)), and which is located, according to orthodox Stoicism, in the heart (Galen, *De foet. format.* 4. 698, 2–9 (= LS 53D)); it is corporeal (Nemesius 78, 7–79, 2, 81, 6–10 (= LS 45C, D)), and specifically breath (*pneuma*) (Calcidius 220 (= LS 53G)). For further discussion see LS 53, Long 1982. Virtue is a disposition of this 'ruling part', and hence can be said to *be* the ruling part appropriately modified; cf. Seneca, *Ep.* 113. 2, DL VII. 89. The qualification 'in a certain state' (*pōs echon*) refers to one of what are traditionally but misleadingly called the four Stoic 'categories' (on these, see LS 27–9).

Contrary to what is commonly suggested about Greek ethics as a whole, the Stoics do not think of the benefits conferred by virtue (or, more generally, by those things that are good) as benefits solely *for* the virtuous agent in question—or indeed, for any particular person. Benefits, in Stoicism, benefit *all* those who are good, whether or not they have any connection with the person conferring the benefit; they are, as one might say, benefits from an impersonal point of view. See Cic. *Fin.* III. 69, Stob. II. 93, 19–94, 6, II. 95, 3–8, II. 101, 21–102, 2, Plut. *Comm. not.* 1068F–1069A, 1076A; and see below on 45–6. In this respect, at least, the Stoics seem to be considerably closer to most modern moral theories than are other ancient ethical systems. (On the general issue of the relation between ancient and modern ethics, see Williams 1985, Annas 1993: esp. ch. 2, sect. 7, and ch. 22.) On the sense in which, on the Stoic view, it is virtue that is beneficial (as opposed to most of the things that would normally occur to us as such), see Annas 1993: ch. 19, sect. 2.

There follows a further threefold distinction among uses of the word 'good'. This is presented as a 'consequence' (*akolouthian*, 25) of the previous definition. This is not meant in any strict logical sense; still, the

threefold distinction does in a clear sense build upon the earlier definition, in that it further specifies the possible relations between goodness
and benefit and the relation to benefit enjoyed by each of the types of
things earlier called good. The same threefold distinction is mentioned
by Stobaeus (II. 69, 17–70, 3), but without examples (and with one
apparent difference from Sextus' account—see below). DL VII. 94 appears to be drawing ultimately on the same material, but differs somewhat from Sextus and Stobaeus; either he is confused (so Tsekourakis
1974: 71), or he is indebted to a partially different Stoic tradition (so
Mansfeld 1989). In either case, Sextus is our most detailed source for
this particular piece of Stoic doctrine. (Atherton (1993: 105–6) is inclined
to regard the threefold distinction as belonging to 'some later phase' of
Stoicism, rather than to orthodox Stoicism; but she neglects the parallel
passages in Stobaeus and DL.)

As Sextus says (30), the three uses of 'good' are progressively broader,
each one including the previous ones. At each stage the required relation
to the central notion of benefit becomes looser; however, as with the
definition in 22–4, a clear connection with the notion of benefit is preserved at all stages. In the 'primary' sense (25), good is the *source* of
benefit, and only virtue itself qualifies as good in this sense. In the second
sense virtuous actions as well as the virtues themselves qualify as good.
The crucial difference between the first sense and the second is the
phrase 'in connection with which' (26, *kath'ho*) as opposed to 'by which
or from which' (*huph'hou ē aph'hou*). When virtuous actions take place,
benefit does (necessarily) result; but it is not virtuous actions themselves,
but the virtues which give rise to them, which are strictly speaking the
origin, or 'spring', from which this benefit occurs. The looser 'in connection with which', unlike 'by which or from which', covers the relation
between virtuous actions and benefit as well as that between virtues and
benefit. Contrary to LS II. 368 (cf. 201), both the first and the second
senses refer to things which give rise to beneficial results, and neither
refers directly to the results themselves (see the next paragraph); the
difference between the first and the second lies in the *ways in which* the
results are specified as arising.

Again, the kind of 'benefit' the Stoics have in mind is not what would
normally occur to us; the 'benefit' which is conferred by a virtue or by a
virtuous action is simply the exercising of the virtue itself. The Stoics'
standard examples are 'being wise' (*to phronein*) and 'being moderate' (*to
sōphronein*); these terms refer to the *exercising* of one's practical wisdom
and moderation respectively, not simply to the *possession* of these virtues

(on this, see Long 1976: 87). (Long has been challenged by Reesor (1983: 78–9) and by Brunschwig (1994a: 163–4). But neither author takes account of the fact that 'being wise' and 'being moderate' are referred to as species of 'right actions' (*katorthōmata*; on this term, see on 200–1 below), and of 'things done' (*energēmata*); see Stob. II. 86, 5–7, II. 96, 18–20.) 'Being wise' and 'being moderate' are referred to by Stobaeus as 'benefactions' (*ōphelēmata*, II. 86, 5–7; cf. II. 97, 18–98, 6) and as the effects of the virtues with which they are correlated (I. 138, 18–21, and cf. 32–3 below). It might seem tempting to identify these 'benefactions' with the virtuous actions referred to by Sextus; but this would be a mistake. For, as he says, a virtuous action (*praxis*)—e.g. an individual wise action—is an 'activity' (*energeia*, 23), and 'activities', for the Stoics, are corporeal (Plut. *Comm. not.* 1084C; cf. Seneca, *Ep.* 113. 23, on what exactly walking is). 'Benefactions', on the other hand, though also designated by a word regularly translated 'action' (*energēma*; see Stob. II. 85, 20–86, 1, II. 96, 18 ff.)—'action' here being used in the sense of a *thing done*, rather than the *doing* of something—are incorporeal 'predicates' (Stob. II. 98, 5–6, and cf. 32 below), as are effects generally (Stob. I. 138, 15–16, Sextus, *M* IX. 211). (On predicates and their incorporeal status, see LS 33, 55, Brunschwig 1994a.) Instead, then, we should understand the exercising of e.g. one's practical wisdom ('being wise') as what *both* the virtue, practical wisdom, *and* individual wise actions (i.e. doings) give rise to. According to Sextus' summary, both virtues and virtuous actions lead to beneficial results; the results, in both cases, are these 'benefactions'. For further discussion of these and related concepts, see Reesor 1983.

According to Sextus' account, as we have seen, the second sense of 'good' *contains* the first. It is in this respect that Stobaeus' much briefer account differs from Sextus'; there it is not suggested that the second sense is included in the first—indeed the opposite is implied. If one of the two is mistaken, I suspect that it is Stobaeus (or his probable source, Arius Didymus); the level of detail in Sextus' treatment inspires greater confidence. But it is also very possible that each of the two classifications had adherents within the Stoic school. The difference between them, after all, is minor. The issue is simply whether, by 'that in connection with which it results that one is benefited', one means to refer *only* to the weaker relation to benefit enjoyed by virtuous actions (see above) or to that relation to benefit *as well as any stronger relation*; the latter reading yields Sextus' account, the former Stobaeus'.

The third sense of 'good', viz. 'able to be of benefit' (27), covers not

only virtues and virtuous actions—both of which, in the earlier definition, were designated as 'benefit'—but also those things which were
designated as 'not other than benefit'; since the 'excellent human being'
for example, has virtue as a part, he or she is 'able to be of benefit' just
as much as is virtue itself. But the phrase 'able to be of benefit' is yet
more non-committal about the way in which benefit ensues than were
the analogous phrases in the first two definitions.

Before closing his discussion of the threefold distinction, Sextus inserts
a brief discussion of Platonic Forms (28–9). Plato and Xenocrates, like
the Stoics, are said to use 'good' 'in multiple ways'; but there is an
important difference in *how* this is true for each group. The passage thus
has the function of clarifying the relations between the various Stoic uses
of 'good' just considered. However, this goal could have been achieved
much more briefly had Sextus wanted (the reference to Platonic views is
simply omitted, with no loss of clarity, in *PH* III (171)); and it looks as
if he may have an ulterior motive in including this material. One possibility is that he hopes, by exhibiting the Platonic position in an unflat-
tering light (see below), to further his subsidiary (and competing) aim of
exhibiting the dogmatists' ineptness at clarifying the concept of goodness.
     The claim that 'the Form is called good in one way and that which
partakes of the Form in another way' (28) is attributed to Plato and
Xenocrates themselves. There is a sense in which this is clearly correct.
For Plato says that particulars are named after Forms; by partaking in
Forms they acquire the names of those Forms (*Parm.* 130e5–131a2; cf.
Tim. 52a5–7, *Ph.* 78d10–e2). The names apply to the Forms strictly
speaking, or without qualification, whereas they apply to particulars only
derivatively and with qualifications (*Ph.* 74a–75a, *Rep.* 479a–d). But it
does not follow—and Plato would obviously contest the suggestion—
that the meanings of e.g. 'good' as applied to the Form and as applied to
particulars 'have nothing in common'; on the contrary, the whole point
of his position is that the latter usage is parasitic on the former. (By the
same token, Sextus is seriously exaggerating when he suggests that the
different usages of 'dog' are *entirely* unrelated.) There is no reason to
suspect that Xenocrates' position on this issue diverged from Plato's—
even though he does appear to have had some innovative views on
Forms, and especially on their numerical basis (see Heinze 1892: frs. 29–
39, Dörrie 1967: esp. 1519–23). Nor does Aristotle criticize Plato on
these grounds, in the course of his many arguments against the theory of
Forms. It is true that he criticizes the notion that there is a Form of the

good by arguing that goodness is, in his sense, 'homonymous' (*NE* 1096a23–9, 1096b14–26; see MacDonald 1989, Irwin 1981). But his point here is *not* that if there were a Form of e.g. good, the goodness of particulars would be merely 'homonymous' with the goodness of the Form; indeed, in summarizing the theory of Forms, he is elsewhere quite happy to say (without taking Plato to task on the issue) that the F-ness of a Form and the F-ness of the corresponding particulars are *not* 'homonymous' (see Alexander, *In Met.* 82. 11–83. 17, with Owen 1957, Fine 1993: ch. 10). Rather, Aristotle's point about the 'homonymy' of the good is that there cannot be a single Form in which all the particulars called good partake, because among the particulars themselves there are many different varieties of goodness. If, then, Sextus' remarks derive ultimately from these Aristotelian arguments, the reflection is a distorted one. But they may perhaps better be understood as a development of another line of criticism offered by Aristotle (and worried about by Plato himself at *Parm.* 133b–134e)—viz. that Forms are too remote from particulars, and the relation between the two insufficiently articulated, for them to do the work which Plato wants them to do; see esp. *Met.* I 991a8–b3 (= XIII 1079b12–1080a2), and on the Good specifically, *NE* I. 1096b26–1097a14. From this it might understandably be *inferred* that, despite what Plato himself says about the semantic connection between 'good' as applied to the Form and 'good' as applied to particulars, the two usages must in fact be unrelated.

Of the three further definitions of the good with which the expository section concludes (30), the second and third are clearly Stoic. This might be guessed from the mention of Zeno, Cleanthes, and Chrysippus immediately afterwards, but is confirmed by other evidence. The Stoics are recorded as defining the indifferent as that which contributes neither to happiness nor to unhappiness (61 below, DL VII. 104); the second definition of the good is an obvious corollary of this. And the third definition is supported by the statement in both Stobaeus (II. 72, 3–6) and DL (VII. 97) that, according to the Stoics, the virtues 'make happiness complete'. Though these two definitions are said to have been offered by distinct groups of people—and the implication is that each is also distinct from those Stoics who defined good as 'benefit or not other than benefit'—there is no reason why any of the definitions need be thought of as excluding or replacing the others. The Stoics not infrequently offered multiple definitions of the same term. Sometimes the definitions refer to distinct uses of the same word (e.g. *cosmos*, DL VII.

137–8, or 'indifferent', 59–61 below), but sometimes they are complementary accounts applying to the same use (e.g. courage, Cic. *Tusc.* IV. 53), and this may be assumed in the present case. The first definition is Aristotelian (*Rhet.* I. 1362a21–3; cf. *NE* I. 1094a18–22). But the Stoics could easily have accepted this also. For they do hold that goods are (by their very nature) to be chosen (DL VII. 101, Stob. II. 97, 18–98, 3); and given the Stoic restriction of good to virtue and what partakes of it, they would obviously have agreed to the qualification 'for its own sake'.

The definition of happiness as 'a good flow of life' (*euroia biou*) is repeated in Stob. II. 77, 20–3, which also names Zeno, Cleanthes, and Chrysippus (as well as 'all their successors') as accepting it. Sextus at 110 below is probably making a sarcastic reference to this definition. On 'happiness' (*eudaimonia*) and its connection with the good in Aristotle and Hellenistic philosophy, see Annas 1993: ch. 1 and the whole of pt. IV.

31–9: Objections to the definitions

Points of text, language, and translation:

[(a) The clause beginning 'according to which' (31), which I have placed in parentheses, is excised by Heintz (1932: 249), followed by Bury. As Heintz says, the logic of the MSS reading *katho legei* '*to agathon*, etc.', 'according to which it says "the good, etc."', is very awkward; 'which' must refer to 'the first signification' and 'it' to 'the definition'. Heintz regards the clause as a gloss, with Sextus himself as the implied subject of *legei*. A far neater and less drastic solution is that of Blomqvist (1968: 97–8), who alters *legei to* to *elegeto*; I have adopted this emendation ('according to which *it was stated* "Good, etc."'). There are two major advantages to this proposal. First, the verb *elegeto* has an easily identifiable subject (the definition itself is the subject). Second, the definition now begins with *agathon* without the article, which is uniformly the practice elsewhere in the chapter (and cf. 184).

(b) *Apiston . . . polemon*, 'interminable war' (36), was altered by Fabricius to *aspeiston . . . polemon* on the basis of Hervetus' translation *irreconciliabile*; Bekker and Bury accept this. But *irreconciliabile* is possible as the translation of *apiston*; cf. *apistos . . . polemos*, Maximus of Tyre, p. 318, 18 Hob.; *apistos echthra*, Eusebius, *De laude Const.* XVI. 766 (wrongly cited as XV. 766 in Mutschmann). In this sense an *apistos polemos* is a war which admits of no *pistis*—i.e. no *assurances* between the two sides which would allow hostilities to cease. Cf. *PH* III. 175, where all editors alter *apiston* to *aspeiston*, although *apiston* again appears in all MSS, and the medieval Latin translation's *incredibile* shows that the translator read *apiston*. In his app. crit. to *M* XI, Mutschmann says that, on the basis of the above parallels, he would restore *apiston* in *PH* III; Mau does not take up this suggestion in his revision of Mutschmann's *PH* text (Mutschmann–Mau 1958).]

(c) 'Its property', 'the property' (35, 37) are strange, implying as they do that the good has only one property. The parallel passage at *PH* III. 173, more sensibly, has 'one of its properties'.

The two objections proposed in this passage are quite distinct in character. The first (31–4) applies to just one small part of the preceding discussion, and is dismissed by Sextus as not necessary for his purposes and implicitly as pedantic (35). As suggested above, it is not clear whether to understand Sextus' inclusion of this objection as designed to undermine (albeit weakly) the definition to which it applies, or, on the contrary, to *support* the definition (by showing the weakness of attempts to undermine it); this reflects the more general ambivalence about the aim of the chapter. The second objection, however, is taken seriously by Sextus, and applies to all the previously mentioned definitions, in addition, it would seem, to all other possible definitions. Only the second objection occurs in *PH* III (173–5). Since the chapter of *PH* III corresponding to this chapter is single-mindedly hostile to attempts to capture the 'conception' of the good, the bad, and the indifferent, it is not surprising that *M* XI's first objection, whose weight as criticism is negligible at best, should not be included.

The word 'benefit' occurs in several different recurring phrases in the first objection. I have translated the various Greek words and phrases as literally as possible, and the result may read somewhat oddly; but there is a point to these diverse usages. In particular, it is initially puzzling that the 'result' of 'generic virtue' is specified both as 'being benefited' (*to ōpheleisthai*, 31, 34) and as 'being of benefit' (*to ōphelein*, 32, 33). The former term is clear enough; virtue is necessarily beneficial, and so the result of virtue is that one is benefited. The more unexpected term 'being of benefit' always occurs in parallel with the phrases 'being wise' or 'being moderate' or both. As noted above, the latter phrases designate the beneficial effects of the virtues practical wisdom and moderation respectively—viz. the exercise of those virtues themselves; and 'being of benefit' serves as the generic term corresponding to these. The beneficial effect of virtue in general will again be the exercise of virtue itself; but since virtue is by definition a form of benefit (22–3), the exercise of virtue in general may be called 'being of benefit'. (It is worth noting that there is no verb corresponding to 'virtue' (*aretē*), as the verbal form 'being wise' (*to phronein*) corresponds to 'practical wisdom' (*phronēsis*).) 'Being of benefit' and 'being benefited' therefore amount, perhaps surprisingly, to the same thing. The Stoics themselves do not talk this way, because they do not conceive of virtue in general as a disposition over and above the specific virtues (see below); it is the authors of the objection who have framed the term 'being of benefit'. But in doing so, they have built on authentically Stoic presuppositions.

Sextus does not tell us, and it is by no means clear, who the authors of the first objection are—though the first sentence of 35 implies that they are dogmatists. This does not appear to be an intra-Stoic dispute, for the Stoics do not seem to use the term 'generic virtue' (*genikē aretē*); it appears nowhere in Stobaeus or DL and at only one other place in *SVF* (*Commenta Lucani*, p. 75 Us., *SVF* III p. 48), in a context which does not suggest a close following of Stoic terminology. It is also not clear whether the second portion of the objection (34), which replies to the rebuttal by the proponents of the definition (33), derives from the original authors of the objection, or whether it is Sextus' (or his source's) own verdict on the inadequacy of the rebuttal. Even if it is the latter, though, the opening of 35 indicates that he regards the issue as nit-picking and unworthy of serious consideration.

In fact the initial objection at 31–2 is not merely nit-picking but thoroughly misconceived. From the fact that the specific virtues do not result in benefit 'pure and simple' (*auto touto*, 32)—i.e. benefit in general *as opposed to* any determinate species of benefit, such as being wise—it does not follow that they do not result in benefit; since being wise, for example, is a species of benefit, for being wise to result *is* for benefit to result. There is nothing to prevent the Stoics from saying any of this. In fact, the reply attributed to them in 33 may be read as making precisely this point; the 'benefit' which, according to the definition, results from good things is, they say, not 'being of benefit in general', but some determinate species of benefit corresponding to the specific character of the good in question. The counter-rebuttal in 34 also contains nothing which need have troubled any Stoic. In Stoic theory there is no such thing as 'generic virtue' *as distinct from* the totality of specific virtues; virtue, whenever it is exercised, will always *take the form of* one of the specific virtues, and hence, contrary to the objection, a specific benefit ('one of the things in one's life') *will* always result from it. (To say this is not at all to deny the very strong interdependence of the virtues in Stoic ethics, on which see LS 61.)

The second objection is divided into two distinct parts; it may be summarized as follows:

(1a) The definitions suggested above, as well as other similar ones which might be imagined, fail in their task of showing us 'what the good is'; instead, they merely tell us one of the properties of the good (35, repeated in conclusion at 37).

(1b) That this is so can be seen from the fact that, though the statements which comprise these definitions are ones with which people will readily agree (35), they do not agree on *what it is* which falls under the definitions (36). If the definitions had succeeded in their task of showing us 'what the good is', there would be no such disagreement; for 'the nature of the good' would be plain for all to see (37).

(2a) If one does not know what X is, one is not even in a position to understand statements which describe the properties of X (38).

(2b) This can be illustrated by examples (38).

(2c) Hence the definitions of the good, which, as argued in (1), merely tell us the properties of the good rather than 'what the good is', cannot even be understood in this depleted role unless one *already* knows 'the nature of the good' (which, if (1) is correct, one will *not* know, since that is what the definitions themselves unsuccessfully attempted to tell us) (39).

It is not immediately obvious why (1b) should be thought to furnish a reason for (1a). Why should the fact that people disagree (even interminably) about what falls under a candidate definition show that the latter is not a genuine definition? Sextus seems to be relying on an assumption to the effect that definitions should enable one to *distinguish* the items that fall under them from those that do not. (The Greek word *horos*, here translated 'definition', had the original meaning 'boundary'; this provides some impetus to the thought that a definition should *mark off*, in a readily discernible fashion, the object or objects conforming to it.) This assumption, though certainly not beyond question, is well known in Plato's early dialogues—a definition of piety, for example, is worth having because it will enable one to spot which actions are pious and which are not (*Euth.* 6e)—and might well have been widely accepted among Sextus' opponents.

Part (2) is not an objection against the definitions *qua* definitions; Sextus takes himself already to have shown in (1) that they cannot succeed in their intended role. Instead, (2) claims to demonstrate that these purported definitions, besides not being definitions, are incapable of being understood. In addition to being inherently implausible, this conflicts with what Sextus said in (1b), that everyone readily agrees to the statements which constitute the purported definitions; to agree to P presumably requires that one understand P. But the main problem is that the argument depends on an ambiguity. Sextus says that unless one knows what a horse is, one will not be familiar with neighing or other distinctive properties of horses. There is a sense in which this is true; if one had never encountered or even heard of horses, neighing would indeed be a mystery. But if 'knowing what a horse is' is taken to entail being in possession of a *definition* of the horse—as it must be if the claim is to support the conclusion—Sextus' statement is clearly false; one does not need to have such a definition in order to know that horses neigh, or to recognize neighing when one hears it. Similarly in the case of the good: if a person was 'without a conception of the good' (39) in the sense of never even having learned how to use the word 'good' or any of the cluster of words in the same semantic range, it *would* be 'idle and profitless' to say to that person that 'good is that which benefits'. But this point lacks any bite, because no normally developed human being is in this position. For Sextus to succeed in showing that these alleged statements of the properties of the good 'aim for something impossible' (37), he instead has to claim that one must know the *definition* of the good before one can understand these statements; this must be what he means by 'it is necessary first to learn the nature of the good itself' (39). But this does not follow from the claim about the person 'without a conception of the good' (in the sense in which that claim is true), and is just as implausible as the statement about the horse, understood in the second way.

Or at any rate, this is implausible unless one is committed to some very strong and special views in ethics and/or epistemology—views which Sextus is hardly entitled to assume himself or presuppose on the part of his audience. For Sextus is not, of course, alone in suggesting that it is necessary to have a definition of X before one can know anything about X. This claim, which appears in Socrates' mouth in at least some of Plato's dialogues, has been labelled 'the Socratic Fallacy' or, less contentiously, the 'Priority of Definition' thesis, and Sextus' argument in (2) is surely a direct descendant of those arguments in Plato which rely on it. For discussion of this thesis, and of the extent to which Socrates or Plato is committed to it, see most recently Beversluis 1987, Vlastos 1990, Benson 1990. For another instance of Sextus' use of it, see *PH* III. 4.

The second part of the objection, then, is defective. (Another argument in this book with a similar structure, and similar shortcomings, occurs at 242-3.) A further confusion appears in the final sentence of 39: what is the referent of 'the thing which is being sought'? The context of the previous sentence suggests that it must be knowledge or understanding of the properties of the good; this is what lack of knowledge of 'the nature of the good' supposedly deprives us of. But it was not knowledge of the *properties* of the good which was being sought by the original proponents of the criticized definitions; rather, it was (of course) an adequate definition of the good.

For comparison of 35-9 and the parallel passage at *PH* III. 173-5, see Appendix A.

40-1: Conclusion and transition

'Those who hold varying opinions' (*tois heterodoxois*, 40) refers back to the conflict in views about the good discussed in 36-7. It is, of course, the dogmatists in general who are meant; Sextus' sly suggestion is that anyone who holds opinions on any subject will be simply one member of a group of people holding competing opinions on the same subject. (*Heterodoxos* can also mean 'holding opinions at variance with the *correct* ones'; but, *pace* Russo, this sense is clearly not one of which a sceptic would avail himself.)

In this short section Sextus tells us that the bad and the indifferent can be treated by analogy with the good. A definition of the bad is mentioned which parallels the definition of the good given in 22; the indifferent is not defined but merely alluded to. By contrast, *PH* III. 176-7 gives three definitions of the bad and briefly states what, in Sextus' view, is wrong with them. More importantly, it includes the three definitions of the indifferent which in *M* XI occur in a different context, at 59-61 (with further elaboration at 62-3). The present chapter, devoted to elucidating the 'conception' of the things to be discussed, is clearly where definitions of the indifferent best belong; the definitions at 59-61 interrupt what is supposed to be an account of divergent views about the good, and specifically about whether health is good (and, if so, whether it is the highest good)—see below.

CHAPTER III (42–109)

In this chapter, the longest in the book, Sextus argues for a negative answer to the question posed in the title. The argument is based on the prevalence of disagreement about what things are good or bad, and the first main section (42–67) is devoted to establishing how widespread such disagreement is, both among ordinary people and among philosophers (though it is the philosophers to whom Sextus devotes most of his attention). Following this is the first and main argument to the effect that nothing is by nature good (or, by implication, bad) (68–78), then a subsidiary argument that nothing is by nature good (79–89), and then an explicit argument that nothing is by nature bad (90–5). The chapter concludes by considering two objections, one by Epicureans (96–8) and one by Stoics (99–109), which appeal to the behaviour of animals, as well as some human behaviour, to try to demonstrate that some things are naturally to be chosen or to be avoided.

The details of the arguments are best considered section by section. It is worth emphasizing at the outset, however, that this chapter does not conclude by *suspending judgement about* whether anything is by nature good or bad; it concludes that *nothing is* by nature good or bad. There is no mention here of the 'equal strength' (*isostheneia*) of opposing arguments, or any other suggestion that Sextus' negative arguments are intended to be balanced against the arguments of the dogmatists to the effect that some things *are* by nature good or bad. As we shall see in the next chapter, the acceptance of these negative conclusions is both consistent with a certain form of suspension of judgement and essential for the attainment of *ataraxia*. The argumentative strategy—indeed, the understanding of scepticism itself—is therefore significantly different in *M* XI from what one would expect from *PH* I and from what one finds in the parallel passages of *PH* III (though *PH* III also, and inconsistently, contains elements of the *M* XI approach—see Appendix A on *M* XI. 68–78, *PH* III. 179–82, and on *M* XI. 79–89, *PH* III. 183–90).

As the title suggests, Sextus nowhere argues that nothing is by nature indifferent; by contrast, the title of the corresponding chapter of *PH* III (179 ff.) is 'Whether anything is by nature good or bad or indifferent', and an argument about the indifferent is included. For a possible explanation of this, see on 90–5; and cf. on 1–2, 21, 40–1, 59–61. On the significance of the term 'by nature' in this context, see on 68–78 below, and Introduction, sect. II.

42–7: General summary of disagreements about the good

[The first quotation in 44 is *Od.* 14. 228 (also quoted by Sextus at *PH* I. 86). In the original context *ergois*, which I have translated 'things', would be better rendered 'activities', 'types of work'; but Sextus' point in using it is a more general one. Sextus is not the only author to quote this line and the one from Archilochus together; cf. Schol. Hom. *Od.* 14. 228, Clement, *Strom.* 6. 2. 7, 3–4. The line from Archilochus is misquoted (and rendered unmetrical) by Sextus; the evidence of these other authors shows that it should read *all'allos allōi kardiēn iainetai.* However, the sense is virtually identical. Portions of this line and a few neighbouring ones have been preserved on an Oxyrinchus papyrus (2310 fr. 1, col. i. 40–8); for the text see West 1989: 12, and for brief discussion Lasserre and Bonnard 1958: 13. The surrounding context is not relevant to Sextus' purposes in either case.]

This section argues in general terms that people disagree about what things are good. Unlike much of the discussion so far, there is no difficulty in following the train of thought; Sextus simply presents some prominent examples of such disagreements, both philosophical and non-philosophical. It is assumed, but not argued, that the same will be true of the bad; good and bad are mentioned together at 42 and 44 (cf. the summary at 68), but we are to understand that the case can be made sufficiently with reference to just one of the two. The observation that people disagree about what is good is presented as in some way contributing to 'the arguments about its existence'—i.e. the arguments about whether there really is anything (by nature) good. It is not immediately clear how it is supposed to do this ('for the purpose of becoming more readily conversant with', 42, is vague); it is not until the argument at 68–78 that it becomes clear that in order for something to be really, or by nature, good, it must, on Sextus' view, be universally *agreed* to be good. The *extent* of the disagreement Sextus wishes to allege is also not obvious from this section; but as we shall see, his argument at 68–78 requires that *nothing* meet the requirement just mentioned. The present section clearly does not establish that; its claim is the much more general one that there is widespread disagreement on the subject. It is the next section, on the specific example of health, which is better understood as doing the detailed work necessary for the following argument (though, as we shall see, it is doubtful whether it actually succeeds in this regard).

    There is nothing in *PH* III corresponding to this section or the next (although certain passages from these sections do have parallels in *PH* III in other contexts—see below); there Sextus moves straight from the chapter on the 'conception' of good, bad, and indifferent to the argument that there is nothing by nature good (the argument which appears in *M* XI at 68–78). Instead, *after* the arguments that there is nothing by nature good, bad, or indifferent, he presents a long account, reminiscent of the material in the Tenth Mode (*PH* I. 145–63), of the differences between the ethical attitudes and practices of different societies (198–234); this is said (235) to result in the sceptic's suspension of judgement about whether anything is by nature good or bad. It would clearly be unnecessary to include both this account of ethical disagreements and the one which appears in *M* XI. But in *M* XI the section on disagreement contributes directly to the arguments that there is nothing good or bad by nature, whereas *PH* III's section on disagreement is separate from those arguments, and directed towards a different end. I suspect that the difference is due to the fact that in *PH* III Sextus is uncomfortable with the arguments that there is nothing good or bad by nature, attributing them much of the time (though not consistently) to other unnamed thinkers; he therefore moves through this material relatively quickly, and then concentrates on a different line of thought which uses observations concerning disagreement in a manner more congenial to *PH*'s general approach.

The conflicting aims which we observed in the previous chapter are recalled one more time at the beginning of this one. Sextus opens by saying that 'the dogmatists did not outline the conception of the good in a convincing fashion' (42); but in 44 he is quite happy to say that both ordinary people and philosophers have a 'common [i.e. shared] preconception' of good and bad, though they differ over what things these concepts apply to. As we saw, it is the second claim which conforms to the official programme of the previous chapter. Indeed, Sextus' point in 44 is highly reminiscent of what he said at 35–6.

The reference to Aenesidemus in 42 is the only one in the book. But there is good reason to think that he was the originator of the style of argument employed in this chapter and the next, even if not its immediate source. The passage of Photius' *Bibliotheca* which is our most detailed source of information about Aenesidemus (169b18–170b35 (= LS 71C, 72L)) contains several notable similarities with the argument of *M* XI, as contrasted with the Pyrrhonism of *PH* (on this, see Introduction, sect. III, and on 118 below, esp. point 3). Paradoxically, the reference to Aenesidemus appears to count *against* the supposition that he is Sextus' immediate source. Sextus seems here to enlist Aenesidemus as an *independent* corroborating voice; this would be somewhat odd if it was Aenesidemus himself who supplied most of Sextus' material.

It is not easy to judge the tone of the analogy in 43. A modern philosopher who compared views about what is good with men's taste in women would be immediately understood as expressing a strongly deflationary attitude towards ethics. But it is not clear whether ancient readers would have had as strong a sense as we do of the cultural relativity of standards of beauty. Plato (*Rep.* 474d–e) and Lucretius (IV. 1153–70) both draw attention to the fact that almost any physical appearance may be judged beautiful by someone. But their point is that infatuation may lead one to a thoroughly *distorted* view of these matters; one may judge all sorts of physiognomies, builds, etc. beautiful which are not really so. Sextus' point—that different societies judge beauty differently—would no doubt be granted easily enough; but it is not clear whether this could have been counted on to strike the ancient reader, as it would strike most modern readers, as a topic on which objectivity is *obviously* not to be attained or even sought.

The view attributed in 45 to 'the Academics and the Peripatetics' also occurs, with many of the same examples, in Arius Didymus' summary of Peripatetic ethics (Stob. II. 136, 9–16) and in Diogenes' life of Aristotle (DL V. 30)—see also *Magna Moralia* 1184b1–4. It is alluded to by Aristotle himself at *Pol.* VII. 1 and *NE* I. 1098b12–14 (cf. *Rhet.* I. 1360b24–8), but, as is pointed out by Annas (1992b: 205), it does not play any significant role in his ethical theory. It is also attributed to Theophrastus by Cicero (*Tusc.* V. 24), as an element in Theophrastus' view that virtue alone cannot guarantee happiness—a view which Cicero attributes to him in numerous other places (*Fin.* V. 12, 77, 85–6, *Acad.* I. 33, 35, *Tusc.* V. 85; for discussion see Fortenbaugh 1984: 218–25). In several of these passages Theophrastus' view is contrasted with that of the Stoics, for whom virtue does suffice for happiness, and who do not recognize as goods the things here referred to as bodily and external goods. So however the details of Theophrastus' view may have marked him out from Aristotle or other members of the Peripatetic school (that they did so is implied by Cicero in *Tusc.* V. 85, *Fin.* V. 12), it is likely that the threefold division of goods was regarded more generally, as it is here by Sextus, as a central point of contrast between Peripatetic and Stoic ethics; on this, see Annas 1993: ch. 19.1—for this general contrast, see also *Tusc.* V. 84–5.

The latter text accords with Sextus in another way; it also says that the position of the Old Academy on this point is more or less the same (*nec multo . . . secus*) as that of the Peripatetics. (By 'Academics' Sextus too presumably means the pre-sceptical Academics—i.e. the immediate successors of Plato.) *Tusc.* V regularly groups together the views of Aristotle, Speusippus, Xenocrates, and Polemo on the question of whether virtue suffices for happiness; cf. 30, 39–40 (which also refers to the threefold division of goods), 87. Cicero is following Antiochus (cf. 21–2), who claimed quite generally that the views of the Old Academy and Peripatos were essentially the same (and also that the Stoics' views, despite appearances, were not substantially different; cf. Cic. *Laws* I. 55 for an application of this to the current issue); see above on 3–6. But we need not suppose that Sextus is also simply reproducing Antiochus' peculiar historical thesis. The threefold distinction is mentioned in passing by Plato himself several times in the *Laws* (697a–b, 743e, 870a–b; cf. *Ep.* VIII. 355b, *Phil.* 48e, *Gorg.* 477c), and was attributed to Plato by Aristotle, according to DL III. 80 (another passage closely resembling the present one; see also Stob. II. 55, 5–13). And Plutarch (*Comm. not.* 1065A) tells us that the Stoics criticized Xenocrates and Speusippus for holding that health is not indifferent and wealth is not useless—i.e. that there are some bodily and external goods in addition to goods of the soul. On this point, at least, the claim of a community of views between the Old Academy and the Peripatetics has some plausibility.

Sextus, of course, shows no tendency to assimilate the Stoics to the philosophers just mentioned; unlike the syncretist Antiochus, he is in the business (at least at this point; cf. on 3–6) of emphasizing the *differences* between philosophies. None the less, he does not stress the differences as clearly as he might. For when he says that the Stoics excluded 'the type of goods having to do with the body' (46), he makes it sound as if the Stoics agree with the other two schools about the other two types of goods; this, of course, is not so, since the 'external' goods recognized by the Stoics are also quite different from the 'external' goods of the Peripatetics and the Academy.

The Stoics' threefold division of goods is also cited by Stobaeus (II. 70, 8–14) and by Diogenes (DL VII. 95). Diogenes seems to be in agreement with Sextus, though at certain points he is less clear; Stobaeus, however, disagrees with Sextus on the specifics. 'Excellent persons and generally those who have the virtues' are cited by Stobaeus as goods which 'neither have to do with the soul nor are external', whereas they seem to count as 'external' goods in Sextus' classification; and Stobaeus cites 'acquaintances' (*gnōrimous*) as external goods. Sextus' summary appears to be more accurate—or at least more precise—on these points. Excellent persons other than oneself (which is what Stobaeus' phrase naturally implies) plainly *are* external to oneself. And the inclusion of acquaintances, without qualification, as external goods seems to neglect what would surely have been a crucial Stoic tenet, that *any* human being who is to qualify, in such classifications, as a 'good' must be an 'excellent' human being. (The inclusion of friends as external goods is not open to the same criticism; on the morally elevated status of 'the friend' in Stoicism, see above on 22–30.) Sextus, on the other hand, makes clear that all those who are to count as external goods must be 'excellent'— even one's parents and children. And there is a clear point in Sextus' classification of 'the excellent human being in relation to himself' as a good of the third type. One is obviously not external to oneself, nor does one consist purely of soul; yet, if one is an 'excellent human being', one has as much reason to regard oneself as a good as to regard other excellent human beings as goods. Not, of course, as a good specifically *for* oneself—it is not clear what that might mean—but as a good for the community of good agents in general. For the Stoics, as noted earlier (see on 22–4), goods or benefits are not goods or benefits solely *for* some given individual. They belong to all who are capable of understanding their beneficial character—i.e. to all who are virtuous, and perhaps even to the universe in general, since the universe itself is rational and ordered for the best.

The items listed as goods correspond largely with those listed when Sextus was explaining the definition of good at 22–4 (cf. 25–7). But the organizing principles are quite different in the two passages; the present passage is concerned purely with the *classification* of goods, whereas the previous discussion had to do with defining the good.

The philosophers who regard 'the type of goods having to do with the body' as 'the most primary good' (47) are the Cyrenaics; see e.g. DL II. 90, Cic. *Acad.* II. 139, *Fin.* II. 18, 39, Quintilian, *Inst. Orat.* XII. 2, 24, Lactantius, *Div. Inst.* III. 7, 7, III. 8, 6–10. The Cyrenaics appear to have been unique in this regard among Greek philosophers (and are frequently contrasted with the Epicureans, whose position on pleasure was both more complicated and less immediately shocking). Many of the anecdotes in Diogenes' life of Aristippus are clearly inspired by the notoriety of this thesis; Aristippus is graphically portrayed as belonging among 'those who are fond of the pleasures of the flesh'.

The material on the Academics, Peripatetics, and Stoics (45–6) occurs, in more concise form, in *PH* III (180–1), in the course of the argument that nothing is by nature good. Since *PH* III has no general section on disagreement (like the present section of *M* XI) preceding that argument, it is not surprising that Sextus would want to include a few more examples of disagreement about what things are good within the argument itself.

Sextus presents the decision in 47 to focus on a single example as motivated by a concern to keep the discussion within reasonable bounds; and he says that he has chosen health because of his own familiarity with the subject. (This is probably one of the very few autobiographical hints in Sextus; for other indications that he was a doctor, see *PH* II. 238, *M* I. 260. It is not certain that 'we' refers to Sextus himself, rather than to Pyrrhonians in general; however, it is not clear why the Pyrrhonist movement as a whole would be 'rather well accustomed' to discussion of health in particular.) But one must also ask what the treatment of the single example of health is supposed to, or can be expected to, accomplish philosophically. As noted above, the argument at 68–78 requires the assumption that *nothing* is universally agreed to be good; the general observation that there is a lot of disagreement about what is good is not sufficient for his purposes. The discussion of health can only do the required job, then, if the case of health is representative of all cases—i.e. if there is as much disagreement about *all* alleged goods as there is about health. It is not unreasonable to assume that Sextus intends us to understand this. On the other hand, he gives no explicit indication, here or anywhere else, that health is to be considered as thus representative, and this is an unfortunate lacuna in his argument. (He comes closer to doing so for the case of folly, which is the counterpart of health in the argument to the effect that nothing is by nature bad; see below on 90–5.) It is not clear, in fact, whether any single example can plausibly be taken to fill this role. (*PH* III. 198 ff., which uses a multiplicity of examples, is perhaps more successful in this respect. But even here, Sextus is forced to do some rather desperate hand-waving; see 233–4.) However, health is perhaps as suitable an example, from an intuitive point of view, as any. For health seems to be as obvious a case of something good as one could hope for; as Sextus says (49), 'all ordinary people' consider it 'a good, indeed the primary good'. If even health fails to achieve universal consent as a good, one might well be inclined to say that nothing will do so. These considerations, however, are by no means logically compelling; for an attempt to fill in this gap more effectively on Sextus' behalf, see below on 68–78.

48–67: The example of health

[Points of text and translation and other points of philological detail:

(a) Sextus does not quote Simonides *verbatim* in 49 (and the lines are quoted by no one else). But it looks as if all he has done is render the original into *oratio obliqua*; simple transformation back to *oratio recta* results in two metrically feasible lines; see Page 1962: 306.

(b) If the text is correct, Sextus presents both the two other verse quotations in 49 as portions of a poem of Licymnius. But the second quotation ('What joy . . .') is in fact from the paean to Health of Ariphron, as is shown by Athenaeus XV. 701F–702B; Sextus quotes the third, fourth, and tenth lines only. (For textual details, see Page 1962: 422–3.) It has been suspected, however, that the text between the two quotations is corrupt (see Page 1962: 396 and point (c) below); if so, Sextus may after all have ascribed the second quotation to Ariphron.

(c) I retain the MSS *hupsistōn* in line 1 of the Licymnius quotation, as against Wilamowitz's emendation *hupsista*, followed by Mutschmann (also Page 1962: 396). Wilamowitz (1886: 192–3) argues that the *hupsēlon* in the line immediately following the quotation only makes sense if Health has already been referred to as 'exalted'. But this is in effect done by the phrase 'queen | Of the most exalted holy throne of Apollo'; there is no need for 'most exalted' to be an epithet directly attached to the noun 'Health'. I do, however, accept Wilamowitz's construal of *poion hupsēlon epipherei* as a question, picking up on an aspect of the description of Health in the previous quotation; Bury and Russo are at best extremely non-literal at this point (contrast Hervetus). The thought is, however, admittedly awkward, and it is possible that the text is corrupt; see point (b) above.

(d) I follow von Staden (1989: 407) in translating *Diaitētikōi* (50) by *Regimen*, rather than *Dietetics*; the contents may well have included more than just dietary matters (see below), and *Regimen* is linguistically just as plausible.

(e) The quotation in 55 is a composite of *Phoen.* 558 and *El.* 944 (which refers to wealth in its original context). Partly because of Sextus' (or Crantor's) curious juxtaposition, the line from *Phoenissae* has been suspected by some editors of Euripides; see Diggle 1994: 113. With Bekker and Bury, I retain the *ho gar* of most MSS in the first line. Mutschmann alters to *ho d'* on the basis of Euripides' own text. This is quite unnecessary; the *gar* is clearly Sextus' addition, designed to connect the quotation to the preceding words. (He also unnecessarily alters the MSS *exiptat'* to *exeptat'* on the same basis; but here the sense is unaffected—the former is simply a later version of the latter.)

(f) The quotation in 56 (a fragment from the lost *Telephus*, as we know from two places in Stobaeus: *Flor.* 93, 19 and 97, 11) contains a lacuna in the first line (printed unfilled by Mutschmann); along with Bekker, Bury, and Russo, I follow Fabricius' emendation of *noson* to *nosounta ge*, which completes both the sense and the metre (for other conjectures see Nauck 1889: 586). The second and third lines also require two textual changes to render them metrical: *alupon echōn* to *echōn alupon* and *biotēn* to *bioton*. All editors since Fabricius have made these changes; but it is far from certain that the text of Sextus, as distinct from the text of Euripides, requires them. Since the sense is unaffected, we need not attempt to settle this question. (The alteration of the MSS *mikran* to *mikr'an* is, however, necessary for the sense, but palaeographically easy.) Even aside from the metrical issue, it is quite probable that Sextus is misquoting; Stobaeus quotes the lines in two different versions, each distinct from Sextus' version but each smoother as Greek. (In particular, the internal accusative *alupon bioton* with *oikein* is awkward, though cf. *IA* 1507–8.) However, the general sense is the same in all three versions.

(g) I retain the MSS *metalabontes* in 57, rather than following Mutschmann's emendation *metamathontes*. *Metalabontes hōs*, 'having been informed that', may seem difficult; but Aristeas 316 has *metelabon . . . dioti*.

(h) I retain the MSS *sullambanomenon* in 61; Mutschmann's alteration to *sumballomenon* is based solely on the parallel passage of *PH*, and is as such groundless. There is no reason to assume that Sextus used the same vocabulary in both works (neither purports, for example, to be direct quotation from the Stoics), and *sullambanomenon* makes just as good sense.

(i) With Mutschmann, I refrain from positing a lacuna in 65; Bury adds *hōs* after *peristaseis*, while Heintz (1932: 249–50) offers a more elaborate supplement derived from the parallel passage of *PH* (III. 192). The thought does indeed become more neatly expressed with either of these additions. But the logical oddity in the MSS version is not excessively surprising in a long sentence like this one, and is not a reason for altering the text; nor does the fact that *PH* III expresses the thought better show that we should alter the text of *M* XI, but simply that Sextus thought and wrote more clearly when he wrote *PH*—which suggests, in turn, that *PH* is the later work.

(j) The *hoti* in 66, deleted by Mutschmann, can easily be retained; see Heintz 1932: 250. However, the sense is unaffected.]

The structure of this section is again easy to follow. The variety of views about whether or not health is good, and what sort of good or non-good it is, is previewed in 48, and then explored in more detail in the same order. No philosopher is cited as holding the first view, that health is the *greatest* good; instead, Sextus has to infer this view from a variety of non-philosophical writings. The remarks quoted in 49–50 are all to the effect that health is a necessary condition for the enjoyment, or the successful functioning, of other things generally considered good. Sextus does not say why this would show that health is the primary good. The thought he is attributing to these authors—not implausibly, to judge from the quotations or summaries which he gives us—is, I suppose, that it is health which renders beneficial whatever else is beneficial; nothing else is beneficial in the absence of health, but health is invariably beneficial and imparts this character to other things. (Socrates makes a similar argument for wisdom in a well-known passage of the *Meno*, 87c–89a.) Given the assumption which Sextus rightly regards as standard (44; cf. 35), that there is a conceptual connection between the good and the beneficial, there would then be a clear sense in which the goodness of health was of a higher order than the goodness of anything else.

On the quotations from Simonides and Licymnius, see philological points (a) and (b) above. Herophilus was one of the most celebrated physicians of the Hellenistic period; his working life was spent in Alexandria, and he probably lived roughly from 330/320 to 260/250 BC; for the evidence see von Staden 1989: ch. 2. We have no other reference to his work *Regimen* (on the title, see philological point (d) above). But several passages refer to his advocacy of exercise for health (T227–9 in von Staden 1989), and this may well have been one of the central topics of the book. Diet was probably another; the Hippocratic *Regimen in Acute Diseases* (*Peri Diaitēs Oxeōn*) is largely, though not exclusively, concerned with dietary matters. (We have some fragments of Herophilus on the subject of diet (e.g. T256 in von Staden 1989); but these may have come from his other work *On Nutriment* (*Peri Trophēs*).)

The 'Academics and Peripatetics' of 51 are the same as those referred to in 45. Despite their disagreement with the Stoics on the sufficiency of virtue for happiness, it is clear from the works of Cicero cited above (see on 45–6) that it was common ground in this debate that virtue was at least superior to all other goods; health would therefore qualify at best as 'a good, but not the primary good'.

Crantor was an Academic who died, at a not particularly advanced age, in 276/5 BC (see Dorandi 1991: 4–5). He was never himself head of the Academy, but was a student of Xenocrates and Polemo, a friend of Crates, and a teacher and lover of Arcesilaus (DL IV. 24–7, *Index Acad.* cols. XVI–XVII). Though he engaged in exegesis of the *Timaeus* (Plut. *De An. Procr. in Tim.* 1012D–F, Proclus, *In Tim.* I, p. 76, 2 Diehl), his main interests, like those of Polemo, appear to have been in ethics; several texts (Plut. *Consol. ad Apol.* 102D, Cic. *Tusc.* III. 12, *Acad.* II. 135) show him to have opposed the Stoic extirpation of the emotions, arguing instead for a positive role for emotions in moderation. (It is possible that he used the term *metriopatheia* to designate this; if so, this is very different from the sceptics' attitude of *metriopatheia*, which was a concession to the fact of inevitable suffering rather than an ethically motivated positive ideal; see on 160–1 below.) It is not clear from what work the story at 52–8 is derived; though he is supposed to have composed 30,000 lines (DL IV. 24, *Index Acad.* col. XVI, 12–14), the only title we know of is *On Grief.* That the passage is something close to a direct quotation (by far the longest we have from Crantor) is, however, likely from the detail with which the story is told, and from the style, which has an elevated character quite unlike Sextus' own writing; on Crantor's interest in style, his efforts as a poet, and his penchant for striking metaphors, see DL IV. 25–7. The passage also contains quotations from Homer (54; *Il.* XIV. 216–17) and Euripides (55, 56; see philological points (e) and (f) above), who are said to have been his favourite authors (DL IV. 26).

The story purports to show that the correct 'rank and value' (51) of the four goods portrayed is: virtue first, health second, pleasure third, wealth fourth. This is the reverse of the order in which the goods are introduced; each good is thus thought of as supplanting the previous one from the title of highest good, while otherwise leaving the ranking undisturbed. But it is far from clear that the story, for all its vivid and engaging character, justifies this conclusion. Reasons are given for ranking pleasure higher than wealth (54–5), and for ranking health higher than these two (56–7—though it is the inferiority of wealth specifically which receives the main focus); but courage is only shown to be superior to wealth (58)—the 'goods' which are liable to be plundered by one's enemies can hardly include health or pleasure. Besides, the basis on which one good is argued to be superior to another is not consistent, and is not always such as to make the claim of superiority convincing. Pleasure is said to be superior to wealth in part because wealth is merely a *means* to pleasure. But courage is said to be superior to other goods because these other goods cannot be retained without it. It is hard to understand this otherwise than as saying that courage is a means to the retention of other goods—which, by the standard applied earlier in the comparison between pleasure and wealth (and in the absence of further discussion), would render it *inferior* to these other goods. (For Aristotle, the highest good cannot be attained in the absence of external goods (*NE* I. 8); but this does not of course show that external goods are *superior* to the highest good.) The case of health, and its superiority to pleasure and wealth, is more complicated. The argument here may seem to be the same as that employed in the case of courage. But Crantor may also be understood, more charitably, as saying that health has an inherently beneficial character which is, so to speak, transferred to pleasure and wealth when it is present (see above on 49–50); in this case health will reasonably qualify as superior to pleasure and wealth (though not on the same grounds as those on which pleasure was argued to be superior to wealth). This reasoning seems more plausible in the case of health versus wealth than in that of health versus pleasure; it would be better to say that pleasure cannot *exist* in the absence of health than that it is 'no use' (56) in the absence of health. In addition, it is not clear why a contrary argument analogous to that employed in the case of pleasure versus wealth might not be constructed for the superiority of pleasure to health—that health 'is pursued by people not for its own sake, but for the sake of the enjoyment and pleasure which result from it' (55).

In summary, while the story may be rhetorically effective, it does not provide a particularly flattering picture of Crantor as a philosopher. A further difficulty is the switch from 'courage' in 57 to 'virtue' in 58. The reason given in 58 for the superiority of courage to the other goods is not readily transferable to the other virtues. It is true that in non-philosophical Greek 'virtue' (*aretē*) is often used to refer specifically to the military virtues (on this, see Dover 1974: 164). But Crantor surely means the final verdict in 58 to place virtue in general, and not only courage, in first place.

Crantor's assignment of health to the second place is said in 59 to be conventional for Academics and Peripatetics. Sextus does not say whether the entire fourfold ranking is also standard Academic and Peripatetic doctrine; but most of it simply follows from what we have already seen them to hold. That virtue comes first would clearly be unquestioned. And if health is agreed to come second, this leaves in doubt only the relative positions of pleasure and wealth. In the passages of Plato's *Laws* which allude to the three types of goods (697a–b, 743e, 870a–b; cf. *Ep.* VIII. 355b, and see above on 45), we are consistently told that goods of the soul are the highest, followed by goods of the body, then external goods; if, as one might in any case expect, the Academics and Peripatetics followed Plato in this, wealth would rank below pleasure, since pleasure is certainly not an external good. The position of pleasure in Crantor's ranking is, however, somewhat peculiar. In order for it to rank below health, it must be a bodily good, and an inferior one at that. But both Plato and Aristotle are very clear that pleasure is not simply a bodily phenomenon. For one thing, both talk of a type of pleasure (the highest type) which is entirely non-bodily, associated with philosophic contemplation (*Rep.* 580d–587e, *NE* X. 1177a22–7). And besides, they both suggest that even what are usually called 'bodily pleasures' are in fact experienced by the soul (*Phil.* 35d, *NE* X. 1173b7–13). These details, though, are unimportant for Sextus' main point, which is simply that a sizeable faction of philosophers considered health a good, but not the highest good.

As noted above, there is no passage in *PH* III occupying the same argumentative role as the present sections (42–67). But the Stoic definitions of the indifferent (as reported in 59–61) also occur in *PH* III (177), in nearly identical language. The context, however, is quite different in *PH* III; the passage comes at the end of the chapter on the 'conceptions' of good, bad, and indifferent. As was also observed earlier (see on 40–1), that is clearly the more suitable place for definitions of the indifferent to go. *M* XI includes them here only because it has neglected to include them in the previous chapter (in keeping with that chapter's general reticence about the indifferent; see above on 21), and needs to explain the term 'indifferent' (as well as 'preferred' and 'dispreferred') before the Stoic claim that health is a preferred indifferent can be properly understood. Here is another respect in which *PH* III is superior in its organization to *M* XI; *PH* III consistently treats the indifferent together with the good and the bad, whereas *M* XI does not (cf. on 90–5).

It is, of course, the third use of 'indifferent' (61) which is relevant to Sextus' discussion of disagreements about health, and which is most common in the doxography; on the connection between happiness and goodness in Stoicism, cf. on 30 above. No other author besides Sextus distinguishes *three* uses of the term 'indifferent'. Both Stobaeus (II. 79, 4–17) and DL (VII. 104–5) distinguish two uses, corresponding to Sextus' first and third uses; both mention Sextus' third use first, then his first use, and then return for further details on Sextus' third use, several times employing similar terminology (which is, however, distinct from that of Sextus). It therefore looks as if Diogenes and Stobaeus are drawing on one source and Sextus on another one. The two accounts need not, however, be regarded as seriously at odds with one another. Sextus' second use, to which nothing in Diogenes or Stobaeus corresponds, covers a relatively unusual type of case; it was no doubt added to an original account including just the two uses which occur in the other authors, probably in response to imaginative counter-examples from Academics or other opponents.

There is a minor error in Sextus' account of the third use. He says that 'virtue can always be used well, and vice badly' (61). But for virtue and vice to be properly distinguished from the indifferents, he should have said that virtue always *is* used well, and vice badly; given the word order in the original, it is possible that he did mean to say this, but lost track of his syntax. This error does not occur in *PH* III. 177.

On the technical term 'impulse' (*hormē*) and its role in the Stoic theory of action, see Inwood 1985: ch. 3, Annas 1992a: ch. 4, Bett 1994b: 194–6.

The Stoics' doctrine that, within the category of the indifferent, some things are 'preferred' and some 'dispreferred' is one of their most initially paradoxical, and did not escape ridicule in antiquity (see e.g. Plut. *Sto. rep.* 1047E–1049A). But the Stoics have good reason for making this further distinction. Things which have 'value' (*axia*) are those which are 'in accordance with nature' (*kata phusin*), and those which have 'disvalue' are those which are contrary to nature; for further details on these terms and their relations with 'preferred' and 'dispreferred' respectively, see on 68–78 below (references to earlier philosophers, point (c)). Since all the Stoics from Zeno onwards (or, at the latest, Cleanthes—see Stob. II. 75, 11–76, 6) included some notion of conformity with nature in their specifications of the ethical end (*telos*), it makes good sense for them to mark out a special class of indifferents which are 'preferred', in the sense defined in 62—of which health is an obvious and often-cited example—and another class opposed to them. The difficulty is that, if aiming for health and the other preferred indifferents is appropriate, and even demanded by the *telos*, it begins to look as if they should be called good. This is part of the point of Aristo's objection (see below).

The example of bending one's finger, which is used by Sextus as a case of an indifferent (in his third use) which is neither preferred nor dispreferred (62), occurs in Diogenes (DL VII. 104) and Stobaeus (II. 79,

11) as an example of the use of 'indifferent' which Sextus lists first (59). The things which are indifferent in Sextus' first use *will* of course be, in his third use, indifferents which are neither preferred nor dispreferred. But it is doubtful whether we should suppose that the Stoics meant to establish conceptual connections among the various uses; the example is probably just a recognized instance, serviceable in various contexts, of something about which one literally could not care less.

Aristo was an unorthodox Stoic of the third century BC, a student of Zeno (DL VII. 18) and a contemporary of Arcesilaus (DL IV. 40). He wrote nothing (except, according to DL I. 16, a few letters), and hence Sextus' information is at least second-hand; but several of his views continued to be discussed, the one reported here being probably the most widely known.

Sextus' treatment of Aristo's position at 64–7 is the most extensive report of his rejection of distinctions within the category of the indifferent, and the only one to offer an argument for the position. The position is, however, frequently alluded to by Cicero—see e.g. *Acad.* II. 130, *Fin.* II. 43, IV. 43, 78, V. 73, *Laws* I. 55. (On the unexpected grouping of Pyrrho with Aristo in some of these passages, see Bett 1994d: sect. VII.) Aristo is represented as making two related points: (a) that to label something as 'preferred' is no different from labelling it as good (or virtually no different—though the force of this concession is not clear) (64); and (b) that the indifferents which according to orthodox Stoicism are preferred should *not* in fact be so regarded, since, for any alleged 'preferred indifferent'—including health, the example under discussion— there will always be circumstances in which it is better not to have it (65–7).

Point (b) does not seem to touch the orthodox Stoics. They themselves stress that, by definition, no indifferent is invariably beneficial (61; cf. DL VII. 102–3), and they would regard examples such as that in 66 as supporting rather than undermining their case. Aristo claims that such variability with circumstances shows that no indifferent is 'by nature' or 'invariably' preferred. But orthodox Stoicism does not speak of health and similar things as being 'by nature' or 'invariably' preferred. One should not always pursue such things—on this, both sides agree; but the point of calling them 'preferred' is that they are *by nature such as to be* (generally) worth pursuing, and the occurrence of special cases in which they are not worth pursuing does not undermine this description. (Nor does it justify attaching qualifications such as 'sometimes' or 'usually' to the epithet 'preferred'; being preferred is not, as Aristo tries to suggest, a characteristic which attaches to things on individual occasions.) Aristo's point (a) is an unsupported accusation; whether it is on target depends on whether the orthodox Stoics have succeeded in creating a theoretical role for the preferred indifferents which leaves them clearly distinct from the category of goods. The Stoics' definitions of the good and of the preferred indifferent seem to distinguish them as clearly as one could wish. None the less, there is some question whether the Stoics manage to keep them apart throughout their ethical thinking; as we saw, the pursuit of the preferred indifferents figured somehow or other in all their numerous different formulations of the *telos*. Indeed, the fact that the Stoics modified their formulations of the *telos* so often suggests that they themselves accepted that there were difficulties in this area. However, it is not at all clear that these difficulties cannot be met (see LS I, comm. on 64, Striker 1991: sect. 3, and cf. on 79–89 below (the choosing of 'choosing itself')).

The figure of the tyrant (66) recurs in 166, again as forcing (this time on the sceptic himself) an extremely difficult and unusual choice or preference (cf. Comm. ad loc.). Essentially the same example, again used to show that health is not invariably good nor sickness invariably bad, occurs at Xen. *Mem.* IV. 2. 32, and this may be no coincidence; on the influence of Xenophon on the Stoics, see DeFilippo and Mitsis 1994. The letter analogy in 67 is perhaps far-fetched—no one would imagine that some letters 'naturally' come before others—but it makes Aristo's point in the strongest way possible, suggesting that the preferability of (say) health over sickness in any given situation is purely due to features of that situation, and has nothing to do with any intrinsic superiority of one over the other. Again, the Stoics would contest this; while agreeing that health is not *invariably* to be valued over sickness, they would still insist that health is by its very nature such as to be usually worth pursuing, and sickness the reverse.

66 includes the first mention of the Stoic 'sage' (*sophos*), and the only one in the book outside ch. VI. On this term and its relation to 'wise person' (*phronimos*) in Stoicism, see introductory remarks to ch. VI.

For comparison of 62–6 and the parallel passage at *PH* III. 191–2, see Appendix A.

68–78: First argument that there is nothing by nature good

Points of language and text:

(a) 'Preconception' (*prolēpsis*), 68. In saying that people do not agree in their 'preconceptions' about the good, the bad, and the indifferent, Sextus appears to be contradicting what he said in 44, that people have 'a common preconception' about the good and the bad. But his use of 'preconception' here is much looser than in 44; what he means is that people disagree on *what things are* good, etc.—and this is of course a point on which he has been consistent throughout. On the Stoic and Epicurean use of 'preconception', see on 21 above. It is not clear how much content was originally thought to be included in *prolēpseis*. But Epictetus takes the *prolēpsis* of good to include the assumption that 'the good is beneficial and choiceworthy' and that one should always pursue it (*Diss.* I. 22. 1); Plutarch implies that a very similar view was taken by Chrysippus (*Sto. rep.* 1041E). Sextus at 44 above seems to be essentially consistent with this Stoic and Epicurean usage, and similar cases are frequent (e.g. *M* IX. 33, 50 on the *prolēpsis* of gods). But elsewhere, as here, he uses the term much more broadly, to refer simply to generally shared opinions (e.g. *M* VII. 443 and always in *PH*—cf. on 21 above), or even to opinions which are *not* generally shared (*M* I. 53), or to *misguided* opinions (129 below).

[(b) The participles *kathestōs* and *psuchousa* may perhaps be read conditionally: 'fire, if it is by nature warming', 'snow, if it chills'. In this case Sextus would not even give the appearance of adopting the view that fire and snow really do have these properties by nature (see below).

(c) There is no need to supply *phusei* before *psuchousa*, 69, as conjectured by Mutschmann and adopted by Bury; *phusei* is frequently to be supplied by the reader in what follows (e.g. *ouden estin agathon*, 78).

(d) 71, 'nothing is good or bad in a way which is common to all'. I read *koinon pantōn* as adverbial; this seems to be the only way to do justice both to the syntax and to the argument.

(e) With Mutschmann, I retain the MSS *panti*, 75, rather than emending to *pantēi* with Bekker, Bury, and Heintz (1932: 250), and decline to adopt Heintz's addition *ou pan* (followed by Bury). The MSS make acceptable sense as they stand. If what seems good to someone is also good for everyone, Sextus says, we ought to be able to spot this; it is *assumed*, given the portion of the argument that has just ended, that this is not true in all cases, and the question now is how, given that it can only be true sometimes, we can tell *when* it is true. Heintz is wrong to claim that the addition makes for a clearer train of thought; the portion of the sentence beginning 'we ought to be in a position to apprehend this' presupposes that some things are in reality good—which is stated by the text as it stands, but not if *ou pan* is added. The alleged back-reference to *ou pan* in 72 is unhelpful to Heintz; for Sextus does not dismiss the possibility indicated by that phrase in 72—his own conclusion is a version of it—whereas he does dismiss the possibility raised at the beginning of 75. It might be suggested that the close parallel with DL IX. 101 (see Appendix A) supports Heintz; DL does have *ou pan* in the corresponding place. However, even apart from this particular point, the parallel in the closing portion of the argument (beginning with the present sentence) is in fact considerably less close than in the preceding portion. Diogenes refers to the 'equal strength' (*isostheneia*) of the opposing arguments; Sextus' strategy, at least as I interpret it, is quite different (see below and Bett 1994c: 157 n. 53, against Janáček 1961). It is therefore not safe at this point to use DL as a basis for changing the text of Sextus.]

(f) I translate *enargeia* by 'plain experience' in 76 and elsewhere. The word occurs once in Plato (*Pol.* 277c), but becomes a technical term with Epicurus, referring to what is immediately evident to the senses (e.g. *Letter to Herodotus*, DL X. 48). But in Sextus' usage, at least, a connection with the senses is not part of its semantic content (as implied by Bury's translation 'sensible evidence'); *M* VII. 141 refers to *tēn dia tēs aisthēseōs enargeian*, 'the plain experience *of sensation*', and *M* VII. 218 refers to *enargeia* as encompassing both sensation and intellect. Rather, *enargeia* designates what is immediately evident, as opposed to what needs to be inferred in some indirect way; *M* VIII. 322 uses *enargēs* together with *prodēlos* and in opposition to *adēlos* (cf. *M* VIII. 145); for another instance of *enargeia* in opposition to *logos* see *M* VII. 200. In addition to the Epicureans, both Theophrastus and the Stoics take *enargeia* to guarantee truth, if Sextus is to be believed (*M* VII. 218, 257); for discussion, see Frede 1983b: 74–6. LS use the translation 'self-evidence', which is consistent with all the above, but sometimes results (as it would here) in awkward English; 'plain experience' seems to me preferable in this respect, while also doing justice to this philosophical background (as well as to the pre-philosophical use of *enargēs*).

This argument is one of the most important in the book. It is here that the first portion of *M* XI's distinctive position is most clearly laid out; the next two arguments both make use to varying degrees of the same general scheme of reasoning, and the conclusion arrived at here is the basis for the discussion in the next two chapters of the superiority of the sceptic's life over the dogmatist's. The argument is based on the prevalence of disagreement about questions of good and bad, which it has been the purpose of the chapter so far to establish. (68 adds 'and indifferent things besides', even though the chapter's announced subject-matter is only the good and the bad; this is presumably due to the incidental focus on the indifferent just above (59–67). On Sextus' vacillation concerning whether to include the indifferent, cf. on 1–2, 21, 40–1, 90–5.) But rather than concluding, as one might expect, that we are forced to suspend judgement about whether anything is in reality good or bad, Sextus here concludes that *nothing* is by nature good. The crucial question for the present is how he thinks he can draw this conclusion. A further crucial question is what the *status* of this argument, as well as the following arguments, is supposed to be. The answer to this latter question, I hold, is that Sextus means to endorse the conclusions of these arguments, and that this is none the less consistent with a certain form of sceptical suspension of judgement; this will be discussed in comments on ch. IV below (see also Introduction, sect. II), but will need to be mentioned at a few points prior to that. (The fact that this section is introduced as giving us 'the things which have been said by the sceptics' (68) does nothing to settle this issue; for the sceptics may *say* a great many things without committing themselves to their truth.) The argument has been widely criticized in recent scholarship (Annas 1986: esp. 9, Annas 1993: 356–7, Striker 1983: 108–11, Hankinson 1994: 65); but most of these criticisms stem from the unwarranted assumption that it must be intended to be consistent with the version of Pyrrhonism presented in *PH* I. The argument should be approached, instead, on its own merits.

The argument purports to show that nothing is by nature good or bad (69–71). But in the detailed discussion at 72–8, including the conclusion at 78, the focus is solely on whether there is anything by nature good. However, analogous considerations would obviously apply to the question of whether there is anything by nature bad—as Sextus himself points out at 90, at the beginning of the one brief argument which does explicitly discuss the bad. Note also that in this section, 'by nature good', 'good in reality', 'really good', and simply 'good' are used interchangeably (see textual point (c) above); the same pattern is repeated elsewhere (e.g. 79, 89, 114).

The argument begins by establishing that if anything is good or bad by nature, it must be so 'for everyone' (69) or 'in relation to everyone' (71); alternatively, its goodness or badness must be 'common to all' (71). And it then allegedly demonstrates, on the basis of disagreement about the good and the bad, that nothing meets this standard. The steps are as follows:

1. Either whatever anyone thinks is good really is good, or this is not the case (72).

2. But the first alternative cannot be correct; for if whatever anyone thinks is good really is so, then, since people's views about what is good, bad, and indifferent vary a great deal, the same thing will be good *and* bad *and* indifferent, which is impossible (72-4).

3. Supposing, however, that the first alternative is ruled out, then if there are *some* cases where what seems good to someone is good in reality, there must be some way of distinguishing between these cases and those where a thing seems good to someone but is *not* so in reality (75; on this transition, see textual point (e) above).

4. Things which are really good—or alternatively, the distinction between real and spurious goods—might be discerned either 'through plain experience' or 'through some reasoning' (76).

5. But that which is really good is not revealed by 'plain experience'. For 'plain experience', by its very nature, precludes dispute about the matter in question; but, as we have seen, there is dispute about the good (76).

6. Nor, however, can real goods be grasped by reasoning. For each school has its own 'private method of reasoning'; hence the items which each of them designates as goods, in accordance with these systems of reasoning, are themselves 'private goods' (77). But 'private goods' are not 'common to all', and hence not good by nature.

7. So there is nothing which is good by nature (78).

It might be wondered whether the dichotomy 'plain experience' or 'reasoning' (step 4) is exhaustive. Sextus conceives of discerning what is really good through 'plain experience' as analogous to, for example, seeing white in normal circumstances (on the strong, but not invariable, association between 'plain experience' and the senses, see linguistic point (f) above). Except those whose perceptions are the object of some definite 'interference' (jaundice, sunglasses, etc.), everyone will see white in the same way (see *M* VIII. 187, 218, 240 for Sextus' formulation of this point); and the same will be true of what is really good, if it is discerned by 'plain experience'—claims about what is really good derived from 'plain experience' will necessarily be unanimous. But it is far from clear that this is the only alternative besides reasoning; it might be the case, for example, that a few people had a special, non-rational insight into what is really good (arrived at, perhaps, through rigorous spiritual training), and that disagreement was the result of most people's lack of this insight.

However, Sextus' neglect of such possibilities is not a serious defect. For, as will become clear below, he is in fact assuming that *agreement* that X is really good is a necessary condition for X's *being* really good. Possibilities such as the one mentioned are therefore ruled out in his mind from the start, and the question of the media by which what is really good might be grasped is not of great importance; the central point is simply that people do disagree about the issue.

Several further interrelated points about the second half of the argument (beginning at step 3) are puzzling:

(a) Sextus begins by talking of our *grasping* or *apprehending* that which is really good; but in step 6 the inapprehensibility of the good apparently drops out of the picture, and the focus shifts exclusively to the *nonexistence* of anything really good. ('Capable of apprehending' (*kataléptikoi*) is, in philosophical usage, a Stoic technical term; on the Stoic 'apprehensive impression' (*phantasia kataléptikē*), see on 182–3 below. But nothing in the present argument turns on a confrontation specifically with Stoicism.)

(b) The conclusion is based on the prevalence of disagreement. But Sextus makes no effort to argue that this disagreement is unresolvable (though even this would seem to show only that we cannot be *sure* what is really good, not that *nothing* is really good); he apparently takes it that the very *existence* of disagreement leads directly to his conclusion.

(c) 'Private good' (step 6): In what sense is the reasoning employed by each school 'private', and the things which this reasoning declares to be goods 'private goods'? All Sextus seems entitled to at this point is that different schools have different views about what is good, established by different methods of reasoning; again, how can it be inferred from this that *none* of these schools has hit upon what is really good?

Some light is shed upon these issues by the beginning of the argument, where the term 'common to all' is introduced (69–71). Fire, Sextus says, warms everyone, not just some people, and snow chills everyone; hence these things may be said to be, respectively, warming and chilling by nature. (He need not be committed to this as a dogmatic conclusion. He could claim to be using these examples purely for the sake of argument, and that counter-instances can be found—e.g. Demophon, *PH* I. 82; see also *M* VIII. 197–9, IX. 242–3, and linguistic point (b) above.) The same, then, ought to be true of good; the effects of that which is *by nature* good should also be uniform for all people. I call this the Universality Requirement. Now, the distinctive effect of the good is to benefit (70); Sextus cites Plato on this point (see below), but it is common ground in Greek philosophy generally (cf. 35–6 for Sextus' acceptance of it as a commonplace, and 22–7 for the Stoics' acceptance of it as true by definition (also DL VII. 103, which again uses the analogy of heat)). That which is by nature good must therefore be beneficial 'for everyone' or 'in relation to everyone'; something which benefits only some people but not others is thereby not good by nature.

It also emerges later that that which is by nature good must be beneficial *on all occasions*, or *in all circumstances*; anything which is beneficial only at certain times is thereby not good by nature (see point 2 on 118 below). This latter aspect of the Universality Requirement is not explicitly stated here, but it is a natural extension of what Sextus does say (see Introduction, sect. II). (It is also apparently presupposed at several points before 118; see on 96–8, 99–109, and on the Recognition Requirement below.) Stated comprehensively, then, the Universality Requirement is the requirement that that which is by nature F must be *invariably* F— F for everyone and in all circumstances; as applied to the present issue, it entails that that which is by nature good must be invariably beneficial.

The Universality Requirement alone, however—whether in the form Sextus actually states it here or in the more comprehensive form appealed to elsewhere—does not solve any of the problems raised above. In all three cases, the following question may still be posed: Could there not be some things which are in fact invariably beneficial, but which not everyone recognizes as such?

Sextus' answer to this question would seem to be 'No'. That is, he is assuming that, in order for something to count as beneficial to a certain person, that person must *regard it as* beneficial; there can be no such thing as a benefit which is not viewed as such by the beneficiary. I shall call this the Recognition Requirement. Unlike the Universality Requirement, the Recognition Requirement is not stated at all in the present passage. But it is clearly at work in the parallel passage of *PH* III (179– 82), where only what 'affects everyone as good' (*pantas kinei hōs agathon*, 179) is considered to be by nature good, but where 'affecting everyone as good' consists in, or at least includes, being regarded by everyone as good (for discussion of this, see Bett 1994*c*: 131); and a precisely analogous requirement is assumed in the argument at 90–5 about whether anything is *bad* by nature (see below). The exact character of the Recognition Requirement is not immediately clear; I have discussed the question in the Introduction, sect. II, but some brief recapitulation may be helpful here. The weakest and most plausible version of this requirement is as follows: in order for one truly to be benefited (or harmed) at time *t*, one must recognize at some time—not necessarily at *t* itself, but perhaps only later, with hindsight or after careful reflection—that one is or was benefited (or harmed) at *t*. And this is sufficient for the needs of Sextus' argument. If this is assumed, then if there is any occasion on which one does not regard oneself (with hindsight, etc.) as having been benefited by some purported good—say, health—one *has not*, on that occasion, been benefited by that good. But this shows that the purported good in question is not invariably beneficial—which in turn, by the Universality Requirement (at least in the comprehensive form discussed just above), shows that it is not really, or by nature, a good.

If the Recognition Requirement as well as the Universality Requirement is operative in the present argument, the three points above become much clearer.

(a) Given the two requirements, the considerations mentioned in step 6 show directly that nothing is really good; things that are not universally recognized as good are not invariably, and hence not really, good. (See also point (b).) Of course, it *follows* that they are not apprehended as really good, either; but since that is not what the argument is primarily attempting to show, it does not need to be made explicit. As was hinted earlier, the topic of how the good might be apprehended or grasped is really not central. It enters the argument at step 3 because the question there is 'Given that only some of the things thought good really are so, how are we to *tell* which these are?' But it turns out that, no matter what method of apprehension one might suggest (including reasoning), the fact of disagreement rules out *anything*'s being really good; hence the project of finding some reliable method of distinguishing, among the things thought good, between the genuine and the non-genuine is abruptly closed down. (On a similar unexpected alternation between 'X cannot be apprehended or known' and 'There is no such thing as X' in other sources for Pyrrhonism, see Introduction, sect. III.)

(b) Given the two requirements, disagreement by itself does lead to Sextus' desired conclusion; any item about which there is disagreement over whether it is really good is *not* really good. For something to be by nature good, it would have to be invariably beneficial; but to be invariably beneficial, it would have to be invariably *regarded as* beneficial— which is certainly not the case if some people *deny* that it is good.

(c) Given the two requirements, the point about 'private goods' can be explained as follows. The various philosophical views about what is good are arrived at by way of idiosyncratic or 'private' schemes of reasoning; since the schemes of reasoning are 'private', the supposed goods which they generate are 'private' as well. Since all the alleged goods arrived at by philosophical reasoning are in this sense 'private'—none of them are universally agreed to be goods—none of them are candidates for being goods by nature.

There may still seem to be a problem. For why should different schemes of reasoning necessarily lead to such extreme disagreement about what things are good? For Sextus to establish in the manner outlined that *nothing* is by nature good, he must establish that there is *not a single thing* which all the schools agree to be good; and this is not established by pointing to the different schemes of reasoning employed by different schools, since the same thing might well be argued to be good in several different ways. In fact, Sextus' own examples at 77 seem to invite precisely this response. Zeno thought virtue was good, Epicurus pleasure, Aristotle health. These are not presented as competing claims about the *highest* good—contrary to Bury's translation, and despite the harsh accusations of Annas (1992b: 205–6); Sextus is well aware that Aristotle does not think that health is the highest good (cf. 51). They are simply examples of things deemed to be good by different philosophers, by means of different schemes of reasoning. (Virtue and pleasure are the obvious cases of things deemed good by the Stoics and the Epicureans respectively. The choice of examples is not nearly so constrained in the case of Aristotle, who has a much more pluralistic conception of what things are good; the example of health, which Aristotle certainly *would* have regarded as a good, is probably suggested by the focus on health in the preceding section.) But all three philosophers mentioned would agree that virtue is good; and in general, why should we suppose that all such things can only be 'private goods', as opposed to being acknowledged as goods by everyone? Sextus would no doubt refer back to his example of health, disagreements about the goodness of which were discussed at 48–67; this appeared to be intended as representative of all cases. But that it is thus representative would itself need to be established.

A more plausible reply can be constructed on Sextus' behalf as follows—though it must be admitted that 77–8 are very compressed, and it is impossible to say how far he was aware of the difficulty, or of this possible response to it. First, the only things which could possibly be agreed by everyone to be goods would be virtue and 'what partakes in virtue'; for these are the *sole* goods recognized by the Stoics (DL VII. 94, 101, Stob. II. 57, 20–2). And possibly there are some who would not even agree that virtue is a good—in which case nothing will be universally agreed to be a good. But, second, even if everyone does agree that virtue is a good, it is certainly *not* true that all will agree in their particular conceptions of what virtue is; each school, by means of its idiosyncratic or 'private' scheme of reasoning, will in fact arrive at a different end-product, even though they may all be called 'virtue'. Virtue-as-conceived-by-the-Stoics, for example, is by no means the same as virtue-as-conceived-by-the-Epicureans; the Epicureans regard virtue as only instrumentally good (LS 21A, L, M, O, P), the Stoics' conception of virtue is far more intellectualist, etc. So there is, after all, nothing whatever which all the schools (let alone people in general) agree to be good; rather, it makes sense to say that, because each school uses its own 'private' system of reasoning, the things which are supposed goods as a result of this reasoning are only 'private' goods. (Sextus does not, of course, consider the possibility that one of these schemes of reasoning might itself be superior to the others; but he would no doubt answer that there is no neutral standpoint from which to judge this question—every standpoint on the issue is 'a party to the dispute' (see e.g. *PH* I. 59, 90).)

The acceptability of the Recognition Requirement is of course debatable. It looks as if Sextus adopts it because the notion of a wholly unexperienced benefit or harm simply seems to him nonsensical; only a dogmatic philosopher, he would probably say, could be attracted to such a notion. (Compare the assumption at work in 79–89 below: the only things that it makes sense to call intrinsically choiceworthy are *positive experiences* of some variety or other. See Commentary ad loc.) For further consideration of these matters, see Introduction, sect. II, and Bett 1994*c*: 134–6. However, if I am right in thinking that Sextus assumes this requirement, the argument is not hopelessly flawed—as has been widely alleged—even if it is expressed (especially at the end) much more elliptically than one might like.

A few more remarks should be made about the term 'private good':

(i) The use of the singular 'private good' is due to the fact that the term is introduced in the context of the examples at 77. In designating virtue, pleasure, and health respectively as goods, each of the three philosophers he has mentioned will be 'introducing a private good'. The singular does not imply that Sextus is thinking of views about the *highest* good, and he is not suggesting that each of them will not adhere to other 'private goods' besides the ones mentioned.

(ii) It has been claimed by Annas and Barnes (1985: 164), and implied by Annas (1986: 9) and McPherran (1990: 132), that Sextus recommends in *M* XI that each of us should pursue our *own* 'private good'. But this is the only passage in the book in which the phrase 'private good' occurs, and there is no suggestion here that 'private goods' are what the *sceptic* will rely on. A 'private good' is simply what is thought by the members of some philosophical school to be good, as a result of some scheme of reasoning 'private' to that school; these goods are 'private' in the sense that they are believed good only by the members of that school (see above). 'Private good', then, is one more term for the apparent or supposed goods which have been the focus of the discussion throughout this section—specifically, for those things supposed good by some philosophical school, employing an idiosyncratic mode of reasoning. The term may mislead, because it sounds as if it refers to a good which is genuine, but in some way restricted. But, as we have seen, Sextus' entire argument proceeds on the assumption that there can be *no* genuine goods which are merely 'private'. The term 'private good' is an oxymoron, coined to emphasize precisely this point. If one could distinguish real goods, or goods by nature, from merely apparent goods 'by reasoning' (77), then *all* philosophical schools could claim to have uncovered what is really good, since they all use reasoning; yet, since each school's reasoning is 'private' to that school, the items which thus pass for genuine goods will all be 'private' as well. This state of affairs is inherently contradictory; and this contradiction is what the term 'private good' is designed to play up.

Several of Sextus' references to earlier philosophers deserve comment:
    (a) Plato never exactly says what Sextus attributes to him at 70. But *Rep.* 379b–c contains an argument that god necessarily does good which relies on the general principle Sextus is discussing, while *Rep.* 335d makes use of roughly the same principle and includes the example of heat. (A similar conflation of the two passages appears to be present in Porphyry, *De Abst.* II. 41.)
    (b) The 'person who said "I would rather be mad than feel pleasure"' (73) is Antisthenes. Sextus refers to Antisthenes (74) as a Cynic. This identification also occurs in DL VI. 13–15, Suda s.v. Antisthenes, and Clement, *Strom.* I. 14. 63, 3, but is in fact very dubious; there is no clear historical connection between Antisthenes and Diogenes of Sinope or other known Cynics (see Giannantoni 1990: iv. n. 24). The statement about pleasure is widely attested elsewhere (e.g. DL VI. 3, Aulus Gellius, *Attic Nights* IX. 5. 3); we are also told that Antisthenes denied that pleasure was a good (Aspas. *In Ar. NE* 142. 8–10), and his statement 'I would shoot down Aphrodite if I could catch her' (Clem. *Strom.* II. 20. 107, 2–3) suggests a particular opposition to sexual pleasure. In other texts, however, this stance against pleasure is qualified; according to

Athenaeus (XII. 513A), he said that pleasure which one does not regret afterwards is good, and Stobaeus (III. 29, 65) reports him saying that 'those pleasures which come after toil are to be pursued, but not those which come before toil' (on his approval of 'toil' (*ponos*), cf. DL VI. 2). For discussion see McKirahan 1994: esp. sect. I, Tarrant 1994: 125–6.

(c) That pleasure is an indifferent (73) is standard Stoic doctrine from Zeno onwards (DL VII. 102; on Zeno specifically, see Stob. II. 57, 18–58, 4, Aulus Gellius, *Attic Nights* IX. 5. 5); that it is not preferred (more precisely, neither preferred nor dispreferred) is said to be the standard Stoic view (Stob. II. 81, 11–15), though this cannot be securely traced back to Zeno. (DL VII. 102 seems to say that it is preferred. But the passage is confused, and Diogenes is generally confused in this area; at VII. 105–6 he conflates the two threefold distinctions outlined below.) Within the category of indifferents, the Stoics distinguished (1) among preferred indifferents, dispreferred indifferents, and those which are neither (Stob. II. 80. 16–21, and cf. 62 above), and (2) among those which are natural (*kata phusin*), those which are contrary to nature, and those which are neither (Stob. II. 79, 18–19). Those which are natural have 'value' (*axia*), and those which are contrary to nature have 'disvalue' (*apaxia*) (Stob. II. 83, 10–11, Cic. *Fin.* III. 20); those which have *much* value (or 'sufficient value', 62) are preferred, and those which have much disvalue are dispreferred (Stob. II. 80, 14–21, II. 84, 18–24, Cic. *Fin.* III. 50–1). Again, it is not clear how much of this doctrine goes back to Zeno, though the passages just cited say that he coined the terms 'preferred' and 'dispreferred' and defined them as stated. (This chronological issue is not insignificant, because one of the Stoics mentioned here, Cleanthes, was Zeno's immediate successor as head of the school.) The category 'neither preferred nor dispreferred' thus encompasses (i) natural things of little value, (ii) things contrary to nature but of little disvalue, and (iii) things of no value or disvalue. The three individual Stoics cited by Sextus appear to be taking different positions on where to classify pleasure among these subclasses. Cleanthes excludes pleasure from class (i) (without specifying as between the remaining two classes). We have no other fragments from Cleanthes on pleasure which might enable us to fill out his views. But this would seem to be contrary to the view attributed to Chrysippus and other Stoics at DL VII. 85–6, according to which pleasure is a 'by-product' (*epigennēma*) of natural growth and development; this clearly implies that at least some pleasures are natural. Panaetius would appear to be more consistent with this standard view, admitting some pleasures to class (i), though relegating others to the least desirable class (ii). For some possible amplification of his position, see Cic. *Off.* I. 105-6, 122; however, Cicero does not pretend to be simply translating Panaetius, but to be following him with some modifications (III. 7). The most puzzling case is Archedemus (probably a rough contemporary of Antipater of Tarsus (see Schmidt 1970)), about whom very little is known in any case; to claim that pleasure is natural but does *not* have value seems to disrupt the usual Stoic taxonomy altogether. Schmidt (1970: 1377) suggests that Archedemus' acceptance of pleasure as natural marks the 'high point' in positive estimations of pleasure by Stoics. But his denial of 'value' to pleasure, together with the armpit analogy, surely points in the opposite direction: contrary to normal Stoic usage, Archedemus is apparently using 'natural' in a way which does not carry a positive evaluation. For some speculations on this matter, see Rist 1969: 48-9, 103-7. Aside from the question of how to classify it, the Stoic conception of pleasure—and especially whether or not the term translated 'pleasure' (*hēdonē*) always designates one of the 'passions' (*pathē*)— is itself the subject of some controversy, into which I cannot enter here; for opposing views, see Gosling and Taylor 1982: 419-27 and LS I. 421, II. 264-5, 343, 405.

(d) It is not clear who Sextus has in mind as the author of the view that 'freedom from pain' (*alupia*) is good (76). For speculations on this, see Spinelli 1995: 249-50.

For comparison of 68-78 and the parallel passages at *PH* III. 179-82 and DL IX. 101, see Appendix A.

79-89: Second argument that there is nothing by nature good

[Textual points and other points of philological detail:
(a) With Mutschmann, I retain *hōs haireton* in 79; Heintz (followed by Bury) deletes it. As I have translated it ('as "thing to be chosen"'), it does not add anything notable to the sentence; but neither does it introduce any difficulties of syntax or comprehension, and the redundancy seems to me harmless.
(b) Bekker (followed by Mutschmann) is surely right to posit a lacuna in 81; Fabricius' attempt to make sense of the text as it stands is intolerably awkward. 'We put off' seems to be the best sense for the lacuna (Bekker's conjecture ⟨anaballometha⟩ to), not Bury's 'we ought to avoid'. The *hōsper* clause must contain some point on which general agreement is to be expected; it is quite unclear why the claim that we *ought* to avoid

eating and drinking should secure such agreement. The point is rather that, if choosing itself is to be chosen, then (absurdly) *all* choosing should be like what *in fact* sometimes happens with eating and drinking; Sextus must be citing as an actual phenomenon the delaying of one's eating and drinking in order to postpone the anticlimax of satiety. *PH* III. 183, referred to by Mutschmann, is not a relevant parallel; there the assumption is, on the contrary, that we hasten to satisfy our hunger and thirst as soon as possible (as in *M* XI. 82).

(c) I do not follow Heintz (together with Bury) in deleting *kata to haireisthai* in 82 as a gloss. If read with *epeigetai*, 'hastens', it is not excessively redundant; it can be taken as adding further emphasis to the main point of the sentence—that choosing something, *per se*, is troublesome rather than desirable.

(d) I do not follow Bekker's addition of *asteion* before *kinēma* in 83 (adopted by Mutschmann); *PH* III. 184 has *asteian kinēsin*, but there is no reason to assume that *M* XI also used this adjective. *Kinēma* is quite intelligible on its own; the character of the psychophysical 'motion' referred to is expanded upon in the following words.

(e) *Akinētōs*, 84: Caizzi (1981a: 254) draws attention to the parallel with *akinētōs* in the fragment from Timon in 1. If she means to suggest that Sextus is *deliberately* echoing Timon here, the point is questionable; the word is not a rare one, and its occurrence here is in no way unexpected, given the context.

(f) Against Mutschmann, but with Bekker (and Bury), I read *psuchēs* in 88 rather than *psuchē*; several MSS read *psuchēs*, and it makes much better sense.

(g) I do not follow Heintz (with Bury) in deleting *kata ton idion logon* in 88. The point of the phrase, in its repeated occurrences in 79–81, is that anything which is in reality, or by nature, good must be *by its very nature* worth choosing. For other examples of this type of usage, see *PH* III. 156, 164, *M* IX. 304, IV. 11. And here, too, the point is that 'the sense or intelligence which grasps that which is to be chosen' is *by its very nature* soul-like; *kata ton idion logon* is not essential to the sense, but it can easily be understood as included for added emphasis.]

This argument has the same conclusion as the previous one (as acknowledged in the final sentence of 89: 'Neither in this way . . .'), and in fact relies in its final stage (89) on the reasoning in 68–78; the 'original difficulty' referred to in 89 is simply the fact of disagreement about what is good, around which the previous argument turned. (The connection here is problematic, however; see below.) Strictly speaking, therefore, this argument does not carry any independent weight. However, it draws for most of its course on considerations quite separate from those employed in the previous argument. The central question it addresses is whether there is anything intrinsically worth choosing—anything to be chosen 'by its own definition' or 'for its own sake'; for this, it is asserted at the outset (79), is a necessary condition of anything's being good—i.e. good by nature. (It is also, apparently, a sufficient condition; in a number of later passages (see esp. 96-109, 112-18) 'good' and 'to be chosen', as well as 'bad' and 'to be avoided', are used interchangeably.) The answer is in the negative, and the argument takes the form of a series of dilemmas, as follows.

If anything is intrinsically worth choosing, this is either (I) 'choosing itself'—i.e. the act of choice—or (II) something other than choosing—something, that is, which is potentially the *object* of choices (80). But (I) is impossible (81-2).

But if it is (II), this intrinsically choiceworthy thing must be either (a) something 'separate from us' or (b) something 'relating to us' (83).

But if it is (a), either (i) this 'separate' object has some effect on us, or (ii) it does not (83). But nothing of which (ii) is true can be intrinsically worth choosing (84-5), and if (i) is true, it is in fact the *effect* which is intrinsically worth choosing and not the object itself—i.e. something belonging under (b) rather than (a) (86). Therefore, (a) is impossible (86).

But if it is (b), this thing 'relating to us' either (1) has no psychological component ('belongs solely to the body') or (2) does have a psychological component (87). But (1) is in effect no different from (aii), which has already been dismissed (87). And if (2) is true, it is the psychological component alone which is intrinsically worth choosing (as distinct from any bodily events which may accompany this) (88). But this leads back to the problem exposed in the previous argument (89).

Alternative I—that 'choosing itself' might be intrinsically worth choosing—is rejected on the ground that if this were so, we would not want to *obtain* the things which we are choosing, since this would deprive us of the opportunity to continue choosing them. This, Sextus argues, is obviously not so; in fact, in so far as choosing something implies not presently possessing it, the state of choosing something is one which a person will want to be rid of as soon as possible. (This is the point about 'the person who is troubled in his choosing of wealth' at the end of 82—

a point picked up in more detail in the next two chapters. On the troubles experienced by non-sceptics who do not have what they take to be good, see ch. IV, *passim*; on the sceptic's own attitude towards choice, see esp. 118, 147, 162–6.) Sextus' conception of choosing here is somewhat peculiar; choosing is pictured not as the discrete act of opting for something, but as an ongoing state—which may be more or less extended in time—of lacking but wanting to have something. Note especially the repeated phrase 'continuing to choose' (*tou eti haireisthai*, 81–2); if choosing were intrinsically worth choosing, the idea is, we would want to do it *for as long as possible*—which would imply, absurdly, that we should postpone getting the things which are the objects of our choices. (Epictetus uses the term *proairesis*, which is regularly translated 'choice', in a somewhat related way, to refer to a settled state which *issues in* choices; see e.g. *Diss.* I. 22. 10, II. 1. 12, where *proairesis* is *distinguished* from 'acts of choice' (*proairetika erga*). Even so, Epictetus uses the verb *haireisthai*, 'choosing', not as Sextus does here, but to refer to individual acts of choice; see e.g. *Diss.* I. 9. 24, II. 9. 20, IV. 2. 3, 7.) A related objection, however, would be open to Sextus even on a more standard conception of choosing; he could say that, since choosing X entails valuing X and trying to obtain it, it would be absurd to regard the choosing of X as intrinsically valuable *rather than* X itself. This is precisely the objection—to which Sextus' actual discussion may well be indirectly indebted—raised by the Academics and others against those Stoics who offered definitions of the ethical end (*telos*) in terms of the 'selecting' (*eklegesthai*) of things according to nature (e.g. Alexander, *Mantissa* 164, 3–9 (= LS 64B), Plut. *Comm. not.* 1070F–1071E, 1072E–F). But in this case it is by no means so clear that the objection is final; on the history of this debate, see LS 64, texts and comm., Striker 1991: sect. 3.

The initial statement of alternatives IIa and IIb—that which is intrinsically worth choosing must be a 'thing separate from us' or a 'thing relating to us'—is somewhat vague. But in the course of the argument it becomes clear that by 'things relating to us', Sextus means states of ourselves ('ourselves' being understood as comprising both body and soul), while by 'things separate from us', he means anything else—anything which is 'external' to ourselves.

The effect on us from the 'external' thing which is envisaged in alternative IIaii is called a 'motion' (*kinēma*). As the subsequent phrases make clear, this is to be understood as a certain type of subjective psychological state. Specifically, it is the adjectives which make this clear; neither *katastēma* nor *pathos*—which I have translated, here and elsewhere, by 'condition' and 'experience' respectively—necessarily designates a subjective state, though both very often do so. (Note that, as the translation of *pathos*, 'experience' is always preceded by the definite or indefinite article; when 'experience' is used generically without the article, the Greek word is either *enargeia* ('plain experience') or *periptōsis*.) However, given the broadly materialist assumptions of Hellenistic philosophy, 'motion' probably also refers literally to a bodily alteration underlying this psychological state. But the argument does not actually depend on any particular view about what is nowadays called the mind–body problem.

Alternative IIa is dismissed on the grounds that 'things separate from us' can be valued only if they affect us experientially in some positive way, and that if this is so, it is the positive effect, rather than the 'external' thing which caused it, which is intrinsically worth choosing. Similarly, alternative IIb1 is dismissed on the ground that a bodily state which had no psychological component or correlate would be one of which we were unaware, and hence would be equivalent to 'external' things which have no positive experiential effect on us. And once IIb2 is left as the only alternative, we are told that psychological states are intrinsically worth choosing only in so far as they are psychological states—their bodily aspect is insignificant. The assumption throughout the argument, then, is that if there are any items intrinsically worth choosing, they are some species of *positive experiences*; whatever else we might normally be inclined to regard as valuable can be valuable only in so far as it results in such experiences. It is perhaps not surprising that a Pyrrhonist—for whom the 'non-evident' is not to be speculated about, and whose aims are *ataraxia*, 'untroubledness', and *metriopatheia*, 'moderate feeling' (*PH* I. 25), which are precisely *experienced* conditions—should assume that value can only reside, if anywhere, in a certain type of experience. Indeed, the enthusiasm with which he adopts this assumption makes it harder for him to argue convincingly that IIb2 is after all *not* a viable alternative, and this helps to account for the argument's awkward final stage (see below). But the assumption is highly questionable. Similar assumptions, though widely held in modern philosophy, have also been widely criticized; in the ancient context such assumptions would be even less likely to be granted. A few might agree with Sextus—the Cyrenaics are a clear example (see e.g. DL II. 86–8)—but many others would not. Both Aristotle and the Stoics, for example, hold that *virtuous activity* is intrinsically choiceworthy; while the state in which one engages in virtuous activity is of course a conscious state, what makes virtuous activity choiceworthy is not the desirability of this conscious state—even though, at least in Aristotle, the virtuous person does find such activity pleasant—but the nobility of the activity itself.

This, of course, raises the question of how important it is for Sextus to convince non-sceptics of his conclusions. The answer to this is not as clear as one might hope; but it is at any rate not obvious that Sextus has reason to care whether an Aristotelian or a Stoic, for example, is persuaded by 'the things which have been said by the sceptics on the subject under discussion' (68). (On this, see also Introduction, n. 28 and accompanying text.) Still, whatever the answer to this question, it is clear from the ensuing discussion (see on 112–18, 130, 140 below) that he does at least endorse the conclusion of this and the neighbouring arguments (as opposed, say, to using it purely as a counterbalance to the arguments of certain dogmatists); it is therefore legitimate for us to question his warrant for relying on the assumption just considered.

There is an unexpected transition in the final portion of the argument. Up to the beginning of 88 Sextus has been speaking of that which is intrinsically worth choosing as being some kind of 'pleasing' psychological state; given this assumption, as we have seen, it has been established that anything which is intrinsically worth choosing must be a 'thing relating to us' which 'belongs to the soul'. One would expect that Sextus would now argue that not even anything which 'belongs to the soul' is intrinsically worth choosing, hence that nothing is intrinsically worth choosing, and hence that nothing is by nature good (cf. 79; this is in fact what happens in the parallel passage of *PH* III (see Appendix A)). But instead, the whole question of what, if anything, is intrinsically worth choosing is forgotten by the beginning of 89, and the argument concludes on quite a different tack, by saying that nothing is by nature good because people's judgements about what is good are in conflict—which appeals, as we saw, to the argument at 68–78. Given this conflict, what seems good to 'each person'—i.e. to any given person—will not seem good to everyone else; so what seems good to 'each person' is not good by nature; so nothing is good by nature. Sextus tries to patch these disparate parts of the argument together in 88, where he insists that those faculties which judge what is worth choosing belong to the soul rather than to the body. This is presented as a consideration in favour of the claim that 'if the pleasing effect . . . extends to the soul, it will be something to be chosen and good as far as the latter is concerned, but not in so far as it is a movement merely of the body'. But, given the previous argumentation, that claim is not in need of further support; and in any case, the kinds of 'pleasing effects' referred to in the preceding discussion are very different psychological phenomena from *judgements about* what is to be chosen (88) or about what is good (89). It looks as if Sextus is at a loss for a way of completing the argument as originally specified, and so is forced to fall back awkwardly on the previous argument to achieve closure. (This is not perhaps surprising, given his single-minded reliance on the assumption discussed in the previous paragraph; in order to show that nothing which 'belongs to the soul' is intrinsically worth choosing, he would in any case have to appeal to very different considerations from those employed so far.)

For comparison of 79–89 and the parallel passage at *PH* III. 183–90, see Appendix A.

90–5: Argument that there is nothing by nature bad

[The text in 90 has been subjected to various more or less drastic additions and subtractions, most of which are unnecessary. First, the MSS reading *apodedotai* makes perfectly good sense; there is no need to alter it, with Mutschmann, to *sunapodedotai*. More significant is the stretch of text from *prōton men* to the end of the sentence, where, among other alleged defects, a lacuna has been posited by several scholars. The main reason for concern seems to have been the thought that the clause beginning *eita epei* cannot be giving, as the received text would require, a second reason why the argument that nothing is by nature bad has in effect been presented by the previous arguments about the good. (For this line of thought, see Heintz 1932: 251–2.) But this is by no means out of the question. The fact that 'it is possible again to rest such a point [i.e. the non-existence of anything by nature bad, as implied by the preceding claim that the bad has been 'done away with'] directly on one example'— as was the case in the argument that nothing is by nature good—shows that similar kinds of considerations operate in both cases, and hence that nothing fundamentally new needs to be said in the case of the bad. The fact that it is possible to rest the point on one example then has to be illustrated, and so the *eita epei* clause also has the effect of introducing the new argument. The 'single example' employed in the case of the good was health (cf. 47); on the analogy between the two examples, see below. There is no need, then, to assume a lacuna. Two small deletions are, however, required. First, either *hoti* or *epei* has to be deleted after *prōton men*; I propose to delete *hoti* rather than *epei* because (i) the

parallel with *eita epei* will then be neater, and (ii) *hoti* seems more likely
to have been added by scribal error—*prōton hoti* is not uncommon in
Sextus (16 occurrences with or without *men*), whereas *prōton epei*, with or
without *men*, occurs only here and at *M* I. 41 (*prōton men epeiper*).
Second, either *to toiouton* or *ton logon* must be deleted; I delete *ton logon*,
which may have been a gloss on the not wholly lucid *to toiouton*. It is also
possible, however, that Sextus himself changed his phrasing in mid-
stream and carelessly wrote both.]

This section begins by giving two reasons why the preceding arguments
against the good also have force against the bad. The second reason
amounts to saying that a parallel argument can be constructed against the
bad (see above and below). The first reason—that when either one of the
good and the bad is 'done away with', so is the other—seems to presuppose the view that opposites are dependent on one another for their
existence. This view was certainly held by the Stoics with regard to
ethical opposites (Aulus Gellius, *Attic Nights* VII. 1. 2–6, Plut. *Sto. rep.*
1050E–F, *Comm. not.* 1065A–B), and can perhaps be traced in Heraclitus
(DK 22B23, 111); but it is not clear why Sextus thinks that he, as a
sceptic, is entitled to assume it. (As with the previous two arguments,
Sextus does mean to *endorse* the assertions made in this section; he is not
arguing *ad hominem*, against the Stoics or anyone else—see on 112–18,
130, 140 below, and Introduction, sect. II.) This is not the only place in
this section where Sextus appears to help himself unjustifiably to Stoic
doctrines; see below.

The explanatory remark 'for each of the two is conceived in virtue of
its holding in relation to the other' is also potentially misleading. Sextus
must mean that bad cannot be conceived of in the absence of its opposite
good, and vice versa (this thought is also apparent in the Aulus Gellius
passage, which quotes Chrysippus). But the phrase 'things conceived in
virtue of their holding in relation to another thing' (*ta kata tēn hōs pros
heteron schesin nooumena*) is elsewhere used by Sextus in a rather different
way, to refer to properties designated by two-place predicates such as
'. . . is whiter than . . .', '. . . is to the right of . . .', etc.; being whiter is
'conceived in virtue of its holding in relation to' the object than which
one is whiter—in other words, the object designated by the term filling
the second place (*M* VIII. 161–2, X. 263–5; for discussion see Barnes
1990*b*: esp. 20–3, Mignucci 1988: 196–7, 204–7). Even if, as Sextus will
later suggest, there is a hidden relativity to goodness and badness, good
and bad are certainly not, in *this* sense, 'conceived in virtue of their

holding in relation to' *each other*. For more on relativity in *M* XI and in Stoicism, see below, linguistic point (a) on 112-18.

As the introductory remarks in 90 suggest, the argument about the bad is in several respects analogous to those on the good—or, more specifically, to the first argument on the good. Just as the distinctive effect of the good is to benefit (70), so the distinctive effect of the bad is to harm (91). The analogy with heating and chilling is again employed, as in 69. There the point was that anything which is *by nature* warming or chilling must be so invariably (the Universality Requirement). But the Universality Requirement is not made explicit here, and in fact it is not needed; for Sextus argues not just that not everyone is harmed by folly, but that *no one* is. The analogy with hot and cold serves simply to make vivid the idea of a thing's distinctive natural effect. The argument does, however, make use of the Recognition Requirement, as did the first argument about the good (see below).

The use of the single example folly is presented as analogous to a procedure employed in the argument about the good. The reference must be to the example of health (cf. 'on a single example' (*epi henos hupodeigmatos*), 47). This was developed in detail as a representative case of something which might be thought obviously good (see esp. 49), but about which there was in fact disagreement concerning whether it is good (48-67). The assumption appeared to be that this was generalizable to all cases; given this supposedly pervasive disagreement, it was then argued that nothing is by nature good (68-78). Folly may seem to be playing a rather different role in the present argument from that played by health in the earlier one. But it is not unreasonable to see this as a greatly compressed instance of the type of argument offered in 48-78 (and the compression is only to be expected if, as Sextus says (90), the job of arguing that nothing is by nature bad has in effect already been done). Instead of first establishing that not everyone regards folly as harmful, and then arguing that—since folly is a representative case, and in virtue of the two requirements—this shows that nothing is by nature bad, Sextus runs these two stages together. He immediately addresses the question of whether folly is by nature bad, arguing that it is not; one crucial part of this argument (94) turns on the fact that those who might be expected to regard folly as harmful do not do so; and this argument is then said to be generalizable to all cases (95).

This argument is indeed superior to the argument about the good, in that it devotes explicit attention to the legitimacy of generalizing from the single case of folly; as we saw earlier, the example of health was clearly intended to stand as representative for all alleged goods, but Sextus did nothing to show that he was entitled to generalize from this one example. Here, in addition to the closing sentence of 95, he presses for the credentials of folly as a 'best case' for his position by saying that the Stoics regard this as the *only* thing which is bad (90); if folly turns out *not* to be bad, it is implied, then nothing will be. Sextus' claim about the Stoics is unfortunately not quite accurate. Orthodox Stoicism holds that 'everything which is a vice or partakes of a vice' is bad, by analogy with the case of good (Stob. II. 57, 20–58, 1, DL VII. 94–5), and folly (*aphrosunē*) is listed as one of four primary vices, each of which corresponds to one of the four primary virtues 'practical wisdom' (*phronēsis*), moderation, justice, and courage (DL VII. 92–3; cf. Stob. II. 60, 9–11). However, the Stoics also define each of these virtues as species of knowledge (*epistēmē*), and the corresponding vices as forms of ignorance (*agnoia*) (Stob. II. 59, 4–60, 4; cf. DL VII. 92–3, *SVF* III pp. 65–7). Now, Plutarch reports that, in what appears to be an earlier version of this view, Zeno defined the three virtues other than practical wisdom as themselves species of practical wisdom (*Sto. rep.* 1034C, *Virt. mor.* 441A); it is therefore not unlikely that he would have defined the corresponding three vices as species of folly. However, no other Stoic followed Zeno in this; the succeeding Stoics, as Plutarch reports, defended Zeno by saying that by 'practical wisdom' he meant 'knowledge', but the standard formulation was clearly deemed preferable (for further discussion and texts see LS 61). Still, Sextus' claim here may be taken as a somewhat loose reflection of the centrality of virtue and vice in the Stoics' conception of good and bad, and of their highly cognitive conception of these virtues and vices. (For further detail on the things which may be called good or bad by 'partaking in' virtue or vice respectively, as opposed to *being* virtues or vices, see 22–7, 40 above, with Comm., and DL VII. 94–5.)

As noted above, the conclusion of Sextus' argument is stronger than one might expect: not just that not everyone is harmed by folly, but that no one is harmed by it. This is because only fools are candidates for being victims of folly, but part of what it is to be a fool is not to recognize one's folly as harmful. In more detail, the argument is as follows:

1. If folly is bad by nature, it must be harmful. Who, then, are harmed by folly? It must be either the wise or the foolish (91).
2. But it is not the wise, since they are 'remote from folly' (i.e. they are not themselves repositories of folly) (92).
3. Suppose, then, that it is fools whom folly harms; they must either

be aware of this folly or unaware of it (92). Sextus here uses the terms 'evident' (*prodēlos*) and 'non-evident' (*adēlos*). These and related terms are elsewhere very important to his characterization of scepticism and his arguments against the dogmatists (in this book, cf. esp. 205, 232–3 with Comm.); but in this instance their wider connotations are of no great significance.

4. But if they are unaware of it, it cannot, in fact, be harmful to them, any more than a 'non-apparent' grief or an 'unfelt' pain could be considered harmful (93). (Here and in what follows Sextus sometimes uses 'bad' and 'to be avoided' where, from the point of view of argumentative clarity, one would expect 'harmful'—e.g. 'it is neither a bad thing nor a thing to be avoided by them'; in summarizing, I have corrected this minor defect.)

5. And if they are aware of it, then if it really was harmful, they would have avoided it as such—they 'ought' to have avoided it in a logical, not a moral sense (94).

6. But this is not the case; fools do not avoid folly, but like everyone else, they take their own judgements, which others may deem foolish, as sound (94).

7. So there is no one whom folly harms; so folly is not by nature bad (95).

The nature of the alternatives posed in step 3 is not immediately clear. Is 'being aware of one's folly' to be understood as (a) being *aware that* one is in a state of folly, or as (b) being aware that one is in a certain state S, which *others* would describe as a state of folly, even though one would not so describe it oneself? There seem to be indications in both directions. The phrase 'that which is called "being a fool" by those who are remote from it' (94; cf. 91, 'those who are called foolish') seems to suggest reading (b). But 'no one will shun as a bad thing folly which is unsuspected' (93) surely means 'no one will shun . . . folly which is not *suspected to be folly*', which accords instead with reading (a). It looks, in fact, as if Sextus has not sorted out these two readings; as we shall see, the argument trades on a shift between them.

Step 4 depends on the Recognition Requirement; indeed, it provides the most explicit evidence in this book that Sextus accepts some such requirement. Sextus makes the uncontroversial point that one will not regard as bad something of which one is not even aware. But he treats this point as tantamount to saying that something of which one is not aware *cannot in fact* be bad ('if it is non-evident to them, it is neither a bad thing nor a thing to be avoided by them'). The latter claim is crucial to the argument; the aim is to show that folly does not harm anyone, not just that it is not viewed as harmful by anyone; but Sextus cannot think himself entitled to this claim unless he assumes that *being regarded as* harmful is a necessary condition for *being* harmful. The analogy with grief and pain suggests that what motivates this requirement is the difficulty of making sense of the notion of a wholly unexperienced benefit or harm. For more on the Recognition Requirement, and its role elsewhere in the book, see above on 68–78 and Introduction, sect. II.

Unfortunately, folly is precisely the kind of case to which the Recognition Requirement—at least, in any remotely attractive form—is clearly inapplicable. For precisely what it is to be in a state of folly is not to recognize things for what they are—including the state of folly itself. One may very well be unaware that one is in a state of folly (as noted just above, this seems the better interpretation of the possibility considered in step 4), and therefore not inclined to regard one's current state as a harmful one. But this plainly is *not* tantamount to saying that one's folly is in fact not harmful, because folly is inherently such as to *conceal* its true character—including, no doubt, its true harmfulness—from its victim. As noted earlier, the most plausible version of the Recognition Requirement would be one in which one's recognition of benefit or harm could be shaped by reflection and hindsight. As we saw, 68–78 (and the parallel passage at *PH* III. 179–82, where the requirement is more overtly operative) can be read as appealing to this version; but this is of course precluded by the situation presupposed here in step 4: that one is (i) in a state of folly, and (ii) unaware of this fact. In this case, therefore, although Sextus seems clearly to be assuming some form of the Recognition Requirement, he does not help himself by doing so.

The treatment of the other horn of the dilemma, in steps 5 and 6, is also problematic. Step 5 is plausible only on reading (a) of step 3. That is, the point must be that one would avoid folly which one *recognized as folly*; if, as reading (b) would have it, one merely recognized that one was in a certain state, which *in fact* was a state of folly even though one did not realize this, it would not be at all obvious that one would see reason to avoid this state. (The words 'if it is recognized by them in an evident fashion' also suggests reading (a) rather than reading (b).) Step 6, on the other hand, only works on reading (b). For the whole point of step 6 is that fools do *not* recognize their state as one of folly; other people may call their state 'folly', but fools themselves think otherwise, and this is *why* they do not avoid it.

A further difficulty with the argument is that most of us are not unequivocally either wise or foolish. (Of course, the Stoics would say that we are. But despite his focus on the example of folly, Sextus is not here arguing only against Stoics (see above); so he is not in a position to rely on the Stoics' very strong assumptions.) Almost all of us, it would seem, are not 'remote from folly', but also not incapable of recognizing, at least sometimes, the harmfulness of our foolish choices. It is (usually) true that foolish choices are not recognized as foolish, and therefore harmful, at the time when they are made. But it is *not* true that, even with hindsight, 'each person accepts his own judgement and deems bad that of the person who thinks the opposite' (94); and it is unclear why retrospective assessments of the wisdom of one's choices should not be allowed a place in the argument. Finally, the 'harm' considered in the argument is solely harm *to the foolish agent*; Sextus does not consider what seems to be a very common occurrence: viz. that people are harmed by the folly of others.

Rather than arguing that folly harms no one, Sextus would have been better advised to argue for the weaker but more plausible conclusion that folly is not *invariably* harmful; given the Universality Requirement, this would have been quite adequate to show that folly is not by nature bad. This is the strategy used in the parallel passage of *PH* III (190). This is very brief; it simply states that none of the things typically regarded as bad are universally regarded as such, and then invokes the Universality Requirement (and, at least implicitly, the Recognition Requirement) to conclude that nothing is by nature bad. (It is not based on folly as a representative case; nor does it appeal, overtly or covertly, to any Stoic doctrines.) This would certainly need some expansion in order to be fully convincing; but it is hard not to see this as an improvement on *M* XI's version.

It is worth mentioning that, unlike *M* XI, *PH* III immediately follows with an argument to the effect that nothing is by nature indifferent (191–3); this too relies on disagreement, the Universality Requirement, and the Recognition Requirement. (The enumeration of disagreements (191–2) parallels *M* XI. 62–6; on the fact that this passage does not quite serve its intended function in *PH* III, see Appendix A.) Despite *M* XI's ambivalence about whether to include the category of the indifferent (cf. on 1–2, 21, 40–1, 59–61), it has been by no means absent from the discussion; why, then, is there no argument parallel to the one in *PH* III? One possible answer is the following. Statements of the form 'X is indifferent' might be thought of either simply as *denying* that X is, in its true nature, either good or bad, or as *asserting* that X has, in its true nature, a certain characteristic, viz. indifference. The concept of the indifferent, as developed by the Stoics, is not obviously determinate as between these two options. Now, understood in the first way, statements of the form 'X is indifferent' need not be in conflict with the outlook of *M* XI (even though the *term* 'indifferent' is one which, given the body of doctrine it could be expected to evoke, a sceptic might well not wish to adopt); for *M* XI is prepared to say that things are not by nature good or bad. So if this was how Sextus understood 'X is indifferent' in writing *M* XI, there would be no reason for him to include an argument to the effect that nothing is by nature indifferent; in fact, if 'indifferent' was equivalent to 'not by nature either good or bad', there would not even be a use for the phrase 'by nature indifferent'. (*PH* III. 191–3, on the other hand, uses the phrase 'by nature indifferent', clearly adopting the other understanding of 'X is indifferent'.)

96–8: *Epicurean objection*

[I have rendered *Hōs an tou hēdeos ou phusei ontos toioutou*, 98, by 'which accords with the pleasant's not being such by nature'. Bury translates this 'just *as though* the pleasant *were* not so by nature' (my emphasis), and Russo follows suit. This may seem closer to the *hōs an* idiom, but it wrongly implies that 'the pleasant's not being such by nature' is counterfactual. Sextus' point, on the contrary, is that people's inconsistent reactions to what has struck them at some time as pleasant is evidence for (or at least, is consistent with) the *truth* of the claim expressed in the *hōs an* phrase. For the same idiom—*hōs an* with genitive absolute—with the same force, cf. 194 below.]

In this short section Sextus mentions a possible Epicurean response to the position as so far developed, and then gives reasons (97–8) why it should not be accepted. The Epicurean view is described in very similar terms, and attributed to Epicurus himself, by both Diogenes (DL X. 137) and Cicero (*Fin*. I. 30); it would appear to be an important element in Epicurean ethics, since, according to these texts, it was used by Epicurus to support his central conclusion that pleasure is the highest good. The slightly unexpected term 'the animal' (*to zōion*) seems to be authentically Epicurean—cf. *Letter to Menoeceus* 128; it is not only the behaviour of non-human animals that is at issue here, but also that of humans in so far as they are acting as natural creatures uncorrupted by society. (As Nussbaum (1994: 106–7) points out, the creature who is just born and 'not yet a slave to opinions' is plainly a human baby; see her ch. 4, sect. II, for discussion of Epicurus' strategy and motivations in this context, also Brunschwig 1986: esp. sects. I and II.)

It may look as if Sextus is attributing the view only to some Epicureans; if so, the restriction would be suspect, given the evidence from Diogenes and Cicero. But his point, rather, is that 'some members of the Epicurean school' appeal to this (standard Epicurean) view 'in confronting such difficulties'—i.e. as a way of rebutting sceptical arguments, such as Sextus has just offered, to the effect that nothing is good or bad by nature; though all Epicureans may have believed in the view in question (and in the parallel passage of *PH* III (194) Sextus himself attributes it to the Epicureans in general), it may well be that only some of them appealed to it specifically for this anti-sceptical purpose. I doubt whether we are in a position to determine who these Epicureans were. The view that nothing is by nature good or bad was already held by Pyrrho (or so I have argued—see Bett 1994*d*), and was also probably advanced by Aenesidemus or at least some other Pyrrhonians (see point 3 on 118 and Introduction, sect. III); it is therefore not clear that there is any single historical period in which the rebuttal of such views would have been of special concern to Epicureans. I see no reason to accept the suggestion of Gigante (1981: 168) that Sextus in 96 may be following a passage of the Epicurean Demetrius Lacon (*P Herc.* 1012, col. 45 in de Falco 1923). The passage in question is making a quite different set of points; most obviously, it says (ll. 4–6) that human beings are 'by nature *receptive of hardships*' (*phusei de ponōn . . . dektikos*), rather than that they naturally avoid hardships. For another example of Epicurean anti-sceptical argument (this time in an epistemological context), see Lucretius, IV. 469–521.

Sextus' reply to this Epicurean argument consists of three points:

1. If the Epicureans were right, then 'even . . . the most despised animals' would have to be considered as having 'a share of the good' (97).
2. Many things which, by common agreement, are worth having can be attained by means of, and only by means of, pain; hence pain cannot be considered something which is by nature to be avoided (97).
3. Things which seem to us pleasant on one occasion often do not seem pleasant on other occasions; hence 'what seems pleasant', or 'the pleasant', cannot be considered something which is universally, or by nature, to be chosen (98).

Point 1 is purely *ad hominem*. Sextus himself does not assert, and is not in a position to assert, that the good is something to which, as a matter of methodology, animals cannot be considered to have access; rather, he extracts from the argument a consequence which he supposes the Epicureans will find disturbing. But even on these terms, the force of his point is very unclear. There is a sense in which the Epicureans could easily accept that animals, even 'the most despised' ones, manage to attain *a share* of the good—i.e. they manage to attain some aspects of what for humans is the highest good. If, on the other hand, Sextus is suggesting that, by this Epicurean argument, animals partake of the good to the same degree, or in the same way, as humans, then the Epicureans would surely deny the claim. The appeal to the natural behaviour of animals, they could say, is designed to show that pleasure is naturally to be chosen; it is quite consistent with this to hold that the distinctive forms of pleasure in which the highest human good consists are at least partly unattainable by non-human animals. This may be a difficult position for them to sustain, given the importance which they assign to the reactions of animals and young children (see again Nussbaum 1994: ch. 4, sect. II, Brunschwig 1986: sects. I and II). But Sextus would at least have to develop his point much further before he could hope for it to be effective.

Point 2 is more successful. Relying on the Universality Requirement (in the comprehensive version in which it applies to circumstances or times as well as to persons—see on 68–78 above), Sextus simply observes that there are plenty of cases in which the results of hardship are valued; assuming that we are not wrong to value these results—and Sextus can surely count on almost everyone's agreement here, including that of the Epicureans (see *Letter to Menoeceus* 129)—this shows that hardship is not invariably, and hence not by nature, to be avoided. (On the sceptic's willingness to make assertions of the form 'Hardship is *sometimes* to be chosen', see below on 118; the present point is not offered as, and need not be understood as, merely *ad hominem*. Cf. Sextus' reply 1b to the Stoic argument immediately following this one.) The phrase 'by nature entirely a thing to be avoided'—cf. 'by nature entirely to be chosen' in point 3—is, however, redundant and misleading. If something is by nature to be avoided, it *is* 'entirely'—i.e. invariably—to be avoided. Sextus makes it sound as if hardship may, despite the preceding argument, be by nature *partially* to be avoided; but this is conceptually impossible, and even if it were not, it would run counter to his conclusion that nothing is by nature bad.

Point 3 is again open to criticism. It too appeals to the Universality

Requirement—for something to qualify as by nature F, it must be invariably F, rather than 'moving us sometimes in this way, sometimes in that way, depending on the circumstances'. But it does not suggest, as one might have expected from point 2 (and as *PH* III. 195 does suggest), that pleasure is sometimes appropriately avoided, and hence is not by nature to be chosen; indeed, it does not cite *any* facts about pleasure in general. Instead, it has to do with the objects which strike us as pleasant; the very same type of thing, Sextus says, may well strike us first as pleasant, then as unpleasant. Unfortunately, this does not show what he needs it to show, that *pleasure* is not by nature to be chosen; it merely shows that things are not always consistently pleasurable. Sextus sees that he is in a weak position here; he says that his observation 'accords with' the conclusion (see the point of translation above), rather than that it demonstrates its correctness—note also the logically unambitious connecting particle 'at any rate' (*goun*), instead of 'for'. In addition, the conclusion itself is stated in two different ways: we are told that 'what seems pleasant' is not by nature to be chosen, and also that 'the pleasant' is not 'such [i.e. to be chosen] by nature'. Neither of these terms is completely clear. But 'the pleasant' is most naturally taken as an alternative expression for pleasure itself, whereas 'what seems pleasant' is more easily taken as meaning 'that which strikes one as pleasant on some individual occasion'. On these interpretations, his observation that things which strike us as pleasant often fail to continue to do so does address the status of 'what seems pleasant' (though even here, it leaves open the possibility that some things which 'seem pleasant' *are* consistently pleasurable—and hence, for all that he has said, perhaps 'by nature to be chosen'); but it does not address the status of 'the pleasant', which is what the argument is supposed to be about. In short, point 3 is both awkwardly expressed and logically unimpressive.

For comparison of 96–8 and the parallel passage at *PH* III. 194–6, see Appendix A.

99–109: *Stoic objection*

[Points of text and translation:

(a) I translate *hopou ge hekateron estin adiaphoron* in 102 by 'seeing that either one is indifferent'. Bury has 'at least where . . .' (cf. Russo), and offers an explanatory footnote. But I fail to follow his explanation; in any case, *hopou ge* elsewhere in Sextus clearly means 'seeing that'—see *PH* I.

50, 206, 238, III. 200, *M* VIII. 278, and LSJ s.v. *hopou*, ii. 2. On the point of this phrase, see below.

(b) I retain the MSS *hōste* in 103, rather than following Apelt's conjecture *allōs te*, as do Mutschmann and Bury. One can make sense of *hōste*, 'so that', by supposing that 102 is parenthetical—as I have marked it—and that 103 is pursuing the theme raised in 101, of the important difference between humans and other animals. The connection is admittedly a little strained; in 101 we are told that animals cannot pursue the fine because they cannot be wise, whereas in 103 the hypothesis is that (despite not being wise) animals do pursue the fine. But this is not out of keeping with the neighbouring text; there are other confusions in the section of the argument at 103–6 (see below).

(c) With Mutschmann, I retain *di'hauto, anthrōpōi d'* in 106; Heintz (1932: 253–4) deletes these words, and is followed by Bury. Heintz argues that the following sentence shows (1) that humanity has not been mentioned here, and (2) that the *same* applies to animals as to humans. Neither point need be accepted. The force of *kai mallon ge* in the following sentence may be 'to an even greater extent than might have been suspected [sc. to be the case *for humans*] from the previous remark', instead of '. . . than in the case of animals'. Heintz also says that there is no reason why what is said (according to the MSS text) of humans should not also be true of animals. But Sextus is picking up two previous suggestions: that of 102, that 'winning and being the leader' is the sole motivating force for animals who fight, and that of the end of 105 (immediately before the present passage), that human beings are just as likely to be *less* noble than animals as to be more noble. Heintz's final argument depends on the mistaken assumption that the speaker (*allos tis*) in 106 is another opponent. But the considerations offered in 106 are never attacked; on the contrary, they lead directly into a number of points (107–9) which Sextus cites in his own favour. *Allos tis* is a friendly bystander.

(d) I translate *diachein* (106) by 'relax', in contrast to Bury's 'thrill'. On this word, see linguistic point (e) on 141–9 below.

(e) A *proupton . . . thanaton* (108) is not a 'conspicuous' death (Bury; cf. Russo), but simply a death which was foreseen; cf. Hdt. 9. 17, Thuc. 5. 99, 111.]

This section, though considerably longer than the previous one, follows much the same pattern. Against the conclusion that nothing is good or bad by nature, it is objected that certain types of animal and human behaviour demonstrate that something is by nature 'to be chosen' (99–100);

and Sextus then offers a number of arguments designed to demolish this suggestion.

The anonymous objectors, 'who believe that only the fine is good' (99), are the Stoics. The word here translated 'fine' (*kalon*) originally referred mainly or even exclusively to physical beauty, and may often, in all periods, be appropriately translated 'beautiful' (see e.g. 43 above). But in Plato and, more obviously, in Aristotle, the word starts to have connotations of the ethically admirable, and this is how the Stoics use it in this context. As Stobaeus explains (II. 78, 1–4; cf. DL VII. 101), the term 'the fine' in the Stoics' statement 'The fine is good' is intended as equivalent to 'virtue and what partakes of virtue' (which are elsewhere named, as we have seen, as exhausting the category of the good—Stob. II. 57, 20–2; cf. DL VII. 94). A more detailed account of this equivalence is given in DL VII. 100; for discussion of the claim, and of the Platonic and Aristotelian precedents, see Tsekourakis 1974: 61–7 (on the ethical connotations of *kalon* in non-philosophical Greek see also Dover 1974: 69–73). The statement itself is widely reported elsewhere (see *SVF* III pp. 9–11), and is the first of the 'Paradoxes of the Stoics', in Cicero's work of that name (*Quod honestum sit id solum bonum esse*).

The argument which Sextus here attributes to the Stoics appears, however, to be unparalleled in other sources. (Cic. *Fin.* II. 109–10, cited as a parallel by Spinelli (1995: 277), does not say that animals are motivated by 'the fine and good'; it merely hazards the suggestion that they may be motivated by aims other than pleasure.) According to Stobaeus (II. 100, 21–2), the Stoics call virtue fine (*kalon*) because it calls (*kalein*) people towards it; the point in 100, that certain types of heroic and self-sacrificing behaviour are explicable only on the supposition that 'the fine and good' has a natural attractive power, fits well enough with this. But the suggestion that *animal* behaviour is also evidence that 'the fine' is by nature to be chosen is very surprising. The Stoics are happy to appeal to animal behaviour in certain contexts: most notably in expounding their notion of 'appropriation' or 'familiarization' (*oikeiōsis*); see e.g. DL VII. 85–6, Cic. *Fin.* III. 16, and LS 57, texts and commentary. But they are very clear that animals do not have reason, and that only rational beings can be ethical. Sextus himself alludes to this point in 101, and one would have thought that it would have prevented any Stoic from arguing in the manner portrayed in 99. Still, Sextus or his source points specifically to the Stoics as the authors of this argument. It is hard to imagine any reason why he would lie about this; there is no reason why he has to consider the objection at all, and in any case, it could easily have been introduced as a purely imaginary one, and most of the counter-arguments would still have been applicable. We must therefore suppose that this ill-advised line of thought did actually appear somewhere in the Stoics' writings.

Sextus' numerous replies to the objection do not include one which would immediately occur to many modern moral philosophers: viz. that the fact that something naturally attracts certain people does not show that it is naturally 'to be chosen'. However, there is nothing surprising in this. For it is assumed throughout ancient ethics that what is perceived as worth choosing by the person whose own nature is properly attuned to the world (and different schools of course disagree about what such a person would be like, or whether any such person exists) *is* in reality, or by nature, worth choosing. The same point of course applies to the Epicurean objection above. On the role and significance of appeals to nature in ancient ethics, see Annas 1993: pt. II.

The replies which Sextus does give may be said to fall into three types. First, he disputes the notion that the animal behaviour cited shows that anything in particular is 'by nature to be chosen' (101–2). Second, he questions the force of analogies between animal and human behaviour; either animal behaviour does not license conclusions about human behaviour, or if it does, the conclusions it suggests are not the ones the Stoics are looking for (103–6). Third, he suggests that, regardless of the force of the analogy, many other explanations can be found for the human behaviour referred to in the objection (106–9). His argument is not always lucid; in more detail, it may best be summarized as follows:

1a. By the Stoics' own admission, animals cannot perceive, and hence cannot be motivated by an awareness of 'the fine and good'; only humans, and for that matter wise humans, can do that (101).

1b. What does seem to motivate animals to engage in the kinds of behaviour referred to in 99 is the desire for 'winning and being the leader'. But this is not universally fine—sometimes the opposite is finer—and so it must be considered indifferent rather than good (102).

2a. If we do suppose that animals pursue 'the fine', then in view of the difference between humans and animals alluded to in 1a (this is the force of 'so that'—see textual point (b) above), it becomes puzzling that humans also do so (103).

2b. Appealing to an analogy between animal and human behaviour will not help to remove the puzzle, since the behaviour of animals could just as well suggest that humans are hedonists as that they pursue 'the fine' (103–4).

2c. If it is objected that humans are *not* entirely like animals, then again, the alleged fact that animals pursue 'the fine' does not show that humans also do so (105).

2d. Along the same lines, one might very well suggest (as proposed in 1b) that animals aim for 'winning and being the leader', and aim for this for its own sake, but also hold that humans aim for the same thing for an ulterior motive—viz. the psychic rewards which come with its attainment (106).

3. In fact, there are many other possible motivations for people to sacrifice themselves in various circumstances, other than their attachment to 'the fine' (106-9). They may be attracted by the psychic rewards which come with the attainment (and perhaps the prospect of the future attainment) of 'glory and praise and gifts and honours' (106; cf. 107). Or they may be motivated by the prospect of some kind of posthumous rewards or by the dreadful circumstances that would await them were they to continue living (108).

Point 1a makes use of the Stoics' own views against them. In this *ad hominem* function it seems quite appropriate; in fact, as noted above, it seems so clearly correct that one must wonder why any Stoic would have appealed to animal behaviour at all in this context. 1b also makes good sense; given the Universality Requirement (again in its comprehensive version; cf. on 96-8 above, discussion of point 2), the fact that being defeated is sometimes finer than winning shows that winning is not fine (or good) by nature (and hence that animal behaviour does not point towards anything which is good by nature). That being defeated is sometimes finer than winning could be illustrated by various types of commonsense examples. But in any case, it would clearly have to be accepted by the Stoics themselves. For them, no specific types of actions are invariably fine or invariably not fine; what makes an action fine is its being informed by virtue, which is the *only* thing which is necessarily fine. (On this, see DL VII. 101-3, which also shows that the Stoics, too, accepted the Universality Requirement, at least for the concepts of good and bad.) The aside, 'seeing that either one is indifferent' (102)—which detracts slightly from the clarity of the argument—must be intended as a reminder of Stoic views on the subject. It is worth mentioning, however, that with the exception of the (non-essential) references to the indifferent, 1b is an argument which Sextus himself would be quite happy to accept; it is not *ad hominem* through and through (so to speak), as 1a is. We have already seen that he is willing to assert that things are not by nature good; on his willingness to make positive evaluative assertions (such as 'being defeated . . . is finer'), provided they are relativized to persons or to times, see on 118 below. On Sextus' attitude towards the indifferent, see above on 90–5, end.

Points 2a–d are rather more problematic. First, the beginning of 106 is misleading. Since both 103 and 105 introduce hypothetical Stoic ripostes by 'if they . . . say', it is natural to suppose that 'And someone else will say', 106, also introduces a point by an opponent. But this is not so; the scenario sketched by 'someone else' is the first of a whole series of scenarios (continuing into point 3) that Sextus himself is prepared to regard as possible or even probable (see also textual point (c) above). A more serious problem, though, is that the whole aim of points 2a–d is misconceived. Sextus is trying to cast doubt, from various angles, on the legitimacy of arguing, on the basis of animal behaviour, to the conclusion that humans aim for the fine. But the Stoics in 99–100 never attempted to argue on the basis of an *analogy* between animals and humans; their point was that *both* (i) certain animal behaviour *and* (ii) certain human behaviour are explicable only on the hypothesis that the fine has a natural motivating force, and is therefore by nature to be chosen.

By contrast, point 3 is at least relevant; as point 1 addressed part (i) of the objection, so point 3 addresses part (ii). It pursues a line of thought suggested by 2d—that whatever may be true of animals, humans may be thought to be motivated, even in the case of fighting or other dangerous activities, by the prospect of some pleasing psychological state. (Compare the assumption underlying the argument at 79–89.) Some of the motivations for self-sacrificing behaviour which Sextus suggests, as alternatives to the perception that the fine is by nature to be chosen, are more plausible than others; the final point, assisted by the quotation from Homer (*Il.* XXII. 62–4), is perhaps the most persuasive. In any case, the general point is a reasonable one; it is by no means clear that the behaviour referred to in the objection has to be explained, as the Stoics allege, in a way which commits one to the existence of anything which is 'by nature to be chosen'.

For comparison of 99–109 and the parallel passages at *PH* III. 193, and 197, see Appendix A.

CHAPTER IV (110–40)

This chapter builds on the results of the previous one. It has been established that nothing is good or bad by nature; the question now is whether one is better off if one accepts this sceptical conclusion or if one believes, on the contrary, that certain things *are* good and bad by nature. It is argued that the dogmatists who hold the latter view are thereby plagued by troubles, whereas the sceptics are as free from trouble as is humanly possible. As the titles suggest, the main focus of the present chapter is on the dogmatists' dire straits, whereas the next chapter concentrates on the sceptic's much more desirable position; but the two topics cannot be wholly separated from one another, and so the subject-matter of the two chapters overlaps to some extent.

This overlap is immediately illustrated by the brief introductory passage (110–11), which states the dogmatists' view and the sceptics' view on the question posed in the title, but then adds a reference to the happier life enjoyed (at least, in their own estimation) by the sceptics themselves. The chapter continues with a more detailed, though still relatively sketchy, account of the differing situations of the dogmatist and the sceptic (112–18). This is followed by an argument to the effect that the dogmatists' pursuit of the things which they take to be by nature good is inherently counter-productive (119–24); then comes an argument against an attempted vindication of the dogmatists' approach (125–30). The chapter ends with a consideration of ways in which the dogmatists themselves might make more bearable the troubles which their own beliefs inflict (131–40); the verdict, not surprisingly, is that they cannot provide any help in this area, and that it is only through scepticism that happiness can be attained—the latter point then being pursued in more detail in the following chapter.

These two chapters have been severely criticized as subject to 'obvious objections' (Striker 1990a: 104; cf. Annas 1986: 9–10, Annas 1993: ch. 17). There is some justice to this reaction; as we shall see, the arguments contain numerous implausible claims and are often misleadingly formulated. But some central criticisms of Sextus here have been misplaced, resulting, as did some criticisms of arguments in the previous chapter, from the unwarranted assumption that *M* XI is attempting (and failing) to present the same form of Pyrrhonism as *PH*.

110–11: Transition and introduction

Points of language:

(a) I have placed 'with a good flow' (*euroōs*) in quotation marks because this is a self-conscious use of Stoic terminology. As we saw in 30, the Stoics defined happiness as 'a good flow of life' (*euroia biou*); Sextus is asking, in a slightly mocking tone, whether the belief that things are good and bad by nature has the consequences which the Stoics (always for Sextus the pre-eminent dogmatists) claim for it.

(b) This passage contains two allusions to the sceptics' self-description as 'enquirers' (cf. *PH* I. 1, 3, 7); 'examination' in 111 is a translation of *skepsis*, the noun from which *skeptikos* is derived (*skepsis* is also used earlier in the same sentence in a phrase designating the sceptics themselves), and 'enquired' in 110 is a translation of the corresponding verb (*eskepsametha*). On the significance of these terms in the present context, see point 4 on 118.

As already noted, this introductory section contrasts the views of the dogmatists and the sceptics about the effects of holding the belief characteristic of the dogmatists—i.e. the belief that there are things which are by nature good and things which are by nature bad. According to the dogmatists it is possible to be happy while holding this belief. Of course, this initial point is a considerable understatement of their position. As Sextus goes on to imply, they think that it is *only* if one holds this belief that one will attain happiness; for happiness requires the discovery of what things are good and what things are bad, followed by the *achievement* of the things identified as good and the avoidance of the things identified as bad. (For more on the 'science relating to life', see ch. VI.) The sceptics claim, on the contrary, that the belief in question leads to unhappiness, and that one does best by being a sceptic. Sextus does not actually say that the sceptic achieves happiness, only that his life is 'easier' than anyone else's. There is perhaps a point to this; though in other places (118, 140) he does say that the sceptic is happy, his final view (see ch. V) is that the sceptic is *less* disturbed than anyone else, not free from disturbance altogether—which naturally suggests (though this, too, is never explicitly stated) that the sceptic is merely closer to happiness than others, rather than being unequivocally happy. On the other hand, the context of the quotation (*Od.* IV. 565), a description of the Elysian fields, might easily be taken to suggest the opposite.

The description of the sceptic in 111 is precisely what one would expect from *PH* I; all the terms used here—'neither affirming nor denying anything', 'examination', 'make no determinations', and 'suspend judgement'—can be matched with key terms in the opening of *PH* I (1–30; cf. 196–9). It should not, however, be assumed that these terms have precisely the same connotations here as they have in *PH* I. We have already seen indications that *M* XI asserts conclusions which would count, by *PH*'s standards, as violations of suspension of judgement; 'suspension of judgement' and related terms should be interpreted, if possible, in such a way as to remain consistent with these assertions. I shall return to this point when commenting on 118 (point 4); by then Sextus' position will have been laid out more fully. It is worth noting immediately, however, that Sextus does not describe the sceptic without qualification as 'neither affirming nor denying anything'; the addition of the word 'casually' (*eikēi*) leaves open the possibility that some carefully considered affirmations and denials may be permitted.

On a similar note, the view that dogmatism leads to unhappiness and scepticism to happiness or its nearest equivalent is said to be something which the sceptics 'teach' (*didaskousin*; cf. 140). This at least suggests that the material which is to follow should be understood as the sceptics' own view, rather than merely a view which the dogmatists are committed to by their own premises (as alleged by Striker (1990*a*: 103)). This is, of course, consistent with the enthusiastic tone with which Sextus goes on to promote the merits of the sceptical outlook. Again, we will need to consider whether Sextus can legitimately put forward such views without immediately violating that outlook; see esp. point 6 on 118 below. For an apparent conflict in *M* XI's attitude towards teaching, see on 216–18.

It is in this passage that the special importance of ethics, as opposed to other areas of philosophy, for the achievement of tranquillity begins to emerge (cf. on 1–2 above). It is beliefs specifically about good and bad which are said to be responsible for the dogmatists' disturbance, and whose absence is said to make possible the sceptics' tranquil existence. As noted earlier, however, this does not mean that the other areas of philosophy simply have nothing to do with sceptical tranquillity. For, first, beliefs in logic and physics are frequently not independent of beliefs about ethics; dogmatic philosophy tends to be systematic, and anyone who has the former type of beliefs is liable to have the latter type as well. Then again, it is stated at the beginning of *PH* I that suspension of judgement about *things in general* leads to tranquillity—just as it was originally hoped that knowledge of things in general would lead to this result (see esp. 8–10, 12, 26, 29, 31–4); by ceasing quite generally to have a stake in how things are, and not merely by ceasing to believe that certain things are good or bad, one will become less disturbed. Whatever other differences there may be between *PH* and *M* XI, there is no reason to think that the two works differ in this respect; that the right attitude towards all subjects, and not merely towards ethics, is necessary for tranquillity appears to have been the Pyrrhonist attitude from the very beginning. It is evident in Timon's crucial report on Pyrrho himself, preserved by Aristocles in Eusebius (*Praep. evang.* XIV. 18. 1–5 (= LS 1F)); on this see Bett 1994*a*: esp. sects. III and IV. It is also suggested by a passage of Photius' report on Aenesidemus (*Bibl.* 169b26–9 (= LS 71C3)), which says that, as opposed to the tormented dogmatist, the Pyrrhonist is happy, and that this happiness is connected in particular with his 'knowing that nothing has been firmly grasped by him'. It is true that, whenever Sextus explicitly addresses the question of why the sceptic is better off than the dogmatist, the issue of beliefs specifically about good and bad is raised. But in *PH* I. 25–30, the only such passage other than the present chapters and their parallel in *PH* III (235–8)—both of which are in books whose subject-matter is, precisely, good and bad— the mention of the belief that things are good or bad, held by the dogmatist but not by the sceptic, is interspersed with passages where tranquillity is said to follow from suspension of judgement in general. One may, I think, conclude that, as Sextus sees the matter, avoidance of the belief that things are by nature good or bad is not *sufficient* for tranquillity—for that, one needs to suspend judgement across the board— but that possession of this belief none the less disrupts tranquillity in an especially dramatic and obvious way, which justifies a special concentration on this topic in the ethical works. In addition, since ethics comes last in Sextus' detailed treatment of the standard areas of philosophy, it may perhaps be assumed that, by this point in the work, we are supposed to have *already* suspended judgement about logical and physical matters, so that beliefs about good and bad are the only potential sources of disturbance which remain.

112–18: The comparative situations of the dogmatist and the sceptic

Points of text, language, and translation:

(a) 'Being in a certain state in relation to something' (*pros ti pōs echein*, 114, *pros ti pōs echontos*, 118) is a Stoic technical term. In Stoic philosophy, the class of things which 'are in a certain state in relation to something' is not, as one might expect, simply identical with the class of relatives (*pros ti*). The difference is explained in a passage of Simplicius (*In Ar. Cat.* 165, 32–166, 29 (= LS 29C—complete text only in LS, vol. II)); for a very full discussion of this passage and surrounding issues, see Mignucci 1988; more briefly see LS I. 177–8, Annas and Barnes 1985: 134–5. (It has usually been assumed that the class of things which 'are in a certain state in relation to something', as treated in the Simplicius passage, is identical with the member of the four Stoic 'categories' which bears the same title; for well-founded doubts about this, see Mignucci 1988: sect. IX.) In Sextus, however, the terms *pros ti* and *pros ti pōs echonta* are regularly used interchangeably, to refer to relatives in general; see *M* VIII. 161–2, 453–6, and 'in relation to this person' (*pros tonde*) in 114 itself. In at least one of these passages (*M* VIII. 453–6) Sextus' *understanding* of relatives none the less appears to conform to the Stoics' concept of *pros ti pōs echonta* (see Mignucci 1988: 169–70; cf. also on 90 above); but this is not true of the present passage. Despite the forbidding terminology, the possibility which Sextus is outlining in 114 and implicitly endorsing in 118 is simply that nothing is *in itself* to be chosen or to be avoided; rather, things can be referred to as 'to be chosen' or 'to be avoided' only *in relation to* certain persons or certain circumstances. This view, and Sextus' acceptance of it, will be explored in more detail below (point 2 on 118).

[(b) Heintz (1932: 254–5) claims that 'in relation to this person' (*pros tonde*, 114) should be emended to 'in relation to this thing' (*pros tode*), because 118, which picks up this line of thought, talks of relativity to circumstances but not of relativity to persons. There is no need to accept this. For one thing, relativity to persons is itself *one case* of relativity to circumstances. More importantly, the main argument that nothing is by nature good (68–78) proceeded, as we saw, by showing that nothing is good for everyone; it is already clear, then, that things can be described as 'to be chosen' and 'to be avoided' not by nature, but only in connection with specific persons. If anything, it is relativity to circumstances which is mildly unexpected, given the terms in which the Universality Requirement was introduced (69–71); see below on 118 (point 2).

(c) There is no need to add 'as bad' (*hōs kakōi*) after 'dejected at bad' in 118, as suggested by Heintz (1932: 255); this can readily be understood by analogy with 'uplifted at good as good'.

(d) Similarly, there is no need to follow Bekker and Bury in adding 'by nature' (*phusei*) with 'good or bad' in the final sentence of 118; the previous sentence, and indeed the whole preceding argument, makes clear that Sextus is talking about things which are good or bad *by nature*. Cf. textual point (c) on 68–78 above.]

This section begins with a simple argument (112–13), as follows:

1. All unhappiness is due to disturbance.
2. All disturbance is due to the intense pursuit or avoidance of things.

3. If one thinks that something is (by nature) good, or is (by nature) bad, one *will* intensely pursue it, in the former case, or intensely avoid it, in the latter case.

4. Therefore, by 1–3, all unhappiness is due to the pursuit of things under the description 'good' and the avoidance of things under the description 'bad'.

5. Hence the person who believes that there are things which are by nature good or bad—i.e. the dogmatist—is bound to be disturbed and unhappy.

There is a minor infelicity in the wording of step 4: 'the pursuit of good things as good' and 'the avoidance of bad things as bad' (113). The first occurrences of 'good' and of 'bad' in these phrases misleadingly imply that the items in question actually *are* good or bad, which is clearly not Sextus' intention; we shall see numerous other examples of this below.

A more serious misstatement occurs in steps 1, 2, and 4. In order for the argument to be valid, 'All x is due to y' should in all three cases be altered to 'All y results in x'. The argument as stated leaves open the possibility that some disturbances do not lead to unhappiness, and that some intense pursuits and avoidances do not lead to disturbance; hence step 5 does not follow from the premises. I take it that Sextus would approve this modification, for the modified steps 1 and 2 are propositions to which he elsewhere strongly assents; throughout this chapter and the next, pursuing or avoiding things 'intensely' (*suntonōs*) is taken to be inherently disturbing (as are 'intense' attitudes of any kind; cf. 116, 146 on immoderate elation), and disturbance is taken to be necessarily productive of, if not identical with, unhappiness. By contrast, step 2 as Sextus states it is false by his own admission; as the next chapter makes clear, some disturbances (the unavoidable ones) are *not* due to any intense pursuits and avoidances, but to hunger, physical pain, and the like.

The remainder of this section (114–18) amplifies the description of the dogmatist's situation just argued for, contrasting it with a much more appealing description of the sceptic's situation. Three formal possibilities are sketched in 114: either (a) *everything* which is pursued (or avoided) is good (or bad) by nature, or (b) *some* things which are pursued (or avoided) are good (or bad) by nature, or (c) *nothing* which is pursued (or avoided) is good (or bad) by nature. (For the equivalence of 'good' and 'to be chosen', and of 'bad' and 'to be avoided', see 79–89, 90–5, 96–109 above.) Option

(a) is included only for the sake of completeness; as Sextus points out in 115, to accept it would be impossible in practical terms, since it would commit one to contradictory attitudes towards the same thing, given that there is disagreement over what things are good or bad. The issue here, of course, is *simply* the consequences of accepting the position, not its truth or falsehood. In ancient philosophy, on the other hand, the practical impossibility of accepting a position is often taken as a demonstration that the position cannot be correct (on this, see Bett 1993: esp. 372–4). This is why, despite their rather different ambitions, Sextus' remarks are reminiscent of some of the considerations Aristotle uses to rule out attempts to deny the law of non-contradiction (see esp. *Met.* 1008b12–18, 1010b1 ff.).

It is options (b) and (c) which are Sextus' real concern. The person who accepts (b) is a dogmatist, and is subject to the disturbances introduced just above (116–17); the person who accepts (c)—i.e. who denies that anything is by nature good or bad, as Sextus did in the previous chapter—is a sceptic, and is free from such disturbances (118). It is this contrast which is to be explored in this chapter and the next. The concluding sentence of 118 seems slightly out of place at the end of the treatment of option (c); but it reminds the reader that it is on option (b) that, for the moment, Sextus means to concentrate. Notice again that it makes no difference for the purposes of this argument whether the dogmatist or the sceptic is *correct*; the question is simply which belief is better for one's peace of mind. In the previous chapter Sextus gave reasons for accepting the sceptical position (c); but what matters now is simply that the sceptic *does* accept (c), while the dogmatist accepts (b). This point applies to the whole of this and the next chapter.

116–17 provides further details on the nature of the disturbances to which the dogmatist is subject. If one thinks that certain things are by nature good, then, if one does not have them, one will pursue them obsessively, and this is disturbing; and if one does have them, one will obsessively take steps to ensure that one retains them, and one will be subject to 'an excess of joy'—both of which are also disturbing. Similarly, with regard to the things which one thinks are by nature bad, if one has them, one will be trying obsessively to get rid of them (the quotation is from *Il.* XIV. 507, with *pōs an* in place of Homer's *hopēi*—the difference in sense is minimal), while if one does not have them, one will be obsessively taking steps to ensure that they do not come upon one. Both the intensity of these disturbances (though the word *suntonos* itself is not repeated here) and their unremitting character are emphasized; if one believes that certain things are good or bad in their very nature, the suggestion is, one cannot but regard it as of immeasurable importance to have them or to be free of them respectively—and this cannot but result in constant activities and attitudes of the kinds described, which in turn are inevitably disturbing. By contrast, the sceptic avoids all such disturbances, by not having the original belief that things are by nature good or bad (118). Sextus should not have said unqualifiedly that the sceptic will live 'without disturbance'; for, as becomes clear in the next chapter, 'what happens by necessity' (pain, hunger, etc.) does give rise to some disturbance—even though the sceptic 'nobly' accepts this, and is better positioned with regard to it than the dogmatist. But the sceptic at least has none of the disturbances which derive from beliefs; cf. 147, where we are told that, at least on this score, the sceptic is 'perfectly happy' (*teleōs . . . eudaimōn*).

In other respects, too, the picture is no doubt highly exaggerated; it does not seem to be true that the belief that certain things really are good or bad necessarily leads to the kinds of tormented attitudes Sextus describes. But there is a good deal of plausibility to the basic claim that there are many things which the dogmatist, because of having this belief, will care much more about than will the sceptic; for a helpful amplification of this point, see Morrison 1990: 216–17. Certainly this is how the issue was understood by the sceptics' contemporaries; for the problem the ancients themselves typically posed in response was how the sceptic could care about anything enough to act at all. Sextus addresses this problem very briefly in 165; there is also an implicit answer to it here in 118, to which we shall return shortly (see point 5 below). Of course, one might also wonder whether it is necessarily *preferable* not to care about things. If caring about things always took the obsessive form portrayed by Sextus, not caring about them might indeed be preferable; otherwise, the lack of firm commitments might itself be seen as a source of anxiety and rootlessness. (On this, see Annas 1986: 23–4.) But ancient sceptics seem to have no cognizance of this kind of existential worry; nor do their opponents propose it as a criticism.

A further oddity, to our eyes, is the suggestion that an 'excess of joy' is objectionable (116; cf. 146). The other effects cited in 116–17 might readily be agreed to be troublesome, at least if present to excess; but one might well think that, in the case of joy, the more of it the better. On this point, however, Sextus is at one with his main dogmatic opponents, the Stoics. One of the Stoics' main reasons for their opposition to the passions (including pleasure) is their violence or excessiveness (see Stob. II.

88, 8–89, 14, Plut. *Virt. mor.* 449C, Galen, *PHP* 4. 2. 10–18 (= LS 65J)).
The position of the Epicureans on this point is less obvious. Epicurus is
very clear on the bad consequences of the indiscriminate pursuit of
pleasures (*Letter to Menoeceus* 129–32); he also regards the 'intense' *pursuit*
of things as very dangerous (*KD* 30, which uses Sextus' word *suntonos*;
on this see Nussbaum 1994: 290–1), and strongly disapproves of erotic
love for this reason (Hermeias, *In Pl. Phdr.* p. 76, Alexander, *In Ar. Top.*
139, 9–13, Cic. *Tusc.* IV. 70; cf. Lucretius, IV); and he regards absence
of pain as the greatest pleasure (Cic. *Fin.* I. 37), or as the 'limit of magni-
tude of pleasures' (*KD* 3). None of these points quite amounts to saying
that an 'excess of joy' is *per se* disturbing. Still, Sextus' claim is clearly
much more at home in a Hellenistic context than it would be today.

118, together with 114, are perhaps the most important sections of the
book for identifying the form of scepticism Sextus is proposing. A number
of major points bearing on this issue now need to be addressed.

　1. As Hankinson (1994: 56–7) observes, 'thinking nothing good or bad
by nature', in the penultimate sentence of 118, is ambiguous; it could
mean 'thinking that *nothing* is good or bad by nature', or it could mean
'*not* thinking that *anything* is good or bad by nature'. The latter reading
is consistent with suspension of judgement over whether anything is
good or bad by nature—and hence with the version of Pyrrhonism
familiar from *PH*—whereas the former is not. But it is clear that the
former reading is the correct one in this case. For the sentence would be
absurdly redundant if read in the latter way. The *previous* sentence says
that the sceptic is happy and 'freed from the trouble associated with the
opinion that something bad or good is present'; the present sentence
then explains the *source* of this freedom from trouble. It would be otiose
to say that the source of one's freedom from the trouble associated with
holding opinion P is one's not holding opinion P. There is a clear point,
however, to saying that the source of one's freedom from the trouble
associated with holding opinion P is one's holding opinion Q—from
which one's not holding opinion P (and therefore not experiencing the
associated troubles) can be easily understood to follow. Besides, we already know that the proponent of the view currently under consideration
does hold that nothing is by nature good or bad. The sceptic in 118 is the
person who accepts the third of the three alternatives presented in 114,
and, according to that alternative, things are 'neither to be chosen nor to
be avoided'. One would therefore expect some mention of this point in
118, and the present sentence is the obvious place in which to find it.

The sceptic, then, is the person who accepts the results for which Sextus has argued in the previous chapter. Cf. 130, 140, where we are again told that disturbance can be avoided only when one comes to understand that nothing is by nature good or bad; coming to *accept* this proposition, not balancing it against its negation, is what leads to the attitude desired by the sceptic. (Indeed, the word *isostheneia*, 'equal strength', used elsewhere in Sextus of opposing arguments on the merits of which one finds oneself suspending judgement, never occurs in *M* XI.) It might be suggested that the sceptic should be taken to 'accept' this proposition only in some attenuated, sceptical way—as a record of the speaker's impressions, for example, rather than as a commitment concerning how things really are. But the content of the proposition itself—'Nothing is *by nature* good or bad'—and the attitudes towards it that Sextus himself either mentions or implies ('thinking' (*doxazein*), 118; 'reason has established', 130; 'we show', 140) rule out this option. We should not, then, interpret *M* XI as essentially consistent with *PH* (as does Hankinson 1994: 66–7 and also McPherran 1990). It does not follow that Sextus has made a silly mistake (as alleged in Annas 1986: 9–10, Striker 1990*a*: 104); that would follow only if *M* XI were *trying* to present the same version of Pyrrhonism as *PH*—which we have no good grounds for assuming.

2. Alongside the denial that anything is good or bad by nature comes the assertion that things are 'at one time to be chosen and at another time to be avoided' (114, 118), or to be chosen or to be avoided 'in relation to' a certain person (114). (Again, it is nowhere suggested that these are anything other than assertions. Though the word 'say' (*legoi*, 118) need not by itself indicate a thoroughgoing assertion (cf. 68 with Comm.), the same word is used in connection with the dogmatist's view just before (116), and there is no indication of any difference between the manners in which these two sets of views are 'said'.) It is, then, acceptable for the sceptic to make assertions about good and bad, provided they are relativized to persons or to circumstances; one may say that something is good *for a certain person* (but not for everyone), or good *in a certain situation* (but not in all situations). Such assertions do not count as assertions to the effect that anything is good or bad *by nature*, or *in reality*, because they violate the Universality Requirement. As we have seen from 68–78 onwards, in order for anything to be good or bad *by nature*, in Sextus' conception, it has to be good or bad *for everyone*. It now becomes clear that the Universality Requirement also demands that something good or bad by nature be good or bad *in all situations*; Sextus is clearly thinking

here of things which are 'at one time to be chosen and at another time to be avoided' for a *single* individual—and which thereby fail to qualify as by nature good or bad. This latter facet of the Universality Requirement was not made clear when it was first introduced, but it is a natural extension of what he did say at 69–71 (cf. Comm. ad loc.), and has in fact been presupposed at several points prior to this (see on 96–8, 99–109, and on the Recognition Requirement at 68–78). It is also true that while the assertion that things are good or bad only in relation to certain persons follows straightforwardly from the argument in the previous chapter, the assertion that things are good or bad only in certain situations does not; variability from person to person (itself inferred from disagreement) was a central theme, but variability from situation to situation was not discussed at all. Again, this omission is relatively minor. The latter kind of variability was emphasized in Greek philosophy as early as the Sophists; it is also, again, an unsurprising corollary of the former kind of variability. For further discussion of these matters, see Bett 1994c: 136–9.

Sextus' view that things which are good or bad only in the relativized ways just discussed are not *in reality* good or bad has been compared unfavourably with an argument by the third-century Epicurean Polystratus to the effect that relative features of things are just as real as non-relative features; Sextus is naïve and confused, it is said, given that Polystratus' subtle position had been developed centuries before his time. (See Striker 1983: sect. III, Annas 1986: 10; cf. Annas and Barnes 1985: 137–8, 164.) This accusation is question-begging. Sextus is employing a different conception of reality from Polystratus; according to Sextus, as we have seen, in order for something to be really F, it must be *invariably* F. Polystratus does not share this conception of reality (and neither do we), but he makes no attempt to argue against it; his argument, while indeed of great interest, has no force as a criticism of Sextus' position. On this, see further Bett 1994c: sect. III.

Viewed historically, Sextus' conception of reality is not as peculiar as it might seem. We have already noted that the Stoics accept something similar, at least for the concepts of good and bad (see above on 102). Sextus' conception also has clear links with that of Plato, for whom, at least in his middle period, the fact that something may equally well be called e.g. beautiful in some circumstances and ugly in others shows that it cannot truly *be* beautiful; for Plato, as for Sextus, relativity or variability disqualifies something from being part of genuine reality. (See esp. *Rep.* V. 476a–480a, also *Phdr.* 247d–e, *Symp.* 211a–b, *Ph.* 78d–e, *Hipp.*

Ma. 289a–c; for Sextus' acknowledgement of common ground with Plato, see 70 above.) It appears that Sextus' inspiration within the Pyrrhonist tradition is Aenesidemus; I take up this issue under point 3.

3. Sextus' use of the sceptical formula 'not more' (*mē mallon*) in 118 does not conform to the explanation of this formula which he gives in *PH* I (188–91). According to the latter passage, 'not more P than Q' is to be understood as meaning 'I do not know whether P or Q' or 'Why P rather than Q?'; i.e. it is intended to express the speaker's suspension of judgement as between the propositions P and Q. This is not what the words 'not more' would naturally be expected to mean. As Sextus there admits, they 'display the character of assent and denial' (191); i.e. it sounds as if, by 'not more P than Q', one is *asserting* that P is the case to no greater extent than Q. And this is precisely how the term is used in the present passage. The sceptic in 118 is not suspending judgement over whether a certain thing is to be chosen or to be avoided; on the contrary, as we have seen, he accepts the view that *nothing* is *either* to be chosen *or* to be avoided. Rather, he is saying what it sounds as if he is saying—that it is *to no greater extent true that* any given thing is by nature to be chosen than it is true that it is by nature to be avoided; the former proposition is 'not more' true than the latter because *neither* of them is (the least bit) true. (For 'not more' in this negating function, cf. DL IX. 75.) Rather than things being *by nature* to be chosen or to be avoided, they are, as Sextus goes on immediately to say, to be chosen or to be avoided only *in certain circumstances*.

I have argued elsewhere that this use of 'not more' is apparent in early Pyrrhonism; indeed, the words are not a recognized sceptical 'formula' at this stage, but are simply normal words, used in the same way as in normal non-philosophical Greek (see Bett 1994*a*: sects. III, V). More importantly for our purposes, it is this standard, everyday usage of 'not more' which appears to have been employed by Aenesidemus. In the passage of Photius' *Bibliotheca* which is our most detailed source of information about Aenesidemus (169b18–170b35 (= LS 71C, 72L)), we are told several times in succession that he favoured locutions of the form 'things are (a) no more (*ouden mallon*) F than G, (b) sometimes F, sometimes G, or (c) F for this person, G for that person' (170a1–11). (On the reliability of Photius' report, including its probable use of Aenesidemus' own language, see Janáček 1976.) The three expressions are evidently supposed to be readily interchangeable; (b) and (c) are the same types of relativizing qualifications as are used here by Sextus, and (a) would *not* be interchangeable with these if it was intended to convey suspension of judgement over whether things are F or G. It should, then, be read in the same way as Sextus' 'not more' statement, as saying that things are to no greater extent F than they are G; in this case (a) simply amounts to the reverse side of the same coin as (b) and (c). Sextus' peculiar redefinition of 'not more' in *PH* I belongs, therefore, to a late stage of the Pyrrhonist tradition; by contrast, *M* XI is in agreement with Aenesidemus and Pyrrho in this respect—another significant piece of evidence for *M* XI's having been composed before *PH*.

We have seen that Sextus' 'not more to be chosen than to be avoided' is to be construed in this context as implying '*neither* to be chosen *nor* to be avoided', and one may well infer that Aenesidemus' 'not more' locutions are to be understood in the same way. Even if this is wrong, however, there is other evidence suggesting that, like Sextus, Aenesidemus did endorse the denial that anything is in reality good or bad; on this evidence, including its complications, see further Introduction, sect. III. As noted earlier (see on 42), there is a problem with the hypothesis that Aenesidemus is Sextus' immediate source; but the indications are that, in important ways, Sextus' position in *M* XI is close to Aenesidemus'. On Aenesidemus, see further Woodruff 1988; however, Woodruff does not mention the common ground with *M* XI.

4. We can no longer postpone the question of how Sextus can claim, as he does in 111, that the sceptics 'make no determinations' and 'suspend judgement'. (Again, compare Aenesidemus, who says that the Pyrrhonist 'determines nothing' (Phot. *Bibl.* 170a11).) The answer is that they do so in the sense that they refrain from attempting any specification of how things are by nature. We have already seen that the relative statements which Sextus asserts do not count as statements purporting to specify the nature of things. Nor, however, does the denial that anything is by nature good or bad. To say that nothing is by nature good is *not* to say that anything *is* by nature of any specific character; it negates a certain attempt to specify the nature of things, but it is not itself an alternative attempt at the same task. In particular, it is not to say that the thing is by nature *not* good. For something to be by nature good, it must be invariably good; but then for something to be by nature *not* good, it must be invariably *not* good—and there is no reason to think that Sextus will allow that anything meets this standard. From the statement that nothing is by nature good, then, no statements of the form 'X is by nature F' follow; in fact, nothing whatever follows about the nature of things *except* that goodness would not figure in the correct account of how things are by nature. This is a perfectly comprehensible sense in

which *M* XI's version of Pyrrhonism may be said to 'suspend judgement' and to 'make no determinations'; it is not the *same* form of suspension of judgement as Sextus practises in *PH*—where the denial that anything is by nature good would count as negative dogmatism—but that by itself is no objection. Nor does Sextus' *argument* for the conclusion that nothing is good or bad by nature involve any violation of this form of suspension of judgement. As we saw, given his conception of what is to count as by nature good or bad (the Universality Requirement) and his requirement for something's qualifying as good or bad for some person on some occasion (the Recognition Requirement), this conclusion can be derived merely from the observation that nothing is universally regarded as good or as bad. And this observation is not itself based on any assertions about the nature of things; it is simply given (or at any rate, Sextus thinks it is) by plain experience.

The sceptics, then, are 'neither affirming nor denying anything casually but bringing everything under examination (*skepsin*)' (111) in the sense that their affirmations and denials are carefully guarded, and are the product of careful scrutiny—not in the sense that they neither affirm nor deny anything at all (and perpetually enquire without coming to any conclusions at all, which is the sense given to *skepsis* at the opening of *PH* I). About the nature of things, they issue no affirmations, and they issue denials only of the form 'X is not by nature F'. And all their other affirmations and denials are hedged about with relativizing qualifications; as Aenesidemus put it, they do not (unlike the Academics of his time) assert anything 'unambiguously' (*anamphibolōs*, Phot. *Bibl.* 169b40–1, 170a28–31). This position is not 'relativism', as that term is usually understood nowadays. Relativism is indeed incompatible with any recognizable variety of suspension of judgement; for suspension of judgement about the real nature of things presupposes the *concept* of 'the way things are in reality, independent of our representations', whereas relativism dispenses with that very concept. (On this, see further Bett 1994*c*: sect. IV with Bett 1989*b*: sect. I.) Rather, Sextus' position in *M* XI is a genuine form of suspension of judgement which none the less permits—and indeed, demands—the assertion of relativities. The idea that sceptics say that things are relative occurs in several ancient authors (Anon. *In Pl. Tht.* col. 63, Aristocles in Eusebius, *Praep. evang.* XIV. 18. 12; Aulus Gellius, *Attic Nights* XI. 5. 7). This characterization is not entirely without merit (as asserted by Annas and Barnes 1985: 97); it fits *M* XI, at least, very nicely.

5. Sextus' willingness to make relativized assertions also provides an

answer to the question raised earlier as to how the sceptic, lacking any beliefs to the effect that things are by nature good or bad, can make decisions and act. He can do so because, though he does not hold that things are good or bad by nature, he does hold that they are 'at one time to be chosen and at another time to be avoided' (118). He can perfectly well conclude, then, that certain things are *on some given occasion* worth seeking or worth avoiding. Since it is nothing about their intrinsic character that makes these things worth seeking or avoiding—it is just circumstances which now render them that way—he cares a lot less about getting or not getting these things than would the dogmatist; it is not, he will say, as if he is seeking anything which *really matters*, or avoiding anything which it is *really important* to avoid, and so he will not be worried if things do not turn out as he planned. All this can go on in the normal, unphilosophical way in which all of us deliberate about things which we do not consider really important, such as which film to go to or whether to go out in the rain. We might object that the fact that something is desirable only on some given occasion does not make it *less* desirable, on that occasion, than something which is invariably desirable. (This objection is suggested in passing by Annas 1986: 10.) Sextus would simply deny this. There is a huge gulf, he would say, between the value and importance one attaches to the things which one thinks are *by their very nature*, or *without qualification*, of a certain positive or negative character, and those which one takes to have that character only contingently and temporarily; so it makes a big difference whether or not one thinks that anything actually belongs in the former category. Again, he could cite Plato as an ally in this view; in any case, I see no reason to say that Sextus is committing an error, as opposed to revealing a basic difference of attitude between him and ourselves.

Note that there is no suggestion here that the sceptic restricts himself to following, or making claims about, appearances; 'X is good for A at *t*' is not a claim about A's impressions, or even about how X appears to A, but a suitably relativized claim about how X is. Because it is suitably relativized, it is not a claim about how X is *in its real nature*. But it still goes beyond the realm of appearances; given *M* XI's standard for something's being a certain way by nature, what is the case by nature and what appears are not exhaustive categories. As Sextus himself said in 18, the sceptic can make ordinary statements like 'It is day', where 'is' does *not* mean 'appears'; 'X is good for A at *t*' is another example of the same thing (cf. on 18–20 above). Once again, the approach is different from that of *PH*, where at least some notion of 'following the appearances' is central—see esp. I. 22–4. Hence the worry expressed by some recent scholars about the 'radical self-detachment' which is thought to be a consequence of the sceptic's attitude is less applicable to *M* XI—if indeed it is a serious worry in the first place; for differing views on this see e.g. Burnyeat 1983, Annas 1993: 357–9 vs. McPherran 1989, Morrison 1990, and esp. Brennan 1994 (which argues that Sextus is *nowhere* committed to a withdrawal from ordinary non-philosophical beliefs). On Sextus' conception of how the sceptic acts, cf. 163–6 with Comm.

6. Finally, questions arise about the status of the argument at 112–18 itself, as well as most of the succeeding arguments in this chapter and the next:

(a) Sextus implicitly identifies happiness (*eudaimonia*) with tranquillity or freedom from disturbance (*ataraxia*); at any rate, he seems to assume that *ataraxia* is both necessary and sufficient for *eudaimonia*, and never displays any awareness that other conceptions of *eudaimonia* existed (most conspicuously Aristotle's) in which tranquillity is by no means central. There are understandable historical reasons for this. The implied identification of happiness and *ataraxia* appears to go back to Pyrrho himself; in the passage of Aristocles cited earlier (Eusebius, *Praep. evang.* XIV. 18. 1–5), we are told that *if one is to be happy* (*eudaimonēsein*), one must attend to three central questions, and that if one approaches these three questions appropriately, the eventual outcome will be *ataraxia*. (On Pyrrho's *ataraxia*, see also the passage from Timon cited approvingly by Sextus in 1 above.) As already noted, Aenesidemus also says that the Pyrrhonist will be happy (Phot. *Bibl.* 169b27), but that the dogmatists are subject to 'continuous torments' (*sunechesin aniais*, 169b24); it does not seem over-bold to infer that Aenesidemus, too, conceives of happiness as essentially a trouble-free or tranquil state. The Epicureans also, of course, conceive of *ataraxia* as, if not identical with happiness, at least the most important component of it—the other component being freedom from bodily pain (e.g. *Letter to Menoeceus* X. 131). Indeed, it looks as if there is no real disagreement between Epicurus and Sextus, since in the next chapter Sextus frequently refers to bodily pain as itself a 'disturbance' (*tarachē*); 'freedom from disturbance' (*ataraxia*) as conceived by Sextus would therefore seem to include both the Epicurean components of happiness. In addition, there is at least a tendency in several later Stoics to connect happiness closely with some form of tranquillity (I deliberately state the relation as vaguely and non-committally as possible); see e.g. Cic. *Tusc.* V. 43, Epict. *Diss.* I. 4. 1, 3, 27–9, IV. 4. 36, Seneca, *Ep.* 85. 2, 24, 92. 3 (but cf. *De Vita Beata*, 15. 2 for a more cautious view);

for further references and discussion see Irwin 1986: 224–8. Against this background (on which see also Striker 1990a), it simply did not occur to Sextus to question the identification of *eudaimonia* and *ataraxia*; this is indeed a limitation, as is pointed out by Annas (1993: 359, 362), but not a surprising one.

It is notable, however, that *PH* never makes such an identification; indeed, the word *eudaimonia* occurs only in the chapter on the 'conceptions' of good, bad, and indifferent (III. 172–5, 177), in summarizing Stoic views. Sextus says that the sceptic aims for *ataraxia*, and does much better in attaining it than the dogmatist (I. 25–30, III. 235–8), but happiness is not mentioned. The reason is presumably that *eudaimonia* is a contentious philosophical notion, *not* always connected with *ataraxia*, and Sextus can well do without it; here I am agreeing with Striker (1990a: 104). Annas (1993: 360) takes Striker to task for assuming that *PH* is later than *M* XI and is correcting it. As I hope this volume demonstrates, the circumstantial evidence for this chronology is weighty. Indeed, the present issue is itself one more piece of evidence. *PH* avoids an objection to which *M* XI is subject, and sticks less closely to the earlier Pyrrhonist tradition; both points favour the view that *PH* is the later work.

(b) Whether or not it is identified with happiness, does not Sextus' account of the sceptic's *ataraxia* imply that he thinks *ataraxia* is *in reality* good? Sextus need not accept this criticism; he can say that *ataraxia* is merely what the sceptic aims for at the most basic level—without having any justification for doing so. (On this, see Nussbaum 1994: 300–6.) The things which Sextus is willing to call 'good for person A' or 'good at time *t*' are those which, in the circumstances in question, turn out to contribute to *ataraxia*. (Compare the Stoic definition of good referred to earlier (30)—'Good is that which contributes to happiness'—and the characterization of the 'science relating to life' at 110 above.) It does not follow that *ataraxia* has to be described as good by nature.

(c) One might also accuse Sextus of dogmatism precisely in that he argues so insistently that scepticism produces tranquillity (and that dogmatism does not). Leaving aside the plausibility of his arguments (and, as we shall see, they are often not very strong), is it legitimate for him to be arguing in this way at all? Again, the evidence on Pyrrho and Aenesidemus suggests that they were willing to argue in this way as well (see the texts cited under point (a) above); one might add that both Arcesilaus and Carneades seem to have asserted that suspension of judgement was at least not incompatible with happiness (*M* VII. 158, 184, and see Bett 1989*a* for the view that these arguments are not merely *ad hominem*). But this does not answer the question. If pressed on this point, Sextus would no doubt answer that his arguments here do not involve him in any commitments regarding how things are by nature. For, he might say, he is not claiming that the sceptical outlook *invariably* contributes to happiness; and, as we have seen, for something to be by nature F, according to *M* XI, it must be invariably F. Scepticism may have contributed to happiness 'up to now' (*achri nun*; cf. *PH* I. 25 for this qualification to the assertion that *ataraxia* is the sceptic's aim); but it is not guaranteed to continue doing so. It is not because of the *nature* of the sceptical outlook that it contributes to *ataraxia*; as the story of Apelles and the sponge in *PH* I. 28 illustrates, *ataraxia* just *happens* to result from suspension of judgement (*tuchikōs*, I. 29; on this see Flückiger 1994). He could answer in the same way to the charge that, by his own arguments, the sceptical outlook itself turns out to be good by nature (since it consistently contributes to happiness; see again under (b)). This answer is, of course, not without difficulties; most obviously, Sextus' own laborious and systematic efforts in composing these works, designed to produce (or to show one how to produce) the sceptical outlook, suggest at least a considerable confidence that *ataraxia will* continue to be the result.

119–24: Argument that the dogmatists' pursuit of goods is counter-productive

Points of translation and text and other points of philological detail:

(a) *Kakia* in 121 is translated 'vice', as conventionally. It should be noted, however, that *kakia* is the abstract noun corresponding to *kakon*, which is throughout translated 'bad'. The qualities of character which Sextus goes on to mention are not only deserving of disapproval—though Sextus certainly assumes that they are—but also qualities which it is *bad for the agent to have*. 'Vice' (at least in philosophical English) suggests the former point but not necessarily the latter (a similar point applies to Bury's misleading translation 'evil' for *kakon* throughout); but it is not clear what other single word would do better. This is, of course, a standard conception of the 'vices' in Greek philosophy—just as virtues are taken to be inherently *good* for the agent; it is also essential for the current argument.

(b) The qualities 'love of money and love of glory and love of victory and love of pleasure' (120) are treated by Sextus as 'vices', in the sense just mentioned. That they are vices is not, however, inherent in the connotations of the terms themselves (unlike, say, 'avarice' or 'obsequiousness'). The English terms are in this respect no different from the Greek terms which they translate; it is not built into the meanings of terms of the form '*philo . . . ia*', 'love of . . .', that one is expected to disapprove of the qualities they designate. Of the items in this list, *philodoxia*, 'love of glory', and *philoneikia*, 'love of victory', are sometimes regarded as positively desirable; see LSJ and Dover 1974: 229–34 (and note the Stoic virtue *philoponia*, 'love of toil', Stob. II. 61, 18–62, 2).

[(c) The 'comic precept' (122) is quoted by no one else; the context, author, and period are unknown (see Kock 1888: iii. 616 (fr. 1255 adesp.)). The tragic line (not really a 'precept', though Sextus' wording implies that it is) is from Euripides' *Danae*. This is the first of six surviving lines, all of them quoted by Stobaeus (*Flor.* 91, 4) and Athenaeus (IV. 159b–c); Sextus himself quotes the first four at *M* I. 279, and smaller portions are quoted by several other authors (for textual details, see Nauck 1889: 456–7 (Eur. fr. 324)). Suitably to Sextus' argument at this point, all six lines consist of inordinate praise of wealth.

(d) With some misgivings, I retain the MSS reading *tina mochthēra* in 124 (retained but marked as corrupt by Mutschmann). The juxtaposition of the plural with the singular *philēdonian* is certainly awkward, but not, I think, intolerably so. Bekker conjectures ⟨*tarachēn*⟩ *tina mochthēran* (but does not actually adopt this suggestion in the text); Bury adopts *mochthēran* and adds ⟨*hexin*⟩ instead of ⟨*tarachēn*⟩. Both of course make for smoother reading. However, the general sense is the same whether or not we adopt either of these changes.]

In this section Sextus argues that the things which are regarded as by nature good must instead be regarded as bad, because of their terrible consequences for those who regard them as good. He starts with a general principle, argued for with examples, to the effect that whatever produces bad consequences is itself bad (119); the argument depends explicitly on a point which we have seen assumed many times, that 'the bad is to be avoided'. He then states that the things which are regarded (by the dogmatists) as by nature good do produce bad consequences, and hence, by the general principle, qualify rather as bad (so that the pursuit of them leads to unhappiness rather than the reverse); indeed, it is claimed that '*everything* bad exists' as a result of the things thought to be by nature good (120). This point is repeated as a conclusion in the final

sentence of 124 (note again 'productive of *all* the bad things'); the conclusion is argued for in the intervening passage.

It turns out to be *from the very pursuit* of these objects that the dreadful
consequences ensue. Thus it is not quite accurate of Sextus to say that
'the *things* which are thought good . . . are in effect bad' (124) (and *hence*
are conducive to unhappiness (120)); the conclusion should really be that
the *belief that* these things are good is bad (*in that* the pursuit of them is
conducive to unhappiness). As in the previous section, it is claimed that
the thought that something is by nature good leads to the pursuit of that
thing in an 'intense' or obsessive way (*suntonōs*, 121, 123); the result is
that, precisely in the act of pursuing what one takes to be good, one
embraces a certain destructive vice (121). This is illustrated by three
examples; the 'intense' pursuit of wealth, glory, or pleasure leads to—or
more accurately, consists in—the destructive vices of 'love of money',
'love of glory', and 'love of pleasure' respectively (122–4). (The fourth
vice named in 120, 'love of victory', is presumably close enough to 'love
of glory' as not to demand separate treatment.)

Even apart from the misstatement noted in the previous paragraph,
this argument is problematic in the extreme. First, it is a drastic overstatement to say that *everything* bad is the result of people's pursuing
what they take to be good. It is also unnecessary for Sextus' purposes; all
he needs to show, and all he could possibly be entitled to conclude, is
that every belief of the form 'X is by nature good' has bad consequences
of the type described. (Compare the misplacing of the word 'all' in the
argument at 112–13; Sextus or his source in this part of the book seems
to have difficulty with the location of universal quantifiers.) Second, the
list of examples of things thought good is very selective; even if it were
true that wealth, glory, and pleasure must always be sought in a self-
destructive frame of mind, it is not obvious why this must be applicable
to *whatever* one thinks is good. (What about the pursuit of virtue, for
example? We shall return to this point in discussing the next two sections.) Third, it is again implausible (see on the previous section) to
claim that the pursuit even of the alleged goods actually mentioned must
necessarily be conducted in this obsessive way. Wealth, glory, and pleasure are perhaps more conducive to such obsessiveness than most other
things normally supposed good; but it is not clear why it is impossible
that one should think these things good and care a great deal about
getting them, but remain level-headed in one's pursuit of them. (Sextus
actually seems to recognize a weakness here when he says that the person
who thinks that wealth is good 'should' (*opheilei*, 122) pursue wealth

intensely—implying that this does not always in fact occur.) To put it another way, it is not clear why the pursuit of these things should necessarily result in, or constitute, qualities reasonably regarded as 'vices'.

This passage is also careless in the extent to which it seems to be adopting a dogmatic position. Sextus at least gives the impression of accepting as his own view the statement that 'that which is productive of something bad is surely to be avoided as also bad' (119), and he takes it that he has *shown* (*dedeiktai*) 'that the things thought good by some of the philosophers are productive of all the bad things' (124); hence the conclusion would appear to be one which 'must be said' (*rēteon*) by him as much as by the dogmatists—yet the conclusion commits one to the existence of things which are (by nature) bad. One may, of course, reply that this conclusion is merely one which Sextus is trying to foist on the dogmatists, given their own beliefs, not one which he is committed to in his own person. But he gives no hint that this is what he is doing, and the way the argument is presented makes it look as if the opposite is the case. (We shall see other cases of the same thing in this and the next chapter.)

The parallel passage of *PH* III is notably more cautious in this last respect; for comparison, on this and other points, of 119–24 and *PH* III. 238, see Appendix A.

125–30: Attempted reply by the dogmatists and its refutation

Points of text, language, and translation:

[(a) 'Are driven for the sake of drinking through pain to pleasure', 126: Here I have adopted Bury's rendering wholesale; the language of the original is curious, and I cannot see a better way of putting it into English.

(b) *Huparchein* in 127, deleted by Mutschmann, can very well be retained; here I am in agreement with Heintz (1932: 255), who points to the close parallel in 141. The effect on the sense is, however, minimal.]

(c) 'In general folly' (*koinōs aphrosunēn*), 128, is odd. It seems to imply that the purportedly bad things previously named are themselves species of folly. This would certainly not be granted by the Stoics, who above all other philosophers regarded folly as bad (see 90–5 above); nor does it seem plausible on any other view. But it is not clear what other force the qualification 'in general' might be intended to have.

(d) On the Stoic and Epicurean use of the term 'preconception' (*prolēpsis*, 129), see on 21 above; on Sextus' own looser usage of the term, see linguistic point (a) on 68–78. Here he is actually talking about *misguided* opinions, which altogether reverses the dogmatists' usage. There is surely an ironic point here; these 'naturally acquired conceptions' on which the dogmatists rely so heavily are in fact no more than unreliable and harmful prejudices. On this, see also Voelke 1990: 188–9.

In this section Sextus presents a possible reply by the dogmatists to the argument as so far developed, and then offers his own counter-response to it. The dogmatists' reply is presented somewhat clumsily. Sextus introduces it in terms which immediately make clear his negative verdict on it ('Nor, however, is it possible . . .', 125), and this makes it sound as if the next point—'for the person who has got wealth . . .' (126)—will be giving reasons *why* the reply is inadequate. In fact, though, this remark and the whole of 126 are a continuation of the reply itself (as if 125 had opened 'Those on the opposite side, however, say that . . .'). 127 then has to repeat Sextus' own negative verdict, and it is only then that the counter-argument begins. The dogmatist reply concedes the conclusion of the previous argument, that the *pursuit* of the things deemed to be good is disturbing and, if one likes, bad; but it then adds that such disturbance by no means attaches to the situation in which one has *obtained* the things in question (which the previous section did not address at all). In this latter situation, it is claimed, one is indeed free of troubles; and the implication, at least, is that the desirability of the situation in which one has these goods more than makes up for the hardships experienced in acquiring them.

As one would expect from the introductory exposition at 112–18, Sextus will have none of this. It is not only the pursuit, he says, but also the possession of these alleged goods which results in massive levels of disturbance; in fact, it is even suggested that the possession is *more* disturbing than the pursuit ('all the more', 'bad things in larger number', 127). But the reason given for this is one which we have not previously encountered. Earlier (116) we were told that the possession of good things was disturbing because it led to excessive joy and to an obsessive concern about keeping them. Now we are told that it is disturbing because other people also possess these goods; one's original aim was to become their *sole* possessor, and when that turns out not to be the case, one is hostile and envious towards the others who also possess them. This point is certainly not stated in a very convincing way. Sextus portrays the awareness that others also have these goods as if it was somehow unanticipated; but why would even the most obsessive seeker of, for example, wealth not be aware from the start that he could not hope to become the *sole* possessor of wealth? None the less, lurking behind Sextus' somewhat unhelpful formulation is a not unreasonable point; at least some things are, or are felt to be, worth having only on condition that few if any other people have them, or have them to the same degree as oneself. 'Glory', one of Sextus' examples in 125 and in the previous section, is an obvious example; indeed, it may be that glory and other supposed goods having to do with reputation *can only* be possessed by a few people at a time. The point also applies quite nicely to Sextus' other example, money; a great many people want not just wealth, but *more* wealth than most other people, and hence are no more satisfied—perhaps even less satisfied—when they merely become wealthy. However, as in the previous section, Sextus' examples are far from representative of all the things usually thought good; it is quite unclear, at least on the surface, why the Stoics would mind if other people had virtue, or why the Epicureans would mind if other people had *ataraxia*. (I say 'on the surface' because one could imagine a Nietzschean type of analysis which concluded that, for example, virtue is really valued only in so far as it allows one to feel superior to the ordinary mass of humanity; but of this kind of dissection of the hidden motives behind moral valuations Sextus, and ancient philosophy generally, had no inkling.)

At 128–9 Sextus adds a parallel argument about the things which are thought to be by nature bad. (This is what he means by 'the bad things themselves' at the opening of 128; these are the things which the dogmatist initially believes to be bad and takes pains to avoid—as opposed to the bad things, mentioned in the previous sentence, which result from the pursuit of what one takes to be good. The phrase is not especially lucid; in addition, Sextus is again careless, as he was in the previous section, about giving the impression of *endorsing* the claim that these things are bad; see also 'bad things in larger number' (127) and 'the vast number of other bad things' (128).) This argument is strictly speaking irrelevant, since the dogmatists' reply in 125 made no mention of things thought to be bad; but it is related to the previous issue, in that it is again concerned to rebut any attempt to differentiate sharply, in respect of desirability, between the situation in which one possesses something (good or bad) and the situation in which one does not. As before, the counter-argument insists that disturbance is caused *both* by the possession *and* by the avoidance of the things which one believes to be by nature bad. The train of thought is roughly the same as in 117. But there is a new element which will become important in the next chapter. This is the idea that, at least with regard to certain things which he thinks bad, the dogmatist experiences disturbance on two levels; there is the disturbance associated with the presence of the thing itself, and there is the disturbance associated with the belief that the thing is by nature bad. It will later emerge that the sceptic is in some cases (including most of the examples in the list at 128) not exempt from the first type of disturbance; but the dogmatist is subject to both types, and the second type, it is claimed, is actually more severe than the first. This last point already appears in the present passage ('as if by a bad thing of greater proportions', 129).

The metaphor of being tossed by a storm (129) recalls Epicurus' language in *Letter to Menoeceus* X. 128 ('the storm of the soul') (on this point, see Voelke 1990: 188). In other respects, too, the arguments in this section and the previous one are very similar to ones which the dogmatists themselves would use against what they take to be mistaken (and primarily non-philosophical) conceptions of what is really good or bad. The Stoics do not hold that wealth, glory, victory, or pleasure are goods; nor do they think that any of the items in the list at 128 are bad. The Epicureans do hold that pleasure is good and pain bad; but even they would say that people who have the wrong views about these things—i.e. most people—will experience far less, if any, of the benefits of pleasure and far more of the bad effects of pain. At least to a large extent, then, Sextus' major dogmatic opponents could simply accept his argument, without conceding that it touches them in the slightest. It is for this reason that the selectivity of Sextus' examples, already noted several times, is particularly damaging. In order to make a convincing case that the sceptic is better off than the dogmatist, he would need to concentrate his critique on the things considered good and bad by the dogmatists themselves, as they themselves conceive of them (e.g. pleasure as conceived by the Epicureans themselves—including prominently *ataraxia*, a goal shared by the sceptics—as opposed to pleasure in the vulgar conception). This would not be by any means impossible; e.g. one might well want to seize on the wildly counter-intuitive character of the Stoic claim that virtue is sufficient for happiness. But, as already suggested, it would need to be done using arguments rather different from the types which Sextus has employed so far. (Versions of this criticism are also offered by Striker (1990a: 103–4) and Annas (1993: 360).) This is not the only place where the interest of Sextus' claims, and the potentials which exist for supporting them persuasively, are not matched by the calibre of his actual arguments for them.

The final sentence of the section (130) reminds us of the allegedly far preferable situation of the sceptic. As already mentioned (see on 118, point 1), this is another passage where the sceptic's view is said to be that nothing is by nature good or bad; unlike in *PH* III (e.g. 235), the answer to the question of whether anything is by nature good or bad is not 'I suspend judgement about that', but 'No'. This, indeed, is said to be something which 'reason has established' (*logou de parastēsantos*); on the nuances of the term *paristanai*, 'establish', in Sextus and in Chrysippus, see Voelke 1990: 189. This sentence, and a similar point in 140, are the only ones in this chapter or the next from which it clearly follows that the sceptic's view about good and bad is *correct*, and the dogmatist's view incorrect. But even here (compare on 114–18, options (a)–(c), above), it is not *required* for the argument that the sceptic's view be correct; the text could just as well have read 'but when *one comes to believe* that none of these things . . .', and the main point would have been the same. As has already become clear, the sceptic of *M* XI *does* believe that nothing is by nature good or bad; so in summarizing the sceptic's view, Sextus, *qua* sceptic, is liable occasionally to say things which entail that it is *true* that nothing is by nature good or bad. But whether or not he does so is irrelevant to the point he is making here.

130–40: Possible dogmatic attempts to alleviate dogmatism-induced disturbances, and their inadequacy

This section begins with a recapitulation of the points Sextus takes himself already to have established (130). As before (see above on 119–24), his formulation is faulty in two ways: (a) it is the 'things thought by some to be goods' which are said to be the culprit, rather than the *belief that* certain things are goods; and (b) the references to 'bad things' are incautious in that they give the appearance of endorsing the view that these things *really are* bad. I take it that 'because of the bad things other bad things come into being' refers back to 128–9; the belief that certain things are by nature bad leads to disturbances which one cannot but regard as also bad. This too is confusing, however, in that the phrase 'masses of bad things' immediately beforehand refers to something different—viz. the disturbances associated with the belief that certain things are by nature *good*.

The remainder of the passage considers three ways in which a dogmatist might be expected to try to mitigate the disturbance experienced by the person who believes that things are by nature good or bad—i.e. the disturbance brought about by dogmatism itself. The three possibilities are set out at the beginning (131–2), and are then examined in order; the second possibility receives by far the most discussion. The three possibilities are as follows:

1. That one should not pursue the good or avoid the bad (131).
2. That one should pursue things other than what one is currently pursuing—such as virtue instead of wealth—since these other things are more valuable than the current objects of one's pursuit (132).
3. That one should pursue things other than what one is currently pursuing, since these other things are less troublesome (and also more useful) (132).

It may be assumed that these possibilities are Sextus' own invention, rather than actual replies by dogmatists concerned about rebutting the sceptical view; we have no evidence of any dogmatists having been sufficiently impressed with a position of the type offered in this chapter to have bothered with a reply at this late stage in the argument. These replies are in principle no more connected with any one dogmatic position than with any other. However, the example offered under possibility 2—that one might switch one's energies from the pursuit of wealth to the pursuit of *virtue* (132)—suggests that Sextus has Stoicism particularly in mind as the target of this section; and this is confirmed by the fact that the terminology in which both the replies and Sextus' dismissals of them are couched is at several other points distinctively Stoic. The connection between virtue and 'the fine' (*to kalon*, 135) is Stoic; see above on 99–109. In addition, the terms 'proper' (*kathēkon*) and 'appropriate' (*oikeion*) are Stoic. An 'appropriate' action is one which accords with one's nature; a 'proper' action is one which there is good reason to do. In Stoic theory the two terms turn out to be coextensive, since what there is good reason for one to do is also what accords with one's nature. On these two terms and the connection between them, see DL VII. 85, 107–9, Stob. II. 85, 12–18, Cic. *Fin.* III. 16, 20–2; for discussion see LS I. 350–4, 364–8, Striker 1991: esp. sects. I, IV, Annas 1993: 96–8, ch. 12, sect. 2. The Stoics also describe the things which are according to nature as having 'value' (*axia*, 132, 138); on this, see on 68–78 above (references to earlier philosophers, point (c)). Finally, the two pairs of terms 'selection and rejection' (*eklogēn, apeklogēn*, 133) and 'choices and avoidances' (*haireseis, phugas*, 133) have precise usages in Stoicism: 'selection and rejection' are exercised towards those indifferents which have 'value' or 'disvalue' respectively, while 'choice and avoidance' are exercised towards things which are good and bad respectively. (For these differing usages, see e.g. Stob. II. 72, 19–22, II. 75, 1–6, II. 79, 1–5, 12–17.) As this last point, especially, makes clear, Sextus is not concerned to be faithful to the precise spirit of all this Stoic terminology; though he is discussing attitudes towards what one takes to be good and bad, he speaks as if 'selection and rejection' and 'choices and avoidances' are equally applicable terms in this context. However, the argument does not depend on his achieving any very accurate portrayal of Stoic ethics; indeed, despite all the Stoic terminology, the argument is not, to repeat, directed purely against the Stoics, but against the dogmatists in general.

Possibility 1 is dismissed in a single sentence (133). It was never a serious possibility in the first place—at least as originally stated; it would make no sense in any ancient ethical theory to suggest that one should *not* pursue the good or avoid the bad, since the good and the bad are by definition the things which one has the strongest reason to pursue and to avoid respectively. It has sometimes been supposed in modern ethics that there is one question having to do with what things are good and what things are bad, and then a *separate* question having to do with what reasons one has to pursue the things identified as good and to avoid the things identified as bad. (This is one of the numerous different views about morality known as 'externalism'; for a recent treatment of 'internalism' and 'externalism', including distinctions among their various forms and plentiful references to further literature, see Brink 1989: ch. 3.) To the ancients this would have been simply unintelligible. But in his dismissal of this possibility, Sextus changes the wording—and so weakens the force of the dismissal. 'It is proper neither to pursue the good nor to avoid the bad' (131) becomes 'It is not appropriate either to pursue the good *intensely* or to avoid the bad [sc. intensely]' (133). As we have seen several times already, it is not clear why the dogmatists are compelled to, or are committed to thinking it appropriate to, adopt an attitude towards the good and the bad which is of the obsessive character described above.

The discussion of possibility 2 (134–8) is a good deal more interesting. Sextus argues that it does not help to change one's views as to what is really most worth pursuing. So long as there is *something* which one takes to be really worth pursuing, the pursuit of that thing, whatever it is, will engender the kinds of disturbances which have been the main subject of this chapter; as the medical analogy in 136 illustrates, the object of one's obsession will be different, but its character will be fundamentally the same. One might suggest, Sextus says (137), that the new disturbance will be less severe than the old one. But if the thought that something is good is what engenders disturbance, there is no reason to suppose that the new disturbance will be less extreme; in fact, since one now thinks that there is something *else* which is worth *more* than the thing by whose pursuit one was previously so disturbed, it seems as if one's level of disturbance should, if anything, increase (137–8).

This argument appears to be intended, at least in part, to address the objection that the choice of examples has so far been too selective and not relevant to the specific claims of dogmatic philosophers. (See on the previous two sections for this complaint.) This is suggested by the new examples considered; 'the fine' and virtue become the objects of one's pursuit, instead of 'wealth or glory or health' (135), just as a Stoic would have advocated. But it is also suggested by the general shape of Sextus' response. One should not imagine, he insists, that it makes a difference *which* things are being singled out as by nature good and bad; there are not, as the dogmatist might try to claim (132), certain items whose pursuit is exempt from the disturbing consequences already discussed.

Striker (1990*a*: 104) objects that in this passage Sextus fails to take account of the fact that, according to the Stoics, virtue cannot be lost, once achieved. (It appears that not *all* Stoics held this view; according to Diogenes, Chrysippus held that virtue *could* be lost (DL VII. 127).) But Sextus could reply that in this argument he never mentions the state in which one has *achieved* virtue; he is talking solely about the state in which one pursues it. If the Stoics are the main opponents envisaged here, this approach has some justification. The Stoics admitted that no actual person—of their acquaintance, at any rate—had achieved the perfect state of wisdom and virtue (Plut. *Sto. rep.* 1041F, 1048E, *Comm. not.* 1076B, Diogenianus in Eusebius, *Praep. evang.* VI. 8. 13 = *SVF* III p. 167); they also held that there was nothing between, on the one hand, wisdom and virtue and, on the other, folly and vice (DL VII. 127, Plut. *Prof. virt.* 75C, *Comm. not.* 1063A–B). Thus the best that any of them, by their own admission, had so far achieved was the unsuccessful *pursuit* of virtue.

One might well wish, however, that Sextus had said something more specific to defuse the idea that the pursuit of the things which are, by the dogmatists' lights, *really* goods is bound to be less disturbing than the pursuit of the things which ordinary opinion mistakenly regards as goods. Again, materials for such an argument might well be available. It may be that money and other supposed goods of that order are often pursued in a frenzied and 'intense' fashion (see above on 119–24). But it also seems that the quest to become a really good person can sometimes lead to anguish, self-loathing, and despair; at any rate, such a quest is by no means necessarily free from disturbance.

Once more, the reply may be that the achievement of *genuine* goods (unlike money, glory, etc.) makes the pursuit worthwhile, even if disturbing (see on 125–9 above). Since at least some dogmatists held that the good had in some cases actually been achieved, Sextus would need to address this point as well—if, that is, he is indeed speaking (as he claims) about the dogmatists in general, and not *just* about the Stoics, and if this section is indeed intended to block the suggestion that his previous arguments depended on leaving out of the story precisely the items which the dogmatists themselves believe to be good. For a version of this objection, see Annas 1993: 360. Annas herself suggests a possible reply (360–1); Sextus might say that even after achieving the alleged good, the dogmatist will not be free of the gnawing worry that the theory which declares it to be the good might not be true. (*Contra* Annas, there is no need for the sceptic to experience any similar worry. The sceptic does not think that suspension of judgement, and then *ataraxia*, are the *correct* or *appropriate* reactions to sceptical argumentation; he or she simply *has* these reactions.) Clearly, then, the discussion could be taken much further than Sextus himself takes it. Still, in this particular argument, unlike some of the surrounding ones, there are at least no readily identifiable blunders.

Possibility 3, like possibility 1, receives very little attention (139). Sextus simply states that this possibility does not achieve the aim which he wants it to achieve—viz. the removal of disturbance; all it does is to *reduce* disturbance. Clearly it is true that it does not altogether remove disturbance; that is how Sextus framed it in 132. What is not so clear is why this entitles him to dismiss it so easily. Of course 'the person who is troubled' would *ideally* like 'to be released from trouble'. But in the absence of that option, it would seem that comparisons between levels of disturbance are not 'absurd', as Sextus claims; the next best thing surely *is* 'to find out what is more troublesome and what is less troublesome', and to achieve the latter. Sextus himself concedes in the next chapter that even the sceptic experiences a certain amount of disturbance in connection with pain, hunger, and the like; his point is precisely that while no one can be utterly free of disturbance, the sceptic gets closer to this ideal than anyone else. It is true that the sceptic is said to be completely free of the disturbances associated with the holding of *opinions*, whereas in the present passage Sextus is talking of a comparison between two opinion-induced disturbances. But it is very hard to see why this should make any difference to the central issue: whatever the *types* of disturbances, surely less disturbance is preferable to more.

This section, and this chapter, ends with another reference to the sceptic's contrasting situation (140; cf. 130). The ending is appropriate, in that several of the distinctive elements of this chapter are repeated. The sceptical position is again said to be that 'there is not anything either good or bad by nature', rather than that the existence of such things is something about which to suspend judgement (cf. 114, 118, 130). The non-existence of anything good or bad by nature is something, Sextus says, which it is necessary that 'we show' (*hupodeixaimen*) to the disturbed person (cf. 'established', 130), and which is a sceptical 'teaching' (cf. 111). It is also something to whose truth Sextus here commits himself (cf. 130)—though again, this is not actually necessary for his argument at this point. Finally, this sceptical position, by contrast with dogmatic positions, is said to 'procure the happy life' (cf. 118).

In support of the view that nothing is good or bad by nature, Sextus quotes a line from Timon. For metrical reasons, this line is usually assigned to Timon's poem *Images* (*Indalmoi*); the line is a pentameter, and *Images* is the only poem of Timon which we know to have been in elegiac couplets. This is the same poem from which the quotations in 1 and (probably) 20 above derive; this, however, tells us very little, since we know virtually nothing else about the poem (see Bett 1994*d*: 330–2 and on 1–2, 18–20 above). But Pyrrho's calm and indifferent attitude is likely to have been a prominent motif; and this line may be giving us part of the basis for this attitude. Sextus implies that, prior to this line, Timon also said something roughly to the effect that 'there is not anything either good or bad by nature'; and the opening word 'But' (assuming, as the metre encourages us to assume, that it is Timon's word, not Sextus' connecting particle) supports this at least to the extent of suggesting that the previous lines included a denial that 'these things' belong to some mind-independent realm. (Here I follow Caizzi (1981*a*: 264); however, I do not agree that 'But' indicates that the state of affairs portrayed is to be deplored. Diggle (1983) suggests that the words 'there is not anything either good or bad by nature' may actually be a further quotation from Timon, or something very close to it; he observes that the simple alteration of Sextus' *esti*, 'is', to *ginetai*—which in this context could also be translated 'is'—yields a second pentameter line. If so, however, the two lines cannot have been adjacent in Timon's original verses; the metre requires pentameters to alternate with hexameters.) In any case, if this is correct, it accords with DL IX. 61, according to which Pyrrho 'said that nothing is either fine or ignoble or just or unjust; and similarly in all cases nothing is the case in reality, but human beings do everything by convention and habit; for each thing is no more this than that'. It also accords with the passage of Aristocles in Eusebius (*Praep. evang.* XIV. 18. 1–5), which explains in more detail Pyrrho's general view that 'each thing is no more this than that', and says that the outcome of adopting this view is *ataraxia*. For further details on the links among these three passages, see Bett 1994d: sect. IV. The present passage, of course, does not say that *Pyrrho* subscribed to the position represented in the quoted line (and its implied context); but the neatness of fit with the other two passages makes this an attractive conjecture. (This is quite different from the situation with respect to Timon's lines on 'the nature of the divine and the good'; see on 18–20 above and Bett 1994d.)

Because of the connection with DL IX. 61, 'by mind' (*noōi*) in the present line is often emended to 'by convention' (*nomōi*) (see e.g. LS 1I). This is possible, but not necessary. With the text as it stands (again, if we trust Sextus' implied information about the context of the line), we are being told that judgements about good and bad do not correspond to any independent reality, but are human inventions or constructions; this is not significantly different from the point in DL IX. 61, and certainly not in conflict with it.

CHAPTER V (141–67)

This chapter is closely connected with the previous one. The purpose of both chapters is to compare the situations of the sceptic and the dogmatist, to the detriment of the latter. As we have seen, the main emphasis in the previous chapter is on the disturbances afflicting the dogmatist; now the focus shifts largely (though again, not exclusively) to the far greater freedom from disturbance enjoyed by the sceptic. It is not suggested that the sceptic is entirely immune from disturbance. (Hence, though this is never made fully explicit, the answer to the question whether the sceptic is 'in all respects happy' is in the negative.) But the sceptic is completely free of those disturbances which derive from the belief that certain things are by nature good or bad; and this also results in the sceptic's being *less* disturbed than the dogmatist even by those sufferings which we are bound to experience whatever we do or do not believe.

The chapter opens with the introduction of this distinction between two potential sources of disturbance, together with a sketch of the situations of the dogmatist and of the sceptic with regard to the first, and of the sceptic alone with regard to the second (141–9). There follows a more detailed discussion of how and why the sceptic, though admittedly vulnerable to disturbances of the second type, those which are not due to belief, is still only moderately affected by them—much less severely affected than is the dogmatist (150–61). The final section (162–7) briefly addresses two versions of an objection commonly voiced against all forms of ancient scepticism: that it is impossible to *live* as a sceptic.

141–9: The two possible sources of disturbance, and the situations of the dogmatist and the sceptic with regard to them

Points of language, text, and translation:

[(a) There is no need to follow Mutschmann in adding *oun* after *men* in the first sentence of 141. Several other chapters do begin with a sentence containing *men oun*; but chs. I and VI, as well as the book as a whole, begin with sentences containing *men* without *oun*—even though *oun* would not have been out of place on grounds of sense.

(b) I follow Heintz (1932: 255) in deleting *logikēn* before *doxan* in 142; I do not, however, accept his transposition of *logikēn* to before *krisin*. (The text which I read is thus the same as in Bury.) The word *logikos* is generally used by Sextus in discussing the details of dogmatic philosophy (for references, see Janáček 1962), and not, as here, in the exposition of the sceptical outlook. Indeed, since it frequently bears an honorific implication, the word would be very out of place here; *doxai* are precisely what it is foolish to have, in the sceptic's view. Besides, as Heintz remarks, *kata doxan* appears numerous other times in this part of the book without *logikēn* (141, 144, 147, 160). Similar considerations, though, tell against placing *logikēn* before *krisin*; a *krisis*, in this context, is just as foolish as a *doxa*, and *kata krisin* appears without *logikēn* in 156. Heintz concedes this last point, and admits that the placing of *logikēn* before *krisin* is less secure than its omission before *doxan*; his alternative suggestion, that *logikēn* may be a gloss on *krisin* (emphasizing the contrast with *alogon aisthēseōs pathos*, 143), seems to me more plausible.

(c) The MSS reading *eikazei* in 148 cannot be correct. The only possible translation in this context would be 'make conjectures' (cf. the Latin translation in Fabricius). But this makes no sense (what is the sceptic supposed in this situation to be conjecturing about?), and in any case sceptics are not supposed to engage in 'conjectures' (cf. e.g. *M* VIII. 324–5 and on *doxa* in point (b) above). Bekker's tentative suggestion *metriazei*, 'is moderate' (adopted by Bury and Russo), is a definite improvement as regards the sense; but it is still not satisfactory. For though the sceptic's moderation in the face of inevitable pain and suffering is certainly a main theme of the following section (cf. esp. 161), it does not seem to be the subject here. The next sentence (148–9), which gives a reason for the statement containing the verb in question, says nothing about moderation, but simply emphasizes that scepticism cannot make these conditions disappear. For this reason I prefer to read *eikei*, 'gives way', as suggested in Pappenheim 1881: 267. Besides being palaeographically easier than *metriazei*, this does result in a statement for which the next sentence can plausibly be seen as a reason; with regard to such conditions, the sceptic simply 'lets it happen'—for the conditions are bound to strike us in any case, whether or not we are sceptics. It is true that *eikein* normally takes an object in the dative (as in *PH* I. 193, which makes the same point), whereas here (unless we also delete *en* and move *de* behind *tois*) it stands alone. But *eikein* also stands alone in *PH* I. 230, and the syntax can be explained by Sextus' desire to maintain a parallelism using phrases beginning with *en* throughout the sentence.]

(d) I render *alogon* in 143 and *alogois* in 148 by 'non-rational', not 'irrational' as Bury translates it (cf. Russo). Though *alogos* can and should often be translated 'irrational', the point here is clearly that we are subject to certain sensory happenings with which reasoning has nothing to do—not that these sensory happenings are somehow *contrary* to sound reasoning.

(e) *diacheomenōi* and *diacheitai* in 149 are translated 'soothed'; Bury's 'overjoyed' (cf. Russo) strikes the wrong note. Literally, *diachein* is to pour away or disperse; in psychological contexts, it refers to a frame of mind, or facial features, which are relaxed or at ease—the relaxation in question often, though not invariably, succeeding a period of tension, anger, or the like. See Epicurus, *KD* 30 (on this, see also Nussbaum 1994: 153–4), Plut. *Alex.* 19, *Prof. virt.* 82F, and 106 above. Of course, there would be no reason for a sceptic to *want* to persuade someone that he or she 'is not soothed'. But that does not affect Sextus' point here, which is simply that the 'non-rational movements' (148) which he is discussing are not amenable to sceptical argumentation; like it or not, they just happen to us. (Cf. 143, where 'pain *or pleasure*' are cited as examples of things which happen to us 'by necessity'.)

This section opens with a characterization of happiness; this is preparatory to the discussion of the two types of possible sources of unhappiness, which is introduced in the closing sentence of 141 (hence 'on the other hand' (*de*); the point of the contrast here is not really explicit. On the use of the phrase 'the things which are said to be good and bad', see below on 141–3). We have already seen Sextus assuming that happiness (*eudaimonia*) is equivalent to freedom from disturbance (*ataraxia*) (point 6a on 118); it should not therefore be surprising to see him simply asserting this equivalence as if it is quite uncontroversial.

The two quotations from Timon, introduced to exemplify the desired attitude, presumably referred in their original context to the extraordinary tranquillity of Pyrrho. What that original context was must remain a matter for guesswork; the lines are quoted by no one else, and Sextus gives no clues as to their provenance. Diels (1901: 201) places them in Timon's poem *Lampoons* (*Silloi*); since this is not the only poem of Timon's from which isolated hexameter lines could derive, I see no basis for this. (*Images* (*Indalmoi*) was in elegiac couplets; it also certainly contained reference to Pyrrho's amazing tranquillity; see on 1–2 above.) Diels also points out that 'When I perceived him, then' (*ton d'hōs oun enoēs*') is based on a Homeric model. The line he quotes is wrongly cited, however, as *Od.* XI. 575 (it is in fact *Il.* XI. 575; this error is repeated in Long 1978*c*: 84 n. 15); and in fact the formula *ton* [or *tēn* or *tous*] *d'hōs oun enoēs*' occurs eleven other times in Homer. Scholars have pointed to another pair of lines in Homer (*Od.* V. 391–2 = XII. 168–9) as the source of the concatenation of 'windlessness' and 'calm' (*nēnemiēisi galēnēs*). It is true that these are the only places in Homer where these two words occur in close proximity. But the correspondence with Timon's line is by no means exact; Pl. *Tht.* 153*c* is just as close (and cf. Aesch. *Ag.* 739), and in any case the use of the words 'windlessness' and 'calm' together is not so recherché as to require explanation by reference to other authors at all. Literary parallels aside, the term *galēnē*, 'calm', is also used in at least two other philosophers' depictions of the ideal attitude—viz. those of Democritus and Epicurus (for discussion of these and other philosophical parallels, see Caizzi 1981*a*: 247–8, Long 1978*c*: 84 n. 15).

The distinction between the two types of potential sources of unhappiness is sketched in 141–3. The treatment is not as lucid as it might be.

Sextus says (141) that the things in question 'are introduced' either by opinion or by necessity, and this way of describing the issue is continued in the following sentences. The language is appropriate only for the second category. Certain things 'are introduced' into our lives 'by necessity'; these are conditions which we are bound to experience simply in virtue of having senses, and reason can do nothing to prevent this. It is not true, on the other hand, that the things listed in 142 'are introduced' by opinion, if that means that it is because of our having certain opinions that we encounter such objects at all. (One may be wealthy or poor, for example, whatever opinions one has or lacks.) What is 'introduced' by opinion is, rather, the *belief that* these things are good or bad; the label 'the things which are said to be good and bad' does not adequately capture this point. In themselves, these things need not lead to disturbance (or at any rate, this is Sextus' claim); it is, instead, this belief *about* them that gives them their status as sources of disturbance. We saw other cases of this type of confusion in the previous chapter (cf. on 119–24, 130–40).

It may also seem surprising that the things which occur 'by necessity' are among those referred to as 'things which are said to be *good and* bad'. But this is consistent with the fact that, as already noted (see linguistic point (e) above), both pain and pleasure are listed as examples of such things; Sextus has in mind both welcome and unwelcome sensory experiences over which we have no control. It is for this reason that he feels the need to supplement the quotation in 143 (from *Il.* III. 66)—which by itself would be applicable only to the unwelcome experiences—with the clumsy addition 'or avoid them'; unfortunately, this does not succeed in making the point he wants to make, which is that the welcome experiences, just as much as the unwelcome ones, simply happen to us whether we like it or not. Welcome experiences which occur by necessity are mentioned only here and at 149 (again, see linguistic point (e) above); the next section, in which the things which occur by necessity are the central topic, concentrates exclusively on the unwelcome variety. It is therefore never made clear why, or even whether, the welcome variety should be considered a source of disturbance. The answer would presumably be that they will be a source of disturbance if one believes that they are by nature good, but not otherwise (cf. 120, 124, 126 on pleasure as one of the things the obsessive pursuit of which results in disturbance). If so, of course, the disturbance itself will have been brought about by *opinion*, rather than by necessity, even though the phenomenon about which the opinion is held occurs by necessity; again, it looks as if Sextus' taxonomy in this passage is too crude to be entirely helpful.

On the three types of alleged goods listed in 142, see on 45 above. These are, of course, just examples; there is no particular significance to the choice of an Academic or Peripatetic scheme of classification.

Sextus now briefly considers the situations of the dogmatist and the sceptic with regard to potential sources of unhappiness of the first type (144–7); since this was the main subject of the previous chapter, this passage has the character of a review, as is noted in the rather awkward and rambling sentence which constitutes 144. 'At present' here refers to the previous chapter; 'earlier, when we discussed the sceptical end' must refer to a discussion in the lost part of the work which originally preceded *M* VII–XI (a discussion which would have paralleled *PH* I. 25–30; the latter passage does indeed deal with the issue in question). On the incompleteness of *M* VII–XI (and on the fact that this and similar back-references in *M* VII–XI are not, as previously often thought, to passages of *PH* itself), see Janáček 1963 and Blomqvist 1974.

With regard to the first type of objects, then, the sceptic is undisturbed (144, 147) and the dogmatist disturbed (145–6); there is nothing unprecedented here. On what it is to 'suspend judgement about everything' (144) in this context, see point 4 on 118. It is not quite clear how to understand all of the several references to 'bad things' in 145. The 'many bad things' which the person 'draw[s] on himself, because of the good things' are presumably the disturbances brought about by the belief that the things in question really are good—disturbances catalogued in more detail in 146. The 'many times more bad things' by which the person is 'pounded, because of his opinion about the bad things' may be either the disturbances which attend the original avoiding of certain things as by nature bad (in this case the point would be the same as in the second sentence of 130, as I interpreted it) or the second-level disturbances consequent upon the belief that the disturbances previously mentioned— those brought about by the belief that some things are by nature good— are themselves bad; or it is possible that both of these are meant. Comprehension of Sextus' exact meaning here is also not helped by the repeated use of 'good things' and 'bad things' as if they were descriptions which he himself endorsed; this is the same careless usage as we saw several times in the previous chapter. On the notion that being 'elated beyond measure' (146) is undesirable, see 116 with Commentary. On the sense in which 'not more' (147) should be understood in *M* XI, see point 3 on 118. Note, finally, that though Sextus describes the sceptic as 'perfectly happy' (*teleōs eudaimōn*, 147), he is careful to qualify this with 'as regards the things thought by opinion to be good and bad'; this leaves open the possibility which is about to be discussed—that things which occur 'by necessity' may detract from even the sceptic's happiness. As we saw, the previous chapter did not tend to include this qualification, leading to some unnecessary overstatements of Sextus' position (118, 140; cf. 160 below).

148–9 begin to address the second category of potential sources of unhappiness, which will be the main subject of the next section. Since we are beings with senses, there are certain things, such as hunger, thirst, or physical pain, concerning which it is not in our control whether we experience them or not, and by which, when we do experience them, we cannot but be disturbed. These 'sensory and non-rational movements' (on the physicalistic implications of 'movements', *kinēmasin*, cf. 83 with Comm.) are not caused by any kind of misguided reasoning; nor can they be eliminated by some more effective form of reasoning—in this respect the sceptic is no better off than anyone else. The sceptic's response in this situation is to 'give way' (*eikei*, 148—if this emendation is correct; see textual point (c) above), to accept these inevitable conditions as they are. The response of the dogmatist is not mentioned until the next section. But it is natural to infer even from this passage that, as is subsequently argued, the dogmatist's response is something *other* than that of simply accepting these conditions as they are, and that the failure to do so leads to a greater level of disturbance than is necessary.

As Nussbaum (1994: 289–90) points out, this passage seems to have been conceived in conscious opposition to the Epicurean view—illustrated most dramatically by Epicurus' letter to Idomeneus on his dying day (DL X. 22)—that philosophical reflection *can* prevent, or at least mitigate, the disturbance associated with physical pain. It is quite possible that Sextus also has the Stoics in mind as targets; in arguing that such things as pain and disease are indifferent (and hence irrelevant to happiness) rather than bad, the Stoics too are attempting, among other things, to convince us that we need not be disturbed by these things—or at any rate, not as disturbed as people generally are. Annas (1993: 361) is surely right that Sextus has a good claim to be more realistic in this respect than the dogmatists.

150–61: Why the sceptic is better off than the dogmatist with regard to 'involuntary and non-rational movements'

[Points of text and language and other points of philological detail:

(a) I retain the MSS reading *kai ei* in 154, rather than altering to *kai eis*, as does Mutschmann (following Bekker). Heintz (1932: 255) is right that *alla toi ge* in the following clause naturally follows *ei* (cf. *M* VII. 65,

VIII. 285, IX. 394, XI. 107, 150). Heintz is, however, being over-subtle when he suggests that *kai ei* should perhaps be altered to *ei kai*. It is true that *kai ei* normally does not commit the speaker to the reality of the state of affairs referred to ('even if'), while *ei kai* normally does ('granted that'). But the distinction between the two is a fine one, and in any case there is no reason why Sextus must make an *explicit* commitment to the reality of the state of affairs referred to in the present case (any more than in 107 or 150 above, where Heintz concedes that analogous changes would be implausible).

(b) Heintz (1932: 255) alters *touto* to *t'auto* in 157, on the basis of a supposed parallel with the first sentence of 128. But the parallel is a false one; the first sentence of 128 introduces an *additional* argument of the same form as the one previously discussed, whereas the final sentence of 157 (as I explain in more detail below) introduces further discussion of a point which is among those *already* raised in the previous sentence, making 'this' an appropriate connective.

(c) Heintz (1932: 256) also proposes adding *monōi* between *ton ponon* and *echetai* in 158, and altering *tōn* to *en men tois* in 160. In both cases this results in a more lucid and neatly expressed train of thought. But this is not a reason for accepting either emendation; this section in any case includes an unusually high proportion of awkward, rambling, and obscurely worded sentences; see esp. 151, 153 (*tina labein anastrophēn eis boētheian*), and the end of 157. Though the passage has no detailed parallel in either of Sextus' other works, its imperfect composition (on which see further below) at least encourages the speculation that it comes from early in Sextus' career.

(d) The quotation in 156 is from an unknown play by Euripides; the complete line (which survives in isolation, in part or in its entirety, in various authors) was *hē phusis ebouleth', hēi nomōn ouden melei.* For details see Nauck 1889: 658–9. The quotation in 159 is from *Od.* XI. 529–30; in accordance with the grammar of his own sentence, Sextus has altered Homer's accusative participles to the nominative, and has (unmetrically) changed Homer's *oute* to *mēte.* The quotation in 161 consists of *Od.* XIX. 163 plus half a line which does not occur in our manuscripts of Homer. However, Clement, *Protrepticus* II. 38 also quotes *Od.* XIX. 163, and adds *all'andrōn genos eisi*; it is therefore possible that Sextus is drawing on a different manuscript tradition to which we do not have access. The thought is proverbial; a more celebrated philosophical use of Homer's line occurs at Pl. *Apol.* 34d. In neither case does the context in the *Odyssey* have any particular relevance to Sextus' point.

(e) 'The idea that the affliction is solely an alien thing, that it is solely a bad thing', 158: The meaning here is not that pain is the *only thing* which is alien and bad, *pace* Russo and Nussbaum (1994: 289). Though the Epicureans do, of course, hold such a view, this remark would be pointless in context; the issue is whether or not one thinks that one's suffering is by nature bad, not whether or not one thinks that *other* kinds of things *besides* such suffering are by nature bad. In any case, the Greek will not easily bear this translation; if this were the meaning, one would expect the masculine *monos*, in agreement with *ponos*, and one would expect the word order to be different. It is far more natural to take *monon* as adverbial ('solely') with the two adjectives 'alien' (*anoikeion*) and 'bad' (*kakon*). On the point of these expressions, see below.]

In this section Sextus elaborates on the sceptic's situation with regard to the second of the two types of possible sources of unhappiness mentioned in the previous section: viz. those which come about 'by necessity'. (Note that it is only inevitable experiences of the *unwelcome* variety which are discussed here; cf. on 141–3 above.) Some initial discussion of this already occurred at the end of the previous section. But that discussion was such as to invite naturally the question put in the dogmatists' mouths at the opening of 150: what is the advantage of scepticism if it is admitted that the sceptic is bound to suffer certain types of disturbances just like anyone else? This question is the more pointed, of course, in view of the fact that at least some dogmatists claimed that one is *not* bound to be disturbed by physical pain and related phenomena (see above on 148–9). Note that the word translated 'be disturbed' in this context is *tarattesthai*, which is the verb corresponding to *tarachē*, the opposite of *ataraxia* (and cf. 155, 157, 160 for *tarachē* itself used of physical suffering). This implies that *ataraxia* includes freedom from physical pain as well as freedom from mental torments. This is different from the Epicurean conception of *ataraxia* (on this, see point 6a on 118). It also appears to be different from *PH* I. 25, where, in outlining the sceptic's end (*telos*), Sextus again distinguishes matters involving 'opinion' and matters of 'necessity', and says that the sceptic's end is *ataraxia* with regard to the first, but something else, *metriopatheia*, with regard to the second. On *metriopatheia*, see further on 161.

The bulk of this section consists of a variety of answers to the question the dogmatists are imagined as posing. One might think that an obvious reply would be that, though sceptics are indeed no better off with regard to physical suffering than other people, they are also no worse off, and that, as argued earlier, they are much better off in other areas—so that, all things considered, scepticism does confer great advantages. One of the replies Sextus gives (the first one) in effect amounts to this. However, the ambition of this section is apparently to show something more specific: viz. that the sceptic is less disturbed than other people even by physical suffering itself. The second half of 150 says that, though the sceptic is indeed disturbed by pain, 'he still bears the distress more easily compared with the dogmatist'; the term 'the distress' here can only refer to pain and other forms of physical suffering (the troubles which occur 'by necessity'), for these are the *only* types of 'distress' to which the sceptic is supposed to be subject. Unfortunately, if this is what Sextus is attempting to show, most of the considerations he offers in support of it are irrelevant. The answers he gives to the question are as follows:

1. The dogmatist is massively and multiply disturbed because of the pursuit and avoidance of things as (by nature) good and bad respectively, whereas the sceptic only has a single disturbance to contend with: viz. physical suffering itself (151).

2. Physical suffering is not in fact 'excessively disturbing' (152–5).

3. Even if the sceptic's physical suffering is extreme, that is not something for which the sceptic is to blame; the suffering is bound to happen in any case, whatever the sceptic does or thinks. Disturbances which are due to the holding of opinions can be blamed on the person concerned; but this does not apply to the present case (156–7).

4. If a sceptic and a non-sceptic are both afflicted by physical suffering (of comparable severity, we may assume), the sceptic will be better off than the non-sceptic; for the sceptic merely experiences the physical suffering itself, whereas the non-sceptic is also disturbed by the belief that physical suffering is by nature bad. In fact, the disturbance due to this belief may even be more severe than the physical suffering itself (158–60).

Of these, only 4 addresses the point Sextus claims to be discussing. Answer 1 simply repeats that the sceptic lacks an *additional* type of disturbance to which the dogmatist is subject. As noted just above, it would make good sense to offer this as a consideration in favour of the general view that the sceptic is better off than the dogmatist; but it is irrelevant—or at least, no effort is made to show that it is relevant—to the specific point being argued here, that the sceptic is better off even with regard to the type of disturbance which they both share. Answers 2 and 3 are irrelevant even to the more general issue. The claim that physical suffering is not excessively disturbing does nothing whatever to differentiate the situations of the sceptic and the dogmatist. And the fact that the sceptic is not *responsible* for his suffering, whereas the dogmatist is at least partially responsible for his, has no bearing on the question of whose suffering is greater.

A few further remarks deserve to be made about each of these four answers. As noted above (see textual point (c)), the wording of answer 1 is highly convoluted. This is not merely a matter of stylistic inelegance; 1 also attributes to the *sceptic* the ambition of 'avoiding and guarding against one single bad thing', and hence, it would seem, the *opinion* that that thing is bad. This error is committed in still more glaring form at the beginning of answer 2—'even this thing which the suspenders of judgement *avoid as bad*' (152); we have seen many other cases in which the belief that things are good or bad appears to be carelessly endorsed by Sextus, but nowhere else does this occur in so stark a fashion. (It might be replied that, on my interpretation, the sceptic of *M* XI does accept that things are good and bad, providing this is appropriately qualified by relativities (cf. point 2 on 118 above); but the answer to that is that the present offending phrase is *not* thus qualified.)

As others have remarked (see Striker 1990a: 104, Annas 1993: 361), the justification offered for answer 2—that extreme pains are short-lived, whereas the more prolonged or everyday forms of discomfort are less severe—seems to be taken over directly from Epicureanism (cf. *KD* 4, *VS* 4, *Letter to Menoeceus* X. 133). Striker is right to remark that this constitutes an admission on Sextus' part that the sceptics are no better off in this respect than the Epicureans.

The assignment of responsibility and blame to the dogmatists in answer 3 makes polemical use of Stoic views. The Stoics insist that, though the universe is ordered deterministically, it is 'in our power' (*eph'hēmin*) whether or not we assent to the impressions with which we are presented; see Cic. *De Fato* 43, Alexander, *De Fato* 182, 9–20 (= LS 62G6–7), Epict. *Diss.* I. 1. 7–12. Hence we are responsible not only for our actions, but also for our beliefs; and the Stoics would have to agree that, if the belief that things are by nature good or bad does indeed result in massive disturbance, it is a disturbance for which the holders of the belief are responsible. (The term 'supposition' (*hupolēpsis*, 157) is also used by the Stoics to designate a certain type of inadequately grounded belief—see Stob. II. 112, 2–5; both Chrysippus and Herillus wrote works 'On Supposition'—*peri hupolēpseōs*, DL VII. 166, 201.) As noted earlier, however, Sextus' argument here seems to be beside the point, which is

not whether the sceptics or the dogmatists are *to blame* for their disturbances, but whose disturbances are the greater and by how much. Again,
the phrase 'for he stirs up for himself a flood of bad things' (157) needlessly makes it look as if Sextus himself holds the belief that the disturbances in question really are bad.

The transition from answer 3 to answer 4, in the final sentence of
157, is again awkward. By 'the things called bad themselves' Sextus
means the things which a dogmatist takes to be (by nature) bad or to be
avoided; the phrase thus refers to one of the categories of object referred
to in the previous sentence ('fashions for himself a mass of objects . . . to
be avoided'), and Sextus' point is that he is going to illustrate the general
claim just made—that the dogmatist creates disturbance for himself—
with reference to this one particular group of objects, the objects which
the dogmatist regards as bad. (Actually, the illustration applies only to a
subset of the objects the dogmatist considers bad—viz. pain and other
'inevitable' physical disturbances.) The word 'themselves' is inserted to
distinguish these objects from the 'flood of bad things' mentioned just
before, which are instead the disturbances which *result from* the pursuit
of some things as good and the avoidance of others as bad. See also
textual point (b) above.

Answer 4, then, develops the notion of 'stir[ring] up . . . a flood of bad
things' which was introduced in the course of answer 3. Here, finally, we
are given a reason for supposing that the sceptic is better off than the
dogmatist (and, for that matter, than ordinary people; see below on 163,
165) even with regard to the physical suffering which both are bound to
experience; this point was hinted at in the previous chapter, at 128–9,
but has never been spelled out before now. The physical suffering is *all*
that the sceptic is troubled by, whereas the dogmatist also holds the
opinion that pain is a bad thing; and this, for reasons with which we are
already familiar, leads to extensive further disturbance—disturbance which,
it is claimed, can actually be *worse* than that which derives from the mere
pain. (The 'movement' mentioned in 159 is, of course, the psychophysical
'movement' which accompanies the cutting—in other words, the suffering itself.) This latter claim also occurs at *PH* III. 236, but without the
melodramatic details of 159; for the general point, see also *PH* I. 29–30.
The term 'alien' (*anoikeion*, 158) is Stoic; it is the opposite of the term
translated 'appropriate' in 132 and 133 (*oikeion*), and refers to that which
is in disharmony with one's nature (see on 132–3 above, and cf. Stob. II.
69, 11–16). Sextus has the dogmatist say that 'the affliction is *solely* an
alien thing' and '*solely* a bad thing' to distinguish the dogmatist's position

from the sceptic's; while the sceptic may accept that things are bad *in certain circumstances but not invariably so*, without thereby being committed to their being bad by nature, the dogmatist holds that physical suffering is *unequivocally* bad—which, as we saw in earlier chapters, *is* tantamount to holding that it is bad by nature—and this is what results in the additional level of disturbance. (See also linguistic point (e) above.) Of course, not all dogmatists do think that physical suffering is bad; the Stoics would say that it is a dispreferred indifferent. But Sextus might well regard this distinction as unimportant for his purposes; for, he could reply, by labelling it dispreferred, the Stoics are still making clear that physical suffering is something which there is, in the nature of things, reason to avoid—and it is the acceptance of *this* view which is supposed to lead to the dogmatists' extra disturbance.

The scene described in 159 might be thought to be nothing but overblown rhetoric on Sextus' part. But it appears that he was not alone in suggesting that the observers at a surgical operation may sometimes suffer more than the patients. A Roman fresco (currently in the Museo Nazionale in Naples) depicts precisely the kind of scene Sextus describes. It shows Aeneas wounded and being attended to by a doctor; Aeneas looks impassive as the doctor cuts into his thigh, while his companion appears to be fainting. (I owe this information to Majno 1991, on the cover of which the fresco is reproduced.)

The argument is summed up in the sentence which covers the second half of 160 and the whole of 161. The claim that 'the person who suspends judgement about all matters of opinion enjoys the most complete happiness' (160) is an overstatement (like those at 118 and 140); it commits Sextus to saying that suspension of judgement is sufficient for happiness, regardless of what bodily disturbances one may be subjected to. Dogmatists might want to maintain that bodily disturbances cannot affect one's level of happiness, but the present chapter has adopted precisely the opposite view. Sextus should have said, as in 147, that suspension of judgement permits the most complete happiness *as far as matters of opinion are concerned*.

The term 'moderate feeling' (*metriopatheia* and cognates) recurs at *PH* I. 25, 30, in the characterization of the sceptic's 'end' (*telos*), and in the passage parallel to the present one, *PH* III. 235–6. In *PH* I. 25 *metriopatheia* in matters of 'necessity' is contrasted with *ataraxia* in matters of 'opinion' (see on 150 above); in *PH* III. 235 the contrasting term applying to matters of opinion is *apathēs*, 'without feeling'. In either case, and in the present passage as well, *metriopatheia* is clearly a second-best state. It is not that moderation is being advocated as desirable *per se*; rather, 'moderate feeling' is the lowest level of feeling one can realistically hope for with regard to physical suffering—by contrast with matters of opinion, where the sceptic manages to achieve a state of no feeling, or no disturbance, at all. Diogenes' account of Pyrrhonism does not include the term *metriopatheia* or any of its cognates, though it does mention both *ataraxia* and *apatheia* as possible candidates for the sceptic's 'end' (DL IX. 107–8). However, it refers to *praotēs*, 'gentleness' (DL IX. 108), as another candidate for the 'end', and this may be closely related to *metriopatheia*; on *praotēs* and the contrast between it and *apatheia*, see Brunschwig 1992: esp. 142–4.

162–7: Replies to two forms of the objection that scepticism cannot be lived

[Textual points:

(a) Von Arnim (*SVF* II. 119) proposed altering *tropon* in 163 to *topon*. For effective arguments against this, see Heintz 1932: 256–7.

(b) Blomqvist (1968: 99–100) proposes altering *tuchon*, 'perhaps', in 166 to *stoichōn*, 'following [the preconception, etc.]'. This is ingenious, but not necessary. *Tuchon* standing alone adverbially is not especially uncommon; see the numerous references in LSJ, s.v. *tunchanō* A. 5. b. And the dative *prolēpsei* depending on the verbs *heleitai* and *pheuxetai*, while a little unusual, is not so unnatural as to demand textual alteration.

(c) With Mutschmann, I retain the MSS *toutōn* in 166, rather than altering it, with Bekker and Bury, to *toutōi*; there is no palaeographic or linguistic difficulty with *toutōn*, and *exōthen* is normally followed by a genitive, not a dative. This makes some difference to the interpretation of the passage, since the singular *toutōi* would obviously refer back to *to sklēron*, 'the harsh situation', whereas the plural *toutōn* more naturally refers to the *pair* of actions being considered, together with their surrounding circumstances (see below).]

In this section Sextus mentions, and then replies to, two versions of the objection that it is impossible to live consistently as a sceptic. The first ('inactivity') is to the effect that scepticism renders human action altogether impossible; the second ('inconsistency') urges that the sceptic will in certain cases be forced to make decisions which cannot be made, one way or the other, without a violation of the sceptical outlook. Such *apraxia* ('inaction') objections, as they were generically known, had been levelled against sceptics since long before Sextus' time. For discussion of Academic responses to them, see Bett 1989a, 1990. The fact that Timon is quoted in the course of one of the objections perhaps suggests that they were already applied against the early Pyrrhonists; the same is suggested by the stories reported in DL (IX. 62) from the third-century Antigonus of Carystus, according to which Pyrrho had to be rescued by his friends from the edges of the cliffs, from under the wheels of wagons, and so on. Aristotle, too, employs objections of this kind against those thinkers who attempted to deny the law of non-contradiction; see *Met.* 1008b12–18, 1010b1 ff., and, for the same 'vegetable' analogy which occurs here in 163, 1008b11–12. This is the only place in Sextus which explicitly addresses *apraxia* objections. The parallel passage of *PH* III omits consideration of such issues altogether; and *PH* I. 21–4, though it does consider in more detail than the present passage how the sceptic can live and act, does not do so in the context of replying to an objection. It is unfortunate that the present treatment of the issue is so brief; as we shall see, interpreting it requires us to venture well beyond the text on several occasions.

It is not in fact immediately clear why consideration of *apraxia* objections should occur at this point in the argument (its omission in *PH* III leaves no obvious gap). Of course, in order for it to be true that the sceptics are happier than other people, they must not be vulnerable to *apraxia* objections; one cannot live happily as a sceptic if one cannot live as a sceptic at all. But the 'Hence' (*hothen*) which opens 162 implies that this issue is connected in some specific way with the matters discussed at the end of the previous section. The connection, admittedly a somewhat oblique one, appears to be this. It has been pointed out in 161 that the sceptic is not immune from all feelings. From a certain point of view, as noted above, this circumstance is to be regretted. However, the implication of 'Hence' is that the sceptic's susceptibility to certain feelings is *also* what ensures that he or she is not 'reduced to inactivity or to inconsistency', as alleged by the authors of the *apraxia* objection. Such feelings can give rise to choices or avoidances, and hence can form the causal antecedents of actions, without constituting *rational grounds* for these choices, avoidances, and actions. The precise form which such feelings take may be shaped by a person's 'ancestral laws and customs' (166, on which more below); given one's cultural background, one may be disgusted by certain burial practices, or seized with admiration at a spectacular performance with the javelin, and these reactions may be reflected in one's behaviour. But at no point does one need to believe that anything is by nature to be chosen or to be avoided; one's natural affects, as structured by one's upbringing in a certain culture, are sufficient to permit action in the absence of any dogmatic beliefs. The connection between this and the foregoing discussion is loose, because the feelings focused on in 161 and earlier were purely bodily feelings associated with illness, surgery, etc.; the feelings which, if I am right, make possible choice and action for the sceptic are presumably not restricted to these, but may include many varieties of affective states (so long as they are 'moderate' and not 'intense'), including, for example, disgust at certain burial practices. (Cf. *PH* I. 23–4, 237–8, where bodily feelings are among the antecedents, but are by no means the sole antecedents, of action for the sceptic. Note also that the Greek word *pathos* is as elastic as the English 'feeling'; the above suggestion does not trade on the idiosyncrasies of an English word.)

This passage is paralleled in some detail by DL IX. 108, from the very end of the life of Pyrrho; it too contains the case of being pressured to do something unspeakable, the distinction between attitudes towards philosophy and attitudes towards ordinary life, and the notion of being guided by laws and customs. The extent of agreement makes it very likely that both passages derive from a common source. However, this information is not as helpful as it might be, since the text of the DL passage is highly problematic in places; for an effort to sort some of it out, see Barnes 1992: 4293. See also Introduction, nn. 46, 48 and accompanying text.

The first objection ('inactivity') is stated in 163 and answered in 165. The objection amounts simply to the charge that the sceptic cannot engage in choices or avoidances. The verb translated 'stays fixed' (*epeichen*) is an ironic dig at the sceptic; it is the verb corresponding to *epochē*, the standard sceptical term for suspension of judgement. Sextus' reply depends on a distinction between 'philosophical reasoning' (*ton philosophon logon*) and 'non-philosophical practice' (*tēn aphilosophon tērēsin*). The sceptic does not use philosophical arguments and conclusions—notably those to the effect that certain things are by nature to be chosen or to be avoided—to guide his conduct; it is in that sense that 'as far as this is concerned he is inactive'. None the less, he can make choices in an everyday, non-theoretical fashion. Sextus does not say precisely *how* the sceptic can do this; so this reply by itself does not tell us very much, nor is it easy, taken by itself, to evaluate. But his answer to the second objection sheds a little more light on this; in addition, one may assume that the topic was discussed in more detail in the lost book or books which preceded *M* VII–XI, and especially in the passage which covered the same ground as *PH* I. 21–4 (or perhaps *PH* I. 25–30; cf. on 167 below). See also point 5 on 118. Notice that the point here is not that philosophy is irrelevant to the sceptic's conduct; despite superficial appearances, this is not some ancient counterpart of the frequent modern practice of 'insulating' one's philosophical from one's everyday attitudes. (On 'insulation', see Burnyeat 1984, Annas 1986: 26–9, Bett 1993.) On the contrary, it is precisely the sceptic's own philosophically generated *attitude* which leads him to avoid relying on philosophical *conclusions* as bases for action.

Sextus here makes it sound as if he is siding against philosophers and with ordinary people. This is a pose which he strikes in some other places: e.g. *PH* II. 102, 246, 254, III. 151, *M* VIII. 158, IX. 49. Whatever its merits in general (for some discussion of this see Barnes 1982*a*, Allen 1990: 2604–5, Brennan 1994), this is disingenuous in the present instance. For the belief which was the centre of attention at the end of the previous section—the belief that pain really is a bad thing—is plainly one which ordinary people hold at least as much as dogmatic philosophers. If Sextus is not going to allow his conduct to be guided by *this* belief, he can hardly claim to be a devotee of ordinary, everyday life as against the purveyors of philosophical abstraction; while it may be true that dogmatic philosophers do 'live in accordance with philosophical reasoning' and that sceptics instead employ a certain form of 'non-philosophical practice', the sceptics' practice is not (as the phrase naturally suggests) the ordinary practice of non-philosophers. For people who are neither dogmatic philosophers nor sceptics will at least some of the time decide what to do on the basis of dogmatic beliefs, such as that pain is by nature bad—even if these beliefs are not themselves the result of philosophical reasoning. (Cf. *PH* I. 30, where it is 'ordinary people' (*idiōtai*), and not dogmatists, who are said to be afflicted with the ills associated with such beliefs.) It may indeed be true that in other respects the sceptic is in accord with the practice, or the attitudes, of ordinary people; for consideration of one aspect of this, see Flückiger 1994. Whether it is *important* for Sextus to be able to make this claim is another question; it is not clear to me that he loses anything significant by giving it up.

The second objection ('inconsistency') is stated at 164 and answered at 166. The example of the autocratic ruler, who forces one to choose or prefer an action or state of affairs which would otherwise be extremely repugnant, is a convenient and vivid one for ancient philosophers. In addition to the parallel passage of DL (see above), the figure of the tyrant occurs earlier in this book (66; cf. *PH* III. 192); Ar. *NE* III. 1110a23–6 also seems to be referring to a similar case, though the details are not spelled out. Such examples were of more than merely theoretical interest— especially, perhaps, to those in the Pyrrhonist tradition; Anaxarchus, the teacher of Pyrrho, was pounded to death at the orders of the tyrant Nicocreon (DL IX. 59; on the significance of this episode see Brunschwig 1993), and Callisthenes, another of the philosophers who, like Pyrrho, accompanied Alexander on his Indian expedition, was put to death on a (probably false) charge of having plotted against him (Plut. *Alex.* 54–5).

The objection is not (as suggested by Annas 1986: 19) that a consistent sceptic will not do the *right* thing in the situation envisaged. Such objections were indeed not unknown in the ancient world; see in particular Aristocles in Eusebius, *Praep. evang.* XIV. 18. 18–20. The point here is rather that, *whatever* the sceptic decides to do in this case, the decision will commit him to the belief that certain courses of action are by nature good and others by nature bad (and hence to inconsistency); the sceptic will make a certain choice, the objector says, and the very making of this choice 'is characteristic of those who have apprehended with confidence . . .'. (On the Stoic notion of 'apprehension' (*katalēpsis*), see on 182–3 below; 'apprehending' things, in the robust and technical sense given to this term by the Stoics, is precisely what sceptics professed never to do.) It is not explained why this should be thought to be so. But we may assume that the reason is something like this: the extremity of this situation forces one to make a decision which is conscious, principled, and based on considerations about which one cares deeply—either that life and freedom from pain must be (or at any rate, may be) preserved, no matter how unspeakable the acts one is required to perform, or that some acts must never be committed, no matter what the consequences. Either way, one's scepticism is thoroughly compromised; for it is scarcely imaginable that either of the principles just mentioned could be adopted in isolation from the belief that certain things are by nature good, or to be chosen, and others by nature bad, or to be avoided.

Sextus' reply is that regardless, again, of *which* choice the sceptic makes, the choice can be made without involvement in any dogmatic commitments. The sceptic will have been raised in a certain culture, in which certain 'ancestral laws and customs' prevail. Given this upbringing, he will come to be favourably disposed towards certain courses of action and unfavourably disposed towards certain others. On any given occasion, these dispositions will express themselves in a 'preconception'—i.e. an attitude, of a type which would be generally shared among conventional people, about the goodness or badness of the course of action under consideration. The sceptic's decisions and actions are determined by these preconceptions, and not by dogmatic opinions, philosophically justified or not. (On 'preconception' (*prolēpsis*), see opening remarks on ch. II, linguistic point (a) on 68–78, linguistic point (d) on 125–30 above; see also *PH* II. 246 for another use of the term in a similar context.)

It might be replied that the sceptic is already involved in dogmatic commitments. For is not a 'preconception' of the kind just mentioned a certain type of impression *that something or other is the case*? And does not action which is based on such impressions commit one to the truth of the propositions in question (e.g. in the tyrant case, that murdering one's parents, or whatever it is one is being ordered to do, is a forbidden act)? Again, Sextus does not tell us how he would respond to this objection; but the answer must somehow be that the sceptic, in having these impressions and allowing them to guide his action, does not come to hold any opinions about the nature of things—not that murdering one's parents is *by nature* forbidden, nor that it is *by nature* better to preserve one's life and one's freedom from pain. This might happen by the sceptic's treating such impressions merely as appearances, rather than as accurately representing an underlying reality. Some such strategy is certainly alluded to in *PH* I. 21–4 (for differing interpretations of Sextus' talk of appearances, see Burnyeat 1983, Brennan 1994). However, we have seen that *M* XI does *not* in general restrict the sceptic to reliance on appearances (see above on 18–20, point 5 on 118). Instead, the sceptic of *M* XI is prepared to make statements about what is to be chosen or to be avoided, provided these statements are relativized to persons or to circumstances; for relativized statements, though they are not statements about appearances, *also* do not count as statements about the real nature of things. And this approach might easily be adopted in the present case. The sceptic, because of his particular upbringing, will be more strongly inclined in the current case to say to himself either (a) 'I must not murder my parents' or (b) 'I have to do what the tyrant says; if I don't, I will be tortured and killed'. Hence he will regard either murdering his parents as to be avoided and defying the tyrant as to be chosen, or vice versa. But these verdicts will refer solely to *this particular case*. Unlike the dogmatist, he does not 'have any further opinion *over and above* (*exōthen*) *these conditions*' (see textual point (c) above); the opinion that he is here said to lack is a *comprehensive* opinion, to the effect that either type of action under consideration is invariably, or by nature, to be chosen or to be avoided. As a sceptic, he will refrain from any such opinion; indeed, if the issue ever arose, he would argue for the *negation* of the view that either kind of action is invariably, or by nature, to be chosen or to be avoided, applying the sorts of considerations laid out in 68–95 above. (In this respect he may of course differ from ordinary people of the same upbringing, whose 'preconceptions', though resulting in the same verdict in this case, could well be expected to involve dogmatic commitments; cf. on 163, 165 above.) Nor will his decision be based on any reasoning from other, more general premisses about what is by nature to be chosen or to be avoided. In fact, it will not be based on *reasoning* at all; it is simply the causal outcome of the play of psychological forces which his upbringing leads him to undergo in this particular case. The impressions experienced by the sceptic will still have motivational force; after all, they are connected with deeply ingrained aspects of his character. But they will present themselves to him merely as stimuli to action, not as rational justifications for action. (Cf. above, on Sextus' apparent implication that feelings, of some unspecified types, are what make choice and action possible for the sceptic; the 'preconceptions' of which Sextus speaks here will be at least one variety of such feelings.) The objection, therefore, will be straightforwardly mistaken—at least, if my reconstruction of it is on the right lines.

The idea that the sceptic's actions are determined by 'laws and customs' occurs in several other places in Sextus (cf. *PH* I. 17, 23–4, 231, 237, *M* IX. 49). In the *PH* passages 'laws and customs' form just one of a total of four categories of 'appearances' by which the sceptic's actions may be regulated; however, of those four, 'laws and customs' are clearly the most relevant to the situation described here. None the less, it is something of an oversimplification to suggest that 'laws and customs' will be the *only* factor affecting the sceptic's decision in this case. It is indeed quite possible that one's 'ancestral laws and customs' could affect one's tendency to obey a tyrant's orders; some cultures, for example, encourage submission to authority, others encourage resistance to it, and some cultures have stronger prohibitions than others against actions which they place in the 'unspeakable' category. But Sextus could easily admit that many other factors might affect the outcome—one's previous relations with the tyrant, one's capacity to endure pain, one's own personal willingness or unwillingness to follow orders, the likely consequences for others if one performs this particular 'unspeakable deed', and so on; all these could be causal factors in one's decision, in addition to 'laws and customs', without committing one to any objectionable beliefs. More generally, it is not clear why 'laws and customs' should have to be a major determinant of the sceptic's actions at all. This point is of some interest because it is sometimes suggested, on the basis of Sextus' emphasis on 'laws and customs', that the sceptic will be a conservative figure who adheres to the *status quo*. There is in fact no reason why this must be so. Someone who was raised by radical critics of the existing order, and who subsequently became a sceptic, or someone who was just congenitally perverse, might well be broadly inclined to do the opposite of what his or her 'ancestral laws and customs' would dictate; there is nothing inconsistent with scepticism in this. In fact, if the evidence is to be trusted, it looks as if Pyrrho did live an extremely unconventional life (see esp. DL IX. 63, 66).

Some have felt discomfort with the fact that Sextus does not give any definite answer to the question of how the sceptic will behave when confronted with the tyrant's orders (see Annas 1986: 19–23, Nussbaum 1994: 313–15). But this, of course, is to look at the matter from the non-sceptic's point of view; one wants some assurance that the sceptic will do what is, by one's own lights, the right thing to do. Sextus quite reasonably has no interest in providing any such assurances. The sceptic will do whatever results from the various psychological forces within him, and there is no way to predict what this will be—hence 'perhaps' (*tuchon*, 166). Anyone who finds this disturbingly arbitrary or disturbingly inattentive to moral demands needs to go back to a much earlier stage in the Pyrrhonists' curriculum—or so Sextus would say.

The quotation from Timon in 164 is the second half of a hexameter line; since it is quoted nowhere else, we cannot tell from which poem it derives. If the context in which it is quoted here accurately reflects its original context, it described the appropriate attitude for the Pyrrhonist to adopt. And if so, the early Pyrrhonist attitude was at least verbally different from Sextus' own. For Sextus' point in this section, of course, is precisely that the sceptic is *not* 'empty of avoidance and choice'; scepticism is perfectly compatible with choice and avoidance—just not with choices and avoidances with which one engages 'intensely' (*suntonōs*, 112–13), and which purport to be based on beliefs to the effect that things are by nature a certain way. If being 'empty of avoidance and choice' (*aphugēs kai anairetos*) is indeed the attitude *recommended* by early Pyrrhonism, then either 'avoidance' and 'choice' must refer specifically to avoidances and choices which are based on commitments incompatible

with scepticism—in which case the difference from Sextus is only verbal—
or the early Pyrrhonists aspired to a level of passivity and indifference to
their surroundings far beyond that described by Sextus. Some of the
evidence relating to Pyrrho seems to suggest the latter interpretation; see
again DL IX. 63, 66, also 67, 68, Plut. *Prof. virt.* 82E–F, Cic. *Acad.* II.
130, and the lines from Timon quoted in 1 above.

167 serves as a conclusion. The second sentence is a conclusion to the
whole of the book so far (part A) and a transition to the remainder of it
(part B; see Introduction, sect. II, beginning). The first sentence is a
conclusion to the immediately preceding discussion. (Appropriately, the
quotation, *Od.* XII. 453, is the last line of Odysseus' account of his
travels, stretching over four books, to Alcinous and his court.) The
'lectures on the sceptical end' may be assumed to be a reference to the
portion of the lost book or books originally preceding *M* VII–XI which
corresponded with *PH* I. 25–30 (on this lost material see Janáček 1963,
Blomqvist 1974). I take it that the reference of 'these topics' (*toutōn*) is
the immediately preceding section, 162–6, on why the sceptic is not
reduced to inactivity or inconsistency; this subject is indeed dealt with
here in a somewhat sketchy and imprecise fashion, and would have
benefited, as we have seen, from a 'more precise' treatment somewhere
else. However, if this is right, the organization of the lost book or books
was at least slightly different from that of *PH* I. For in *PH* I the issue of
how the sceptic can act does not occur in the chapter on the sceptic's
'end' (25–30), but in the chapter immediately before that, on the sceptic's criterion (21–4). (The lost material on the 'end' did, however, also
cover at least some of the same ground as *PH* I. 25–30; cf. on 144 above.)
   Before leaving these chapters (i.e. this and the preceding one), it is
worth considering in general terms the relation between *M* XI and *PH*
III on the issues considered here. The discussion in *PH* III is drastically
shorter (only four numbered sections, 235–8); why is this? Striker (1990a:
104–5) says that it is because Sextus realized that the arguments in *M* XI
were full of difficulties, and so drastically reduced their scope in *PH* III.
Assuming that Striker is right about the order of the two works (on this,
see point 6a on 118), this is no doubt at least part of the answer. We have
seen that many of the arguments for the conclusion that the sceptic enjoys
a much greater degree of tranquillity, or happiness, than the dogmatist
are faulty; we have also seen that there are dangers in the very business
of *arguing* that tranquillity is the result of the sceptic's procedures—
dangers which it is not clear whether Sextus can ultimately escape (see

point 6c on 118). *PH* III offers at least some improvements on the arguments of *M* XI (see point 6a on 118, Appendix A on *M* XI. 119–24, *PH* III. 238). It also, as Striker remarks, adds at least a mention (though without any serious attempt at refutation) of the view held by some Stoics that genuinely good things cannot be lost once achieved (238)— a view which Sextus would have done well to consider at some point in *M* XI. But the most obvious difference is that a great deal of argumentation, much of it dubious, is omitted. *PH* III does not go to great lengths, then, to try to *show* that the sceptic is better off than the dogmatist; it just briefly sets out the comparative situations of the sceptic and the dogmatist, and then leaves the aspiring sceptic to *discover* the truth of this by experience. This may well be a better strategy. Aside from the dangers mentioned above, the arguments in *M* XI would have had to be very substantially improved before Sextus could hope that they might be generally persuasive. As we saw in the previous chapter, there are resources for some improvements here; but it is doubtful whether these extend far enough for the purpose. And in any case, the question who is the more free from suffering—the sceptic or the dogmatist—is a question more appropriately settled by experience than by abstract reasoning. A few incisive remarks, stimulating readers (or so it might be hoped) to check for themselves, could well be more effective than a long set of elaborate arguments.

However, the shortcomings of these two chapters of *M* XI are not the only reason why most of the material contained in them has not found its way into *PH* III. The other reason is much less embarrassing: viz. that, as we have seen, the two books put forward two different versions of Pyrrhonism. The sceptic of *M* XI asserts that nothing is by nature good or bad, and is willing to assert that things are good or bad *for certain people* or *in certain circumstances*; the notion of suspension of judgement and the Pyrrhonist stock phrase 'not more' are to be understood in a manner consistent with this. (See points 1–4 on 118.) All this is different from the model of Pyrrhonism presented by *PH*. As a result, many parts of *M* XI's discussion could not have been incorporated into *PH* III without inconsistency; this is not a matter of omitting *bad* arguments, but of omitting arguments which are out of keeping with *PH*'s revised form of scepticism. In some places *PH* III does inadvisedly retain such arguments from *M* XI (see Appendix A on *M* XI. 68–78, *PH* III. 179–82, and *M* XI. 79–89, *PH* III. 183–90); but in this case Sextus has resisted the temptation, and the end-product is therefore consistent, albeit much briefer.

CHAPTER VI (168–215)

This chapter and the next, on whether a 'skill relating to life' exists and whether, if it does exist, it can be taught, stand apart from the rest of the book. Prior to this point, the argument has been continuous and cumulative from the beginning. But the previous chapters contain no forward references to these last two chapters (110 mentions a 'science relating to life', but with no indication that the topic is going to be taken up in more detail later); and there is only one clear back-reference in these chapters to the previous material (185; 178 has been thought to contain another such reference, but this is uncertain—see below). This lack of explicit connection is in keeping with the distinctness of the subject-matter. One may even suspect, for this reason, that these chapters are drawn from a different source from the previous five chapters; though this matter probably does not admit of being settled conclusively, we shall see other reasons for suspecting the same thing. (In comparing and contrasting the two parts of the book, I shall follow the practice used in the Introduction; chs. I–V will be referred to as part A, chs. VI–VII as part B.)

The point of this chapter is simply to argue, in a number of different ways, against the notion of a 'skill relating to life'; the arguments begin after a brief section of transition and introduction (168–73). The first argument is to the effect that it makes no sense to follow any particular 'skill relating to life', because of the unresolvable disagreement among the proposed candidates for this title (173–7). Second, it is argued that all the candidates proposed by the dogmatists actually increase human distress rather than reducing it (178–80). There follows an argument against the Stoics specifically; they must admit that there is no such skill, because the existence of such a skill depends on the existence of the 'apprehensive impression', and there is no such thing (180–3). The next argument is again to the conclusion that the 'skill relating to life' does not exist; such a skill would have to be either directed towards the securing of goods distinct from itself, or it would have to be itself the good—but neither alternative, it is argued, is possible (184–7). Then we are told, in an argument again directed against the Stoics in particular, that such a skill is valueless, since it is not or cannot be used (188–96). After this it is argued that practical wisdom (*phronēsis*), the Stoics' candidate for this skill, cannot be one, since it does not give rise to any distinctive action (197–209). The final argument purports to demonstrate that practical wisdom cannot be the 'skill relating to life', since it does not benefit anyone, even those who possess it (210–15).

The heavy concentration on specifically Stoic views is due to the fact that it was the Stoics who were most serious, and most explicit, in employing the notion of a 'skill relating to life' (indeed, the term itself seems to be theirs); for more on this, see on 168–73 below. It will be noticed that some of these arguments are to the conclusion that such a skill does not *exist*, while others are to the conclusion that it could not be *adopted* or would be of no *use*. But in light of the last argument just listed, it is clear that Sextus would regard the latter type of argument as really a species of the former; any alleged 'skill relating to life' which is not beneficial to at least some people cannot qualify as genuine. Thus, despite initial impressions, the title does properly cover the entire chapter.

Some points of translation which apply throughout part B (and indeed the whole book): *Phronēsis* is translated 'practical wisdom', and the corresponding adjective *phronimos* is translated 'wise' or, when appropriate, 'wise person'. *Sophos* is translated 'sage' whenever it occurs in a Stoic context (i.e. everywhere except 21—'the wise (*sophon*) Epicurus'—and the verse quotation in 172—'what wisdom' (*ti sophon*)); with the exception of that in 66, these occurrences are solely in the present chapter. Sextus appears to use *sophos* and *phronimos* more or less interchangeably in this chapter; several times he switches very rapidly between *sophos* and *phronimos* or *phronēsis*—see esp. 199, also 201, 206, 210, 215. This is legitimate in that, in Stoic theory, all and only *sophoi* are *phronimoi*; this follows from the interdependence of the virtues and of virtue and knowledge. But in Stoicism *sophos* is the broader term, covering not just knowledge of what to do; the Stoic sage is said in quite general terms to have knowledge of the true (see e.g. *M* VII. 38–45, esp. 42, 44)—which would include, incidentally, the forms of knowledge which constitute all of the virtues, not just the virtue of practical wisdom.

It must be admitted that part B is in some ways of less interest than part A. Of course, many of the individual arguments are of intrinsic interest, and many passages are of considerable doxographical value. However, the distinctive Pyrrhonist position which we have seen developed in part A is almost entirely off-stage for the rest of the book. Sextus argues against positions to which the dogmatists are committed, but devotes little or no attention to elucidating the spirit in which he is doing so, or, more generally, to questions about what it is like to think and act as a sceptic. It is, on the other hand, not quite fair of Annas (1993: 356 n. 11 (cf. 396 n. 34)) to complain that part B fails to include any detailed discussion of specific ethical theories, and that 'a golden opportunity to discuss central ethical issues is frittered away in trivialities'. If the notion of a 'skill relating to life' is fundamentally flawed, Sextus is under no obligation to discuss the details of what, according to the Stoics or others, that skill might consist in; and if his arguments succeed in showing that this notion is fundamentally flawed, they are not, for his purposes, trivial. Whether or not they do succeed is another question; but there is at any rate no inherent problem with his approach. For Sextus' preference for general arguments rather than specific ones, see *M* VII. 262, VIII. 337a–338, IX. 1–2 (III. 18), with Caizzi 1992*b*: 287–92.

168–73: Transition and introduction

[Textual points:

(a) Along with Lloyd-Jones and Parsons (1983: 391), I adopt Usener's conjecture *elpidodōtai*, 'givers of hope', in the first quotation from Timon (171); the MSS read *epidolōtai* (printed and obelized by Mutschmann) or *epidolotai*. Fabricius, followed by Bekker and Bury, read *aipudolōtai*, 'utter tricksters' (cf. Hes. *Works and Days* 83). But this seems to have less point in context; 'givers of hope' connects this fragment more closely with Sextus' immediately preceding remarks, and it is not to Sextus' purpose to suggest (or to quote a line of Timon which suggested) that the dogmatists are *intentionally* leading impressionable youths to destruction.

(b) I follow Mutschmann's text in the second quotation from Timon (172). The only significant change from the MSS is *matēn* for *mathein* in l. 4. Lloyd-Jones and Parsons propose several other changes, but for what seem to me insufficient reasons.]

In this section Sextus introduces the dogmatists' pretensions to possess a 'skill relating to life', and indicates that he is going to demolish these pretensions. The transitional sentence which forms most of 168 is not as informative as one might like about the motivation for embarking on this new topic. If the topic of good and bad things—'whose difficulties', as Sextus said just before (167), 'stretch over almost the entire subject of ethics'—has already been covered, and if the dogmatists' position has already been shown to be both mistaken and destructive to those who believe it, what is the point of devoting a separate discussion to the notion of a 'skill relating to life'? This looks like an example of Sextus' not uncommon practice of offering additional specific arguments for some conclusion, even though this conclusion can already be seen to follow from earlier arguments on a distinct or a more general topic; see 216 below, also e.g. *PH* II. 134, 193–4, I. 62, 78, and see Spinelli 1995: 342 on the phrase 'in a parallel way' (*ek parallēlou*). The parallel passage of *PH* III is closer to being explicit that this is the purpose; it opens by saying 'It is clear from what has been said before that neither could there be any skill relating to life' (239), and briefly indicating why this is so, but then goes on to give specific arguments for this very conclusion. By contrast, *M* XI's 'there is nothing to prevent us' gives us very little idea of why we should pursue this issue. Sextus' inadequate explanation of the connection between this material and that which has preceded again suggests (see above) that he has united two originally unrelated discussions—in other words, that part B derives from a different source from part A. In any case, the more polished transition in *PH* III suggests that it, and not *M* XI, is the later, revised version.

The term 'skill relating to life' (*technē peri ton bion*) is in origin Stoic, as might be guessed from Sextus' comment (170) that the Stoics 'say straight out' (*antikrus phasi*) that practical wisdom is a skill relating to life (see Stob. II. 66, 19–67, 2, Cic. *Fin.* IV. 16). Virtue is also referred to by the Stoics as a skill—*Anecdota graeca Paris.* I. 171 (Cramer) (= *SVF* III p. 51), Stob. II. 62, 15–20, Alexander, *Mantissa* 159, 34. A skill (*technē*) is defined, in turn, by the Stoics as a 'system made up of apprehensions organized together' (*sustēma ek katalēpseōn suggegumnasmenōn*) and directed towards some useful end ([Galen], *Def. med.* XIX. 350; cf. *Scholia in Dionys. Thrac.* 108, 31–3 (= *SVF* II. 94), and 182 below), or alternatively as a 'system made up of principles (*theōrēmatōn*) organized together' (*Anecd. gr. Paris.* I. 171). We are told by Olympiodorus (*In Pl. Gorg.* 12, 1 (= *LS* 42A)) that the first definition was devised by Zeno; the same passage also ascribes variant definitions to Cleanthes and Chrysippus, but these are less informative than, and not in conflict with, those just cited. On skills as composed of 'principles', see again Stob. II. 62, 15–20; cf. DL VII. 125. A skill, then, is a systematic and articulable practical body of knowledge. And a skill relating to life is a systematic and articulable body of knowledge which is directed towards the proper or effective living of life in general.

According to Sextus, it is practical wisdom (*phronēsis*) specifically, rather than any of the other virtues, which is designated by the Stoics as the 'skill relating to life'. This seems to be confirmed by Stob. II. 66, 15–67, 2 (though there may be a difficulty with the text; see LS 61G, vol. II), and is more generally in keeping with the definition of practical wisdom as 'the science (*epistēmē*) of things which are good and bad and neither' (170; cf. DL VII. 92) and with the statements in Stobaeus that practical wisdom is concerned with actions which are proper (*kathēkonta*,

II. 60, 12) and with 'considering and doing what should be done' (II. 63, 11–12). Though practical wisdom, for the Stoics, is only one of four central virtues, all of which are species of *epistēmē* (on this, see on 90–5 above), the distinctive job of practical wisdom is nevertheless that of determining what one should or should not do, in any circumstances. (For discussion of the relations among the virtues and the senses in which, for the Stoics, they are a unity, see Ioppolo 1980: ch. 8, Schofield 1984, Annas 1993: 79–84.) In this respect it resembles practical wisdom as conceived by Aristotle (*NE* VI. 1140a25–8); however, Aristotle (at least on most interpretations of his ethical theory) would resist the notion implicit in the Stoics' use of the term *technē*, and also the term *epistēmē*, in this connection, that practical wisdom can be systematized. (He actually denies both that practical wisdom is a *technē* (1140b24–5) and that it is *epistēmē* (1142a23–4), but for other reasons.) It is unfortunate that we are not told specifically how the Stoics conceived of the systematic character of practical wisdom. But it is tempting to link this with their strong interest in ethical rules, on which see Mitsis 1993 and Annas 1993: ch. 2, sect. 4. We should not, however, imagine the Stoic ethical 'system' as having a strictly algorithmic or deductive character; ethical rules, however useful, were not exceptionless in Stoicism, and the wise person's insight was always required to guarantee correct choices. This is well discussed in Vander Waerdt 1994; and see below on 190–4, on the (very occasional) acceptability of even incest and cannibalism.

On the Stoics' conception of *technē* more generally, its links with *epistēmē*, and contrasts with Aristotle in these respects, see also Isnardi Parente 1966: 287–307; on their motivations for employing the notion of *technē* in connection with that of virtue, and the difficulties they faced in doing so, see Striker 1991: sect. 3. The connections between virtue and both knowledge and skill were a major preoccupation of Socrates, and the Stoics would undoubtedly have regarded their claims here as developments of Socratic ideas; on this see Striker 1994, and on the Stoics' admiration for, and identification with, Socrates in general, see Long 1988.

Sextus also includes Epicurus among those who 'promise to impart a certain skill relating to life' (168). There is no evidence that Epicurus or his followers actually used this term (Cic. *Fin.* I. 72, which talks of Epicurus' neglect of the specialized arts in favour of the much more important 'art of living', does not purport to be quoting or even paraphrasing any Epicurean's actual words); their application of the term *technē* seems to be restricted to the things which would normally be regarded as skills. However, the characterization of philosophy attributed to Epicurus in 169 is consistent with *Letter to Menoeceus* X. 122; note also that *dialogismos*, 'debate', appears to be an Epicurean term of art (see Sedley 1973: 13). The Epicureans are said to have defined a skill much more loosely than the Stoics, as 'a method achieving what is useful in life' (*Scholia in Dionys. Thrac.* 108, 27–9 (= Usener 1887, fr. 227b)); on this definition philosophy would certainly seem to qualify as a skill. It is actually not clear whether the Epicureans, or all Epicureans, even insisted on a skill's being useful; Philodemus offers a definition of a skill in which usefulness is not a requirement (*Rhet.* 2, *P Herc.* 1674 col. XXXVIII, p. 123, 2–15 Longo)—on this, see Blank 1995. Still, Philodemus' definition does not seem to contain any additional feature which would rule out philosophy's being a skill. Thus, although the Epicureans did not label philosophy a 'skill relating to life', it does not look as if they would have had any theoretical reason for objecting to that label. However, as was mentioned earlier, the Epicureans are really not Sextus' main interest in this chapter; most of the arguments which follow have the Stoics as the main targets, and several of them can *only* be understood as directed against the Stoics.

By Cicero's time, the idea that philosophy is a 'skill relating to life' appears to be regarded as a commonplace (see *Fin.* I. 72, III. 4; and cf. Apuleius, *Dog. Plat.* II. 9. 234, where Plato is said to regard justice as a skill relating to life). But the sceptics themselves do not go along with this tendency, avoiding any suggestion that their argumentative procedures are a *technē*; for this, they would no doubt say, would immediately smack too much of dogmatism. The beneficial effects of sceptical argument are said to occur, instead, 'by chance' (*tuchikōs*, *PH* I. 29). On this see Flückiger 1994 and point 6c on 118 above. Sextus also, of course, conducts a lengthy attack on the more specialized *technai* in *M* I–VI.

The claims that only the sage is rich and that only the sage is beautiful, which Sextus presents as a corollary of the thesis that practical wisdom is a skill relating to life (170), are among what were known as the Stoic 'paradoxes' (and were so called by the Stoics themselves—Cic. *Paradox. Sto.* 4). These are Stoic positions which sound wildly counterintuitive, but which can be argued to follow from certain central Stoic doctrines. The first claim is one of those addressed in Cicero's work actually entitled *Paradoxa Stoicorum* (42–52), but both are widely reported elsewhere; see e.g. Cic. *Acad.* II. 136, *Fin.* III. 75, Stob. II. 101, 14–20, Alexander, *In Ar. Top.* 147, 16–20, 134, 13–16. The Stoic paradoxes generally involve stretching or transforming to some degree the usual senses of their central terms; this is clearly true in the present cases (as is commented upon in both the passages just cited from Alexander), where partial redefinitions of the terms 'rich' and 'beautiful'—which are not, however, wholly divorced from their normal employment—force us to reconsider what things are really worth valuing. But in other cases, such as the first of Cicero's *Paradoxa Stoicorum* (6–15), 'only what is fine is good', the 'paradox' resides less in the idiosyncratic use of terms than in the arresting character of the Stoic doctrine itself.

There is one minor confusion. Sextus has the Stoics saying that those who have achieved the 'skill relating to life' are 'the only ones who are beautiful, the only ones who are rich, the only ones who are sages'; the text then goes on to *argue* that these people are the only ones who are rich and beautiful, but to *assume* that they are sages. The latter assumption is in no way surprising; what is surprising is that 'sages' should initially have been grouped with 'rich' and 'beautiful', as if this was something which needed discussing. For this reason Heintz (1932: 257–8) suggested adding *epeiper* before the final phrase of that sentence, yielding the sense '*since they are* the only ones who are sages'. But in the absence of any disagreements or other difficulties in the MSS, it seems preferable to regard this as a defect in the train of thought—of a type of which there is unfortunately no shortage in *M* XI—rather than as an error in the transmission of the text.

A more serious difficulty occurs in one of the syllogisms of which the paradoxes are the conclusions. There is no problem with the first syllogism; but the idea that only the sage is 'worthy of love' (*axieraston*), which is crucial to the second syllogism, is contradicted by other evidence about Stoic views on love. (Bury translates this word 'lover of the valuable'—cf. Russo. But this misses the point of the argument, which is clearly that the beautiful person is regarded by common sense as justifiably *inspiring* love.) Persons who are 'worthy of love' are those with whom the sage will be in love, but these are not themselves sages; rather, they are young persons with a strong *potential* for developing virtue (see DL VII. 129(–30), Plut. *Comm. not.* 1073B, Stob. II. 115, 1–4; cf. Stob. II. 66, 6–8, 11–13, and for discussion see Schofield 1991: 28–35, 112–14). As a result, Plutarch (polemically but not without justification) actually attributes to the Stoics the view that the sage is *not* 'worthy of love' (*Comm. not.* 1073A). Sextus or his source may be irresponsibly foisting on the Stoics an argument which they would unanimously have rejected (this is the view of Schofield (1991: 113)). But this syllogism may, alternatively, reflect a variant Stoic view, not otherwise preserved, which attempted better to justify the paradoxical conclusion; as Schofield remarks, it is difficult both to claim that only sages are beautiful and to do justice—as the texts just cited show that the standard Stoic view attempted to do—to the role which beauty (the beauty of those who are not, or not yet, sages) plays in inspiring love.

Sextus' initial response (171) to the claim that philosophy can supply a 'skill relating to life' is uncompromisingly negative; such claims are 'in no way true', for reasons which 'we can learn' by way of the arguments to follow (173). The remainder of the work contains little, if anything, to make one doubt that this is Sextus' own considered verdict. One set of arguments in this chapter can be read as *ad hominem*, as showing the Stoics what follows from their own views (see on 180–3 below); but the rest give every appearance of being endorsed by Sextus himself. This raises the question of whether Sextus should be accused of violating his own scepticism in this portion of the book. One might try to rescue him by suggesting that he means his negative arguments to be juxtaposed with the dogmatists' own positive arguments, leading precisely to *suspension of judgement* on the question as to whether a skill relating to life exists or can be taught. Sextus often clearly does argue in this fashion in the other books of *M* VII–XI; see *M* VII. 443, VIII. 298, 476–7, IX. 137, 191–2, X. 168 for explicit references to this approach. But he gives absolutely no indication that this is the spirit in which he is offering these arguments in *M* XI; and the flat declaration, never subsequently qualified, with which he opens the entire sequence of arguments in part B—that what the dogmatists say is false—makes this interpretation very difficult to credit. (On the differences between *M* VII–X and *M* XI, see further Introduction, sect. V.)

But whether Sextus has violated the sceptical outlook depends, of course, on what the sceptical outlook is taken to be; and another possibility is that *M* XI's distinctive form of scepticism does, after all, allow Sextus to endorse the negative conclusions in part B, just as it allowed him, in part A, to endorse the conclusion that nothing is good or bad by nature. What suspension of judgement appeared to rule out, in the earlier portion of *M* XI, was any attempt at specifying how things are by nature—not the advancing of any statements whatever as true or false (see point 4 on 118). It is by no means clear that the denial that there is any skill relating to life, or that even if there were it could be taught, constitutes a violation of suspension of judgement as *M* XI understands that notion; for it does not look as if any statement of the form 'X is by

nature F' follows from these denials. Indeed, the whole question of how
things are by nature seems quite remote from the discussion in part B;
the very term 'by nature' (*phusei*) occurs only three times in the rest of
the book (twice in 241, once in 248), and in contexts which clearly
commit Sextus to nothing anti-sceptical. So in issuing his negative conclusions in these chapters, Sextus is not in any obvious conflict with the
variety of scepticism we have already found developed in part A. It is
notable that the parallel portion of *PH* III does make some attempt to
reconcile these arguments with what we have seen to be the more de-
manding form of scepticism adopted in that book; see esp. 241 ('there
will not be any skill relating to life *as far as what they* [i.e. the dogmatists]
say is concerned'—i.e. they fail to prove that there is such a skill), 249
('neither *can anyone affirm that* it [i.e. the skill] exists'), 278 ('the skill
relating to life is *perhaps* non-existent').

It looks, then, as if Sextus' apparent endorsement of almost all the
arguments in part B is at least prima facie defensible. It is unfortunate,
however, that Sextus gives very little indication that he has devoted
attention to the issue (cf. introductory remarks to this chapter); whatever
interpretation we offer, it cannot be said clearly to capture his intentions,
but is better understood as an account of what he *could* say if pressed on
the question raised above.

The quotations from Timon in 171–2, which Sextus introduces as graphic
portrayals of the havoc wrought by the dogmatists' unfulfillable promises, appear in no other ancient source; we are wholly dependent on
Sextus' account of their original context. Diels (1901: 201–2) places them
in the *Lampoons (Silloi)*; unless Timon wrote another poem in hexameters
of which we know nothing, this must be correct. For the numerous
Homeric parallels in the second, longer quotation, see Diels 1901: 202,
Lloyd-Jones and Parsons 1983: 392; many of these Homeric passages are
from Book V of the *Odyssey*, where Odysseus endures a storm at sea and
shipwreck after escaping from Calypso's island. As Diels (1901: 202)
points out, there is no contradiction in the second quotation between ll.
5–6 and ll. 7–8. The speaker is bemoaning his *descent* from a situation of
relative comfort into 'wretched strife and poverty'; the people who are
'three and four times blessed' are those who never had any resources to
squander in the first place. If Sextus is reporting the context accurately,
the 'wretched strife and poverty' itself probably symbolizes the speaker's
dashed hopes for achieving the good life through philosophy. This is in
any case suggested by the references just before to the speaker's lack of

wisdom and sense, and by the remark '*As to my mind* I am a beggar' (*ptōchos men phrenas eimi*); note also that the words translated 'at leisure' (*eni scholēi*) might also (or instead?) be translated 'at school'.

These are the last quotations from Timon in the book. This accords with the fact that the quotations from Timon in *M* XI all have to do with desirable or undesirable attitudes or ways of life (cf. on 1–2 above); this general topic has been a major focus of attention so far, but is largely lost in the somewhat abstract and rarefied arguments which constitute part B.

173–7: First argument against the 'skill relating to life'

[Textual point:

I follow Mutschmann's text throughout 175, reading *ison to*—as do all the MSS except one, which reads *ison tōi*—and otherwise leaving the MSS unchanged. A number of conjectures have been offered to improve the text; but the sense is quite acceptable as it stands. The *ētoi*, with nothing answering it until *leipetai* two sentences later, is certainly clumsy; but it is far from unintelligible.

The sentence beginning *akolouthei*, in particular, has been the subject of conjectures; the matter is discussed by Heintz (1932: 258–9). However, the reading *ison to* of most MSS (as opposed to *ison tōi*), which Heintz rejects, is quite intelligible, with *ison* adverbial and the articular infinitive *to pasais thelein hepesthai* the subject of *akolouthei*—'for one's being willing to follow all of them is equally a consequence'. That is, suppose that one has reason to follow some given skill S, which is 'any one whatsoever' (i.e. arbitrarily selected); it is a consequence that one might just as well follow some skill *other* than S, and this consequence holds 'equally' for *all* the skills other than S. (Strictly speaking, then, the text should say 'one's being willing to follow all the others'; but this can easily be understood as a minor oversight—compare the careless but very common use of 'all' for 'all the others' in modern English.) *Why* does this consequence hold? The answer is given in the next sentence; what reason could there possibly be for choosing any one skill (again, assuming that the selection is arbitrary) over any other? It is true that this means that the verb *akolouthein* is used in this passage both of adopting or 'following' a certain skill and of something's 'following' as a logical consequence. *Pace* Heintz, this point seems to me to carry no weight whatever; both usages are common, and the shift between the two senses presents no difficulty in comprehension.]

The argument may be summarized as follows:

1. There are many different alleged 'skills relating to life' offered by the various philosophical schools. One might adopt all of them or one of them or none of them (173).

2. One cannot adopt all of them, since they offer incompatible prescriptions (174).

3. If one is to follow just one, which one is it to be? It might be either any arbitrarily selected one or one which there is some reason for preferring over the others (175).

4. If it is any arbitrarily selected one ('any one whatsoever'), one might just as well adopt all of them; for, by hypothesis, there is no reason for preferring one over the others (175). (The adoption of all of them has, however, already been dismissed; this point is implied rather than stated. For further details on this stage of the argument, see textual point above.)

5. One must therefore follow one which there is some reason for preferring over the others ('the one which has been preferred'). But what could be the basis for this preference? Either the skill itself or some other skill (176).

6. But the skill itself cannot provide the basis for preferring it to other skills; for again, this reasoning would equally allow every skill to count as justifiably preferred (176).

7. But if it is judged preferable by some other skill, the same questions will arise about the credentials of this second skill (177).

8. Hence one cannot reasonably follow either all these skills or just one; so one must follow none (177).

This argument is of a multiply dilemmatic form, which is very common in Sextus; previous examples in this book have been the arguments at 68–78, 79–89, 90–5. Most of it presents few difficulties (at least, if I am right about the text; see textual point above). One might object that, strictly speaking, the possibility of adopting *many* skills (less than all, but more than one) should have been considered; but the objection to this would obviously have been the same as to the alternative of adopting all of them (step 2). One might also say that it is not clear why what judges a certain skill to be preferable to the others, according to the final stage of the argument (step 7), should have to be another *skill*; why should this role not be filled by some form of reasoning or experience which is not itself a skill? But this issue, too, is unimportant; for it is clear that, whatever the nature of the faculty which is thought of as making this judgement, Sextus will raise the very same questions about its credentials; its verdict will be in disagreement with those proposed by other second-order skills or faculties in favour of other first-order skills, and so it will itself be in need of some warrant for judging its verdicts preferable.

Step 7 is, however, significantly incomplete as stated. No reason is given why some third-order skill could not actually do the job of judging the second-order skill under consideration trustworthy in selecting some particular first-order skill. Sextus is, of course, assuming that the task of certifying some skill as trustworthy can never be discharged—that the process of seeking a method for resolving a disagreement, only to find that this method is itself one of many possible conflicting methods, will go on indefinitely. This assumption would certainly need to be justified. However, it is quite possible that, if asked, Sextus would have been able to go at least a considerable distance towards providing the needed justification. For this style of argument is closely related to that of the Five Modes, ascribed by Sextus to the 'later sceptics' (*PH* I. 164–9) and by Diogenes to the otherwise virtually unknown Agrippa (IX. 88; cf. 106, the only other mention of his name); and the Five Modes may fairly be regarded as one of the Pyrrhonian sceptic's most powerful tools. On the Five Modes and their philosophical strengths and weaknesses, see Barnes 1990*c*.

177 contains the only occurrence of the word *kritērion* in the book, apart from a back-reference to a work entitled *On the Criterion* (232), which is presumably *M* VII, a book devoted exclusively to the question of whether there is any criterion of truth. On Sextus' treatment of the criterion, see Brunschwig 1988; on the criterion in Hellenistic philosophy generally, see Striker 1974, 1990*b*. Elsewhere in Sextus the word appears not uncommonly in contexts like the present one, where the argument centres around unresolvable disagreement and other related devices of the kind which figure in the Five Modes (see e.g. *PH* I. 114–17, II. 88–9, III. 34–6, *M* VIII. 26–9, 118–22). For this reason it is not surprising that the word should not have appeared in *M* XI before now. For, though part A certainly contained much emphasis on ethical disagreement, no arguments before this one were based on the *unresolvability* of this disagreement. (For another passage featuring unresolvable disagreement in part B, see 229–30.) In the central arguments for the conclusion that nothing is good or bad by nature, it was the very *existence* of disagreement, rather than the lack of any criterion for settling it, which was the main issue (see above on 68–95).

The willingness to use arguments from unresolvable disagreement might perhaps be seen as another indication that part B is drawn from a source different from that of part A. For one might suppose that these arguments became central to Pyrrhonism not during the phase dominated by Aenesidemus (with which the earlier chapters of *M* XI appear to be strongly associated—see point 3 on 118 above and Introduction, sect. III), but only during the later, Agrippan phase. However, this line of thought is no more than speculative. The appropriateness of arguments from unresolvable disagreement may vary with the subject-matter; certainly there is nothing inconsistent in using such an argument in this context, but arguing in a quite different fashion about the good, the bad, and the indifferent (see Introduction, sect. V, esp. n. 55 and accompanying text; cf. on 205 below). It is also probable that the sceptics' *use* of arguments from unresolvable disagreement, circularity, etc. considerably predated their schematization by Agrippa.

For comparison of 173–7 and the parallel passages at *PH* III. 182, 239, see Appendix A.

178–80: Second argument against the 'skill relating to life'

Point of translation:

'Method' in 178, 179 is a translation of *agōgē*. This word can refer to a way of life and also to a method of arguing. In this case both nuances seem to be present; the 'methods' in question are of course methods of living, but methods of living which are themselves certified by philosophical argument (cf. 257 with Comm.).

This argument contributes little to Sextus' overall purpose. The claim is that no skill relating to life can do other than increase human misery, since the effect of all such skills is to intensify already existing deleterious urges. This claim is wholly dependent on the arguments in ch. IV which maintained that love of wealth, pleasure, or glory (the same examples were employed) is a cause of unhappiness, whether or not one achieves the object of one's craving—see especially 125–30; without the amplification provided by these earlier arguments, the remarks here have the status of bare assertions. But there are further difficulties in connecting these remarks with the aims of the present chapter. First, this argument has nothing specifically to do with the dogmatists' pretensions to have a *skill* for regulating one's life; it is a much more general argument (as were the arguments in ch. IV) about the bad effects of dogmatism.

Second, as we observed in discussing ch. IV, the focus on the examples of wealth, pleasure, and glory largely misrepresents the character of dogmatic conceptions of the good; dogmatists would entirely agree with Sextus that the right approach is not to attempt to *satisfy* people's desires for these things—thereby only intensifying these desires—but to extirpate or, at the very least, to moderate and redirect them. Sextus seems to recognize that there is a problem here; for he takes the trouble to connect the various 'passions' he mentions with named dogmatic philosophies. But the effort is very unconvincing. It is true that wealth and glory would qualify as necessary external goods in Aristotle's ethics (see e.g. *NE* I. 8, X. 8). But these goods are strictly subordinate to the good of virtuous activity; and the virtues of which such activity is the exercise ensure that one's attitude towards wealth and glory is appropriately subdued. To suggest that 'the lover of wealth or the lover of glory has his desire kindled all the more by the Peripatetic philosophy' (179) is frankly absurd. Still more absurd is the idea that the Stoic pursuit of virtue will render yet more obsessive a person's 'love of glory'; virtue, in the Stoic conception, simply has nothing to do with external rewards and reputation. Even the claim that 'the lover of pleasure is further inflamed by Epicurus' method' (179) wilfully misconstrues the Epicurean conception of pleasure; again, pleasure of the 'inflamed' variety is precisely what the Epicurean will avoid (see e.g. *Letter to Menoeceus* X. 131–2). Finally, of course, to suggest that '*every person* is in the grip of a certain passion' (178)—which dogmatic philosophies will then only feed to a frenzy—is exaggerated and implausible. In fact, Aristotle remarks that it is only people who are already *beyond* the youthful, passionate period of their lives (which some people never outgrow) who can profitably study ethics (*NE* I. 1095a4–11).

The clear connection between this passage and the arguments in ch. IV recalls the question of the relation between part B and part A. It has been suggested above that Sextus may here be drawing on a different source from that which he used in part A, thereby uniting two originally separate discussions. This is not disproved by the present passage. First, it is not impossible that the same general argument could have appeared in two different sources. But even if one rejects that hypothesis, it is still possible that there were two different sources, but that Sextus himself added the present passage to the original material, drawing on the arguments he had already written up in ch. IV. As we have seen, this argument does not really belong in this context; it is neither helpful nor relevant. In addition, the linking sentence which begins 178 is awkward, and may well be an imperfect attempt to attach originally extraneous material. What are 'the reasons mentioned before'? Bury and Russo take this to be a reference back to the arguments in ch. IV, and this may be correct. But ch. IV never used the term 'skill relating to life'. More importantly, the reason 'which will be stated as the argument moves forward' (i.e. 179–80 itself) will then be simply a truncated version of the *same* arguments which are being referred back to, rather than a separate reason, as the text suggests. The other alternative is that 'the reasons mentioned before' refers to the immediately preceding argument (173–7); yet this argument did not purport to demonstrate that reliance on a single skill relating to life results in *unhappiness*. The attempt to integrate this passage into the surrounding material, then, is somewhat inept; this strengthens the possibility that it was added in a fit of mis-guided enthusiasm to a text in which it originally had no place. See also on 180–3, beginning.

PH III has no passage corresponding to this one; if I am right that *PH* III is later, Sextus will have thought better of this enthusiasm and taken the passage out again. This would make sense not only because of the difficulties discussed above, but also because *PH* III does not contain the arguments which appear in ch. IV of *M* XI, on which the present passage depends.

180–3: Third argument against the 'skill relating to life'

Points of translation and text:

(a) Various translations are current for the Stoic technical term *katalēptikē phantasia*, which I have rendered 'apprehensive impression'. 'Appear-ance' and 'presentation' are common for *phantasia*, and 'cognitive' is common for *katalēptikē*. 'Impression', though etymologically less close than 'appearance', seems to me best to capture the character of the Stoic concept (here I am agreeing with LS I. 239). 'Apprehensive', on the other hand, seems to me preferable on etymological grounds. It preserves a link with the original sense of the root, that of literal grasping (which has resonance for the Stoics—see e.g. Cic. *Acad.* II. 145); it also pre-serves the link with *katalambanein*, 'apprehend' (see e.g. 38 above).

[(b) Heintz (1932: 259–60) suggests adding *te* in the first sentence of 183—*hē ⟨te⟩ katalēptikē phantasia krinetai*, etc.—on the basis of numer-ous parallel passages. This may well be correct; however, the sense is unaffected.]

In this section Sextus turns his attention to Stoic views in particular, and argues that if one is to base one's conclusions on what the Stoics say, one should conclude that there is no such thing as a skill relating to life, or at least that one cannot possess it. Unlike the rest of the arguments in this chapter, then, these arguments need not be seen as endorsed by Sextus himself; they merely claim to demonstrate what the Stoics are committed to (cf. on 171–3 above). (Sextus is not, however, as clear as he might be about this orientation; 'not even in this case will *we* accept it' (180) makes it look as if the argument is *not* simply showing us what must be conceded by the Stoics.) Two comments are worth making about the opening sentence (180). (a) This section is here presented as proceeding on the assumption that a previous argument was faulty; we are to assume, contrary to previous results, that there *is* a single skill relating to life. This is a common enough sceptical strategy. But in this case it is a misrepresentation; for the effect of the following argument is that, at least on the Stoics' showing, there is *no* skill relating to life. The words 'not even in this case will we accept it', in this very sentence, already contradict 'even if we concede that . . .'. Sextus should instead have said 'But even if it is agreed that the Stoic view of the skill relating to life is superior to all the others', or something of the kind. (b) The reason given for not accepting the Stoics' account of the skill relating to life is that it produces 'many and varied disasters'. Again, this misrepresents the argument; the point is instead that the skill relating to life does not exist, and the considerations offered in favour of that point have nothing to do with disasters. This characterization would apply better to the immediately preceding argument than to the present one. If I was right to speculate that this last argument was added by Sextus himself to the material appearing in his source (see the final paragraph on the previous section), the point about 'many and varied disasters' is probably also an addition by Sextus; in the desire to effect a smooth transition between the two arguments, he misleadingly portrays them as having more in common than they actually have. (Note also that 'even if we concede that there is one skill relating to life, and this one is agreed upon' is naturally understood as referring back to the argument at 173–7—a further reason for thinking that 178–80 is an insertion into the original material.)

In both respects the parallel passage of *PH* III (240) is much more successful. Here Sextus says 'However, even if *they were all to say*' that there is a single such skill (i.e. even if the previous argument from disagreement did not apply), such as the Stoic one, which 'seems to be more impressive than the others', none the less 'absurdities will follow' (absurdities which bar us—or more precisely, bar the dogmatists—from accepting that there is any such thing). This avoids the difficulties in both (a) and (b) above. Sextus does not involve himself in any conflict between 'conceding' and 'not accepting' the same proposition; and he does not say anything inappropriate about 'disasters'. It is hard to imagine that Sextus could have first written the sentence in *PH*—which does the job of transition very nicely—and then, in *revising PH*, produced the garbled sentence in *M* XI. The opposite hypothesis, that the sentence in *PH* is a revision of the one in *M* XI, seems vastly more plausible.

Most of this section centres around the concept of the 'apprehensive impression' (*phantasia kataleptike*). There are three different arguments:

1. To possess the Stoic skill relating to life would require that one be a sage; but the Stoics are *not* sages. Hence they cannot possess the Stoic skill relating to life; hence they also cannot teach it to non-Stoics (181).

2. Given the Stoics' definition of a skill, in order for there to be any skill, there must be 'apprehensive impressions'. But there are no such impressions; hence there are no skills, and so specifically there is no skill relating to life (181–2).

3. By the Stoics' own account of the 'apprehensive impression', such impressions are 'unknown'—i.e. one cannot know, of any given impression, whether or not it is 'apprehensive'; it follows that there can be no skills (183).

The claim in argument 1 that the Stoics are not sages is not merely a piece of sceptical sarcasm. It was the Stoics' own contention that the sage had never existed, or was at any rate extraordinarily rare (Plut. *Comm. not.* 1076B, Sextus, *M* VII. 432, IX. 133, Diogenianus in Eusebius, *Praep. evang.* VI. 8. 13 (= *SVF* III p. 167)), and their own admission that they themselves were not sages (Plut. *Sto. rep.* 1048E, Sextus, *M* VII. 433). The latter admission is all that Sextus uses here; he is working on the reasonable assumption that the Stoic skill could originate only among Stoics, and hence that if the Stoics themselves do not possess it, neither can anyone else. The Stoics' exceptionally high standards for wisdom or virtue, coupled with their insistence that there is nothing between wisdom or virtue and folly or vice (DL VII. 127, Plut. *Comm. not.* 1063A–B), make them tempting targets for arguments like this one. In reply, they might stress the possibility of *progress towards* wisdom and virtue; 'progress' (*prokope*) is mentioned in both the passages just cited (see also Stob. V. 906, 18–907, 5). But it is not clear how helpful this would be in responding to Sextus' allegation.

On the definition of a skill on which argument 2 relies—a 'system made up of apprehensions'—see on 168–70 above. Argument 2 is simple in form; the crucial claim is that there is no such thing as an 'apprehensive impression' (*kataleptikē phantasia*). The statement 'neither is every impression apprehensive . . . nor is any one of them' recalls the argumentative strategy of 173–7 above; but in this case the device is largely decorative. For it is the second half of the claim which has by far the greater weight; the first half would be conceded on all sides, and in any case follows from the second half. The claim that '*according to them*, no skill can be put together' is not, of course, meant as a literal summary of what the Stoics said; it is, rather, a statement of what Sextus thinks they are compelled to say. (For this usage of 'according to', cf. on 8–14 above.) The conclusion that there is no skill relating to life should also apply only 'according to them'. Again, Sextus does not really make this clear; see above on 180, and compare the more circumspect *PH* III. 241.

The 'apprehensive impression' is one of the central concepts of Stoic epistemology. There are, for the Stoics, both sensory and non-sensory impressions (*phantasiai*), and impressions are propositional in character; whenever, in English, one could speak of having an impression that P, it will be appropriate to speak of having a *phantasia* that P. An apprehensive impression is an impression which is in some sense guaranteed to be correct about its subject-matter; such impressions can thus serve as a criterion of truth—i.e. as a method of distinguishing what is true and what is not (*M* VII. 227, DL VII. 54). An apprehensive impression is defined as an impression which (i) arises from what is, (ii) as it is, and (iii) is of such a kind that it could not arise from what is not (see e.g. Cic. *Acad.* II. 77, Sextus, *M* VII. 248). There are some difficulties in understanding 'what is' (*huparchontos, quod est*), of a kind which are very familiar in Greek philosophy (cf. on 219–23 below); does this phrase refer to what *exists*, i.e. a real object as opposed to an illusory one, or does it refer to what is *really the case*? Points (i) and (ii) seem to favour the former understanding—point (ii) would seem to be idle if 'is' in (i) meant 'is the case'—whereas the latter understanding is clearly preferable for (iii)—the requirement that such impressions merely not derive from a *fictional object* would be much too weak for them to serve as a criterion of truth. But the general point is clear; an apprehensive impression is bound to be correct—the proposition to which it corresponds is bound to be true. The sense in which this last point is intended is, however, also open to debate, and this is more significant. One might suppose that (a) such impressions are 'bound to be correct' in the sense that there is some feature of them which is discernible to the person whose impressions they are, and which *certifies* to this person that they are correct. Alternatively, one might suppose that (b) their necessary correctness consists simply in their being caused by their objects in the right way—i.e. in such a way that there is no room for inaccuracy to be introduced. If (a) is right, it follows that the agent is aware of which of his or her impressions are apprehensive; if (b) is right, this does not follow, and will surely not always be the case. The evidence bearing on the question of which was the Stoics' real view is not easy to interpret, and it is at least possible that they (or at any rate the earlier members of the school—for the view did not remain static) did not notice the distinction between the two. For texts and discussion see LS 39–41; see also Frede 1983*b* and Annas 1990*b* (whose view the present sketch most closely resembles). Sextus himself gives a relatively lengthy account of the 'apprehensive impression' at *M* VII. 227–60, and a critique of it at *M* VII. 401–35.

In favour of the view that (a) must have been at least part of what the Stoics intended is the fact that the sceptics, both Academic and Pyrrhonian, argue against the Stoics in ways which clearly have force against (a) rather than against (b); they insist that there are no true impressions which are not such that there are false ones indistinguishable from them. This is Sextus' point in the present passage, in what I signalled above as the important part of the argument; no single impression can be apprehensive 'because of the impossibility of discriminating among them' (182). For the Academics' use of this type of argument, see Cic. *Acad.* II. 77–8, Sextus, *M* VII. 154, 164; for more extensive instances of Sextus' use of it, see *M* VII. 401–11, 415–21, 427–9 (and cf. *PH* III. 241). For their part, the Stoics did not accept these arguments as settling the matter; the debate between Stoics and sceptics on this topic persisted throughout most of the Hellenistic period. (As often, Sextus' own involvement in the topic seems to be somewhat anachronistic.) And this suggests that (a) cannot have been all that the Stoics wanted to say (if it had been, the debate would have been over in the first round), but that (b) also captures some aspect of their view. If so, of course, the coherence of the view itself comes into question; for (a) and (b) are incompatible. On the other hand, both have strong attractions, and would understandably be hard to give up; (b) has the advantage of plausibility and of immunity to these sceptical arguments, while (a) presents us with a criterion of truth which we can actually use to settle what is true—as (b) does not.

Argument 3 proceeds by showing not that there is no such thing as an 'apprehensive impression', but that 'the apprehensive impression is unknown'. Given the nature of the considerations which establish it, this must mean that no impression can be known to be apprehensive. As we have just seen, it is not clear whether it *follows* from this that there are no apprehensive impressions; if interpretation (a) is correct, it does follow, but if interpretation (b) is correct, it does not. But this may not be important for the present argument. The conclusion of the argument appears to be that there is no such thing as a skill (not that skills are 'unknown'); this is how 'skill . . . is destroyed' is most naturally understood. But this may plausibly be thought to follow even from the claim which is actually stated: that we cannot *tell* which impressions are apprehensive. For if this is so, and if, as Sextus says, a skill is 'a system of apprehensions', it follows that one cannot tell, of any given set of impressions to which one has assented (see the definition of 'apprehension' (*katalēpsis*) in 182), whether or not it is a skill. But it is plausible to suppose that there can be *no such thing as* a skill of which one cannot tell whether or not it is a skill. After all, one of the most important things about skills is surely their predictability in producing their intended results (see 207 below for Sextus' own exploitation of this point); such predictability can hardly be said to obtain if one cannot even say whether what one is in possession of is a skill or just a set of routines with no basis in any true grasp of things.

That it cannot be known which impressions are apprehensive is established by a form of circularity argument. How can one (reliably) judge that any given impression is apprehensive? One would have to be able to discern that it 'comes from an existing thing and corresponds with the existing thing itself in the manner of a stamp and a seal' (183). (On 'existing' as the translation of *huparchon*, see on argument 2 above; this is clearly what is required in the present context, in which only clauses (i) and (ii) of the definition appear. For the stamp and seal metaphors, cf. *M* VII. 250–1, 426.) But how can one discern this? One would have to be able to discern that the impression which reveals this object to one is, in fact, an apprehensive impression—which is what one was trying to discover in the first place.

The only obvious answer to this is that there is something about the *manner* in which apprehensive impressions present themselves that conveys the fact that they are such; one does not need, *per impossibile*, to have some *independent* perspective on whether or not the object is as the impression represents it as being. This takes us back to interpretation (a) above. But against this, as we have noted, the sceptics have a barrage of examples all tending to the same conclusion: apprehensive impressions are not distinguishable from non-apprehensive ones by way of some phenomenologically accessible feature of the former. It is not clear what else the Stoics could say in response. Interpretation (b) is not subject to the same sceptical objections; but unfortunately, it concedes the point which is at issue here: viz. that one cannot be sure which of one's impressions are the apprehensive ones. The Stoics might at this point reconsider their definition of a skill as a system of *apprehensions*; perhaps some system of reasonable beliefs would be sufficient. But whatever the Stoics might think of this in general, it would be disastrous in the crucial case of the skill relating to life; for this, as we saw, is identified with practical wisdom, and it is central to Stoic ethics that practical wisdom is a form of knowledge. So if I am right that an alleged skill of which one cannot *tell* whether or not it is a skill is no skill, argument 3 is a powerful one—more powerful than argument 2, since it does not turn on an interpretation of the Stoic doctrine which may well be less than fair. Even if I am not right, Sextus has at least established that no skill can be known to be such, which would surely be unpalatable to the Stoics—again, particularly in the case of the skill relating to life.

For further comparison of 180–3 and the parallel passage at *PH* III. 240–2, see Appendix A.

184–7: Fourth argument against the 'skill relating to life'

This argument is again to the effect that there is no such thing as the skill relating to life—or, in the variant terminology employed in this section, no such thing as the science (*epistēmē*) relating to life. (On the close connection between *epistēmē* and *technē* in Stoic theory see Isnardi Parente 1966: 287–307; cf. on 170 above.) Sextus gives the initial impression that this argument, like the last one, is directed specifically against the Stoics; he refers in the opening conditional (184) to 'the science relating to life—that is, practical wisdom', and he characterizes this science as 'capable of contemplating things which are good and bad and neither', which is a clear reference to the Stoics' definition of practical wisdom (cf. on 170 above). On the other hand, he says just below this that 'some of them' say, in defining (*horizomenoi*) the good, 'Good is virtue or what shares in virtue' (184). Now this is not a view which, as far as we know, was held by some Stoics and rejected by others; to the extent that Sextus is reproducing a Stoic view, it is one which was common ground among Stoics generally. (He is not, it appears, being quite accurate. For the Stoics do not *define* the good in this fashion; rather, virtue and what shares in virtue are the only things which *qualify as* goods according to their definition of the good as 'benefit or not other than benefit' (see Stob. II. 57, 20–58, 1, DL VII. 94–5, 101, and on 22–7 above). But this is unimportant for the present argument.) Hence 'some of them' cannot very well mean 'some of the Stoics'; it seems that it must mean 'some of those who purport to offer a science relating to life'. Sextus is thus not consistent about the targets of the argument. This argument in fact seems to apply to anything claiming to be such a science, and not just to the Stoic candidate for this title; for any such alleged science would surely present itself as capable of discerning what is good and bad. Although Sextus speaks as if the science relating to life is, specifically, practical wisdom, the form of the argument does not depend on his doing so. In fact, the argument might well be considerably more successful against certain opponents other than the Stoics; see below on the Stoics' capacity to resist the conclusion.

The argument is presented in the form of a simple dilemma. The goods which are the subject-matter of the science are either distinct from the science itself, or simply are the science itself; but neither alternative is possible. No new argument is offered against the first, more intuitively acceptable alternative. Instead, we are simply referred back to the arguments in ch. III to the effect that nothing is by nature good or bad (185). (The third possibility, 'neither [good nor bad]', is not repeated here, because this was not included in the argument in ch. III; see on 90–5, end, also on 1–2, 21, 40–1.) Note that these arguments are unabashedly presented as having *shown* good and bad things to be *non-existent* (*edeixamen, anuparkta*); there is no hint that the outcome of these arguments was, or was intended to be, suspension of judgement about that issue. As we have seen repeatedly, this portrayal of these arguments is correct; see esp. on 68–95, point 1 on 118. (This may be one reason why nothing corresponding to this argument appears in *PH* III; for *PH* III—at least officially—does wish to suspend judgement about the existence of good, bad, and indifferent things. If *PH* III is a revision of *M* XI, Sextus would have felt the need to modify this part of the argument—if he retained it at all; and this, coupled perhaps with the perception of other imperfections (see below), may have led him to abandon it.)

As noted earlier (see introductory remarks on this chapter), this is the only unambiguous reference to part A from within part B. If one is attracted by the hypothesis that these two rather disparate portions of the book are drawn from different sources, the present passage creates no difficulty for that hypothesis; it is perfectly possible that this back-reference is an insertion by Sextus, replacing some other argument for the first horn of the dilemma which he found in his source. One point in favour of this possibility is that the arguments referred back to, against the existence of anything by nature good or bad, actually suffice to eliminate *both* of the two alternatives Sextus here offers the dogmatist; if nothing is in reality good, there can no such thing as a science of good things, *whether or not* the science is distinct from the good things. The present argument thus becomes very lopsided—to the extent, in fact, that it is misleading to structure it in the form of a dilemma; the original presence of another argument with a more limited target, namely Sextus' first alternative, therefore has some plausibility.

Sextus now turns to the second alternative: that the science relating to life might itself be the good which is its subject-matter. This is dismissed (186–7) by means of a principle which seems at first sight very plausible: the subject-matter of any science must exist prior to the science itself— in order for there to be a science, there has to be something already there for the science to study. This is illustrated by a variety of examples to which the principle clearly does apply; and the principle is then said to apply to the case of practical wisdom itself. (Strictly speaking, Sextus should not have said 'music does not exist prior to these' (186), but 'these exist prior to music'; his statement leaves open the possibility that music and its subject-matter might come into existence simultaneously.)

However, the application of this principle to practical wisdom would be resisted by the Stoics. Cicero, in the Stoic portion of *De Finibus*, explicitly contrasts wisdom (*sapientia*) with skills such as helmsmanship and medicine precisely on the ground that the former is not directed to anything external to itself, but simply to its own exercise (III. 24; cf. Seneca, *Ep*. 85. 31–2). The same point is apparent from the *Carneadea divisio*, Carneades' classification of actual and possible views about the ethical end. In one especially informative summary of this classification (Cic. *Fin*. V. 16 ff.), we are told that Carneades insisted on the very same point as Sextus: that every skill must be directed towards something other than simply its own exercise; this point, which is used as an organizing principle for the subsequent classification, is introduced by Carneades as part of a strategy to embarrass the Stoics, who are committed to holding the opposite. (On this, see Lévy 1992: pt. IV, ch. 1, LS I, commentary on 64; it is worth noting that Carneades' criticisms by no means silenced the Stoics on this issue.) It might be objected that the Stoics misrepresent their own position, since practical wisdom is very far from exhausting the category of good things; there are the other virtues, the actions in accordance with them (and with practical wisdom itself), and various other items. But given the unity of the virtues in Stoicism, there will not be any exercise of virtue which is not in some respect an exercise of practical wisdom (see Stob. II. 63, 6–24, and cf. on 170 above); thus the Stoics can indeed claim that there is no subject-matter for practical wisdom which is independent of practical wisdom in the way both Sextus and Carneades urge. The Stoic position may or may not have been defensible; for an argument that it was not (or not entirely), see Striker 1991: sect. 3. But at any rate, Sextus' argument, if directed against the Stoics (see above on how far this is true), is not successful as it stands; for the Stoics would simply deny that the principle invoked by Sextus is generalizable in the way he supposes.

The Stoics and the sceptics were not the first to consider these issues. Plato's *Charmides* contains a discussion of the question of whether a science must always be *of* something distinct from itself (165c–169c). By the end of this discussion, Socrates professes himself unable to say what the answer is, but the possibility that temperance (*sōphrosunē*) might be a science of which no such requirement holds is at any rate not dismissed out of hand; it is arguable that Plato is actually convinced that this is true, and is struggling, or inviting his readers to struggle, to understand *how* it can be true. A similar but briefer discussion occurs at *Euthydemus* 291d–293a; cf. *Cleitophon* 409a–410a. The Stoics no doubt took some inspiration from Plato, or from Socrates, on this matter (cf. on 170 above); for a brief discussion, see Striker 1994: 246–51. In this case the sceptics are likely to have done the same; for the considerations which, in the *Charmides*, seem to favour a negative answer to the question are highly reminiscent of those employed by Sextus.

188–96: Fifth argument against the 'skill relating to life'

Points of text and translation:

(a) For *diatribai* (190), translated '*Discourses*', as the title of a book by Zeno, see DL VII. 34. (This is missed by Bury.)

[(b) With von Arnim (*SVF* I. 251), followed by Bury, I adopt Bekker's tentative suggestion *epithumēsas* for the second occurrence of *epethumēsas* in 190, and delete the word *ē* in the following clause; I cannot find an acceptable sense for the MSS readings, which Mutschmann retains.

(c) With Mutschmann, Bury, and Russo, I accept von Arnim's alteration of the MSS *eph'hōi heuren* to *euphrainen* in 191, and Fabricius' addition of *ek tou huiou teknopoieisthai kai ton patera* in 192, on the basis of the parallel passages in *PH* III. 246. Though I have elsewhere rejected textual alterations based on parallels with *PH* (cf. 48–67, point (i); 79–89, point (d); and point (d) below), the changes seem to me justified here because (1) the text in the MSS of *M* XI is clearly defective—in the one case the protasis of the conditional lacks a verb, and in the other the *hōste* clause lacks a verb—and (2) the passages in question are quotations from another author, so that there is at least a prima facie expectation that they will be identical.

(d) I retain the MSS reading *epoisousin* in 194. Mutschmann alters to *easousin* on the basis of the parallel with *PH* III. 248. But *M* XI, unlike *PH* III, also contains the word *to mnēma*, 'the monument', which makes at least as good sense as the object of *epoisousin* as of *easousin*. As in the previous case (point (c) above), both purport to be quotations from the same passage of Chrysippus; so (at least) one of them must be mistaken —and this is true even with Mutschmann's alteration. But one cannot assume that the error is in the transmission of the manuscript rather than in the original copying of Chrysippus' text by Sextus or his source. *Easousin* is admittedly preferable in the general context of lack of continuing concern about one parents' dead bodies. But this merely suggests that *M* XI is less likely to give the authentic text of Chrysippus; it has no bearing on who made the mistake, if that is what it is.]

This section again has the Stoics exclusively as targets, though this is not made clear in the introductory passage (188). There are other problems, too, concerning the relation between this passage and what follows. The conclusion for which Sextus announces that he is going to argue is that 'there is not any skill relating to life'; but this is not the conclusion actually reached, which is that the skill relating to life is useless (196). Again, the transition between 188 and 189, where the details of the argument begin, is far from smooth; it is quite unclear until the end of the argument why the Stoics' views about the guidance of children, etc. should even be thought relevant to the claim that the skill relating to life does not give rise to any 'action' (*energēma*). Furthermore, this introductory passage very closely resembles the introduction to the next section (197)—which, by contrast, is entirely suited to the argument which it previews (cf. the conclusion in 209, which neatly recapitulates the train of thought in 197). The only significant differences are that (a) 197 specifies the Stoic practical wisdom as the purported skill under discussion, as 188 does not; and (b) the point in 197 is that there is no action 'peculiar to' (*idion*) practical wisdom, whereas in 188 it is claimed that the skill relating to life does not give rise to any action at all. The second difference accurately reflects differences in the arguments that follow. But the very substantial repetition reads oddly, to say the least. (By contrast, *PH* III has only one occurrence of a parallel set of remarks (243).)

All these difficulties may be plausibly explained by the hypothesis that Sextus himself has introduced the anti-Stoic polemic which constitutes the main body of this section into the material drawn from his main source, and that he has attempted, with by no means complete success, to adapt the introduction to the next section (which would have been the next thing he saw in his main source) to the purpose of introducing this one. The Stoics' views about incest and cannibalism have no obvious connection with the topic of skills (and their efficacy in Sextus' argument is extremely limited—see below); so it is inherently likely that they did not belong in the discussion originally. Sextus simply cannot resist bringing them in, largely as a rhetorical device to undermine the Stoics' credibility.

It has been argued by Schofield (1991: ch. 1) that 189–94, the passage which reports the Stoic views, is taken more or less *verbatim* from Cassius the sceptic. The reason for thinking this is the close connection which, according to Schofield, exists between this passage and a set of criticisms of Zeno ascribed to this little-known sceptic at DL VII. 32–4, together with a set of criticisms of Chrysippus at DL VII. 187–9 which may plausibly be argued to have been originally (i.e. in Diogenes' source) a continuation of 32–4. Schofield's thesis is not inconsistent with any of the above, and it might be true. However, his argument is tenuous at a number of points (see Hahm 1992: 4131–4, esp. n. 135, Inwood 1992: 211–13, Vander Waerdt 1994: n. 60).

The general form of the argument is very simple. The Stoics' writings include recommendations of the most outrageous practices one can imagine (190–4). But they cannot seriously be proposing that these recommendations be implemented; aside from their abhorrence, no society would permit such practices (195). (Or at least, no non-mythical society; the quotation is from *Od.* IX. 297—with Homer's participles altered to infinitives—and occurs, as one would expect, in the course of an account

of the Cyclops' meal.) But if there is no expectation that they will be
implemented, then these recommendations are pointless. Hence the skill
of which these recommendations are the product is useless (196). (The
analogy with blindness and deafness recurs several times in the next
chapter; cf. 235, 238, 245, 247.) The conclusion only follows, of course,
if these recommendations are representative of *all* manifestations of the
skill relating to life. Even on the most uncharitable possible reading of
the quotations from the Stoics, this is plainly not so. Hence the argument
is very ineffective.

The early Stoics' willingness to sanction incest and cannibalism and
the apparent licentiousness of their sexual attitudes are widely attested.
In addition to the present passages, Sextus himself alludes to these
matters at *PH* I. 160, III. 201, 205–7; see also DL VII. 34 (which
specifically confirms that 'erotic matters' were discussed in Zeno's *Discourses*), 121, 188 (which confirms that incest was discussed in Chrysippus'
Republic and cannibalism in his *On Justice*), Plut. *Sto. rep.* 1044F–1045A,
Philodemus' *On the Stoics* (see the edition of Dorandi (1982)), and other
texts collected in *SVF* I. 247–56, III pp. 185–7. This appears to be one
aspect of the Cynic legacy of Stoicism (Zeno, the founder of the school,
was a student of Crates of Thebes—DL VI. 105, VII. 1, Numenius in
Eusebius, *Praep. evang.* XIV. 5. 11), which is discussed in Mansfeld
1986—see esp. 343–51; Philodemus' *On the Stoics* seems to be designed
to embarrass the Stoics of his own day by emphasizing the strong connections between early Stoicism and Cynicism. This work also indicates
that later Stoics did indeed feel discomfort with this side of early Stoicism, and tried in various ways to deny it or downplay its significance
(on this, see also DL VII. 34).

The important question is what place these seemingly shocking ideas
had in the philosophies of Zeno and Chrysippus; here it is necessary to
distinguish to some extent (1) the references to incest and cannibalism
(191–4), attested for both thinkers, from (2) Zeno's advocacy of indiscriminate sexual activity (190). (1) Two points should be emphasized.
First, it follows from Stoic views about the good, the bad, and the
indifferent that incest and cannibalism will be indifferent (see *PH* I. 160
for Chrysippus' admission of this in the case of incest). As we have seen
(above on 22–30, 59–67), the Stoics hold that virtue and vice and 'what
share in' them are the only things which are good and bad respectively,
on the ground that these are the only things which are invariably beneficial and harmful respectively; everything else is indifferent. Though
the Stoics also hold that some indifferents are 'preferred' and others
'dispreferred' (on this, see also on 68–78, references to earlier philo-

sophers, point (c)), it none the less follows that, for all types of action which qualify as indifferent, there will be circumstances in which they are appropriate (*oikeion*), and in which it will be proper (*kathēkon*) to pursue them, and circumstances in which they are inappropriate. (On the terms *oikeion* and *kathēkon*, see on 130–40 above; and note that Sextus' longest quotation (194) derives from a work by Chrysippus entitled *Peri tou Kathēkontos*, '*On What is Proper*'.) This will be true, then, even of incest and cannibalism; they cannot be considered absolutely prohibited. This does not, of course, imply that they are appropriate other than in very exceptional circumstances. DL VII. 121 says that the sage 'will even taste human flesh *in certain circumstances* (*kata peristasin*)'; and Origen, *Contra Celsum* IV. 45 (= *SVF* III p. 185) describes an extremely unlikely situation in which, according to the Stoics, incest would be justified. Sextus (like Philodemus) implies that the Stoics recommend these as everyday practices; but this impression could easily have been created by selective quotation. (The quotation from Chrysippus' *Republic* in 192 is perhaps the most difficult in this respect. But even here it is not stated that incest should take place as a regular occurrence, but merely that social arrangements should be such that it does sometimes appropriately take place. The passage might then have continued with an account of the special circumstances in which this is true.) For more on this, see Vander Waerdt 1994: 300–1, LS I, comm. on 67.

The second point is that several of the works from which Sextus takes his quotations are works of political philosophy; Chrysippus' *Republic* and *On Justice* are named, and it is also likely that Zeno's sanctioning of incest occurred in his *Republic*. (As Philodemus' discussion, among others, attests, the *Republic* was the work of Zeno's which caused particular embarrassment to later members of the school.) In this case, many of the remarks quoted will probably have belonged to discussions of ideal societies composed solely of wise persons. (For differing accounts of the character of Stoic political philosophy—which none the less agree on this central point—see Schofield 1991, Vander Waerdt 1994, LS 67.) To say that these practices may sometimes be permitted in an ideal society of wise persons—i.e. persons who have an unerring sense of what is appropriate on any given occasion—is very different from recommending them to ordinary people.

(2) There is also reason to believe that Zeno's scandalous views about sex, as reported in 190, occurred in the context of his political philosophy. In his *Republic*, Zeno apparently accorded to *erōs* an important role in fostering a harmonious society (Athenaeus 561C = LS 67D); and it was in the *Republic* that he said that the sage would love (*erasthēsesthai*)

young persons with a strong potential for virtue (DL VII. 129). The same work also advanced a view highly reminiscent of the first quotation in 190, viz. that any man should be able to have sexual relations with any woman (DL VII. 131). But again, this is said to hold only 'among sages'—which would certainly affect the character of the relationships among the parties; it is not a prescription for free love in the here and now. One should also note that Plato's *Republic*, Book V, contains similarly surprising sexual prescriptions; malicious excerpting of Plato's text could certainly have produced an effect just as shocking as that achieved by Sextus and others—yet we know that advocacy of sexual licentiousness was very far from being Plato's intention. On the centrality of love in Zeno's political philosophy, see Schofield 1991: ch. 2.

Sextus' claim that the passages quoted in 190 have to do with 'the guidance of children' could be a distortion for polemical purposes. But a strong educational component in homosexual alliances between men and boys is taken for granted in Plato, and this is certainly not just his own invention (on the social background see Dover 1978). It is by no means improbable that Zeno's remarks here, having to do with actual or potential sexual partners younger than oneself (this is guaranteed by the words *paidika*, 'boy-friend', and *erōmenos*, 'beloved'), did occur in the context of a discussion of education. The original purpose of the second set of remarks quoted in 190 is very obscure (and this is the only passage which is not also quoted in *PH* III); as a piece of salacious dialogue, it suits Sextus' purpose, but there is no discernible doctrine to be extracted from it.

To sum up, these passages from Zeno and Chrysippus are quoted out of context, and it is probable that the impression conveyed by Sextus is misleading. In particular, it seems to be a drastic oversimplification to offer the Stoics just two options: either they want the young to put these precepts into practice or they do not (195); their true purpose in saying these things appears to have been far too complex to permit a simple choice between these options.

For comparison of 188–96 and the parallel passage at *PH* III. 245–9, see Appendix A.

197–209: Sixth argument against the 'skill relating to life'

Points of text and translation:

(a) I translate *ergon* throughout this section by 'action' (cf. *ergon*, *energēma* in 188). *Ergon* is standardly used from at least as early as Plato to refer to whatever it is that a skill brings about, and it is frequently translated 'product' in such cases. (See e.g. Annas and Barnes 1994 in their translation of the parallel passage of *PH* III.) But 'action' (in the sense of a *thing done*) is just as acceptable as a rendering of the Greek word, and seems to me preferable in this context. The examples of *erga* which are central in this section—giving health, honouring one's parents, etc.—clearly are actions in this sense; it is a little strained to refer to them as 'products', which more naturally suggests some tangible objects which are the outcome of the processes in question. Of course, if one restricts the term *technē* to skilled capacities to produce artefacts—as Aristotle does (*NE* VI. 4)—then 'products' will be an appropriate word by which to refer to what a *technē* brings about. However, as we have seen, the Stoic conception of *technē* is much broader than this (see on 170 above).

[(b) Heintz (1932: 260) proposes adding *tines* before *phasi* in the first sentence of 200—'some say' instead of 'they say'; this would be consistent with 206 ('there are others who think'; cf. 208, 'these people, too'), and the parallel passage of *PH* III (243) does contain *tines*. Neither point, though, is a reason for changing the text; the inconsistency is not severe, and it is just the kind of minor point which could easily have been corrected in a revision—another slight indication, perhaps, of the relative order of the two works. (I also see no reason to follow Heintz in regarding the suggestions at 200 and at 206 as representing *competing* Stoic positions; they are quite compatible and even complementary; see on 206–9 below.)

(c) With Mutschmann, I read *to diaphorōs ginomenon* in 204, not *ti diaphorōs ginomenon*, as do Bekker and Bury; the MSS diverge on this point. The difference is slight, but the sense of *to* seems to me marginally preferable.

(d) I translate *meta . . . poiotētos* in 204 by 'with quality'. *Poiotēs* does of course mean 'quality'; but I am not aware of any other case where it is used, as 'quality' often is in modern English (including in the phrase 'with quality'), to refer to *high* quality. However, I do not see how else to understand it in the context. Russo ('con classe') appears to be thinking on the same lines (and cf. Hervetus' *cum certo qualitate*); Bury's 'on a definite plan' seems to bear no relation to the text.

(e) All editors since Bekker have altered the MSS *einai* to *ēn* before *akolouthon* in the first sentence of 205. The logic is better with *ēn*, but this is not a compelling reason for accepting the emendation—see point (f) below; I retain *einai*.

(f) Heintz (1932: 260) suggests numerous changes in 205–6: (i) altering *oude to apo atechnou* (205) to *kai to apo atechnou*, (ii) deleting *aphanē* in *tēn kath'hekaston aphanē diathesin* (205), (iii) adding *panta* after *to homologein* (first sentence of 206), or perhaps adding *phanai* after *diapherein d'auta* (at any rate, adopting some device to make the *men* and *de* in this sentence genuinely parallel). Changes (ii) and (iii) (adding *phanai*) are followed by Bury. None of these changes is necessary. All of them result in greater clarity (on (iii) in particular, no doubt Sextus did mean to say something like 'but *to claim* that they differ' rather than 'but that they differ'). But the text is quite intelligible as it stands; and the fact that the thought is not expressed as clearly as it might be does not show, or even suggest, that Sextus did not write what appears in the text (cf. e.g. point (i) on 48–67, point (c) on 150–61). (The same may be said of Bury's unnecessary adding of *auto* before *apodeixeōs* in 203.)

(g) The MSS *mē hupo tou sophou* does not need to be altered, as it is by Mutschmann, to *hupo tou mē sophou* in 206; the sense, however, is unaffected. On this unexpected idiom, see Heintz 1932: 165–7.]

This section and the next are directed solely against the Stoics. Sextus does not say so, but it is assumed for the rest of the chapter that, if there is a skill relating to life, it is practical wisdom (and there are no countervailing considerations suggesting a wider set of targets—cf. on 184 above). Sextus' basic point in this section is a simple one. There are no characteristic actions which are the outcome of practical wisdom; any skill surely does give rise to some set of characteristic actions, so practical wisdom must not be a skill. The point is made in 197–9; the rest of the section then considers, and rejects, two possible replies to the basic argument (200–6, 206–9).

The basic argument is stated in syllogistic form in 197; the two premisses are then justified in 198 and 199 respectively. The division of skills into theoretical, practical, and productive (197) is initially surprising. The tripartite division theoretical, practical, productive is of course Aristotelian in origin; but Aristotle himself restricts skills to the productive sphere (*NE* VI. 4). However, in the Hellenistic period the term *technē* seems to have lost the exclusive connotation of a productive capacity; as we saw, neither the Stoic nor the Epicurean definitions of *technē* had anything specially to do with production (see linguistic point (a), and on 170 above).

The major premiss, that every skill has some 'action peculiar to itself', is established in 198. Any action which is performed equally by someone who possesses a certain skill and by someone who does not cannot be an action which is the outcome of the skill in question; it therefore follows (this is not stated but left for the reader to discern) that those actions which *are* the outcome of the skill in question must be actions which are 'peculiar to' the skill itself—i.e. actions which cannot be performed *other than* in the exercise of the skill itself. This is illustrated by two examples and then generalized. In preparation for the subsequent stages of the argument, the general principle is then applied to the case of practical wisdom. Sextus does not state this last point quite correctly. He says that an action performed both by the wise and by the non-wise 'could not be an action *peculiar to* practical wisdom'. This is of course true—trivially so; but it is in principle compatible with this statement that there might be actions which are not *peculiar to* practical wisdom, but which none the less are the *outcome* of practical wisdom—precisely the negation of what the general principle, stated in the previous sentence, would entail. What he needs to say, and is in a position to say, is that an action which both the wise and the non-wise perform could not have practical wisdom as its source (assuming that practical wisdom is a skill—again, this is not stated but implied), from which it follows that any actions which do have practical wisdom as their source must be 'peculiar to' it.

The minor premiss is argued for in 199 by way of the claim that any type of action which might be considered to have practical wisdom as its source is also performed by those lacking such wisdom. Hence no actions can be specified as the actions 'peculiar to' practical wisdom. Sextus does not commit himself as to whether there actually are any actions which are the outcome of practical wisdom ('seems to be brought about', 'if we regard'), and he does not need to. If there are no such actions (or, in other words, if there is no such thing as practical wisdom), practical wisdom will certainly not meet the requirement for a skill which is stated in the major premiss. But if there are such actions, they will not, according to the argument for the minor premiss, be actions which are 'peculiar to' practical wisdom—in which case practical wisdom will still not be a skill, according to the test contained in the major premiss.

The argument for the minor premiss may seem very feeble; why should the Stoics agree that the wise person will not do anything which is not also done by those who are not wise? But there is a sense in which the Stoics would be happy to accept this. If actions are described without reference to the dispositions which give rise to them (and without reference to the particular way in which they are done—see below), it is indeed plausible that there will be no actions of which it can be said that only the wise will perform them; in this sense what the wise do will be 'common to' those who are not wise. ('Honouring one's parents' might not seem a promising case of an action described in this type of way. But I assume that Sextus has in mind some set of *performances* which together could be said to constitute 'honouring one's parents'—visiting them, or allowing them to visit oneself, on appropriate occasions, not being rude to them, remembering their anniversary, etc.—irrespective of the frame of mind in which they are done.) What is distinctive about Stoic wise persons is not any unique types of gross behaviour, but the spirit in which, or the motivations with which, they perform the actions which they do perform; so if this is what Sextus means by 'action', he appears to be right that no action is 'peculiar to' the wise person. However, the Stoics will answer that, if one expands one's description of the actions so as to include reference to the dispositions which give rise to them—and it is not clear why one should not do this—the wise person's actions *are* distinctive ('returning money virtuously', for example, as opposed to returning money for base motives, such as fear of antagonizing one's business partners). Sextus considers this response immediately below; whatever one thinks of his counter-argument, he at least recognizes that the present argument, as it stands, is not watertight.

For comparison of 197–9 and the parallel passage at *PH* III. 243, see Appendix A.

As just noted, the first response that Sextus attributes to the Stoics (200–1) is this: the crucial difference between the actions of the wise and of those who are not wise is precisely the wisdom or lack of wisdom with which they are done. 'Caring for one's parents' is something both the wise and the non-wise may do; 'caring for one's parents . . . from practical wisdom' is something which, obviously, only the wise can do. Thus, if the dispositions which give rise to the actions are included in the description of the actions themselves, the actions of the wise are indeed 'peculiar to' them, admitting of the distinctive description 'the *performance from the best disposition* of each of the things performed' (201).

There is ample evidence to confirm that Sextus is accurately summarizing the Stoic position. The difference, in Stoic terminology, between 'right deeds' (*katorthōmata*)—i.e. the actions of the person who has achieved virtue or wisdom—and actions which are merely 'proper' (*kathēkonta*) is, we are told, simply that the former are expressions of virtue or wisdom, whereas the latter need not be (though 'right deeds' are *also* 'proper'—the terms are not mutually exclusive). See e.g. Cic. *Fin*. III. 59 (which uses the example of returning a deposit; cf. 199 above), Stob. V. 906, 18–907, 5. For discussion see Tsekourakis 1974: 44–60; LS I, comm. on 59; Vander Waerdt 1994: 274–6. Even the medical analogy is likely to have been employed by the Stoics themselves; cf. Plut. *Sto. rep.* 1037E.

Sextus' counter-argument against this Stoic response (202–6) is long-winded and repetitive (the essentials are captured in a single sentence in the parallel passage of *PH* III (244)); the whole of 202, for example, could with advantage have been omitted. The basic point is epistemological; if the actions of the wise person are distinctive because of the disposition which gives rise to them, how are we to tell which actions are in fact those of a wise person (203; cf. 205)? If there is nothing in the overt characteristics of these actions to mark them as those of a wise person— and it is assumed, at least initially, that this is the case—identifying these actions is impossible. (At the beginning of 203, it would have been clearer and more precise for Sextus to say 'there is an action peculiar to the wise person', rather than 'there is not an action common to both the wise and those who are not such'.)

It is by no means clear that this is an adequate rebuttal to the Stoics. For they are forced to accept the conclusion only if there are no observable indications whatever of the fact that a certain action is the product of a wise disposition. Sextus assumes throughout most of the passage that this must be so; but there seems to be no good reason why we should agree. For one thing, even if the bodily movements of a wise person and of a non-wise person in a certain situation are indistinguishable, wise persons—and therefore, the actions of wise persons—might well be identified by the kinds of justification they give of these actions before or after the fact; their *attitudes towards* their actions could be revealed by what they say about them rather than by any feature intrinsic to the actions themselves, and this might suffice to demonstrate the character of the dispositions which gave rise to the actions. Though this move might be blocked by a more general scepticism about our knowledge of other minds, nothing that Sextus says in the present passage seems to rule out this response.

But it is in any case not obvious why the Stoics should concede that the actions of the wise are behaviourally indistinguishable from those of other people. (I leave aside the fact that speech itself is a form of action, which already suggests, in light of the point just made, that there is a class of actions peculiar to the wise—viz. certain of their speech-acts.

Though the notion that speech is a form of action is not unheard of in ancient philosophy—see e.g. Pl. *Crat.* 387b8–9—it is not clear whether Sextus would be prepared to regard speech-acts as relevant to the present argument; we are dealing, he might say, with the supposedly distinctive *accomplishments* of the skilled person, and mere talk does not come under this heading.) Curiously enough, Sextus himself suggests a way in which the actions of the wise and of the non-wise might be held to differ. In 204–5 he claims that the medical analogy employed by the Stoics (201) actually works to their disadvantage; the reasons given are as follows. It was suggested that what was distinctive about the doctor was giving health 'in a medical fashion'—i.e. as a result of medical expertise; other people may give health (e.g. other people besides doctors, or even besides medical practitioners in general, may administer injections), but they will not do so 'in a medical fashion'. Now, either giving health 'in a medical fashion' is distinguishable from the ordinary person's giving of health by some aspect of the *way* in which the actions in question are performed by the doctor as opposed to the ordinary person (204); or this is not the case. If it is the case, then there are, after all, actions peculiar to the doctor—e.g. the quick and painless administering of injections, as opposed to the clumsy and uncomfortable administering of injections; and if so, there ought to be analogous actions which are peculiar to the wise person. If, on the other hand, this is not the case, then the epistemological problem raised earlier will apply (205).

What is puzzling about this argument is that it should be thought to count *against* the Stoics. For it looks as if the Stoics can simply accept the first alternative, and thank Sextus for suggesting it; i.e. they can agree that the wise person's actions do have a certain style about them by which they differ observably from the otherwise identical actions of those who are not wise. If types of actions are individuated in a relatively coarse-grained way, as is done by most of the ancient sources—so that, for example, all cases of 'honouring one's parents' or of 'returning money deposited' are considered to belong to the same type—then the same actions (i.e. actions of the same type) will indeed be 'common' to the wise and to ordinary people. But there is no reason why the performance of these actions 'from the best disposition' may not result in their being performed in a distinctive and behaviourally discernible fashion, so that, by a more fine-grained taxonomy of actions, the actions of the wise do differ from those of ordinary people. Sextus speaks as if the Stoics are committed to denying this ('they have admitted right away that there is some action apparent which is peculiar to the doctor', 205). But it was not the Stoics, but Sextus himself, who earlier insisted on these actions being 'common' to the wise and the non-wise. On some ways of individuating types of actions, the Stoics will be willing to accept this; but it is difficult to see why they are bound to accept it no matter how fine-grained the system of individuation. It looks, then, as if Sextus is seriously confused; it also looks as if the Stoics are untouched by his argument.

It is interesting that 205 contains the first occurrence in the book of the word 'non-apparent' (*aphanēs*); the word occurs again only in 255, in a context which explicitly recalls this passage. This is no accident; for the contrast between what is apparent and what is non-apparent or 'non-evident', so important elsewhere in Sextus, has played virtually no role in the argument prior to this point. The idea that sceptics should rely solely on appearances applies in *M* XI only to a very limited degree (see above on 18-20, and point 5 on 118). And the arguments in ch. III concerning what, if anything, is by nature good or bad had nothing to do with the impossibility of our penetrating behind the appearances concerning these things; on the contrary, in 92-3, the only passage prior to this point (except for a quotation at 50) containing the related term 'non-evident' (*adēlos*; cf. *mē phainomenēn*, also translated 'non-apparent'), Sextus maintains that an allegedly bad thing which is 'non-evident' *is not in fact* a bad thing at all. The very notion of there being a truth about good and bad which is 'non-apparent' is alien to the spirit of ch. III's argument (see esp. on 68-95 above).

Again, it may be tempting to see these differences as further evidence that part B derives from a different source and a different phase in the history of scepticism from part A (see above on 173-7, end). But again, this is far from obvious. The contrast between the apparent and the non-apparent certainly had some role in the thinking of Aenesidemus, to whom it is plausible to trace the style of argument in part A; it figures in several of Aenesidemus' Eight Modes against causal explanation (*PH* I. 180-4). As noted earlier (on 173-7), the appropriateness of a certain style of argument may vary with the subject-matter. If my interpretation was correct, the arguments against the existence of anything by nature good or bad appealed to what I called the Recognition Requirement (see on 68-78, 90-5, also Introduction, sect. II); this explains why the possibility of 'non-apparent' truths about good and bad had no role in these arguments. But there is no reason to suspect that Sextus means the Recognition Requirement to apply to anything other than benefits or harms (on this, see also Introduction, sect. V); hence the suggestion that a person's skilled dispositions may be 'non-apparent' is perfectly compatible with the arguments employed in ch. III.

A second Stoic response is offered at 206–7; the wise person's actions have the distinctive features of 'consistency and order' (*diomalismos, taxis*). As the explanation and analogy in 207 make clear, this is not a property of individual actions, but of sets of actions over time; the wise person will reliably perform the same actions, or the same sequences of actions, in the same circumstances, whereas ordinary people's actions will be fickle and unstable. This seems to be a further way in which the actions of the wise may be held to be behaviourally distinguishable from those of ordinary people (see above on 202–6). Indeed, one of the suggestions in 204 was that the wise person's actions might differ in being done 'in an orderly manner' (*meta taxeōs*); the present response appears to be a development of this point. This response is in no way incompatible with the previous one (cf. textual point (b) above); the consistency and order of the wise person's actions are very naturally understood as the *result* of their being the expression of the 'skilful disposition' (200), practical wisdom. Nevertheless, there are reasons for thinking that this second response was developed by a distinct and later group of Stoics, very possibly in reaction to criticism.

First, Sextus refers to the originators of the second response as 'others' (206; cf. 208). This is not quite as straightforward as it might be, since the authors of the previous response are referred to simply as 'they' (i.e. the Stoics in general); see textual point (b) above. However, Sextus' slightly confusing language is understandable if we think of the first response as the standard Stoic view, originated by the early Stoics but maintained throughout the school's history, and the second response as a later addition—the authors of which are therefore 'other' than those of the first response (even though they are also among those who *accept* the first response). Second, it looks as if, beginning with Antipater in the second century BC, Stoic definitions of the ethical end (*telos*) began to incorporate a reference, which earlier definitions had not included, to consistency in action; see Stob. II. 76, 11–15, Clement, *Strom.* II. 21. 129, 2, and for amplification Tsekourakis 1974: 44–60. We are told by Plutarch (*Comm. not.* 1072F) that Antipater developed a new specification of the end under pressure from the Academic Carneades; Sextus' arguments in 202–6 may well be ultimately indebted to Carneades. It should be repeated, however, that this emphasis on consistency is not a *replacement* of previous views (Tsekourakis is occasionally misleading here). Even in the early Stoa, consistency was regarded as a characteristic of the wise person's actions (see e.g. Stob. II. 60, 7–8, V. 906, 18–907, 5); the second response represents no more than a new emphasis, perhaps prompted by a need to provide some more easily recognizable mark of the wise person's distinctness.

A couple of Stoic terms in this passage are worth drawing attention to. (a) The 'intermediate skills' (*mesai technai*, 207) are those skills which, unlike the skill relating to life, are not inherently either good or bad; in other words, they are skills of the everyday variety. For this use of 'intermediate', see Cic. *Acad.* I. 37, Simplicius, *In Ar. Cat.* 284, 32–4 (= *SVF* II. 393, end), and for further references and discussion Pohlenz 1972: ii. 73–4, Isnardi Parente 1966: 330–1. (b) 'Right deeds' (*katorthōmata*) are by definition the actions of the wise person; one does not rise to the level of performing 'right deeds' until one has fully achieved virtue. For references to texts and discussion, see on 200–1 above. This is the only occurrence of this word in the book.

Sextus introduces his counter-arguments to this second Stoic response in 208. The claim that his opponents are 'plainly not oriented in accordance with the nature of things' seems incautious for a sceptic; but this is clearly not a philosophically loaded use of the term 'the nature of things', and the expression is probably just borrowed carelessly from the argumentative usage of non-sceptics. There are two counter-arguments:

1. Given life's vicissitudes, it is simply not realistic to suggest that anyone can or should proceed through life adhering to some single and consistent 'order of life' (208).
2. The wise cannot be spotted by the non-wise, as one would expect them to be, by way of this 'order of life' which they allegedly possess (209).

Argument 1 seems to beg the question. An 'order of life' which is not sensitive to the variability of circumstances is of course liable to run into trouble when applied over an extended period; but it would take considerable further argument to show that *no* consistent manner of acting, no matter how subtle in its recognition of life's complexities, could be maintained in the real world. The Stoics' position may be bold, but it cannot be merely *asserted* to be unrealistic.

Argument 2 may also seem very weak. For it seems open to the Stoics to reply that those who are not wise cannot be expected to be in a position to grasp the consistency and order exhibited in the actions of those who are; the fact that this consistency and order is not apparent to

ordinary people is no reason for doubting its existence. But Sextus may
be on stronger ground here than might initially appear. If, as was suggested above, the point of this second response was to provide some
more tangible distinguishing feature of the wise person's actions, the
Stoics are not in a position to avail themselves of this reply; if this
distinguishing feature of the wise person's actions is accessible only to
the wise themselves, it will be of no help in silencing the critics. So if the
debate is to advance beyond a stalemate, the Stoics will have to appeal to
something of which even those who are not wise can be made aware.
Again, however, it is by no means out of the question that they might be
able to do this; see above on 202–6. Argument 2, then, though it succeeds better than argument 1 in putting the Stoics on the defensive, is
also inconclusive.

The final sentence of 209, while it serves as a conclusion to the whole
of this section, is worded in a way which is influenced by the immediately preceding argument 2. It is this argument which has just shown
that 'there is no action peculiar to practical wisdom *from which it* [i.e.
practical wisdom] *is apparent*', and which needs the premiss 'every skill
is apparent from the actions peculiar to it' in order to yield the conclusion
that practical wisdom is not a skill relating to life. (Compare 197–9,
where there is no mention of things' being or not being 'apparent'.)

For comparison of 206–9 and the parallel passage at *PH* III. 244, see
Appendix A.

210–15: Seventh argument against the 'skill relating to life'

Textual points:

(a) I retain the placing of 'good' (*agathon*) and 'bad' (*kakou*) that
occurs in the MSS in 210; both Mutschmann and Bury switch to *kakon*
and *agathou*. The sense is perfectly acceptable. The person with practical
wisdom has 'self-control in his impulses towards the good and in his
repulsions from the bad'; i.e. he is self-controlled *in that* his impulses are
towards the good and his repulsions are from the bad. Of course, that is
not what we usually understand by self-control. But the Stoic conception
of self-control is by no means the same as the usual one (see below).
Indeed, that is precisely part of Sextus' point in the subsequent argument; if (as the Stoics would indeed want to maintain) the sage has
impulses only towards the good and repulsions only from the bad, it is
not correct to call him self-controlled (211–12). Moreover, the MSS

error in 211—where *agathon* and *kakou* clearly *have* been substituted for
kakon and *agathou*—is much more easily understandable if *agathon* and
kakou actually did appear in similar phrases a few lines earlier. (There is
a similar textual dispute in the parallel passage of *PH* III (273), where the
MSS do not agree; see app. crit. in Mutschmann–Mau 1958, also Annas
and Barnes 1994.)

(b) I retain the MSS reading *kakodaimonesteros*, 'more unhappy', in
215. Mutschmann alters to *kakodaimonestatos*, 'most unhappy', citing the
parallel passage in *PH* III. 277. (Bury reads *kakodaimonesteros*, but translates 'most unhappy'; Russo is similarly overgenerous, translating 'più
sventurato di ogni *altro* mortale' (my emphasis).) 'More unhappy than all
human beings' is of course logically odd; but the substitution of phrases
such as 'than all human beings' for 'than all other human beings' is
ubiquitous in everyday English, and I see no reason to think that the
Greeks did not do the same (cf. textual point on 173–7 above). The
difference between 'more unhappy' and the more accurate 'most unhappy' is of just the kind one would expect if, as I have argued, *PH* III
is the later, revised version.

[(c) Blomqvist (1968: 100) argues for altering *aphrodisiōn* to *aphrodision*
in 212. This is probably correct; however, the translation is unaffected.]

This final argument states its conclusion in a quite general form ('there
is not any skill relating to life', 215), even though the skill relating to life
is assumed throughout to be practical wisdom specifically. The suggestion made at the beginning of the chapter (esp. 168–70), that a skill
relating to life is something which the dogmatists in general claim to
offer, has been dropped (as we have seen, it was inconsistently maintained over the course of the chapter); practical wisdom is referred to in
the closing sentence (215) as 'what has been deemed to be the skill
relating to life'. Nevertheless, the argument has nothing specifically to do
with the Stoic conception of practical wisdom; it centres instead around
the concepts of benefit and self-control (*egkrateia*, often translated 'continence'). The two central premisses and the conclusion are again presented initially (210; cf. 197), followed by more detailed discussion.
(This style of presentation is very common in Sextus, even though it has
not loomed large in *M* XI so far—but see 71, 79 above; we shall find
several examples in the next chapter.) The first premiss, that a skill
benefits the person who possesses it more than it benefits anyone else
(210; cf. 215), is assumed not to need argument; it is the second premiss,
that practical wisdom is of no benefit to the person who possesses it, to

which Sextus devotes the whole of the subsequent discussion. (This pattern in particular is common; see e.g. *M* VIII. 166, IX. 232, 375–6, and 218, 224 below. Often this is because the first premiss is a disjunction, presented as obviously exhausting the possible alternatives; unfortunately, the first premiss in the present argument is by no means so self-evident—see below and Appendix A.) It is also assumed that the benefits which practical wisdom supposedly affords are a function of the wise person's being self-controlled; this is stated in the first sentence of 210 (cf. textual point (a) above). The argument which follows is therefore mainly directed to showing that the wise person derives no benefit whatever from being self-controlled; the steps are as follows:

1. To be self-controlled is either to lack all untoward impulses, or it is to have such impulses but to overcome them—i.e. to prevent them from achieving expression in action (211).

2. But the first alternative is senseless; people who lack all untoward impulses cannot be described as self-*controlled*, since there is nothing for them to control (211, illustrated with examples in 212).

3. But if the second alternative obtains, then the practical wisdom in virtue of which the wise person has self-control is of no benefit. (a) If the wise person has untoward impulses, this already shows that practical wisdom has failed to help; for it has failed to quell these impulses (this is presumably what is meant by 'practical wisdom was of no benefit to him right when he was in a state of disturbance and in need of help', 213). (b) If the wise person does not allow expression to these impulses, the disturbance which they cause by their very presence cannot even be alleviated, as it is in the case of lesser mortals, by satisfying them; hence the wise person's self-control actually results in his being *more* disturbed and unhappy than other people (213–14).

This argument makes several points which in themselves have some plausibility; but it entirely misses its target. On the familiar Aristotelian conception of continence (see esp. *NE* VII. 1151b32–1152a3), step 2 is unexceptionable. Then again, it seems reasonable to say that a person who has wayward impulses over which self-control needs to be exerted is worse off than someone in whom no such inner conflict arises (this too is clearly Aristotle's view); if the wise person's condition were the former, it might well be viewed as less than optimal, and this provides some support for step 3a. As for step 3b, we can surely go along with it at least to the extent of allowing that repression can lead to unhappiness; people who habitually deny expression to their impulses may in this sense be 'more disturbed' than people who do not.

No doubt these points admit of much further discussion. However, there is no need for us to pursue the issues; for even if Sextus is entirely correct in what he says here, the Stoics are not touched in the slightest. First, they would certainly deny that the wise person is self-controlled in the sense treated in step 3. Someone who genuinely possesses practical wisdom and the other virtues is not subject to impulses which need to be controlled; such impulses belong to those who are still subject to the passions. A passion, according to the Stoics, is an 'excessive impulse' (Stob. II. 88, 8; cf. Galen, *PHP* 4. 2. 10–18 (= LS 65J)), and in the wise person all such impulses have been eradicated. (More strikingly, passions are also described by them as a certain type of mistaken *opinion*; but this need not occupy us in the present context. On the passions in Stoicism, see LS 65, Nussbaum 1994: ch. 10.) But the Stoics would also deny the conceptual point made in step 2. For their conception of self-control is very different from Aristotle's; self-control is a virtue (DL VII. 92), which the wise person therefore possesses despite lacking the impulses just mentioned. It is defined as 'a disposition which cannot go beyond what is in accordance with correct reason, or a state incapable of being worsted by pleasures' (DL VII. 93); Sextus himself reports a similar definition at *M* IX. 153. This definition makes no reference to the presence of wayward impulses which need to be controlled (though Plutarch characteristically tries to argue that the Stoics ought to, or are bound to, admit these into their account (*Virt. mor.* 449C)). The definition specifies that the wise person who has self-control does not ever *do* the kinds of things which lesser persons are tempted to do, and often do do; it is quite compatible with this that wise persons themselves are not even tempted to do these things. Sextus relies on a conception of self-control which is no doubt based in common sense; the Greek word *egkrateia*, like the English 'self-control', does normally have the connotation of *mastery over* something in oneself. But the Stoics do not share this conception. In any case, even aside from this, the Stoics have no reason to grant the assumption underlying Sextus' whole argument: that the benefit conferred by practical wisdom is due to the self-control which is an aspect of it. This assumption is in fact quite arbitrary; many other ways can be imagined in which practical wisdom might be held to benefit those who possess it.

Step 3b contains ideas which are reminiscent of the discussions in chs. IV and V of the disturbances suffered by the dogmatist; there is the idea that having a craving for something (which is the species of impulse Sextus seems to have in mind) is intrinsically disturbing, and there is the equation, implied here if not actually stated, between disturbance and unhappiness. But these similarities are not enough to show that the present argument has simply borrowed material from earlier in the book; the latter equation was widespread in the Pyrrhonist tradition (see point 6a on 118), and the former idea is not even peculiar to Pyrrhonism. Besides, the idea that one's disturbance is reduced by getting the thing which one craves (214) is actually in tension with an important theme in those earlier chapters (see esp. 125–7). The present passage is thus entirely compatible with the hypothesis that part B draws on a different source from part A.

The parallel passage of *PH* III contains an explicit reference (277) to the portion of the book corresponding to chs. IV and V of *M* XI (235–8). Sextus mitigates the tension just alluded to by stressing that it is the person who *thinks he has a skill relating to life* who is troubled by the presence of both good things and bad things; by contrast, the person whose disturbance is 'weakened' by getting what he or she craves and thinks good is 'the inferior person' (*phaulos*). This is not wholly convincing, however; for in the earlier passages it was the belief that things are by nature good or bad which was responsible for the trouble in question, and this belief can hardly be thought to be unique to dogmatic philosophers (cf. on 163, 165 above). None the less, it is interesting that *PH* III connects the two different portions of the book to a greater extent than does *M* XI (for another case of this, see Appendix A on *M* XI. 173–7, *PH* III. 182, 239). This fact is another small point favouring the view that *PH* III is the later version; other things being equal, one would expect that greater cohesiveness, not less, would be the result of a revision.

For further comparison of 210–15 and the parallel passage at *PH* III. 274–7, see Appendix A.

CHAPTER VII (216–57)

In this final chapter Sextus argues that even if (contrary to the arguments of the previous chapter) there is a skill relating to life, it cannot be taught. The structure of the discussion is clearly previewed in the introductory section (216–18), and the plan laid out there is precisely followed in the remainder of the chapter. The arguments are divided into those having to do with teaching and learning in general (219–43) and those having to do specifically with the teachability of practical wisdom, the skill relating to life according to the Stoics (243–56) (on the prominence accorded to Stoicism in this portion of the book, see on the previous chapter). In the former category there are said to be difficulties having to do with the subject-matter to be taught, the teacher, the learner, and the means by which the teaching is to take place (218). With regard to the subject-matter to be taught, it is argued that (a) neither what exists nor what does not exist is taught (219–23), (b) neither the corporeal nor the incorporeal is taught (224–31), and (c) neither what is true nor what is false is taught, nor either what is skilled or what is unskilled (232–3). There follows an argument against there being either teachers or learners (234–8), then an argument against there being any feasible means of teaching (239–43). Concerning the teachability of practical wisdom specifically, there is just one extended argument (243–56): the first part of this is adapted from the general argument in 234–8 against teachers and learners, while the second part introduces new considerations to show that wise persons are unable to perceive folly (as they would need to do in order to teach those who are not wise). The chapter ends with a sentence which serves as a conclusion to the whole book, and indeed to the entire work of which this book is a part (257).

The introductory remarks on the previous chapter covered a number of points which apply to this chapter as well; but a couple of points may be added. First, while most of the arguments in this chapter are paralleled more or less closely by arguments in *PH* III—and this is no surprise—the arguments on teaching and learning in general also have a parallel in the general introduction to *M* I–VI (*M* I. 9–38); the similarities here are generally more exact. This is the only case in the writings of Sextus where all three of his works contain extended passages covering the same material. It is clear from explicit back-references that *M* I–VI is later than *M* VII–XI (*M* I. 35, III. 116; for some less obvious instances, see Blomqvist 1974); I will suggest in what follows, and in Appendix A, that comparisons among these three passages favour the conclusion that *PH* is the latest of the three works.

The topic of teaching and learning, and specifically the teaching and learning of virtue, has a long history in Greek philosophy; Sextus' comment at the beginning of 217, that 'the arguments about learning, among the philosophers, are many and varied' (cf. *M* I. 9), appears to signal his recognition of this fact. The Stoics' interest in this topic is clear from DL VII. 91, where several different Stoics are said to have written to the effect that virtue is teachable; but the topic was already an old one by

their time. The question whether virtue can be taught is at the centre of
two of Plato's best-known dialogues, the *Protagoras* and the *Meno*, and
occupies him in several others as well. 'Concerning wisdom and virtue,
whether they are teachable' is also the title of one section of the *Dual
Arguments* (*Dissoi Logoi*), a work composed under strong Sophistic influence probably around 400 BC. Interest in this topic was initially aroused
in large part by the novel educational activities and aspirations of the
Sophists; the development in the fifth century of specialized bodies of
knowledge, or 'skills' (*technai*), was no doubt another stimulus towards
reflection on the nature of teaching and learning and on what kinds of
things could be taught or learned. Several of Sextus' arguments may well
be indirectly indebted to the paradox raised by Meno in the dialogue
bearing his name (8od–e). But the arguments in this chapter also give
the impression of having been institutionalized within the sceptical tradition itself; there is a routine and often almost mechanical character
about the way they are expounded.

216–18: Transition and introduction

Unlike the previous chapter (see on 168 above), this chapter starts with
two sentences (216) which neatly effect the transition from the previous
material, and successfully motivate that which is to follow. On Sextus'
habit of introducing arguments 'for good measure' (*ek perittou*), even
though their conclusions already follow from previous arguments, see
again on 168. The ways in which 217–18 preview the rest of the chapter
have already been mentioned.

Sextus says that he is going to 'teach that [the skill relating to life] is
unteachable' (216). This is put in a deliberately paradoxical way, but is
not, considered on its own, self-refuting; it is not by way of the skill
relating to life itself that he proposes to impart this teaching. However,
since the majority of his arguments to this conclusion are directed against
the possibility of teaching and learning in general, his words here do,
after all, invite criticism. (The paradoxical formulation of *M* XI. 216 is
avoided in the parallel passages *M* I. 9 and *PH* III. 252. If I am right that
M XI is the earliest of the three, this may be because he later senses that
there is a problem here.) It is possible that Sextus would be willing to
accept the charge of self-refutation, and contend that his arguments still
leave us in a position such that there is no teaching or learning; he offers
a precisely analogous defence of his proof that there is no such thing as
proof (*M* VIII. 480–1, and see McPherran 1987). Though he gives no

indications that this move has occurred to him, it might be judged acceptable in the present case. However, this issue naturally leads to more general questions about the sceptic's attitude towards teaching.

For this is not the only place in which Sextus suggests that the sceptic does engage in some variety of teaching or learning. A better-known case is *PH* I. 23-4, where he says that one of the four main ways in which the sceptic's everyday life is regulated is the 'teaching of skills' (*didaskalia technōn*); but we have also seen in *M* XI itself that Sextus is prepared to ascribe certain 'teachings' to the sceptic—cf. 111, 140 with Comm. If his outlook is to be coherent, some distinction needs to be drawn between the kind of teaching which is acceptable to the sceptic and the kind which is here argued to be impossible. One might try to draw the requisite distinction as follows: the kind of teaching which is impossible is the imparting of bodies of theoretical knowledge, such as the dogmatists claim to possess, whereas the kind of teaching which is possible is the inculcation of abilities, or systematic sets of activities, through supervised practice. Sextus refers to scepticism itself as an 'ability' (*dunamis*, *PH* I. 8), rather than as a doctrine; and his preference for the Methodic school of medicine over the Empiric school (*PH* I. 236-41)—or at least some segment of the Empiric school—seems to be based on his portrayal of Methodism as *simply* a set of treatments to be applied in appropriate circumstances, not a set of doctrines (positive or negative) in which those treatments are supposed to be grounded. (On the complex issues surrounding these two schools and Sextus' discussion of them in this passage, see Frede 1983*a*, 1987*a*.) By contrast, the teaching which, in the present chapter and its analogues in *PH* III and *M* I, is argued to be impossible is assumed to concern some 'subject being taught' (218); and this seems to mean some object, or set of objects, about which information is to be imparted to the learner (or sometimes this information itself), rather than some activity in which the learner is to be trained.

This approach may work for *PH*. Unfortunately, it will not cover the uses of the word 'teach' in 111, 140 above, where it is clearly the *propositions* argued for in this book itself which are said to be taught by the sceptic. In addition, as we saw, it was taken to be crucial to the attainment of happiness that the 'teaching' in question be *successful*—i.e. that one *accept* the content of this 'teaching'. Merely omitting the *word* 'teach' in these passages will not solve the problem; for, in any normal sense of the word, teaching is in fact what is happening in that part of the book. Nor can I can see any further distinction among uses of the term 'teach' which would allow us to reconcile these passages with the arguments in

ch. VII. Sextus does not seem to have noticed that there is a problem
here; either his source also did not notice, or part B derives from a
different source from part A (a conclusion for which we saw some possible support in the previous chapter). On the paradox at 216 and its
implications, see also Voelke 1990: 191–4.

For comparison of 218 and the parallel passages at *M* I. 9 and *PH* III.
252, see Appendix A.

219–23: First argument that there is no subject taught

Textual points:

(a) I retain the MSS reading *epei toi*, 'since in fact', in the fourth
sentence of 221, rather than emending to *epeita*, 'then', as does
Mutschmann, following Rüstow. It is true that this introduces a new
argument for the conclusion just stated. But as Heintz (1932: 260–1)
shows, Sextus does sometimes use *epei*, 'since', in this position, introducing additional considerations in favour of what has already been
argued on other grounds (e.g. *M* X. 164).

[(b) I do not accept Heintz's supplement ⟨*to gar on ouk echei allo ti*⟩
in the first sentence of 223, accepted by Mutschmann and Bury. The
sense is quite acceptable, albeit a little inelegant, without it; Sextus is
simply assuming, rather than stating, that any attribute other than that of
being existent must be non-existent. (On this reasoning, see below.) The
supplement is lifted from the parallel passage of *PH* III (258); on the
illegitimacy of changing the text of *M* XI solely on the basis of parallels
with *PH* III, see above on 48–67, point (i); 79–89, point (d).]

In this section Sextus argues that there can be no subject-matter for
teaching or learning, because neither (I) what does not exist nor (II) what
exists can be taught. (I) is argued for on several different grounds:

a. What does not exist has no attributes, hence not the attribute of
being taught (219).

b. What does not exist is not true, and so not real (220).

c. What does not exist cannot give rise to any impressions (220).

d. If what does not exist were taught, everything which was taught
would be false (221).

e. If what does not exist were taught, this would be either (i) in virtue
of its being non-existent or (ii) in virtue of something else; but neither
alternative is possible (221).

There is just one argument for (II): what exists would have to be taught either (i) in virtue of its being existent or (ii) in virtue of something else; but neither alternative is possible (222–3).

Some remarks on the terms 'exist', 'existent', etc. are in order. In this section I use these terms to translate *esti*, *on*, etc.—i.e. forms of the Greek verb which is most non-committally translated 'is', 'being', etc. 'Is' is obviously the right translation for the numerous predicative uses of *esti*; but use of these non-committal translations throughout would have made for an almost unreadable English version. Unfortunately, when *esti* is used non-predicatively, it can mean at least two different things; sometimes 'exists' is an appropriate translation (at least in the Hellenistic period and beyond—it is debatable how far this is true in earlier Greek philosophy), and sometimes 'be so', 'be the case', or 'be true' (the 'veridical' usage). In most of the arguments in this section, 'exists' seems to be the translation best suited to the reasoning employed. But in (Ib) and (Id) the veridical usage would have been more appropriate. (The shift between these two usages is made easier by the fact that the term 'the subject being taught' (*to didaskomenon pragma*) could refer either to the *entities* being *taught about* or to the set of *propositions* having to do with these entities which the teacher is attempting to get the learner to grasp; the former reading clearly fits the translation 'exists' for *esti*, and the latter the translation 'is the case'.) However, it would be intolerable to switch translations several times in the course of a single section; I have therefore, with some misgivings, translated by 'exists', etc. throughout.

That what does not exist cannot form the subject-matter of any teaching is hardly controversial, and Sextus really does not need to devote five separate arguments to establishing it; 219–21 are tedious and, in the case of (Ib) and (Id), somewhat repetitive. Arguments (Ia) and (Ic) need no comment. (Ib) and (Id), as just noted, trade on the flexibility of the Greek verb *esti*, but also on some flexibility in the word *alēthes*, translated 'true'; while 'true' is clearly the best single translation here—the Stoic definition is unequivocally a definition of 'true' (more on this below)—the word can also mean 'genuine', 'real'. The same kind of flexibility also affects *huparkton*, *huparchei*, translated 'real', 'is real'; most commonly these terms refer to what really exists, but in the Stoic definition of 'true' *huparchei* must refer to what is really the case (see below)—'is real' is my attempt at a compromise between the two. Again, there are inevitable shortcomings with my translations, as there would be with any attempt

to render the same Greek words with the same English words throughout the section. One simply has to bear in mind that ancient Greek is in
general quite willing to use the same terms for what we regard as the
importantly distinct concepts of reality, existence, and truth. Hence the
moves from 'exist' to 'be true' and from 'be true' to 'be real' in 220; and
hence the claim in 221 that 'the true belongs among the things which
exist and are real'. Though Sextus is clearly exploiting the flexibility of
these terms, one need not therefore accuse him of being underhanded.

Sextus says in the course of (Ib) that 'learning is of things which are
true'. If this means, as one would naturally suppose, that only true
propositions are learned, it is false—unless he is assuming a restricted
conception of teaching and learning, according to which the inculcation
of, say, creationism or astrology does not count as the teaching of it, and
the process of becoming aware of, and accepting, its content does not
count as learning it. That his conception is thus restricted is suggested
by 231, where it is assumed that only things which are 'undisputed' can
be taught (and cf. 232).

The Stoic definition of 'true' recurs with virtually identical wording,
along with a correlative definition of 'false'—'that which is not real and
is in opposition to something'—in *M* VIII. 10, and receives some discussion later in that book (85–6, 88–90); it is not attested by any author
other than Sextus. 'Is in opposition to' (*antikeitai*) is the normal Stoic
word for being the contradictory of some proposition. As one would
expect, then, it is propositions which are true or false (cf. DL VII. 65);
what a true proposition is 'in opposition to' is the false proposition which
is its negation. So what the Stoics must mean here by 'what is real' (*ho
huparchei*) is 'what is really the case'; it is this feature which differenti-
ates true from false propositions. Here, at least, there are none of the
ambiguities which were exercising us just above. For further discussion
see Long 1971: esp. 91–4, LS I, comm. on 34.

I said 'the Stoic definition of "true"' rather than '. . . of truth' because
the Stoics also draw a distinction between 'truth' (*hē alētheia*) and 'the true'
(*to alēthes*); on this, see Sextus, *PH* II. 80–3, *M* VII. 38–45, with Long
1978*b*. On the Stoic habit of omitting the article in definitions ('true
is . . .' rather than 'the true is . . .'), cf. linguistic point (a) on 31–9 above.

As noted above, argument (Ie) is in the form of the dilemma. The first
horn of the dilemma is unproblematic. But why, in arguing against the
second horn, does Sextus baldly assert that 'the "something else" exists'?

Two possible answers suggest themselves. One is that the expression
'something else', if it is to be used meaningfully, must have some existing
referent. If this is what Sextus had in mind, the Stoics would disagree;
according to them, *not* all the items which qualify as 'somethings' exist
(see on 224 below). The other possible explanation is that something
which is other than the property of being non-existent must itself be
other than non-existent—i.e. it must exist. This explanation is more
likely in view of the fact that the second horn of the dilemma which
comprises argument II seems to proceed in an exactly parallel fashion.
Here it is simply assumed, without explanation, that any attribute other
than that of being existent must be non-existent (223; on the text of this
passage, see textual point (b) above). This assumption is clearly false,
involving a confusion between, on the one hand, the identity of a certain
attribute, and on the other hand, the attributes which in turn belong to
that attribute; a thing may possess many attributes which exist, but
which are not themselves the attribute *of existing*. Indeed, Sextus' own
very next words, '*every* attribute of it is existent', suggest this point. If
argument (Ie) is relying on the same type of assumption, it is just as
flawed—even though the claim being advanced in this case, that there
are no non-existent properties of a thing, is in itself difficult to object to.
    The first horn of argument II is by no means immediately clear; what
is the force of the crucial claim that 'it is necessary that there be something untaught, in order that from this learning may come about' (222)?
One might think the point is that only things which have *not yet* been
taught (to someone) can be taught (to that person). But Sextus can also
be understood as making the Aristotelian point (cf. *Post. An.* I. 1) that
teaching and learning have to proceed on the basis of knowledge which
is already present prior to this teaching—and which is therefore, at least
as regards this particular episode of teaching, 'untaught'. It is quite clear
in the parallel passage of *PH* III (257) that this is the operative assumption; it seems easiest (in the absence of any clearly preferable interpretation) to read *M* XI's argument as invoking the same assumption. In
either case, in order for the argument to be valid, 'taught' and 'untaught'
must be understood as shorthand for 'taught/untaught to person A at
time *t*'; otherwise it could be objected that the same subject-matter could
be both taught (to some people and/or at some times) and untaught (to
other people and/or at other times).

A further unsatisfactory feature of this section is the concluding statement, 'none of the things *which exist* is taught' (223). This contradicts

the approach of this whole series of arguments, which is to countenance
(even if only to dismiss) the possibility that there may be things which do
not exist. The contradiction is plain even from the sentence of which this
statement is the final portion. Sextus should have said simply 'nothing is
taught'; in the parallel concluding sentence in *PH* III. 258, this is what
he does say. (The passage in *M* I does not include a similar concluding
sentence.)

For further comparison of 219–23 and the parallel passages at *M* I. 10–
14, *PH* III. 256–8, and DL IX. 100, see Appendix A.

224–31: Second argument that there is no subject taught

[I retain the MSS reading *sōma* at the end of 224, rather than altering
to *sōmata*, as does Mutschmann, following Heintz. The sense is quite
acceptable—'sayables are not body', i.e. are not corporeal—and the text
cited to justify the change (*M* I. 20) is not precisely parallel. (Bury
retains *sōma*, but translates as if the text read *sōmata*.)]

This section begins with an abrupt and unprepared reference to the
'somethings'. As mentioned earlier (see above on 8–14), the 'something'
is the highest genus in Stoic ontology; as Sextus says (224), it covers not
only corporeals, which according to the Stoics are the only things which
exist (*einai*), but also incorporeals (Alexander, *In Ar. Top.* 301, 19–25
(= LS 27B)), which merely 'subsist' (*huphistasthai*, Procl. *In Pl. Tim.*
271D (= LS 51F))—viz. place, time, void, and 'sayables' (Sextus, *M* X.
218; cf. *M* XI. 230—on 'sayables', see below). (It is arguable that fictional
entities and limits are also regarded as 'subsisting' and as 'somethings'—
see LS 27, 50 and, against this view, Brunschwig 1994*b*: 96–9; but this
need not concern us here.)

  Why does Sextus suddenly refer to the 'somethings'? The answer is
given by the parallel passage of *M* I, where, *between* the material corresponding to the last section and that corresponding to the present one,
there is a discussion of whether what is taught is 'something' or 'not-
something' (15–18); given this intervening section, the reference to the
'somethings' in *M* I. 19, corresponding to *M* XI. 224, is entirely natural.
The version which included this extra section is evidently the original
one. Since *M* I is later than *M* XI, it must have been Sextus' source
which contained the fuller version preserved in *M* I; when composing *M*
XI, he chose to omit the argument about the 'something' and the 'not-

something', but in composing *M* I he chose to include it. In composing *M* I Sextus has returned to the original source, and has followed it more closely than he did when composing *M* XI; see Appendix A on 219–23 and parallel passages. (*PH* III does not mention the 'somethings'; again, it is less beholden to the original source than are the other two works.)

It is extremely difficult to summarize this argument in a way which is neat and concise as well as being true to the text; Sextus' reasoning does not stay on a single clear track, and is in places repetitive. But a schematic version might look like this:

What is taught must be either (I) body or (II) incorporeal; but neither is possible (224).

(Ia) On the Stoic view, body is not taught, since what are taught are 'sayables', which are incorporeal (224).

(Ib) What is taught must be either sensible or intelligible; but body is neither, so it cannot be taught (225). For:

> (i) Body is not sensible (226).
>
> (Digression from (i): Even if it were sensible, it still could not be taught (227).)
>
> (ii) Body is not intelligible, and so on this count, too, cannot be taught (228).

(Ic) Suppose that (as the standard view would have it), there are bodies, some of which are sensible and some intelligible. Then, if body is taught, either sensible bodies or intelligible bodies are taught (229). But:

> (i) Sensible bodies are not taught (229).
>
> (ii) Intelligible bodies are not taught (229).
>
> (iii) So body is not taught (229).

(II) Nor is the incorporeal taught (230–1).

Conclusion: Nothing is taught (231).

Note that (Ia), (Ib), and (Ic) are *separate* arguments for the same conclusion—body is not taught; (i)–(ii) within (Ib) and (i)–(iii) within (Ic) are of course individual steps of those arguments.

There is no difficulty in the reasoning in (Ia). The argument, of course, has force only against the Stoics, since the doctrine of *lekta* is exclusively theirs; but we have seen that the Stoics are the opponents Sextus has especially in mind throughout this part of the book. *Lekta* (I borrow the translation 'sayables' from LS) are, to put it as uncontroversially as possible, what get said in linguistic utterances. It may seem tempting to identify them with the meanings of sentences (and of some, but probably not all, parts of sentences); see e.g. Mates 1953: ch. 2. But the evidence suggests rather that they are, at least primarily, the *states of affairs* which declarative sentences express. (It is not clear how this is to be extended to non-declarative sentences such as questions, commands, etc., to which there may well also have been thought to be *lekta* corresponding—see DL VII. 66–7; the situation of the 'incomplete' *lekta*— those corresponding to certain parts of sentences—is also complicated.) See *M* VIII. 11–12, 70, DL VII. 57, and for discussion LS I, comm. on 33 (34), Frede 1994*b*.

In saying that 'sayables' are what is taught, Sextus is clearly thinking of 'the subject being taught' as the *content* of teaching. But for the rest of this section, in considering whether body or the incorporeal are taught, he seems instead to have in mind the *objects* about which teaching occurs. This is a particularly clear example of a phenomenon which recurs throughout much of the chapter; on the ambiguity of 'the subject being taught' (*to didaskomenon pragma*), see above on 219–23.

In introducing (Ib) Sextus refers to *Against the Physicists*, and implies that the reasoning which is to follow will be reproducing arguments already made in that book. *M* IX. 437–9 does contain an argument to the effect that body is neither sensible nor intelligible. Unfortunately, only one part of that argument is paralleled in the present passage: (i) employs the same reasoning as *M* IX. 437, but (ii) has nothing to do with *M* IX. 438–9. Instead, (ii) is close to another passage of *M* IX (369), which is on a quite different topic; as a result, the relevance of the reasoning in (ii) is not easy to see (we shall return to this point). However, it is plausible to suppose that Sextus is not here merely borrowing from his own previous work. This is not just because it is hard to see why he would have borrowed *one half* of a pertinent argument and then substituted an argument of very doubtful relevance in place of the other half; there is some more direct evidence. *M* IX. 437 mentions only the first of the two definitions of body given here; and the parallel passage of *M* I (whose argument (19–29) has precisely the same structure as the present section) mentions (21) two other definitions besides those given here, neither of which occur in *M* IX. 437. There is also the digression following (i) (in both *M* XI and *M* I (23)), to which nothing in *M* IX or X corresponds. It looks, then, as if Sextus is drawing on a source other than his own *M* IX. The obvious supposition is that it is this source which has combined these two ill-matched halves of the argument, and that Sextus has uncritically reproduced the reasoning which he found there—while also noticing that this reasoning resembles some passages in *Against the Physicists*. (The extra examples in *M* I—together, perhaps, with the fact that *Against the Physicists* is not mentioned this time—also suggest, again, that he has returned to this source in composing *M* I, rather than following *M* XI.)

The first definition of body in 226 is said be due to Epicurus. That size and shape were essential features of body in Epicureanism (together with weight, which Democritus did not recognize) is confirmed by Plutarch, *Plac. phil.* 877E; cf. Sextus, *M* X. 240, which mentions all three features together with resistance. *M* XI's second definition is also said in *M* I. 21 to be Epicurean (and to be used by them to distinguish body from void). But Galen, *Qual. inc.* XIX. 483, 13–16 (= LS 45F) ascribes the same definition to the Stoics. These points are not, however, incompatible; Sextus' detail about the function of the definition inspires some confidence in his report, but this does not show that the Stoics, or some Stoics, did not accept the same definition (see Mueller 1982: 75–7).

(Ibi) is very unconvincing. The claim that it is the function of reason rather than of the senses to 'grasp everything which is grasped by way of a conjunction of several things' (226) is vaguely reminiscent of the argument in the *Theaetetus* (184b–186d) which finally demolishes the thesis that knowledge is sensation; here it is shown, among other things, that certain mental operations which involve the comparison of several sensory properties must be the operations of reason. But in the *Theaetetus* the whole point is that the comparisons in question are between the deliverances of *different* senses, whereas the features which figure in the definitions of bodies in 226 are all accessible to both sight and touch. If the point is that anything which has multiple related properties is inaccessible to sensation, it is absurd. If, on the other hand, the point is that understanding the *concept* of body requires understanding several different concepts and the relation between them, which only reason can accomplish—and this is suggested more clearly in the parallel passage of *M* I (22), but is possible for our passage as well—it is true but plainly irrelevant; one does not need to understand the concept of body in order to sense bodies.

Following (Ibi), Sextus inserts an argument (227) which is not strictly relevant to his agenda at this point, though it clearly is germane to the general project of showing that nothing can be taught. The main point here is that the perception of sensory qualities is not something we are taught; it just happens naturally. The argument fails, because there are many other things about sensible objects which might be held to be

teachable besides their immediately obvious sensory qualities. From the
fact that 'no one learns to see white', etc., it does not follow that 'of
sensible things *nothing* is taught'. Of course, if 'sensible things' *means*
'the sensory qualities of things'—and the Greek *aisthēta* can certainly
mean this (cf. e.g. Ar. *De An.* II. 6)—then this does follow; but it still
does not follow that nothing having to do with *bodies* can be taught—
which is what Sextus is attempting to establish. In this connection, the
phrase 'body is not taught' and related phrases are clumsy and unhelpful;
they close off from the start a possibility which appears obviously to
obtain: viz. that some features of bodies can be the object of teaching,
and some cannot.

Having argued that body is not sensible, Sextus turns to the possibility
that it is intelligible (228). One would expect him now to argue that body
is not intelligible (cf. 225). What he presents himself as arguing is instead
that body cannot be taught 'as an intelligible thing'; i.e. that it cannot be
taught in virtue of being intelligible. In this respect my step (Ibii) in the
summary above is perhaps over-generous; it draws on the parallel at *M*
I. 24—'it remains to say, then, that body is intelligible and in this way
teachable'—which succeeds better at situating this stage of the argument
within the original plan. In neither case, however, is the fit perfect; it
looks as if the digression in 227 (*M* I. 23) has somewhat diverted Sextus
or his source from the argument promised.

Whether (Ibii) purports to argue that body is not intelligible or merely
that it cannot be taught *qua* intelligible, it is very hard to see how the
considerations offered in 228 are supposed to support the conclusion. As
noted earlier, these considerations echo *M* IX. 369–70, which belong in
an argument to the effect that body cannot be conceived. In the present
passage, too, the claim is that the obvious way of attempting to conceive
body, viz. as a combination of three dimensions, will in fact result in
one's conceiving something incorporeal—from which it will follow (though
this is not stated) that body cannot be conceived. The argument is in any
case questionable. From the fact that none of the three dimensions,
considered on its own, amounts to body, it does not follow that each of
the three dimensions is incorporeal (and hence that the amalgam of the
three is incorporeal); rather, each of the three dimensions is, precisely, an
aspect of body. It is perhaps doubtful, however, whether either Sextus or
his dogmatic opponents would have had the analytical resources to sort this
out. (A more detailed version of this argument occurs at *M* III. 83–91.
But here, too, Sextus refuses to consider any possibilities besides (1) each
of the three dimensions is itself body, and (2) each of them is incorporeal.)

The more pressing question, though, is why this argument is inserted here. If body cannot even be conceived, it does of course follow that it cannot be the subject of any teaching (and this point, too, is made more explicit in the more extensive treatment of this topic in *M* I. 24–5); but how is this supposed to be related specifically to body's being *intelligible*? I can only assume that since this reasoning talks of the *conceiving* (*noein*) of body, Sextus confusedly supposes that the possibility is thereby being entertained that body is something intelligible (*noēton*) *as opposed to* something sensible. Again, he would have done better to borrow from *M* IX. 438–9, which would have led to a clear completion of (Ib); however, as noted above (see on 225), it looks as if the problem may derive from Sextus' source rather than from Sextus himself.

(Ic) seems to overlap very considerably in subject-matter with (Ib). The transition in the first sentence of 229 is very awkward, giving no indication that, or why, much the same ground is being retraced; again, my presentation in the summary above bends over backwards to give Sextus a sensibly constructed argument, and it again relies on the parallel passage in *M* I. 26, which, while not completely clear, goes much further than *M* XI. 229 in justifying the presence of (Ic). (Ici) is similar in its force to the digression at 227—and similarly problematic. (Icii) cites the 'as yet unresolved disagreement about it' (*anepikriton mechri tou nun peri autou diaphōnian*). As is clear from the remainder of the sentence, the 'it' here should refer to intelligible body—i.e. to that kind of body, or those aspects of body, which can only be known about through the intellect, not through the senses; read literally, the 'it' refers to the intelligible in general, but it is intelligible *body* which is the subject here. (*M* I. 27 avoids this unclarity.) It is not immediately specified why the presence of unresolved disagreement guarantees unteachability; but this is explained at 231 (on which see below), following the similar reference to unresolved disagreement in 230 (step II). On the character and power of Pyrrhonist arguments from unresolved disagreement, see Barnes 1990c: ch. 1.

Those who say that intelligible body is indivisible (*atomon*)—i.e. that there is a level, below that which is accessible to the senses, at which body is indivisible—are, of course, the atomists, both the Epicureans and their fifth-century forerunners Leucippus and Democritus. Those who say that intelligible body is (i.e. that there is a level, of which only the intellect can be aware, at which body is) 'without parts and smallest' are the Epicureans specifically; see Epicurus, *Letter to Herodotus* X. 56–9, with Furley 1967: pt. I and LS I, comm. on 9, II, comm. on 9A. Those who say that intelligible body is 'composed of parts and can be divided to infinity' (i.e. that body is infinitely divisible, so that any portion of body, no matter how small and inaccessible to the senses, can be said to be composed of parts) are the Stoics—see Stob. I. 142, 2–6, DL VII. 150, with Todd 1973*a*, LS I, comm. on 50—and Aristotle—see *Phys.* 231b15–18, 232a23–5. This leaves the view that intelligible body is 'divisible'. This may be just a loose (and redundant) reference to the Stoic/ Aristotelian view. But that may be too charitable; for there seems to be some confusion in Sextus or his source. The parallel passage at *M* I. 27 sets out the same first pair of alternatives, but then presents the second pair of alternatives as *subspecies* of the view that 'it is divisible'. This makes sense if and only if it is body in general, rather than 'intelligible body', which is being referred to as divisible (and the wording of the second pair of alternatives in *M* I is clearly tailored to this); yet it is quite unclear who might be thought to hold that body *in general* is *in*divisible. The difficulty in both passages no doubt stems partly from the fact that the notion of 'intelligible body' is never properly pinned down; hence the exact reference of the 'it' is never really made clear—as was already suggested by my rather tortuous paraphrases just above (and see the previous paragraph).

As was observed earlier (see on 173–7 above), arguments from unresolved disagreement are surprisingly rare in *M* XI; the presence of a few such arguments in part B, and their complete absence in part A, might lead one to believe that the two portions of the book derive from different strata in the history of Pyrrhonism. While such considerations are not entirely without weight, they are far from decisive; see also on *aphanēs*, 'non-apparent', 205; the present passage contains nothing novel in that respect. On the other hand, it is striking that in *PH* III the notion of unresolved disagreement, as well as the paired notions of the apparent and the non-evident, is central to the entire passage corresponding to the present section. Corresponding loosely to *M* XI. 229 (but much more closely than to 227–8, which is the parallel cited by Mutschmann, Bury, and Russo) is *PH* III. 254. This states that the subject being taught must be either apparent or non-evident—but that it is not the former, because what is apparent does not need teaching, nor the latter, because the non-evident is subject to unresolved disagreement, hence not apprehensible, hence not teachable. This argument is then referred back to in the brief passage which parallels *M* XI. 224–31 as a whole; Sextus simply says (255) that what is taught is either corporeal or incorporeal, but that since (as just shown) each is either apparent or non-evident, neither can be taught. So even where *M* XI does use arguments from unresolved disagreement, *PH* III does so in much larger measure; that *PH* III should draw more extensively on a strategy made systematic by the later sceptic Agrippa is only to be expected if *PH* is the later work (see Appendix A on *M* XI. 180–3, *PH* III. 240–2).

As noted above, step II, that the incorporeal is not teachable, makes use of the same strategy based on unresolved disagreement (the parallel passage at *M* I. 28 does the same, though at slightly greater length). That unresolved disagreement should entail unteachability, which is not self-evident, is here briefly justified (231). But the justification amounts merely to claiming that what is taught must be 'undisputed'. It is not clear why this should be accepted—a look at contemporary higher education would seem to refute it immediately—unless the ancient sceptics (or perhaps the ancient Greeks generally) assume a much more rigorous standard than we do for what is to count as teaching and learning; cf. above on 220, 'learning is of things which are true'.

On the four Stoic incorporeals, see on 224 above. That Platonic Forms are incorporeal is obvious enough, though the word 'incorporeal' (*asōmatos*) itself is rarely used by Plato (only six times, and then not always in connection with Forms—see e.g. *Ph.* 85e); two texts which make the point clearly are *Symp.* 211a5–7 and *Rep.* 476a4–7.

For further comparison of 224–31 and the parallel passages at *M* I. 19–29 and *PH* III. 254–5, see Appendix A.

232–3: Third and fourth arguments that there is no subject taught

To round off his discussion of 'the subject being taught', Sextus adds two very brief arguments: nothing either true or false can be taught (232), and nothing either skilled or unskilled can be taught (233). I group them together because they are similarly skeletal; Sextus wants to maximize the number of arguments on this issue, but not to engage in further detailed discussion.

As noted earlier (see on 220), that what is taught is not false does *not* seem to us 'immediately apparent'; Sextus seems consistently to assume that teaching can only have truths as its subject-matter, but it is not clear how this assumption should be explained or justified. What is true is then said not to be taught because it is 'intractable' (*aporon*). This is the adjective corresponding to *aporia*, which is the state of not knowing where to turn, intellectually speaking, to which Socrates famously reduces his

interlocutors; Sextus himself also frequently describes his own procedure as that of raising *aporiai*, 'difficulties' (e.g. in this book, 1, 234; cf.
257). By analogy, what it means to say that the true is *aporon*, 'intractable', is that there is no way to deal with it or to get a secure grasp of it.
Why is this supposed to be so? Sextus refers us at this point to his work
On the Criterion; this must be his name for *M* VII, which is wholly
devoted to casting doubt on the idea that a criterion of truth exists.
Summing up the consequences of *M* VII's argumentation at the beginning of *M* VIII, Sextus says 'That, if there is no clear criterion, truth also
is necessarily made non-evident at the same time (*sunadēleitai*) is immediately apparent to everyone' (2). And he presumably has something
similar in mind here; the true is 'intractable' in the sense that (owing to
the lack of a clear criterion) there is no way of settling uncontroversially
what is true and what is not. (Cf. 231, where it is claimed that what is
taught must be 'undisputed'.)

   In talking of what is taught as being either 'skilled' (*technikon*) or
'unskilled' (*atechnon*), Sextus must be thinking of a skill as consisting
of a body of knowledge rather than of a set of activities (cf. on 170, 216
above); it is truths, not types of behaviour, which are said to be either
'apparent' or 'non-evident'. It is not obvious that what is unskilled does
not need learning. This partly depends, of course, on what exactly qualifies as a skill; but it seems as if one might very well *need to learn*, say, the
way to Larissa (Socrates' example at the end of the *Meno*), yet this
information (at least, by itself) could hardly be said to form part of the
content of any skill. That what is immediately apparent is untaught has
been discussed in the previous section (229; cf. 227). That 'non-evidentness'
guarantees unteachability has also been implied above in 229, where non-
evidentness and unresolved disagreement are assumed to go together.
This would obviously require considerable further argument; Sextus is
here merely gesturing towards the considerations he needs. But the kind
of further argument he would use can be found in abundance in the
logical works (*M* VII–VIII) in particular. One might also question whether
the dichotomy 'apparent'/'non-evident' is exhaustive. But this is standardly
taken for granted in Sextus; see e.g. *M* VIII. 144–8, VII. 358, 369 (also
PH III. 254–5, the parallel passage discussed in connection with the
previous section). At *M* VIII. 17–31 the possibility is raised that things
might be partly apparent and partly non-evident; but it is quickly de-
cided that this does not constitute a genuine third alternative. On some
complications in Sextus' conceptions of the apparent and of the non-
evident, see Allen 1990: pt. 4.

For comparison of 232–3 and the parallel passages at *M* I. 29–30 and *PH* III. 253, see Appendix A.

234–8: Argument that there are no teachers and no learners

As Sextus remarks at the outset (234), this argument is superfluous, in that the absence of any teachable subject-matter already entails that there are no teachers or learners. On Sextus' habit of including such extra arguments 'for good measure', see above on 168, 216. To say that 'the subject being taught' has been shown to be 'intractable' (*aporos*) is a slight understatement; what has in fact been argued is that 'the subject being taught' does not exist (and this is suggested even in the next phrase: 'together with it are *eliminated* both the teacher . . . and the learner').

In 235 Sextus offers four possible scenarios in which there might be teachers and learners, and eliminates three of the four for obvious reasons. (On skills as consisting of 'principles' (*theōrēmata*, 235, etc.), see on 170 above.) This part of the argument bears a considerable resemblance to *M* VII. 55, which is part of an argument attributed by Sextus to Anacharsis the Scythian; for reservations about this attribution, see Spinelli 1995: 391. The remainder of the present section then addresses the interesting fourth possibility: that the skilled person might be the teacher and the unskilled person the learner. An argument against this fourth possibility is offered in 237–8; but prior to that Sextus also says that the skilled person has been 'subjected . . . to difficulties along with (*suneporētai*) the principles of the skill' (236). This may be a reference to the just completed arguments against the 'subject being taught'; it may alternatively refer to the previous chapter arguing against the 'skill relating to life'. (The latter is the view of Blomqvist (1974: 11), who observes that the parallel statement at *M* I. 33 apparently refers back to *M* XI; if the first alternative were correct, this would be pointless.) In the latter case Sextus has forgotten that he is currently engaged in general arguments, not those having to do specifically with the skill relating to life.

The argument against the fourth possibility is a dilemma. Suppose that someone is taught, thereby changing from being unskilled in some area to being skilled. What is the condition of the person at the time when this change takes place—skilled or unskilled? Neither is possible. That one cannot *become* skilled (in some area) if one is already skilled (in that area) is obvious enough, and the final sentence of 238 adds little or nothing to what was said in 237; the denial of the other possibility is not obvious, and is stated in 237 and then justified in 238.

The analogy with people blind or deaf from birth begs the question. Someone blind or deaf from birth will never come to see or hear; that the unskilled person is in the same situation is precisely what needs to be shown. Sextus claims that the unskilled person is '*defective* (*pepērōmenos*) as regards the grasp of skilled principles' (238), which suggests some constitutional incapacity, analogous to congenital blindness or deafness; but this is mere bluff—an unskilled person is someone who *has not* acquired a certain skill, not necessarily someone who is *incapable* of doing so. This unwarranted assimilation is still more explicit in the parallel passage at *M* I. 34, where the unskilled person is said to be 'in a state of blindness and deafness (*tetuphlōmenos kai kekōphōmenos*) with regard to the skilled principles'. (Of course, a person *logically* 'cannot', *while being unskilled*, possess the skill in question; but that says nothing about the person's potential to *become* skilled.) The qualification 'in so far as he is unskilled' makes it sound as if being skilled or unskilled admits of degrees. But this consideration is not introduced in such a way as to allow it to make any difference; whatever the degree to which one is unskilled, one cannot, according to the argument, advance in the slightest towards a higher level of skill. If the argument were directed solely against the Stoics' conception of wisdom and virtue, it would be more forceful (see below on 243–7); but in this general form, and without the Stoics in particular as the targets, it cannot be judged successful.

For all its inadequacy, this argument belongs to a lengthy tradition in Greek philosophy; it is related more or less closely to a whole series of arguments against the possibility of change which were deployed not only by the sceptics themselves, but also by numerous predecessors. Sextus devotes a considerable part of *Against the Physicists* to the topic of change or 'motion' (*kinēsis*)—*M* X. 37–168; *M* I. 35, which immediately follows the passage corresponding to the present argument, actually cites what appears to be this portion of *Against the Physicists* as offering additional support for the conclusion just argued for. In a number of the arguments considered in *Against the Physicists*, as in the present argument, it is alleged that a certain change in something must take place when the thing is in one of two states (which are taken to exhaust the possibilities), and both states are then argued not to admit of the change in question. The closest analogue to the present argument is at *M* X. 106–7, but see also X. 87, 143. The argument in the latter passages is ascribed by Sextus to Diodorus Cronos. But it is also ascribed to Zeno of

Elea by DL IX. 72 and Epiphanius, *Adv. Haer.* III. 11. The attribution
to Diodorus leads Barnes (1982*b*: 276) to doubt whether the argument
goes back to Zeno. However, the argument is described by Sextus as
'well-worn' (*periphorētikos*, 87); and this, coupled with the derogatory
tone in which Diodorus is referred to (*houtos*, 'this man', is disrespectful
in Greek), at least suggests that the argument was already current by
Diodorus' time. Whatever the truth of this, Zeno was certainly the
author of a number of paradoxes concerning motion, and two of those
which survive have as their conclusions that motion is impossible; see
Barnes 1982*b*: ch. 13, Kirk *et al.* 1983: ch. 9. Zeno's arguments, in turn,
were intended to support the conclusions of Parmenides, who denied the
possibility of change in general.

   Another well-known argument against a certain kind of change, much
closer to the topic and the structure of the present argument, is that
raised at Pl. *Meno* 80d–e. In Socrates' formulation, this paradoxical
argument states that one cannot search either for what one knows or for
what one does not know; in the first case there is no search to be
conducted, and in the latter case one does not know what it is for which
one is searching. The seriousness with which Plato takes this argument
is measured by the fact that in response to it he constructs the dramatic
and elaborate doctrine that all learning is recollection of truths already
known before birth. Aristotle, too, takes the trouble to discuss it in *Post.
An.* I. 1, and his solution to it can also be applied, in general outline, to
Sextus' argument here: it is necessary to distinguish ways in which, or
degrees to which, things may be understood or known about. The paradox in the *Meno* does not countenance this (though cf. on 242 below),
and neither, in any serious way, does Sextus. The strong family resemblance between the two arguments suggests that this is a place where,
directly or indirectly, Plato has influenced the Pyrrhonist tradition.

For comparison of 234–8 and the parallel passages at *M* I. 31–5 and *PH*
III. 259–65, see Appendix A.

239–43: Argument that there is no 'means of learning'

This argument completes the general portion of the chapter. For the use
of 'intractable' (239), compare 234 with Comm. Sextus proposes two ways
in which learning might be thought to take place, and then gives reasons
for rejecting each. As before, 'plain experience' is a translation of *enargeia*.

On the significance of this term, see linguistic point (f) on 68–78 above. As noted there, there is indeed a conceptual connection between *enargeia* and what is evident or immediately apparent; the dismissal of 'plain experience' as a mode of learning on the ground that its objects are simply apparent (240) is therefore quite legitimate. (On the apparent as unteachable, cf. 229.) It is not clear what is added by the intermediate step, according to which the objects of plain experience are 'revealed'; the assertion that what is apparent is 'grasped by everyone in common' (for a similar point, cf. 76) is also not really necessary here. One might try to object that it is perfectly possible to *learn* things by plain experience—and the Greek verb *manthanō* seems no different in this respect from the English word 'learn'. However, Sextus is talking throughout the chapter of that species of learning in which one is instructed by a teacher.

'Discourse' is a translation of *logos*. When the dichotomy *enargeia/logos* appeared earlier (76), *logos* was translated 'reasoning'; but in this case the argument clearly requires some term designating spoken language. The second half of the argument poses two further nested dilemmas (241). The language through which, by hypothesis, teaching takes place must either signify something or signify nothing, and the second option is plainly hopeless; but if it signifies something, it does so either by nature or by convention. Each of the latter two possibilities deserves a little more examination.

The notion that language signifies 'by nature'—i.e. that there is something in the world independent of human norms which causes some given set of phonemes to have some particular signification—may also seem obviously absurd. Certainly Sextus' observation (241; the same point occurs in *PH* II. 214 as well as in the parallel passages in *M* I and *PH* III) that each speaker is comprehensible only to that limited group of people who speak the same language seems sufficient to render it highly questionable; in *M* I. 37 the point is extended to dialects of Greek, as well as to different non-Greek languages. (The assumption that what is the case by nature must be the case universally is familiar from part A; see esp. on 68–78.) But this view had been taken quite seriously by a number of earlier thinkers. The topic of 'correctness of names' was first explicitly addressed by some of the fifth-century Sophists; while it is not easy to say exactly what this topic amounted to, it seems at least to have included the ambition of having objects in the world referred to by terms which were, in some sense, naturally appropriate to them. For discussion of this, see Bett 1989*b*: 154–6, and for a partially different view, Baxter

1992: 147–56. Against this background, Plato's *Cratylus* takes up the question of whether names are natural or conventional, and, while not finally endorsing the former alternative, gives it extended consideration. Here already, though, the observation that there are different languages and dialects is taken as a point in favour of the opposite view that names are conventional (385d–e). The fact that the same things have different names in different languages is acknowledged in the discussion of the 'nature' view; but this can only be interpreted as an indication that some names are less naturally correct than others (431c–e). (Cratylus refuses to allow that an incorrect name is a name at all; but Socrates argues against him several times on this point.) Democritus also argued in favour of the 'convention' view, on the basis that the same thing may be designated by several different terms within the *same* language; see Procl. *In Crat.* XVI (= DK 68B26). The Stoics, on the other hand, maintained the 'nature' view (Origen, *Contra Celsum* I. 24 (= LS 32J)), and, in the spirit of the *Cratylus*, indulged in etymologies on this basis; see e.g. Chrysippus' explanation of the word 'I' (*egō*) in Galen, *PHP* 2. 2. 9–11 (= LS 34J)—and note the two sets of books on etymology among Chrysippus' titles at DL VII. 200. It is not clear how, if at all, the Stoics handled objections like Sextus'.

The 'convention' view is attacked (242) with another strategy resembling Meno's paradox (cf. on 237–8 above). This passage is discussed by Glidden (1994); however, Glidden mistakenly supposes that Sextus is talking specifically about the learning of language. Rather, he is talking about learning in general *by way of* certain considerations concerning the knowledge or lack of knowledge of language. It is not immediately clear what this argument has to do with the view that language signifies by convention. The connection, I take it, is this: if language signifies by convention, then what any given set of words signifies is not, as it were, simply built into the words themselves (as it would be if language signified by nature); to understand what is being said, one needs to have prior knowledge of how the words in the language map on to what they signify. (I deliberately leave vague whether, by 'what they signify', one should understand the objects which words refer to, the facts which they state, or something else again; I shall return to this issue.)

Suppose, then, that a lecturer is addressing a class; Sextus' argument will go as follows:

1. If the students know 'the things with which the words are correlated', they will certainly grasp what the lecturer is talking about. But this is not because of having been *taught* these things by what the lecturer

said ('them', in the phrase 'through being taught by them', must refer to the speaker's *words*); rather, it is by being reminded of these things, which they already knew before hearing the lecturer.

2. If, on the other hand, the students do not 'know the things with which the words are correlated', they will fail to grasp anything at all (since they will not even grasp what the lecturer is saying).

The structural similarity with Meno's paradox is clear—though Meno's paradox has nothing specially to do with language. The solution offered by Socrates in the *Meno* is that we do have prior knowledge of the things into which we are enquiring, but that this does not mean that there is no room for any process describable as learning, for we still need to *recollect* what we know. Unlike Socrates, Sextus does not count recollecting as learning. But this is because Socrates is talking about things known in previous lives, and now known only latently; coming to recollect this deep-seated knowledge will be an arduous process of (re)discovery, probably achievable only by the kinds of techniques we normally refer to as teaching. Sextus, by contrast, is talking about the immediate and effortless recollection of things already known (overtly) in this life.

The paradox in the *Meno* has often been dismissed as childish. But it is arguable that, given Socrates' assumptions, or given its context in the dialogue, it is serious and well-motivated. For example, if one assumes the 'priority of definition' thesis (and that the *Meno* does assume this is agreed by interpreters who otherwise differ considerably about 'priority of definition' in early Plato (see Benson 1990, Vlastos 1990)), then it may well look as if the only two options are the ones given by the paradox. See also Nehamas 1985. But whatever may be the case with the *Meno*, Sextus' argument here is subject to criticism (cf. on 35–9, an argument with significant similarities to this one).

The problem is that the phrase 'know [or apprehend] the things with which the words are correlated' is multiply ambiguous. The 'things' might be (a) the objects to which the words refer, or (b) the facts, or states of affairs, which the words describe. (For the Stoic view that what is signified by language is facts or states of affairs, see on 224 above ('sayables'), and see esp. *M* VIII. 11–12.) And 'know the things' might mean (i) 'have knowledge *of* those things' which the words refer to or describe, or it might mean (ii) 'know *which* things' the words refer to or describe (in other words, know the language to which the words belong). Either of (i) and (ii) might be combined with either of (a) and (b). There is also, in the case of i(a), a question about how strongly to understand the 'knowledge of' the objects. But however one reads the argument, either step 1 or step 2 is false.

Let us begin with i(a). If 'knowing the objects' means having a comprehensive understanding of the objects, step 2 is false; one can know what objects are referred to by certain terms, and thus understand sentences using those terms, without having a comprehensive understanding of those objects. Though I am extremely hazy about the nature of particle accelerators, I can fairly be said to know what 'particle accelerator' refers to; hence I can understand (non-technical) sentences using the term, and so am in a position to learn more about particle accelerators. If, on the other hand, 'knowing the objects' simply means knowing some very general facts about the objects (such as I know about particle accelerators), sufficient for one to understand sentences using the words which refer to those objects, then step 1 is false; by no means all the sentences which I am capable of understanding about particle accelerators will simply recall to my mind things I already know about them.

On reading i(b), step 2 is false. That is, it is false that, if one does not already know the fact which a certain sentence expresses, one will fail to understand that sentence. (In order to know a certain language, one does not need to know every fact which is expressible in that language.)

On reading (ii) (and here the distinction between (a) and (b) makes no difference), step 1 is false. That is, it is false that, if one knows *which* objects or facts a certain string of words refers to or describes—in other words, if one understands what is being said—that string of words can have nothing to teach one; understanding a sentence is not *incompatible* with receiving new information by means of it.

The argument, then, is devious. On any interpretation there is something wrong with it; yet, for each of the two steps, there is more than one interpretation which renders it correct. As often elsewhere, one might accuse Sextus or his source of intellectual dishonesty, or of sheer lack of brainpower. Sextus might reply, however, that the point is not that his arguments be in some abstract (and dogmatically defined) sense valid or sound; what matters is rather the *effect* these arguments have on the reader—and there may well be readers who will find this admittedly disputable argument disruptive of their dogmatism. This is certainly the approach advertised at the end of *PH* (III. 280–1); on the therapeutic aspect of sceptical argument, and the departure from the usual canons of rationality which it entails, see Nussbaum 1994: ch. 8, sect. 3. But it is doubtful whether Sextus can avail himself of this response in this book. As we have seen, in part A of *M* XI he is willing to, and needs to, endorse the arguments he advances (see esp. points 1–4 on 118 above), while in part B he at least gives the impression that he mostly wishes to do so (see on 171–3, 216 above).

For comparison of 239–43 and the parallel passages at *M* I. 36–8 and *PH* III. 266–8, see Appendix A.

243–56: Argument that practical wisdom, or the skill relating to life, in particular cannot be taught

Points of translation and text:

(a) 'Grasp', which appears frequently in this section, translates sometimes *lambanesthai*, sometimes *antilambanesthai*. It is not always clear whether these words indicate the simple awareness (sensory or otherwise) of something, or whether some *understanding* of the object in question is implied. (The same is true of 'perceive' (*theōrein*)—see below.) 'Grasp sounds' (247) may seem awkward; but it draws attention to the ambiguity just referred to (which here seems to me to be particularly striking). Besides, *antilambanetai* appears again later in the sentence ('grasp things which are wisely said and done'), and here 'grasps' seems quite appropriate.

[(b) Mutschmann marks *ei d'apo toutou*, etc. in 252 as corrupt, and conjectures that some words may have been lost; Bury (cf. Russo) excises *ei d'apo toutou . . . analogistikēn*. Other editors have also suspected the text at this point; see Mutschmann's app. crit. It is possible that these words are a gloss (which, I take it, was Bury's justification—this is not explained); certainly the sense is fine without them. But I see no compelling reason to assume so; the sense is acceptable without any changes. Nor do I see any compelling reason to think that the text is in disarray. The MSS diverge considerably on the opening of this passage; but of the various choices they offer, *ei d'* is clearly the most satisfactory, and is adopted by all editors. I therefore read Mutschmann's text, but without his reservations. *Toutou* refers back loosely to (*ouden*) *tōn ontōn* in the previous sentence; 'this' is any one of the objects (for it makes no difference *which* object one has in mind) by means of which the grasping of folly has been, or might be, attempted through 'transition from experience'. And one can understand *poieitai metabasin*, from immediately before, in the clause beginning *ētoi*. The point, then, is that any instance of 'transition from experience' would have to proceed from *something like* the object one is thus attempting to grasp—as is clear from the account in 250–1, all three forms of transition require this—so that if, as just stated, there is *nothing* like folly, no such transition can take place.]

Sextus now turns to considering the teachability of the skill relating to life specifically. As in much of the previous chapter, it is assumed that, if there is a skill relating to life, it is practical wisdom, as maintained by the Stoics. (The claim that 'folly is not, *according to them*, capable of perceiving these things' (246) may suggest that Sextus is merely drawing out the implications of Stoic views, without meaning to commit himself to the conclusion of the argument. If so, he is not as clear about his motivations as one might hope; nowhere else in the argument is any such caution expressed—even at 250–1, where he exploits a Stoic doctrine (see below) about which he might well be expected to suspend judgement. On this general issue, see on 171–3 above.) Sextus says that he is going to 'transfer (*metapherein*) the difficulties to the so-called skill relating to life' (243), which makes it sound as if what follows will be simply an application of arguments already rehearsed to this specific case. This is not what we were led to expect at the beginning of the chapter (217), and in fact only the first part (244–7) is closely related to the previous discussion; the majority of this section (248–56) employs considerations not previously mentioned. However, the whole section forms a single argument dismissing all four of the possible pairs of candidates for the roles of teacher and learner: wise person teaching wise person, fool teaching fool, fool teaching wise person, wise person teaching fool. And this general structure is certainly an application of the reasoning at 235–8 above. As in 235, the first three possibilities are quickly ruled out (244–5), and on grounds very similar to the ones used there; the remainder of the section then addresses the possibility that the wise person teaches the skill relating to life to the fool. On 'folly' (*aphrosunē*) as the opposite of practical wisdom, see on 90 above.

This fourth possibility, too, is initially argued against on familiar grounds. Most of 246–7 is adapted from 237–8, with the fool taking the place of the unskilled person and the wise person that of the skilled person. There is nothing here corresponding to the part of the earlier argument which stated that the unskilled person cannot become a skilled person *while he is a skilled person*. But the analogy with people blind or deaf from birth reappears, in company with the general idea that the fool is in no position to effect a change in his condition from folly to practical wisdom. As was noted earlier, the argument at 237–8 appears to trade on an unwarranted 'all-or-nothing' conception of possessing a skill. But it is at least arguable that Sextus is on stronger ground in arguing thus against specifically Stoic views. For the Stoics insisted that there is nothing between folly or wisdom (on this, see on 181 above); and their picture of how one can progress from the one to the other, while still remaining (wholly) in a state of folly, is paradoxical. Nor is Sextus being entirely unfair when he states that 'folly is not, according to them, capable of perceiving' (246) the things which are good and bad and neither. At any rate, a lengthy paragraph in Stobaeus (II. 104, 10–105, 6) appears, in hearty agreement with this sentiment, to cut off the fool from all prospect of achieving virtue; only the wise person (*sophon*) is said to be capable of this (II. 105, 1–2)—which makes it hard to see how the Stoics could escape the force of Sextus' argument. On the Stoic definition of practical wisdom as a 'science of things which are good and bad and neither', see on 170 above, and DL VII. 92.

In contrast to the rest of 246–7, the first sentence of 246 draws on the argument against the 'means of learning'; it appeals to the idea used in 242, that one cannot learn if one does not know the things which are being talked about. That is a deliberately ambiguous formulation; as we saw, it was just such ambiguities on which the argument traded in 242. And the same is true of the present sentence. What is meant by 'the fool . . . will only hear what is said'? It might mean that the fool will hear the wise person speaking, but will perceive this merely as noise rather than as meaningful language; or it might mean that the fool will merely understand the words. The former claim seems highly implausible (at least, if 'fool' is given the very broad extension which it has in Stoicism); but it is not obvious, if the latter claim is meant, why it is supposed to be impossible that the fool should learn something.

At 248–55 Sextus adds an extra argument against the fourth possibility, that the wise person might teach the fool, which does not draw on any materials from earlier in the book. The central point here is that, in order for this to happen, the wise person would have to be 'capable of perceiving folly', but that this is not possible. It is not immediately obvious what is meant by 'capable of perceiving' (*theōrētikē*) in this context. *Theōrein*, the verb from which the Greek term derives, can mean 'to look at' or 'to observe', but it can also mean 'to contemplate'. To judge from the argument which follows, and especially from the numerous other cognitive verbs used in connection with folly ('gain knowledge of', 'grasp', 'understand', 'apprehend', 'recognize'), it appears that what is being asked is both that the wise person know, of any case of folly with which he is presented, that that is what it is, and also that he have some understanding of what folly is like. (Cf. linguistic point (a) above, on 'grasp'.) Both requirements, incidentally, seem plausible as necessary conditions for effective teaching.

In any case, an argument is mounted to show that the wise person is not 'capable of perceiving folly'. This argument is somewhat ramshackle;

more interpretive effort than usual is needed in order for a systematic train of thought to be discerned. With this proviso, it may be summarized as follows:

1. Those who are wise have either (a) retained their original folly and had practical wisdom superimposed upon it, or (b) have *exchanged* their original folly for practical wisdom (248).

2. (a) is clearly impossible, since it would entail the simultaneous possession of opposite dispositions (249).

3. Suppose, then, that (b) is the case. If so, their original folly is no longer present in them to inspect, and hence cannot be known about (249).

4. In confirmation of 3: There are various possible routes by which things can be apprehended, none of which can apply in the case of the wise person's attempted apprehension of folly (250–2).

5. Possible objection to 3: The wise person can understand the folly of others by means of his own practical wisdom (despite not having folly present in himself) (253). But against this,

6. The folly of others would have to be apprehended either by itself— i.e. purely as a disposition, independently of any of the actions to which it gives rise—or by way of the actions to which it gives rise; but neither alternative is possible (253–5).

In his statement of the initial dilemma in 1, Sextus asserts that practical wisdom is acquired by 'training and practice', and that 'no one is this way by nature'. This would have been entirely uncontroversial, so that the absence of any argument for it is unsurprising (a similar point is spelled out in more detail at *M* VII. 146, but still without any serious attempt at justification). None the less, it is interesting that *PH* III. 250–1 does contain a brief argument against practical wisdom's arising in people by nature. This occurs in a different place (see Appendix A on *M* XI. 218, *M* I. 9, *PH* III. 252), but can perhaps be read as another example of *PH*'s greater unwillingness to issue unguarded assertions.

Step 2 is difficult to object to. Possibility (a) does seem to require that one be 'simultaneously wise and foolish', and in the same respects; barring some very strange case of split personality, this can be eliminated. However, step 3 and the remainder of the argument which develops from it neglect what seems a very obvious possibility. Why should the wise person not retain the *memory* of what his own earlier folly was like? In that case the understanding of folly would not be a matter of grasping some new object with which one (currently) has no acquaintance—as this entire phase of the argument seems to assume; it would simply be a matter of recalling some knowledge which one already has (a process which Sextus himself referred to just above, 242). It might be said that one does not have an *understanding* of folly while one is actually in a state of folly; but it is not clear why this should preclude one's developing a *retrospective* understanding of one's own previous folly, based on memories of one's earlier actions and states of mind, by means of the wisdom which one later comes to possess. A resourceful sceptic could no doubt produce further difficulties for this picture; but Sextus does not even consider it.

Step 4 makes use of a schema which is plainly empiricist in orientation. In speaking of it as a schema of ways in which 'the apprehension (*katalēpsis*) of every object' (250) may take place, Sextus suggests that it is a theory of how knowledge is acquired; and the use to which it is put in 252—viz. consideration of the question of how the wise person can come to have knowledge of folly—seems to bear this out. However, numerous other passages, both in Sextus himself and in other authors, make clear that this was originally a theory of the formation of concepts. *M* III. 40–2, VIII. 58–60, and IX. 393–5 are closely related to 250–1 (the latter especially so), while *M* IX. 45 reproduces part of this material; all four passages use the same examples as here, and all quote the same description of the Cyclops (*Od.* IX. 191; in some cases part or all of the next line is added). But all these passages offer this as an account of how concepts are acquired from experience. In fact, this has not been wholly expunged from the present passage. Though 250 (unlike *M* IX. 394) talks of Socrates being 'identified' (*gnōrizētai*) from his portrait, the centaur and the Cyclops are clearly examples of things which come to be *conceived* (not known about) through 'transition from experience'. Unlike any of the other passages, the present passage is confusing in its use of '*analogical* transition' (250) as the generic term, when analogy is also one of the *species* of transition.

The theory has its closest parallel in Stoicism. DL VII. 52–3 reports (though in Diogenes' usual telegraphic style) a more extensive classification of ways in which, according to the Stoics, concepts come to be formed—which, however, includes all the species of transition mentioned by Sextus, again with the same examples. See also Cic. *Fin.* III. 33; *notiones* is Cicero's translation for the Stoic term *ennoiai*, 'conceptions' (cf. III. 21)—on these, see on 21 above. However, the Epicureans seem also to have adopted a related view, and it is not clear which was the original one; DL X. 32 reports that, on the Epicurean view, 'all conceptions (*epinoiai*) come about from sensations, empirically and by analogy and by resemblance and by composition'. In adapting this account to serve as a classification of ways in which we can come to know things, Sextus is not fundamentally transforming it; for what kinds of 'conceptions' we have of things and what kinds of knowledge we have about them are, as one might expect, related topics for the Stoics. 'Conceptions' seem to include, as part of their content, a certain amount of general knowledge about the objects of which they are the conceptions; see linguistic point (a) on 68–78 above. And 'apprehensive impressions', in turn (on these, see on 180–3 above), have a conceptual content which is dependent on the 'conceptions' we have previously acquired (see Schofield 1980: 291–8, LS I, comm. on 39).

Sextus' account is none the less unduly restrictive, either in the number of methods it offers for acquiring knowledge, or in its interpretation of the scope of each of these methods. He assumes that knowledge 'by experience' covers only knowledge of sensory qualities, and he simply asserts that 'none of the things which exist is like folly' (252). But it is arguable (and the Stoics themselves would be in a good position to argue) that, on a broader conception of knowledge 'by experience', one *can* come to know about folly by experience; it is also arguable that there *are* other things which are in some respects like folly—such as disease, one of the Stoics' own favourite analogies—and that one can come to have some understanding of folly by some form of 'transition' from these. If it is objected that this construes 'experience' and 'transition from experience' too loosely, then the reply is that, if they are construed narrowly, they do not exhaust the possibilities; there may be other ways in which we can come to know things than the ways listed. For example, Diogenes includes, as part of his longer list (VII. 52–3), 'privation' (*sterēsis*) as one way in which we may conceive something. Why should we not adapt this, too, to the case of acquiring knowledge; why should the wise person not acquire some understanding of folly by imaginatively subtracting his own wisdom and pondering the result? It looks, then, as if Sextus' argument is both hasty and incomplete.

Even apart from this, it is not clear how, as a sceptic, he is entitled to advance what looks like a piece of dogmatic epistemology. It might be suggested that he is revealing to the Stoics the difficulties in their own views. But the problem with that is that he does *not* seem to be recounting the Stoics' own views; as just noted, the Stoics had a longer list of ways in which one can extrapolate from experience, and theirs was a list of methods of concept formation, not methods for acquiring knowledge.

Nor is there any indication that he intends this account to balance a Stoic or other dogmatic account of these matters, thereby inducing suspension of judgement about the whole topic (indeed, this type of strategy is not hinted at anywhere in the book; see on 171-3 above); in any case, given the incompleteness of his own account, the balance would seem to be very uneven. So it is not easy to see how else to read this portion of the argument than as advancing an ill-advised theory about the acquisition of knowledge; certainly Sextus gives us no help on this question.

Step 5 introduces the final escape route which Sextus imagines being attempted; step 6 then closes off this route. The argument here draws on material from the previous chapter, as Sextus at one point remarks (255). The idea that a disposition 'on its own'—i.e. in isolation from any of its behavioural manifestations—is 'non-apparent' (aphanēs), and hence inaccessible to us, occurs in 205. And the idea that practical wisdom and folly are not behaviourally distinguishable from one another is the main theme of the entire argument at 197-209; the analogies with medicine and painting also occur there (197, 201, 204-5; cf. 188). As we saw, there is room for questions about this argument; though it exploits a genuine, and genuinely surprising, aspect of Stoic ethics, we are not obviously bound to accept its conclusion.

For comparison of 243-56 and the parallel passage at PH III. 270-2, see Appendix A.

257: Conclusion

In a single sentence, Sextus here concludes both M XI and the entire work of which it is the final book. As Janáček (1963) has shown, this work must have included more than just M VII-XI; it also included, prior to these books, a general section on the Pyrrhonist outlook, corresponding (how closely we cannot say) to PH I. Hence it is legitimate for Sextus to claim that he is closing his 'entire exposition of the sceptical method', rather than just his examination of the three standard parts of philosophy. The term 'method' (agōgē) was used earlier in connection with dogmatic philosophies, or at least certain aspects of them (see 178, 179 with Comm.). But here the term seems intended to signal the difference between scepticism and dogmatic philosophies. Scepticism is a 'method'—a method of living and also a method of conducting philosophical discussion—and that is all; it is not a set of theories or doctrines purporting to explain the nature of things and to *justify* some particular method of living. Cf. *PH* I. 8, where scepticism is described as an 'ability' (*dunamis*) rather than as a theory.

It has been suggested by Janáček (1948: 24–5) that the particle *kai dē*, which I have translated 'then', may be intended to indicate that this is *not* the end of all discussion, but that some continuation is to be expected— viz. *M* I–VI. This is very unlikely. First, as just noted, the present sentence sums up the 'entire exposition of the sceptical method', which seems to rule out any continuation. Second, the introduction to *M* I–VI gives no hint that it is to be viewed as the continuation of some work or series of works already begun. It is true that *kai dē* can often be used to introduce new material. But in such cases the material being introduced is *mentioned* in the sentence containing *kai dē*; this would not be so on the current hypothesis. It is clear that this is another use of *kai dē*: viz., as Denniston (1954: 251) puts it, as 'Marking the provision or completion of something required by the circumstances'. In such cases the following sentence—if there is one—*will* of course typically begin a new topic; but, *pace* Janáček, it is no part of the function of *kai dē* itself, in this usage, to suggest that this is about to occur.

Coming immediately after the detailed argument about whether the wise person is 'capable of perceiving folly', this very brief conclusion to the entire work is extraordinarily abrupt. There is no conclusion to the portion of the book covering the skill relating to life, and no transition from this portion of the book to the general conclusion (cf. 167 above). By contrast, the transition at the end of the section of *PH* III corresponding to *M* XI. 243–56 is smooth (see Appendix A on *M* XI. 243–56, *PH* III. 270–2); and the transition from the final section of detailed argumentation to the conclusion of the entire work (which in *PH* III comes a page or two later, at 278–9) is also clear and elegant. These observations suggest two things. First, as is so often the case, the ineptness of *M* XI compared with the polish of *PH* III makes it very hard to believe that *M* XI is the later, revised version; the reverse is much more plausible. Second, the abruptness of *M* XI's conclusion suggests that, for part B, Sextus has been drawing on a source which did not itself belong in a treatise devoted specifically to the ethical part of philosophy. Part A clearly does draw upon a source specifically in ethics; but part B might easily have been based, for example, on a work about skills. If so, having reached the end of the part which he wants to excerpt, Sextus would be obliged to add a conclusion of his own, which would remind the reader of the general purpose of the work. The final sentence gives the impression of having been tacked on in precisely this way. If this is correct, the end of the book supports the conclusion to which the introduction to part B, and the almost complete lack of connection between part B and part A, already pointed (see on 168 above, and introductory remarks to ch. VI): *M* XI is patched together, with less than complete success, from two different sources.

APPENDIX A:
Further Analysis of Parallel Passages

This appendix discusses similarities and differences between sections of *M* XI and *PH* III (as well as, in some cases, *M* I and DL) that have not been covered in the Commentary. The Commentary engaged in such comparisons where this was germane to the interpretation of the sections of *M* XI under discussion. The comparisons made here do not bear on the detailed interpretation of *M* XI, but are none the less relevant to the order of composition of the two works—a matter which, as I have urged, should affect our broader views about the place of *M* XI within Sextus' works and within Pyrrhonian scepticism as a whole. Arguments, or steps within arguments, are sometimes referred to by number; the numbers are those employed in the elucidation of *M* XI in the corresponding sections of the Commentary. In this and other ways, the appendix is dependent on the Commentary, and should be read in close conjunction with it.

M XI. 35–9, *PH* III. 173–5

The most obvious difference between these passages is in the order of the argument; in *PH* III step 2 is placed between steps 1a and 1b. The effect is to make 2 part of the same argument as 1, rather than, as in *M* XI, an additional line of thought not strictly relevant to the main point. But it creates strains of its own; this unified argument is more tortuous and unwieldy than anything in the *M* XI passage. 2 is subject to the same criticisms as in *M* XI. In addition, *PH* III makes a concession at step 2b which in effect gives the game away. At 174 Sextus says: 'Just as the person who is without a conception of horse neither knows what neighing is, nor can come through this to a conception of horse, *unless he were previously to encounter a neighing horse*, so . . .'; the italicized clause admits (surely plausibly) what the argument as a whole is concerned to deny, that experience of the properties of a thing *can* perfectly well precede, and lead to, a general understanding of the nature of that thing. No reason is given why an analogous escape clause should not apply in the case of the good and its properties. This is not a case, then, where *PH* III can be judged clearly superior in its reasoning to *M* XI (or vice versa); the two arguments differ in various ways, but both are problematic.

Mutschmann, Bury, and Russo all claim that *PH* III. 175 is paralleled by *M* XI. 44. This is a mistake; it is *M* XI. 35–6 which is parallel with *PH* III. 175— note the phrase 'interminable war' (*apiston polemon*) and the list of goods— virtue, pleasure, freedom from pain, 'something else'—which occur in both these passages but not in *M* XI. 44.

M XI. 62–6, *PH* III. 191–2

The *PH* passage, though clearly a briefer summary of the same material, occurs
at a quite different point in the argument (as does the passage corresponding to
M XI. 59–61; see Comm.). It forms part of an argument to the effect that
nothing is by nature indifferent, which immediately follows the arguments that
nothing is by nature good or by nature bad; on this argument and on the absence
of any analogous argument in *M* XI, see Comm. on 90–5. The name of Aristo
is omitted, being replaced by an anonymous 'some people'. And in the tyrant
example, instead of 'healthy' and 'sick' there occur 'rich' and 'poor'; the latter
perhaps make for a more likely example—a tyrant is not likely to exempt people
from service on grounds of ill health—but *M* XI has to use the example of
health, since that is the topic of discussion. I suggested (see Comm.) that *M* XI.
59–61—the three definitions of the indifferent—are in a considerably less suitable place in the argument than the corresponding passage in *PH* III (177). By
contrast, there is no such incongruity in most of 62–7 (the definitions of 'preferred' and 'dispreferred' at 62 are a possible exception); on the other hand, *PH*
III. 191–2 does sit a little oddly in its context. To provide an effective argument
that nothing is by nature indifferent, Sextus needs to show that nothing is
universally agreed to be indifferent; and immediately after this passage (193), this
is precisely what he asserts. But the dispute between the orthodox Stoics and
Aristo is not about which things are indifferent, but about what *kinds* of indifferents
there are. Sextus glosses over this difference with the ambiguous introduction
'Similarly there is not anything by nature indifferent because of *the disagreement
about the indifferents*' (191). It is at least quite possible that Sextus has pressed
into service in *PH*, for an argument which had no analogue in *M* XI, a passage
which he had already used in *M* XI for another purpose (but which, in turn, was
not needed for that purpose in *PH*); it would not then be surprising if the
passage fitted somewhat awkwardly into its new context. On this, see further
Introduction, sect. IV.

M XI. 68–78, *PH* III. 179–82, DL IX. 101

The account of ethical disagreements in the *PH* passage is longer than the one
in *M* XI, and is paralleled in part by another passage of *M* XI (see Comm. on
45–6). There are two other differences, both crucial. First, Sextus says at *PH* III.
179 that things which affect people by nature have the same effect, not on
everyone *tout court*, but on 'all those who are, as they say, in a natural state'
(*pantas . . . tous kata phusin, hōs phasin, echontas*). On the damaging effects of this
concession on the argument's consistency, see Hankinson 1994: sect. 5. Second,
at *PH* III. 182, immediately after the conclusion that nothing is by nature good,
Sextus adds that the disagreements previously mentioned force us to *suspend
judgement* about what (if anything) is by nature good. (On this, see also on *M* XI.

173–7, *PH* III. 182, 239 below.) The latter claim is of course consistent with *PH*'s general policy (in the ethical section, cf. III. 235); but it is inconsistent with the conclusion just reached, even though Sextus presents it as complementing that conclusion. (The conclusion that nothing is by nature good is not, as one might try to suggest, *one party* to the disagreement from which the suspension of judgement results. Rather, it is a *lesson* extracted from the fact of disagreement— as in *M* XI; yet the very same disagreement is then said to produce suspension of judgement.) On both counts, then, *PH* III is inconsistent where *M* XI is consistent. Sextus recognizes that there is a problem, and tries to compensate; at *PH* III. 178 he introduces the argument by saying that 'some argue' that nothing is by nature good (cf. *phasin*, 'they say', twice in 179). But he does not maintain his distance; in 179 he also adopts the argument as his own ('as we shall show', *hōs hupomnēsomen*). The uncomfortable status of the argument in *PH* III is most easily explained, I suggest, by the hypothesis that Sextus is taking over *en bloc* a section of material which was originally at home in a book expressing a different outlook—viz. *M* XI. In *M* XI, which on this hypothesis is the earlier of the two, the acceptance of the conclusion is quite permissible for the sceptic, whereas in *PH* III it is not; Sextus makes an effort to adapt the argument to its new environment, but does not entirely succeed. (If, on the other hand, *PH* III is the earlier work, we must suppose that Sextus first borrowed this less than ideally suited material from some other author, and then changed his mind in such a way that this material came to be entirely congenial to the view he now wanted to express; this is not impossible, but it is clearly a much less economical explanation of the data.) See also Introduction, sect. IV, Bett 1994*c*: 154–6, and on *M* XI. 79–89, *PH* III. 183–90 below.

Another striking parallel is DL IX. 101 (from the life of Pyrrho, much of which is a summary of later Pyrrhonism). Though much shorter, this corresponds much more closely—in structure, language, and choice of examples— with *M* XI. 69–78 than with *PH* III. 179–82 (despite an important difference in the ending, which again tries to assimilate the argument to a variety of Pyrrhonism more akin to that of *PH* (on this, see also Comm., textual point (e) on 68–78)). This may be explained by supposing either that Diogenes (who is later than Sextus; see IX. 116) is copying *M* XI or that both derive from a common source. Judging by this passage alone, it is hard to decide between these options; but in a number of the many other cases of correspondence between DL IX. 74–108 and Sextus, the hypothesis of a common source seems clearly preferable (see Barnes 1992: esp. 4272). If this is correct, it provides another strong reason for thinking that *M* XI is earlier than *PH* III. For if *M* XI is much closer to DL than is *PH* III, this means that *M* XI is much closer to the common source than is *PH* III, which in turn makes it highly likely that *PH* III is a revised version of *M* XI, rather than the other way round. On this, and more generally on Sextus' heavy reliance on earlier sources, see further Introduction, sect. IV; on Diogenes' unexpected conclusion that 'the good by nature is unknowable', see Introduction, sect. III (and cf. Comm. on 68–78, 'puzzling point' (a)). Another parallel

between *M* XI and Diogenes' life of Pyrrho is *M* XI. 219–23 and DL IX. 100;
see below.

M XI. 79–89, *PH* III. 183–90

The argument in *PH* III has virtually the same dilemmatic form as that in *M* XI;
the only structural differences are its neater finish, on which more below, and the
use (arguably also an increase in clarity) of the trilemma 'belonging to the body
alone' / 'belonging to the soul alone' / 'belonging to both', instead of *M* XI's
dilemma 'belonging to the body alone' / 'belonging to the soul'. But as before, in
PH III Sextus vacillates between claiming the argument as his own ('as I have
argued', 190) and attributing it to unnamed others ('some people say', 183),
whereas in *M* XI he shows no signs of not endorsing it, and makes clear later
(112–18, 130, 140) that he has endorsed it. *PH* III wavers for the same reason as
in the previous case; the conclusion, that nothing is good by nature, counts as a
sceptical conclusion by *M* XI's standards, but not by those of *PH*. But there is
a particular unwillingness in *PH* III to make commitments regarding the character of the soul and the body—perhaps the most theoretically loaded aspect of the
argument; 185–6 contains no fewer than seven disclaimers ('they say', 'it is said',
'according to them', etc.). No such caution is apparent in the corresponding
passage of *M* XI (87–8). This is problematic, in that, despite differences between
the outlooks of the two works, dogmatic assertions about the soul and the body
are just as contrary to *M* XI's version of suspension of judgement as to *PH*'s.
Another significant difference, as noted above, is that *PH* III does complete the
argument according to the structure promised at the beginning and developed in
what follows (see the conclusion, 190, to which nothing in *M* XI corresponds).
Instead of referring back to the previous argument based on disagreement, Sextus
ends by giving reasons why that which is to be chosen cannot belong to the soul
(186–9); it is not clear that the soul even exists, or if it does, that it can be
apprehended, and in any case, the various dogmatic theories of the nature of the
soul all leave it mysterious *how* that which is worth choosing can reside in the
soul.

    PH III's argument, then, seems in certain respects cleaner and more careful
than that of *M* XI; it is at least tempting to conclude that *PH* III's is an
improved, and therefore later, version. *PH* III's ambivalence about whether to
endorse the argument (like the ambivalence in the previous argument) also points
in the same direction; the simplest explanation is that *M* XI first presents an
earlier variety of Pyrrhonism (a variety akin to that of Aenesidemus, if I am right;
see Introduction, sect. III), and that *PH* III then uneasily tries to integrate
arguments from this variety of Pyrrhonism into its own distinct, and later,
framework. It might be objected that these are two *incompatible* arguments for
the same conclusion. But *PH* III's ambivalence, compared with *M* XI's decisive-
ness, has to do with its transplanting an *entire stretch* of text from the context in
which it belonged into a context in which it does not easily belong; *PH* III's

neater organization, on the other hand, has to do with its reworking of some of the *details* of the argument. On this, see also Introduction, sect. IV. A further possible indication of the relative order of composition is the isolated occurrence of the phrase 'by its own definition' (*kata ton idion logon*) in *PH* III. 183. In *M* XI this phrase is part of the argument's standard vocabulary; its single appearance in *PH* III reads oddly, and is most naturally explained as the result of incomplete editing in the preparation of the revised, condensed version.

M XI. 96–8, *PH* III. 194–6

The passage of *PH* III is considerably superior. It avoids the unfortunate locution 'by nature entirely', and is as a whole clearly expressed and lucidly organized. More important, it omits *M* XI's point 1 altogether, and substitutes for point 3 an argument closely analogous to point 2; just as pain or hardship can often produce results which we value, so pleasure can often produce painful or troublesome results, and hence cannot be considered by nature good. (In fact, Sextus claims (195) that *every* pleasure—i.e. every type of pleasurable activity— has some pain attached to it.) Finally, it adds the observation that numerous philosophers actually choose hardship *rather than* pleasure (196)—which, in view of the two requirements assumed in the original argument that nothing is by nature good (to which Sextus here refers), leads to the same conclusions. That Sextus first wrote *PH* III. 194–6 and then later substituted the messy discussion at *M* XI. 96–8 seems highly unlikely; the reverse is far more plausible. The same conclusion is suggested by the occurrence of the plural 'animals' (*ta zōia*, 194) instead of *M* XI's 'the animal'. As I observed (see Comm.), the singular seems to be Epicurean usage; one would expect the earlier work to stick more closely to the language of the sources on which Sextus is drawing, and the revised later work to be more independent in its language.

In *PH* III, Sextus is careful to point out that the argument depends on certain views held by the objectors, to which Sextus himself would not want to be committed ('according to them', 'they say', 195). It is only point 1 in *M* XI which is subject to any such restriction (see Comm.). This difference reflects the general difference between the forms of Pyrrhonism presented by the two books; see above on *PH* III's discomfort with the arguments that nothing is by nature good.

M XI. 99–109, *PH* III. 193, 197

PH III. 193 briefly examines roughly the same objection as is treated in *M* XI. The objection is introduced by 'if someone should say', rather than identifying any particular authors. This might be taken to suggest an ambivalence on Sextus' part about whether the Stoics really did advance this type of argument (see Comm. on the oddity of their doing so). But this would be too hasty; *PH* III is not infrequently less specific than *M* XI about the authorship of an idea (e.g. 181, 192; cf. *M* XI. 73–4, 64). The suggestion is that courage is by nature to be chosen because certain animals, as well as certain humans, are naturally courageous. Sextus' answer is simply that it would be as plausible, if not more plausible, to argue that *cowardice* is naturally to be chosen, since a greater number of animals are naturally cowardly, and so are most humans. (Of course, if this were true, it would still contradict the conclusion that nothing is by nature good; but Sextus assumes that his reply will instead induce the opponent to abandon this line of argument altogether.) There is also a passing reference to the Stoic position in 197, where Sextus says that 'those who say that the virtuous life is by nature good' are refuted by the fact that some philosophers choose 'the life with pleasure'; disagreement, he says, rules out claims to the effect 'that something is by nature such and such'—i.e. claims of the form 'X is by nature F'. This argument relies, as have several previous arguments from both books, on the Universality Requirement combined with the Recognition Requirement. (It comes immediately after, and its structure is identical with, Sextus' final reply to the Epicurean objection; see above.) None of points 1–3 from *M* XI occur in *PH* III at all. So whichever book was composed first, the passage in the later work represents a major overhaul of the one in the earlier work; given the difficulties in at least one portion of the *M* XI passage (see Comm.) and the comparative neatness of the discussion in *PH* III, the supposition that the latter is a greatly revised version of the former seems preferable to the reverse.

M XI. 119–24, *PH* III. 238

The penultimate sentence of *PH* III. 238 is very similar in structure to the final sentence of *M* XI. 124; both are conditionals, with double protases of similar content, and the apodosis of both states that certain things (with which the dogmatist is in some way involved) are bad. But in *PH* III the first protasis, to the effect that what is productive of bad is itself bad, is never independently asserted, as it is in *M* XI (119); hence Sextus is not committed to accepting the apodosis. *PH* III is also free from an inaccuracy of *M* XI. Instead of saying that 'the *things* thought good . . . are productive of all the bad things', and that 'the *things* which are thought good . . . are in effect bad' (*M* XI. 124), *PH* III. 238 says: 'the *confidence that* these things are by nature good and those bad produces disturbances', and '*supposing and being convinced that* something is good or bad in respect of its nature is bad and to be avoided' (see Comm. on why the latter formulations are more apt). Finally, *PH* III avoids *M* XI's peculiar and unsupported claim that the things thought good are responsible for *everything* bad ('produces disturbances' instead of 'are productive of all the bad things').

M XI. 173–7, *PH* III. 182, 239

PH III. 182, which belongs in the first argument that nothing is by nature good (the one that parallels *M* XI. 68–78), is structurally similar to *M* XI. 173–7. It is also the passage to which the final sentence of *PH* III. 239, the only portion of

PH III which directly parallels *M* XI. 173–7, refers back; in 239 Sextus says that since the dogmatists do not all propose the same skill relating to life, they are subject to the argument from disagreement 'which I put forward in the things which were said about the good'. As was noted earlier (see on *M* XI. 68–78, *PH* III. 179–82 above), *PH* III. 182 fits uneasily into its immediate context, in the middle of arguments to the effect that nothing is by nature good; but it fits nicely with *PH* III's general aim (with which the latter arguments are in tension) of suspending judgement about whether anything is by nature good or bad. If *PH* is the later work, it looks as if Sextus has moved the argument which he previously used here at *M* XI. 173–7 back to an earlier position in *PH* III. It would not have been appropriate in that position in *M* XI—for arguments from unresolvable disagreement are alien to part A of *M* XI (see Comm. on 173–7); but it now is appropriate (with adaptation to the different subject-matter) because of the different version of Pyrrhonism being advanced in *PH*. As a result, he no longer has a complete argument in *PH* III. 239, and so needs to refer back to an argument already employed. This has the incidental effect of linking the two portions of the work more closely in *PH* than in *M* XI; on their lack of connection in *M* XI, see Comm. on 168.

M XI. 180–3, *PH* III. 240–2

Versions of all three of *M* XI's arguments appear in the parallel passage of *PH*. Argument 1 and the introduction to argument 2 (240–1) read in essentially the same way as their occurrences in *M* XI. 181 (with the exception of *PH*'s clearer presentation of the status of the argument; see Comm.). But what appears as the main body of argument 2 in *M* XI (182) is broken up in *PH*. The argument against the apprehensive impression comes first (241), and the restatement of the bearing of this argument on the skill relating to life comes at the end (242). Between these two passages he inserts argument 3 (242). We are thus given two juxtaposed arguments against the apprehensive impression, followed by a single common statement as to their bearing on the main topic; we are also spared *M* XI. 182's tedious rehearsal, in very close proximity, of *two* accounts of the dependence of the skill relating to life on apprehensive impressions. *PH* III shows the same superior organization and articulation noted elsewhere; again, the presumption that it is the later work is strong.

Other features of the *PH* passage suggest the same thing. The first argument against the apprehensive impression (241) is different from, and more extensive than, that which appears in *M* XI's argument 2; instead, it is closely related to *M* VII. 427–9, which is one of Sextus' many arguments against the Stoic criterion of truth. The crucial difference (between *PH* III's argument and *M* XI's) is that its conclusion is not that '*there is no* apprehensive impression', but that the apprehensive impression is 'undiscoverable' (*aneuretos*)—i.e. that no impression can be definitively found to be apprehensive. As we saw above, this is a much safer conclusion to argue for, since it does not depend on a contentious interpretation of the Stoic doctrine; another effect is that the conclusion is now the same as that of argument 3, making the juxtaposition of the two arguments all the more appropriate. It is at least tempting to see these differences as improvements. In addition, the relation to *M* VII at least fits very comfortably with *PH*'s being the later work. For, as just noted, the passage in *M* VII is embedded in a longer discussion; it is one of a series of arguments against the apprehensive impression, and it is immediately followed by an objection (430–2). It is very natural to suppose that Sextus, in seeking to improve *M* XI's brief discussion of the apprehensive impression, would turn for help to the long sequence of arguments which he had already compiled on that very topic, extracting one which served his purpose especially well. (It is worth noting that a version of argument 3 also appears in *M* VII, immediately before the passage just considered (426). This may well have been the immediate source of *M* XI. 183, which could easily have been inserted into the material in his main source; the continuity of the passage is fine without it.)

Finally, we should note that *PH* III's version of argument 3 (242) contains an explicit reference to one of the Five Modes, the mode of circularity (*ho diallēlos tropos*; cf. *PH* I. 169). As already noted, the Five Modes are associated with a later phase in the history of Pyrrhonism. Though *M* XI. 183 does use the same argument from circularity, it does not use the later Pyrrhonist technical term 'the mode of circularity' (neither does *M* VII. 426), but makes the same point in more everyday language; other things being equal, one would expect that the work which used the later technical term is the later work, and that the other work is drawing on sources dating from a period before the terminology of the Five Modes became common currency.

M XI. 188–96, *PH* III. 245–9

The passage of *PH* III does not contain *M* XI's troublesome repetition of near-identical introductory material in two successive arguments (see Comm.). There is just one occurrence of this material, and since it is closer to the introduction to the next section in *M* XI (197), I will postpone further mention of it. But the material in the main body of this section also occurs in a different place in *PH* III—*after* the arguments which appear in the next section of *M* XI, and as a supplementary argument for the same conclusion, that there is no action peculiar to the skill relating to life. In *PH* III Sextus first offers several arguments, all paralleled by arguments in the next section of *M* XI, which claim to demonstrate that whatever the wise person does, ordinary people do as well (243–4). The scandalous quotations on incest and cannibalism follow immediately, together with the assertion (rather more concise than in *M* XI. 195–6) that the Stoics will never actually do what they talk about in these quotations (249). The conclusion is then stated as follows: 'But if they absolutely do not do these things, whereas the things which they do do are common to ordinary people as well, there is no action peculiar to those suspected of having the skill relating to life' (249). The scandalous quotations are thus neatly integrated into the larger argument. They are offered as the final possible way in which it might be shown that there are actions peculiar to the person who possesses this skill; they certainly do describe some actions which are not 'common to ordinary people as well'—but then they fail to serve the required purpose, because, it is claimed, these actions are not, after all, ones which anyone, even the person who has the skill, will actually perform. Incest and cannibalism do not, therefore, have to serve, as they very implausibly do in *M* XI, as *typical* cases of actions to which the skill relating to life will lead; they are mentioned simply as a last-ditch effort, after other efforts have failed, to find *some* actions distinctive to the person possessing this skill.

That this is the point of including them is not made explicit when they are introduced (245) (though *leipetai legein*, 'it remains to say', does suggest that some form of last-ditch effort is forthcoming). But in other respects the treatment of this material in *PH* III is much more effective than its treatment in *M* XI. It is very difficult to understand the bungled discussion in *M* XI as representing Sextus' *revision* of the judicious and clearly constructed discussion in *PH* III.

M XI. 197–9, *PH* III. 243

PH III's version is much the shorter of the two. The two premisses are stated initially, as in *M* XI. 197; the second premiss is justified, in considerably fewer words, by means of the same examples as in *M* XI. 199; and then the conclusion is stated. It is not clear that anything is lost by this brevity; in fact, several minor shortcomings present in *M* XI (see Comm.) are avoided in *PH*'s treatment. No argument is offered for the first premiss; but it might well be maintained that the premiss itself is no less intuitively appealing than the considerations offered in its favour in *M* XI. 198. The only other obvious difference is that the first premiss reads 'every art *seems* (*dokei*) to be apprehended from the actions which are produced peculiarly by it'. The word 'seems' is presumably included to avoid a dogmatic statement about the requirements for something to be a skill. This is no surprise; as we have seen, *PH* III is generally more cautious in these chapters (and indeed throughout the ethical section); see Comm. on 171–3.

M XI. 206–9, *PH* III. 244

PH III has a single sentence followed by a quotation. The single sentence corresponds to the entire first half of the paragraph in *M* XI (up to 'seems rather like a pious wish', 208); it covers the Stoic response and the beginning of argument 1. The quotation (*Od*. XVIII. 136–7) occurs instead of the notably clumsy final sentence of *M* XI. 208. The focus of *PH* III's version of argument 1 is slightly different; it is the inconstancy of human nature, rather than the changeability of circumstances, which is held to render the Stoic response unrealistic. But the argument is subject to the same objection. There is nothing corresponding to *M* XI's possibly more promising argument 2.

M XI. 210–15, *PH* III. 274–7

The two passages are extremely close to one another (more so than in any other
case we will examine, though some of the passages of *PH* corresponding to
sections of *M* XI's ch. VII are also very similar); unlike most of the parallels we
have looked at, there is no shortening in the *PH* passage, and the wording is
virtually identical most of the time. But in *PH* III the passage occurs in a quite
different place. It comes in a separate chapter at the very end, after all the
discussion of whether there is a skill relating to life and whether it can be taught,
which is directed to the separate question 'whether the skill relating to life
benefits the person who has it' (273) (i.e. even if it is conceded that this skill does
exist and can be taught); the conclusion drawn is therefore not, as in *M* XI, that
there is no skill relating to life, but simply that this skill, if it exists, is harmful
rather than beneficial. The reason for this difference in organization is, I think,
clear. In *PH* III Sextus does not want to commit himself to the principle that, for
any body of techniques or practices to *count as* a skill, it must be beneficial to the
person who has it; hence the role of the argument must be different from that
which it occupies in *M* XI, where Sextus has no qualms about adopting this
principle and using it to relate the argument to the question of whether a skill
relating to life exists. Two reasons may be suggested for this greater caution.
First, the principle is not entirely uncontroversial. Some Epicureans appear to
have been willing to deny that skills had to be useful at all; on this see Blank
1995. And even if it is agreed that skills must be useful to someone, it is not
obvious that the principal beneficiary has to be the person who possesses the
skill; indeed, Socrates in *Rep.*, Book I, insists, against Thrasymachus, that skills
work to the benefit of people or objects *other* than the possessor of the skill
(341c–342e, 345b–346e). Second, the principle, whether controversial or not,
commits one to a position about the character of genuine skills. We have seen
that the more stringent form of scepticism in *PH* makes Sextus more unwilling
to commit himself, including on questions having to do with skills, than he is in
M XI (see Comm. on 171–3); it is not at all surprising that, in this case as well,
PH III should avoid a commitment which *M* XI adopts. (Another neat example
of the same phenomenon is provided by comparing the final words of the present
chapter—'it must be affirmed that there is not any skill relating to life'—with
the final words of the corresponding chapter of *PH* III—'no one can affirm of it
that it exists' (249). Compare also *M* XI. 213, 'inferior people', with *PH* III. 276,
'those *said to be* inferior'.)

M XI. 218, *M* I. 9, *PH* III. 252

M XI. 218 is closely resembled by portions of both other texts. An interesting
exception is that *M* I. 9, introducing the list of things which must be 'agreed
upon', says that 'four things must first be agreed upon', whereas *PH* III. 252 says
that 'three things must first be agreed upon'; *PH* III then goes on to list the

teacher and the learner as a single topic, while *M* I, like *M* XI, lists them as separate topics. As will be clear from the introductory survey of ch. VII's arguments (see Comm.), it is *PH* III's classification which more accurately reflects what follows; the teacher and the learner are treated simultaneously—and this is the same in all three works. (For this reason the difference in *PH* III's statement of the conclusion, that there is no *teaching*, rather than no learning, is insignificant.) As often before, it seems plausible to interpret *PH* as having introduced a small revision in the interests of greater clarity; in this case what follows, if this is correct, is that *PH* is later than either of the other two works.

PH III also differs from *M* XI in that the upcoming arguments are presented as a continuation of the topic previously addressed—viz. whether there is a skill relating to life. In 250 Sextus says that if there is a skill relating to life, it comes into being in people either by nature or by teaching and learning. The first alternative, nowhere mentioned in *M* XI, is eliminated in 250–1; 252 then introduces the second alternative. At 272, at the end of the arguments on teaching and learning, the dilemma is recalled, and the conclusion given as 'the skill relating to life . . . is undiscoverable'. The effect is to make the treatment of these issues in *PH* slightly more comprehensive and slightly more unified; but both ways of connecting the material of the present chapter to what preceded it seem perfectly acceptable in light of Sextus' usual procedures.

M XI. 219–23, *M* I. 10–14, *PH* III. 256–8, DL IX. 100

Comparisons here are extremely complicated. I shall summarize the main points of similarity and difference, and then attempt to make some sense of the situation.

PH III. 256–8 contains argument (Ib), with very similar wording to that of *M* XI; one noteworthy difference is that *PH* III says that 'teaching *is thought* (*dokousin*) to be of things which are true' (256) instead of 'learning *is* of things which are true' (*M* XI. 220). (On 'teaching' instead of 'learning', see above.) Otherwise there are no arguments in *PH* III corresponding to *M* XI's part I (and a good thing, one might add, given their redundancy). There follows a version of the first horn of argument II (257). In the text as transmitted, this appears to be unintelligible; with Mau's supplement, based on the Latin translation, it is intelligible and closely related to *M* XI. 222 (see Mutschmann–Mau 1958). The second horn of argument II (258) is *longer* than in *M* XI; the reasoning is spelled out in a little more detail (cf. Comm., textual point (b)). Argument II is then supplemented (258) by an appeal to previous considerations concerning the apparent and the non-evident; Sextus is in a position to do this because this section in *PH* III is at the end of the arguments about the subject-matter of teaching and learning, not at the beginning.

M I includes arguments (Ia) and (Ic) (11–12), and arguments reminiscent of, but not closely related to, (Ib) and (Id) (12–13). There follows an argument reminiscent of, but again significantly different from, II(i) (14); this argument contains the strikingly unsceptical claim that 'existing things are apparent to

everyone' (*tōn ontōn pasi phainomenōn*). Finally, *M* I differs from the other two
works in that the entire argument is set up as a dilemma: either what exists is
taught 'by existing' (*tōi einai*), or what does not exist is taught 'by not existing'
(*tōi mē einai*, 10). If 'by existing' and 'by not existing' mean the same as what *M*
XI means by 'in virtue of being existent' (222) and 'in virtue of being non-
existent' (221), this explains why *M* I contains nothing corresponding to (Ie) or
(IIii), both of which envisage possibilities other than those expressed in *M* I's
main dilemma.

The parallel passage in DL IX. 100 is very brief. It opens with a statement of
the same main dilemma as appears in *M* I, with identical wording. That what
exists is not taught is then justified by the same surprising 'unsceptical claim' as
appears in *M* I. 14; what exists is apparent to everyone, hence it is not subject to
teaching. That what does not exist is not taught is justified by argument (Ia). The
wording is virtually identical with that of *M* XI. 219 (note in particular *hōst'oude
to didaskesthai*, 'and hence not that of being taught'); *M* I's version is somewhat
more expansive.

The similarities between Diogenes and Sextus are too close to be coincidental.
It is very likely that they are each reproducing material from the same earlier
source, rather than that Diogenes is copying Sextus (on this, see Barnes 1992).
(Whether they are both drawing on the same *immediate* source is another issue,
which is much more difficult to settle—and which may be affected by the
question of whether part A and part B of *M* XI themselves derive from different
sources (on this, see Appendix B). But for the present purpose, it is enough to
be clear that both Diogenes and Sextus are indebted, in these passages, to the
same *ultimate* source.) If so, it looks as if Sextus directly consulted his source
while composing both *M* I and *M* XI; the similarities between *M* I and DL are
greater, but the common wording in one phrase of DL and *M* XI is enough to
establish that *M* XI drew directly on this source as well. Now, the structure of
the arguments in his source must presumably have been that shared by *M* I and
DL. If so, Sextus used this source in composing *M* XI, but altered the structure
of the arguments he found there. In composing *M* I (which we know to be the
later work), he then returned to the source, rather than drawing on *M* XI, and
(at least in the respects about which we can judge) stuck to it more closely than
he did when composing *M* XI.

In contrast with the other two passages in Sextus, *PH* III. 256–8 has no exact
correspondences with DL IX. 100; hence we need not suppose that it was
composed with direct consultation of the earlier source. Either *PH* III is a
revision of *M* XI, or vice versa; it is far more probable that revision would result
in greater departure from the earlier source than in greater assimilation to it (cf.
on *M* XI. 68–78, *PH* III. 179–82, DL IX. 101 above). This passage therefore
provides strong evidence that *PH* III is the later work. The same thing is
suggested by several points already mentioned. *PH* III's expanded version of
II(ii) may plausibly be seen as an attempt at improvement; and its statement of

the conclusion is plausibly understood as a correction of the corresponding, but badly worded, statement in *M* XI (see Comm.). Finally, the addition of the word *dokousin* in *PH* III. 256 (see above) reflects the generally more non-committal outlook of *PH* III as compared with *M* XI, which, I have argued, is in turn associated with a later version of Pyrrhonism (see esp. Comm. on 171–3, and point 4 on 118).

It is also plausible to suppose that *PH* III, which apparently is not directly indebted to the earlier source at all, is later than *M* I, which is. But the reasoning here is far less decisive than in the case of *PH* III versus *M* XI, since it is *not* the case that one of *PH* III and *M* I is the revised version of the other; I am relying simply on the general assumption that the more independent work is liable to be the later one (an assumption to which the comparison between *M* XI and *M* I may indeed be a counter-example; see above).

M XI. 224–31, *M* I. 19–29, *PH* III. 254–5

These parallels have been discussed in the course of examining the arguments (see Comm.); just a few points are worth adding. First, we have seen that, though *M* XI and *M* I proceed through essentially the same steps, *M* I is at many points the clearer and better organized of the two. Whether or not *M* I consistently stuck more closely to the source than did *M* XI (see Comm. on the beginning of this section for one clear case of this), this supports the general presumption with which I have been working throughout, that the better-composed work is, other things being equal, likely to be the later; for our reasons for thinking that *M* I is later than *M* XI are independent of such considerations. Similar considerations might lead us to conclude that *PH* III. 254–5 is later than either the present section or *M* I. 19–29; for it avoids all of the fallacies and obscurities to which the present section and, to a lesser extent, *M* I. 19–29 are subject. However, the difference in length and character between *PH* III. 254–5 and the other two texts makes the inference hazardous in this particular case. Still, *PH* III's apparently much greater freedom from the constraints of Sextus' original source again suggests strongly that it is later than *M* XI, and less strongly that it is later than *M* I (see on the previous section, also Comm. on the beginning of this section and on 229). This freedom extends to reordering the arguments as well as to re-creating them; while *M* I has all of *M* XI's arguments in the same order (with occasional extra portions), *PH* III. 254–5 comes *before* the passage parallel to the previous section.

M XI. 232–3, *M* I. 29–30, *PH* III. 253

Here the arguments in *M* I are identical to those in *M* XI. *PH* III. 253 corresponds to *M* XI. 232, but only loosely (and the argument is at the beginning, not the end, of the discussion of 'the subject being taught'); there is nothing in *PH*

III corresponding to 233. It was argued on the basis of earlier sections that *M* XI and *M* I are following the same source; if we assume that this is still true here (and the systematicity of the discussions in both books encourages this supposition), we should conclude that *PH* III again manifests a greater originality and independence than the other two books.

M XI. 234–8, *M* I. 31–5, *PH* III. 259–65

Apart from its slightly greater length, there are no notable differences between the *M* I passage and that of *M* XI. It is another story with *PH* III. The same four possibilities are offered, and the same three quickly dismissed, as in *M* XI. 235. But the dismissal of the possibility that the skilled person might teach the unskilled person takes much longer, and employs arguments which are considerably more complex—and which, whatever their merits, are not open to the accusation of simple question-begging (see Comm.). Most of them turn on the implausibility of specifying any particular point as the point at which one ceases to be unskilled and becomes skilled; the analogy with people blind and deaf from birth is also used (264), but in a less obviously objectionable way.

M I. 35's supplementary reference to *Against the Physicists* (see Comm.) suggests that Sextus already perceives the inadequacy of the argument which the present section and *M* I. 31–4 share; but the passage in *PH* III is most easily interpreted as a later, more thorough overhaul of this part of his discussion, in light of a fuller recognition of this inadequacy. It is rare for a section in *PH* III to be longer than the corresponding section in *M* XI; and it is difficult to see why, if the generally more expansive *M* XI were the later of the two, Sextus would have abandoned the more elaborate and subtle treatment in *PH* III for the briefer and cruder treatment. The same considerations tell in favour of *PH* III's being later than *M* I; the case here is, however, less powerful, since it is not clear that Sextus had the earlier of the two (whichever that is) in mind when composing the later.

M XI. 239–43, *M* I. 36–8, *PH* III. 266–8

The three passages are extremely close to one another; in no case are there more than minor verbal differences. In some cases, however, the formulations which occur in *PH* III and not in the other two works are clearer and less awkward— as one might expect if it is the most mature version: e.g. 'will not be capable of teaching (*didaskalikos*) anything' (*PH* III. 267), instead of 'will not be a teacher (*didaskalos*) of anything' (*M* XI. 241; cf. *M* I. 37); '*such as* Greeks [understanding] barbarians and barbarians Greeks' (*PH* III. 267), instead of 'Greeks [understanding] barbarians and barbarians Greeks' (*M* XI. 241; cf. *M* I. 37). *PH* III also differs from the other two works in including a second, separate argument against the 'means of learning' (269), based on the impossibility of 'apprehension' (*katalēpsis*; for this term, see Comm. on 180–3).

M XI. 243–56, *PH* III. 270–2

The *PH* passage is considerably briefer. As in *M* XI. 244, the four possibilities are initially presented (270); but in *PH* Sextus does not even bother to mention the reasons why the first three are to be ruled out, calling this 'superfluous' (*peritton*)—as indeed it is, since the equivalent three possibilities were discussed in the general argument at 259–65. Following this, the two texts are almost identical for some time. The analogy with people blind or deaf from birth is then omitted (it too was used in the general argument (264)); instead there is a reference back to the general argument against the means of learning (272). *M* XI's argument against the wise person's being able to 'perceive folly' is also completely absent; given the difficulties we observed in this argument (see Comm.), a good case can be made that the passage is better without it. One may well feel the same about the other omissions just noted; however, since *PH* in general is more concise than *M* VII–XI, one cannot infer on this basis alone that *PH* III is the revised version. However, the *PH* passage adds a concluding sentence (272) which neatly sums up the entire portion of the book dealing with the skill relating to life, and prepares the way for the transition to the next topic (on this additional section in *PH* III, see above on *M* XI. 210–15, *PH* III. 274–7; on the concluding sentence in *PH* III. 272, see also on *M* XI. 218, *M* I. 9, *PH* III. 252). *M* XI has nothing corresponding to this; 256 serves as a conclusion to the whole of this particular section, but there is no general conclusion to this part of the book. Here, I think, we do have evidence that *PH* III is the revised version (see Comm. on 257).

APPENDIX B:
On the 'Common Source or Sources' Employed by Sextus and Diogenes

It is plausible to suppose that Diogenes is drawing on a single source throughout DL IX. 90–101, which includes almost all the parallels with *M* VII–XI (on this, see Barnes 1992: 4269 n. 149). But this passage includes both the parallels with *M* XI (DL IX. 101 with *M* XI. 68–78, DL IX. 100 with *M* XI. 219–23); yet one of the *M* XI passages is in part A, and the other is in part B. So if, as I have suggested may well be the case, part A and part B derive from different sources, at most one of the *M* XI passages can be drawing on the same *immediate* source as the corresponding passages in DL. In at least one case DL and *M* XI must be drawing on two *different* texts which are themselves ultimately indebted to the same source; it will thus be only in an extended or indirect sense that Sextus and Diogenes can be said in this case to be following a 'common source'. This may be considered excessively complicated. But the kinds of parallels which actually exist between Sextus and Diogenes could perfectly well also have existed in a lost earlier generation of Pyrrhonist texts; and if some of these earlier texts did little more than rearrange previously written material, it would not be at all surprising that some argumentation and language should persist unchanged through two or more generations of sources.

In fact, this more complicated scenario should probably be invoked for *both* the parallels between *M* XI and DL. For the immediate source for DL IX. 90–101 appears to be some sort of concise summary of major Pyrrhonist arguments. But if part A and part B of *M* XI are each drawing on a single main source, these sources cannot be concise summaries, but must be extended discussions, of the same general character as the discussions Sextus produced with their use. And that part A and part B each have a single main source is itself probable. This is favoured by the continuity of the argument within each of the two parts; each part consists, with minor exceptions, of a single clear structure, within which every section has a clearly understandable function, and each appears to be homogeneous in its assumptions. (Compare e.g. *M* VII, where the long doxographical section (46–262) could easily have been taken from a source separate from that of the rest of the book; part A and part B of *M* XI contain few such detachable portions.) The combination of part A and part B forms a not particularly felicitous patchwork; but part A and part B individually do not look like patchworks at all. So if Sextus was drawing on a variety of sources throughout *M* XI, we would have to suppose *both* that he was highly accomplished (at this stage in his career) in smoothly uniting materials from different sources—the materials within each of the two parts—*and* very inept at doing so—in making the connection between the two parts. It seems more plausible to suppose that there are two, and only two, main sources for the book.

APPENDIX C:
The Views of Karel Janáček

As noted in the Introduction (sect. I), my conclusions about the order of composition of Sextus' works run counter to the standard view. It is usually thought that *PH* is the earliest of Sextus' works, followed by *M* VII–XI and then by *M* I–VI. Traditionally, this was because it was thought that *M* VII–XI contained numerous back-references to *PH*, just as *M* I–VI contains back-references to *M* VII–XI.[1] But this view was demolished by Janáček 1963, the paper which established that *M* VII–XI are incomplete; the back-references in *M* VII–XI are not to passages of *PH*, but to passages of the lost book or books which originally preceded *M* VII–XI. None the less, it is due largely to the influence of Janáček himself that the orthodoxy that *PH* is the earliest work continues to prevail.

Janáček is the author of a large number of minute studies of Sextus' style and vocabulary.[2] He has been convinced throughout his long career that *PH* preceded *M* VII–XI. At least from 1963 onwards, he has held that this standard picture of the order of composition is justified on stylistic grounds alone (Janáček 1963: 277).[3] However, his support for this view is surprisingly weak. He certainly succeeds in showing that there is a large number of stylistic *differences* between *PH* and *M* VII–XI; and he constantly asserts or presupposes that this is due to a development in Sextus' style between *PH* and *M* VII–XI. But there is precious little in the way of *argument* that the stylistic differences favour this chronology. To the extent that there is argument, it consists in claiming that the style of *M*

---

[1] See e.g. Brochard 1923: 318–19.

[2] A complete list of Janáček's writings on Sextus and Pyrrhonism may be found in the bibliography of Barnes 1992. By far the most comprehensive are Janáček 1948 and Janáček 1972.

[3] It does not seem to have been noticed that this is not true of Janáček's earlier writings. In Janáček 1948, his major early work in this area, he says at the outset that there is 'no reason to doubt the truth of *external evidence*, according to which the chronological order of Sextus' works is *PH*, *M* VII–XI, *M* I–VI' (8, my emphasis); he then proceeds to compare the style of the three works, but particularly *PH* and *M* VII–XI, on the basis of the unquestioned *assumption*, not itself based on stylistic considerations, that this is the order of composition. What is the 'external evidence' to which Janáček here refers? He offers no clue, and, in the usual sense of the term 'external evidence', there is none; the *only* evidence is that provided by the works themselves. If he is referring to the supposed cross-references between works, then this 'external evidence' is precisely what he himself demolishes in Janáček 1963; if not, the 'evidence' in question is simply illusory. The original basis for Janáček's chronological view is thus somewhat obscure. However, by 1963 his picture of Sextus' stylistic development has apparently acquired its own momentum, despite the dubiousness of its starting-point.

VII–XI is *better* than the style of *PH*.[4] But often, at least, this is highly disputable; Janáček's own evidence frequently does not have to be read in the way he suggests. For example, in a chapter examining Sextus' statements at the conclusions of arguments (Janáček 1948: ch. 10), it is shown that the concluding sentences of *M* VII–XI tend to be analysable into discrete segments, which together precisely recapitulate the preceding argument; those in *PH*, on the other hand, tend to bear a less exact relationship to the stages of the prior reasoning. Janáček describes *PH*'s concluding sentences as 'primitive', and those of *M* VII–XI as 'better' and as exhibiting 'the greatest perfection' (45–6). I, at least, have the opposite impression; *M* VII–XI's sentences seem more pedantic and repetitive, while *PH*'s seem no less adequate as concluding statements, but more relaxed and suggestive of an author more assured of his powers of argument and of communication. Again, Janáček points to the larger vocabulary employed in *M* VII–XI: e.g. *M* VII–XI uses the words *hōsautōs* ('in the same way') and *homoiōs* ('similarly'), whereas *PH* uses only *homoiōs*; this, he says, is a clear indication that *PH* is earlier (Janáček 1972: 10). There is no need to accept this. In ordinary English, 'similarly' and 'in the same way' are largely interchangeable, and the same is true of *hōsautōs* and *homoiōs* in Greek; in fact, the senses given in LSJ for these two words largely overlap. I am not aware of any loss in elegance or lucidity suffered by *PH* as a result of using only one of the two. The mere fact that *M* VII–XI uses two words where *PH* uses one does not show that *M* VII–XI is stylistically an improvement on, and therefore later than, *PH*.

Even if we were to agree, however, that the style of *M* VII–XI is better than that of *PH*, this still would not show that the standard chronology is correct, because of a point discussed earlier—which Janáček himself has done more than anyone else to bring to our attention. Sextus' works draw heavily on other authors, even to the extent of sometimes copying whole phrases or sentences. The earlier work, whichever it is, is therefore not genuinely representative of Sextus' *own* writing style at all; its style is at least partially the style of its

[4] The only possible exception that I can find is this. One of Janáček's articles (1959) suggests that *PH* shares several stylistic characteristics with DL, and that with respect to these features *M* VII–XI differs from both. In light of my remarks about the significance of parallels between Diogenes and Sextus (see Introduction, sect. IV), it might be concluded (though Janáček himself does not press the point in this article) that *PH* is closer to the common source or sources, and therefore earlier, than *M* VII–XI. However, the common ground cited between DL and *PH* is by no means distinctive enough to force us to this conclusion; this is clear from Barnes 1992: sect. 10, which reconsiders most of the types of evidence cited here by Janáček. Besides the cases examined by Barnes, Janáček mentions (56–7) a transitional phrase of a type which is common in *M* VII–XI ('it remains to say that . . . —which is also impossible'), but which is absent in parallel passages of DL and in *PH*. But this too proves nothing. DL and *PH* are both much more concise than *M* VII–XI; the common source might easily have contained such transitional phrases, and DL (or his immediate source) and *PH* might both have omitted them (they are generally unnecessary for comprehension of the argument, and in fact are often tediously redundant).

unknown source or sources. It is the later work, if any, which can be thought to show us Sextus' own style; here he revises his own earlier work and, whether or not he consulted his original sources again, presumably tended to a much greater extent to express matters in his own words rather than in those of the sources. The degree to which the language of at least some of Sextus' works is contaminated by the language of other authors thus makes any claims about developments in Sextus' own style quite untrustworthy. If Sextus' source on any given topic had a style which was in some respects better than his own, then it would be the earlier work, not the later one, which would in those respects be stylistically superior; so even if *M* VII–XI is stylistically superior—a point on which we are by no means bound to agree—it could just as well be the earlier work.[5]

Janáček's stylistic studies are of interest for many reasons. But they do not have the chronological consequences he claims for them, and it is time to stop citing him as an authority on the order of Sextus' works. There is thus no fundamental obstacle to the view for which I have argued throughout, that *M* XI is earlier than the ethical section of *PH* III.

[5] It might be objected that a precisely parallel objection could be raised against one of my main arguments. Suppose I am right that the ethical portion of *PH* III is superior to *M* XI in the clarity of its organization and the cogency of its arguments; why should that show that *PH* III is later, rather than that Sextus' source was a better expositor of philosophical argument than he was? But the two cases are not analogous. For it is reasonable to assume that Sextus was much more concerned and self-conscious about the nature and the force of his arguments than he was about the kinds of linguistic minutiae with which Janáček mostly deals. First, most philosophers are more concerned about this; second, Sextus never gives the impression of being a self-conscious stylist (in the way that, e.g., Plato obviously is), whereas he clearly is highly self-conscious about the marshalling of his arguments; and third, Sextus himself tells us that it is not the sceptic's business to worry about linguistic niceties (*PH* I. 207; cf. 191). So, if we agree to suppose that the style of *M* VII–XI is better than that of *PH*, and that Sextus would also have agreed if asked, it by no means follows that *M* VII–XI is later. Achieving the best possible style is simply not one of his priorities; even if his source's style was better than his own, he had no particular reason to hang on to as much of it as possible in his later work. By contrast, he has every reason, at every stage of his career, to make his exposition as cogent as possible. If the frequently much more clearly organized and cogently argued *PH* III had come first, he would have had every reason, however much or however little he owed this clarity and cogency to his source, to preserve them and, if possible, enhance them in his revised version—not to bungle them, as we would have to say he had done if *M* XI were the revised version. Unless he was very obtuse indeed, and learned nothing whatever from the writings which he used as his sources, we may fairly infer that the work which is much better argued is later than the one which is much less well argued.

BIBLIOGRAPHY

I. Editions and Translations of Against the Ethicists

BEKKER, I. (1842). *Sextus Empiricus* (Berlin).

BURY, R. (1936). *Sextus Empiricus*, vol. III. Greek text with facing English trans. (Cambridge, Mass., Loeb Classical Library).

FABRICIUS, A., and HERVETUS, G. (1840). *Sextus Empirici Opera Graece et Latine*, vol. II. Greek text with notes by Fabricius, Latin trans. Hervetus, rev. Fabricius (Leipzig). Originally published 1718. Latin trans. originally published 1569.

MUTSCHMANN, H. (1914). *Sexti Empirici Opera*, vol. II (Leipzig, Teubner).

RUSSO, A., rev. INDELLI, G. (1990). *Sesto Empirico Contro I Fisici, Contro I Moralisti.* Italian trans. with notes (Rome/Bari).

SPINELLI, E. (1995). *Contro Gli Etici.* Greek text (from Mutschmann), Italian trans., introduction, and commentary (Naples).

II. Editions and Translations of Other Ancient Sources

ANNAS, J., and BARNES, J. (1994). *Sextus Empiricus: Outlines of Scepticism* (Cambridge).

CAIZZI, F. DECLEVA (1981a). *Pirrone: Testimonianze* (Naples).

DEICHGRÄBER, K. (1965). *Die griechische Empirikerschule*, 2nd edn. (Berlin/Zürich). Originally published 1930.

DIELS, H. (1901). *Poetarum Philosophorum Fragmenta* (Berlin).

DIGGLE, J. (1994). *Euripidis Fabulae*, vol. III (Oxford).

DORANDI, T. (1982). 'Filodemo. Gli Stoici (PHerc. 155 e 339)', *Cronache Ercolanesi*, 12: 91–133.

FALCO, V. DE (1923). *L'epicureo Demetrio Lacone* (Naples).

FORTENBAUGH, W. (1984). *Quellen zur Ethik Theophrasts* (Amsterdam).

GAUTHIER, R., and JOLIF, J. (1958–9). *L'Ethique à Nicomaque: Introduction, Traduction et Commentaire*, 3 vols. (Louvain).

GIANNANTONI, G. (1990). *Socratis et Socraticorum Reliquiae*, 4 vols. (Naples).

HEINZE, R. (1892). *Xenokrates: Darstellung der Lehre und Sammlung der Fragmente* (Leipzig).

JANÁČEK, K. (1962). *Sexti Empirici Opera*, vol. IV—Indices (Leipzig, Teubner).

KOCK, T. (1888). *Comicorum Atticorum Fragmenta* (Leipzig).

This bibliography includes all the works cited in the Introduction and the Commentary except those given in the List of Abbreviations, and no others.

LASSERRE, F., and BONNARD, A. (1958). *Archiloque: Fragments* (Paris, Budé).

LLOYD-JONES, H., and PARSONS, P. (1983). *Supplementum Hellenisticum* (Berlin/New York).

MARCOVICH, M. (1986). *Hippolytus: Refutatio Omnium Haeresium, Patristische Texte und Studien* 25 (Berlin/New York).

MUTSCHMANN, H., rev. MAU, J. (1958). *Sexti Empirici Opera*, vol. I (Leipzig, Teubner). Mutschmann's edition originally published 1912.

NAUCK, A. (1889). *Tragicorum Graecorum Fragmenta*, 2nd edn. (Leipzig).

PAGE, D. (1962). *Poetae Melici Graeci* (Oxford).

STADEN, H. VON (1989). *Herophilus: The Art of Medicine in Early Alexandria* (Cambridge).

USENER, H. (1887). *Epicurea* (Leipzig).

WEHRLI, F. (1967–78). *Die Schule des Aristoteles: Texte und Kommentar*, 2nd edn., 10 vols. + 2 supplements (Basel/Stuttgart).

WEST, M. (1989). *Iambi et Elegi Graeci*, 2nd edn. (Oxford).

III. Secondary Literature

ALLEN, J. (1990). 'The Skepticism of Sextus Empiricus', *Aufstieg und Niedergang der Römischen Welt*, II.36.4: 2582–2607.

ANNAS, J. (1986). 'Doing without Objective Values: Ancient and Modern Strategies', in M. Schofield and G. Striker (eds.), *The Norms of Nature* (Cambridge), 3–29.

—— (1990a). 'The Hellenistic Version of Aristotle's Ethics', *Monist*, 73: 80–96.

—— (1990b). 'Stoic Epistemology', in S. Everson (ed.), *Companions to Ancient Thought 1: Epistemology* (Cambridge), 184–203.

—— (1992a). *Hellenistic Philosophy of Mind* (Berkeley/Los Angeles/London).

—— (1992b). 'Sextus Empiricus and the Peripatetics', *Elenchos*, 13: 203–31.

—— (1993). *The Morality of Happiness* (Oxford).

—— and BARNES, J. (1985). *The Modes of Scepticism* (Cambridge).

ATHERTON, C. (1993). *The Stoics on Ambiguity* (Cambridge).

AUSLAND, H. W. (1989). 'On the Moral Origin of the Pyrrhonian Philosophy', *Elenchos*, 10: 359–434.

BARNES, J. (1982a). 'The Beliefs of a Pyrrhonist', *Proceedings of the Cambridge Philological Society*, 208: 1–29.

—— (1982b). *The Presocratic Philosophers*, rev. edn. (London). Originally published 1979.

—— (1989). 'Antiochus of Ascalon', in M. Griffin and J. Barnes (eds.), *Philosophia Togata: Essays on Philosophy and Roman Society* (Oxford), 51–96.

—— (1990a). 'Pyrrhonism, Belief and Causation. Observations on the Scepticism of Sextus Empiricus', *Aufstieg und Niedergang der Römischen Welt*, II.36.4: 2608–95.

—— (1990*b*). 'Scepticism and Relativity', *Philosophical Studies* (Ireland), 32: 1–31.

—— (1990*c*). *The Toils of Scepticism* (Cambridge).

—— (1992). 'Diogenes Laertius IX 61–116: The Philosophy of Pyrrhonism', *Aufstieg und Niedergang der Römischen Welt*, II.36.6: 4241–4301.

BAXTER, T. (1992). *The Cratylus: Plato's Critique of Naming* (Leiden/New York).

BENSON, H. (1990). 'The Priority of Definition and the Socratic Elenchus', *Oxford Studies in Ancient Philosophy*, 8: 19–65.

BETT, R. (1989*a*). 'Carneades *Pithanon*: A Reappraisal of its Role and Status', *Oxford Studies in Ancient Philosophy*, 7: 59–94.

—— (1989*b*). 'The Sophists and Relativism', *Phronesis*, 34: 139–69.

—— (1990). 'Carneades' Distinction between Assent and Approval', *Monist*, 73: 3–20.

—— (1993). 'Scepticism and Everyday Attitudes in Ancient and Modern Philosophy', *Metaphilosophy*, 24: 363–81.

—— (1994*a*). 'Aristocles on Timon on Pyrrho: The Text, its Logic, and its Credibility', *Oxford Studies in Ancient Philosophy*, 12: 137–81.

—— (1994*b*). Review of Annas 1992*a*, *Ancient Philosophy*, 14: 192–200.

—— (1994*c*). 'Sextus' *Against the Ethicists*: Scepticism, Relativism or Both?', *Apeiron*, 27: 123–61.

—— (1994*d*). 'What did Pyrrho Think about "The Nature of the Divine and the Good"?', *Phronesis*, 39: 303–37.

BEVERSLUIS, J. (1987). 'Does Socrates Commit the Socratic Fallacy?', *American Philosophical Quarterly*, 24: 211–23.

BLANK, D. (1995). 'Philodemus on the Technicity of Rhetoric', in D. Obbink (ed.), *Philodemus and Poetry: Poetic Theory and Practice in Lucretius, Philodemus, and Horace* (New York/Oxford), 178–88.

BLOMQVIST, J. (1968). 'Textkritisches zu Sextus Empiricus', *Eranos*, 66: 73–100.

—— (1974). 'Die Skeptika des Sextus Empiricus', *Grazer Beiträge*, 2: 7–14.

BRENNAN, T. (1994). 'Criterion and Appearance in Sextus Empiricus: The Scope of Sceptical Doubt, the Status of Sceptical Belief', *Bulletin of the Institute of Classical Studies*, 39: 151–69.

BRINK, D. (1989). *Moral Realism and the Foundations of Ethics* (Cambridge).

BROCHARD, V. (1923). *Les Sceptiques grecs*, 2nd edn. (Paris). Originally published 1887.

BRUNSCHWIG, J. (1986). 'The Cradle Argument in Epicureanism and Stoicism', in M. Schofield and G. Striker (eds.), *The Norms of Nature* (Cambridge), 113–44.

—— (1988). 'Sextus Empiricus on the *kritērion*: The Skeptic as Conceptual Legatee', in J. M. Dillon and A. A. Long (eds.), *The Question of 'Eclecticism'—Studies in Later Greek Philosophy* (Berkeley/Los Angeles/London), 145–75.

—— (1992). 'Pyrrhon et Philista', in M.-O. Goulet-Cazé, G. Madec, and D. O'Brien (eds.), *'Chercheurs de Sagesse': Hommage à Jean Pépin* (Paris), 133–46.

BRUNSCHWIG, J. (1993). 'The Anaxarchus Case: An Essay on Survival', *Proceedings of the British Academy*, 82: 59–88.

—— (1994*a*). 'On a Stoic Way of Not Being', in *Papers in Hellenistic Philosophy*, trans. J. Lloyd (Cambridge), 158–69. Originally published as 'Sur une façon stoïcienne de ne pas être', *Revue de Théologie et de Philosophie*, 122 (1990): 389–403.

—— (1994*b*). 'The Stoic Theory of the Supreme Genus and Platonic Ontology', in *Papers in Hellenistic Philosophy*, trans. J. Lloyd (Cambridge), 92–157. Originally published as 'La Théorie stoïcienne du genre suprême et l'ontologie platonicienne', in J. Barnes and M. Mignucci (eds.), *Matter and Metaphysics, Fourth Symposium Hellenisticum* (Naples, 1988), 19–127.

—— (1994*c*). 'The Title of Timon's *Indalmoi*: From Odysseus to Pyrrho', in *Papers in Hellenistic Philosophy*, trans. J. Lloyd (Cambridge), 212–23. Originally published as 'Le Titre des "Indalmoi" de Timon: d'Ulysse à Pyrrhon', *Recherches sur la Philosophie et le Langage*, 12 (1990): 83–99.

BURNYEAT, M. (1980). 'Tranquillity without a Stop: Timon frag. 68', *Classical Quarterly*, 72 (NS 30): 86–93.

—— (1983). 'Can the Skeptic Live his Skepticism?', in M. Burnyeat (ed.), *The Skeptical Tradition* (Berkeley/Los Angeles/London), 117–48.

—— (1984). 'The Sceptic in his Place and Time', in R. Rorty, J. Schneewind, and Q. Skinner (eds.), *Philosophy in History* (Cambridge), 225–54.

CAIZZI, F. DECLEVA (1981*b*). 'Prolegomeni ad una raccolta delle fonti relative a Pirrone di Elide', in G. Giannantoni (ed.), *Lo Scetticismo Antico* (Naples), 93–128.

—— (1986). 'Pirroniani ed Accademici nel III Secolo A.C.', in *Aspects de la Philosophie Hellénistique*, Fondation Hardt vol. 32 (Geneva), 147–83.

—— (1992*a*). 'Aenesidemus and the Academy', *Classical Quarterly*, 42: 176–89.

—— (1992*b*). 'Sesto e gli Scettici', *Elenchos*, 13: 279–327.

—— (1993). 'L'Elogio del Cane. Sesto Empirico, *Schizzi Pirroniani* I.62–68', *Elenchos*, 14: 305–30.

CRIVELLI, P. (1994). 'The Stoic Analysis of Tense and of Plural Propositions in Sextus Empiricus, *Adversus Mathematicos* X 99', *Classical Quarterly*, 44: 490–9.

DEFILIPPO, J., and MITSIS, P. (1994). 'Socrates and Stoic Natural Law', in P. Vander Waerdt (ed.), *The Socratic Movement* (Ithaca, NY/London), 252–71.

DENNISTON, J. (1954). *The Greek Particles*, 2nd edn. (Oxford).

DIGGLE, J. (1983). 'A New Verse of Timon of Phlius?', *Liverpool Classical Monthly*, 8: 143.

DILLON, J. (1977). *Middle Platonism* (London).

DORANDI, T. (1991). *Ricerche sulla cronologia dei filosofi ellenistici* (Stuttgart).

DÖRRIE, H. (1967). 'Xenocrates 4)', in *Paulys Realencyclopädie der Classischen Altertumswissenschaft* (Stuttgart), IXA2: 1512–28.

DOVER, K. (1974). *Greek Popular Morality in the Time of Plato and Aristotle* (Oxford/Berkeley).

—— (1978). *Greek Homosexuality* (London).

EBERT, T. (1987). 'The Origin of the Stoic Theory of Signs in Sextus Empiricus', *Oxford Studies in Ancient Philosophy*, 5: 83–126.

—— (1991). *Dialektiker und frühe Stoiker bei Sextus Empiricus: Untersuchungen zur Entstehung der Aussagenlogik, Hypomnemata*, 95 (Göttingen).

FERRARI, G. A. (1981). 'L'immagine dell'equilibrio', in G. Giannantoni (ed.), *Lo Scetticismo Antico* (Naples), 337–70.

FINE, G. (1993). *On Ideas: Aristotle's Criticism of Plato's Theory of Forms* (Oxford).

FLÜCKIGER, H. (1994). 'Der Weg zum Glück in der pyrrhonischen Skepsis und im griechischen Roman: Die Beobachtung des *bios* gegen die Erkenntnis der Philosophen', *Museum Helveticum*, 51: 198–205.

FREDE, M. (1983*a*). 'The Method of the So-Called Methodical School of Medicine', in J. Barnes, J. Brunschwig, M. Burnyeat, and M. Schofield (eds.), *Science and Speculation: Studies in Hellenistic Theory and Practice* (Cambridge), 1–23. Reprinted in M. Frede, *Essays in Ancient Philosophy* (Minneapolis, 1987), 261–78.

—— (1983*b*). 'Stoics and Skeptics on Clear and Distinct Impressions', in M. Burnyeat (ed.), *The Skeptical Tradition* (Berkeley/Los Angeles/London), 65–93. Reprinted in M. Frede, *Essays in Ancient Philosophy* (Minneapolis, 1987), 151–76.

—— (1984). 'The Skeptic's Two Kinds of Assent and the Question of the Possibility of Knowledge', in R. Rorty, J. Schneewind, and Q. Skinner (eds.), *Philosophy in History* (Cambridge), 255–78. Reprinted in M. Frede, *Essays in Ancient Philosophy* (Minneapolis, 1987), 201–22.

—— (1987*a*). 'The Ancient Empiricists', in *Essays in Ancient Philosophy* (Minneapolis), 243–60.

—— (1987*b*). 'The Skeptic's Beliefs', in *Essays in Ancient Philosophy* (Minneapolis), 179–200. Originally published as 'Des Skeptikers Meinungen', *Neue Hefte für Philosophie*, 15/16 (1979): 102–29.

—— (1994*a*). 'The Stoic Notion of a Grammatical Case', *Bulletin of the Institute of Classical Studies*, 39: 13–24.

—— (1994*b*). 'The Stoic Notion of a *Lekton*', in S. Everson (ed.), *Companions to Ancient Thought 3: Language* (Cambridge), 109–28.

FURLEY, D. (1967). *Two Studies in the Greek Atomists* (Princeton).

GIGANTE, M. (1981). *Scetticismo e Epicureismo* (Naples).

GLIDDEN, D. (1994). 'Parrots, Pyrrhonists and Native Speakers', in S. Everson (ed.), *Companions to Ancient Thought 3: Language* (Cambridge), 129–48.

GLUCKER, J. (1978). *Antiochus and the Late Academy, Hypomnemata*, 56 (Göttingen).

GOSLING, J., and TAYLOR, C. (1982). *The Greeks on Pleasure* (Oxford).

HAHM, D. (1992). 'Diogenes Laertius VII: On the Stoics', *Aufstieg und Niedergang der Römischen Welt*, II.36.6: 4076–4182.

HANKINSON, R. J. (1994). 'Values, Objectivity, and Dialectic; The Sceptical Attack on Ethics: Its Methods, Aims, and Success', *Phronesis*, 39: 45–68.

HEINTZ, W., ed. HARDER, R. (1932). *Studien zu Sextus Empiricus* (Halle).

HOUSE, D. (1980). 'The Life of Sextus Empiricus', *Classical Quarterly*, 30: 227–38.

INWOOD, B. (1985). *Ethics and Human Action in Early Stoicism* (Oxford).

—— (1992). Review of Schofield 1991, *Bryn Mawr Classical Review*, 3: 208–13.

IOPPOLO, A.-M. (1980). *Aristone di Chio e lo Stoicismo antico* (Naples).

IRWIN, T. (1981). 'Homonymy in Aristotle', *Review of Metaphysics*, 34: 523–44.

—— (1986). 'Stoic and Aristotelian Conceptions of Happiness', in M. Schofield and G. Striker (eds.), *The Norms of Nature* (Cambridge), 205–44.

ISNARDI PARENTE, M. (1966). *Techne: Momenti del pensiero greco da Platone ad Epicuro* (Florence).

JANÁČEK, K. (1948). *Prolegomena to Sextus Empiricus* (Olomouc).

—— (1959). 'Diogenes Laertius and Sextus Empiricus', *Eunomia*, 3 (= *Listy Filologické*, 82 suppl.): 50–8.

—— (1961). 'Diogenes Laertius IX 101 und Sextus Empiricus M XI 69–75 (–78)', in F. Steibitz and R. Hošek (eds.), *Charisteria F. Novotny Octogenario Oblata*, Opera Universitatis Purkynianae Brunensis (Facultas Philosophica), vol. 90 (Prague), 143–6.

—— (1963). 'Die Hauptschrift des Sextus Empiricus als Torso erhalten?', *Philologus*, 107: 271–7.

—— (1964). 'Eine anonyme Schrift gegen die Astrologen', *Helikon*, 4: 290–6.

—— (1972). *Sextus Empiricus' Sceptical Methods* (Prague).

—— (1976). 'Zur Interpretation des Photius-Abschnittes über Aenesidemos', *Eirene*, 14: 93–100.

KIRK, G., RAVEN, J., and SCHOFIELD, M. (1983). *The Presocratic Philosophers*, 2nd edn. (Cambridge). Originally published 1957.

LÉVY, C. (1992). *Cicero Academicus: Recherches sur les Académiques et sur la Philosophie Cicéronienne* (Rome).

LONG, A. (1971). 'Language and Thought in Stoicism', in A. Long (ed.), *Problems in Stoicism* (London), 75–113.

—— (1976). 'The Early Stoic Concept of Moral Choice', in *Images of Man in Ancient and Medieval Thought: Studies Presented to G. Verbeke* (Louvain), 77–92.

—— (1978a). 'Sextus Empiricus on the Criterion of Truth', *Bulletin of the Institute of Classical Studies*, 25: 25–49.

—— (1978b). 'The Stoic Distinction between Truth and the True', in J. Brunschwig (ed.), *Les Stoïciens et leur logique* (Paris), 297–316.

—— (1978c). 'Timon of Phlius: Pyrrhonist and Satirist', *Proceedings of the Cambridge Philological Society*, NS 24: 68–91.

—— (1982). 'Soul and Body in Stoicism', *Phronesis*, 27: 34–57.

—— (1988). 'Socrates in Hellenistic Philosophy', *Classical Quarterly*, 38: 150–71.

MACDONALD, S. (1989). 'Aristotle and the Homonymy of the Good', *Archiv für Geschichte der Philosophie*, 71: 150–74.

MCKIRAHAN, V. TSOUNA (1994). 'The Socratic Origins of the Cynics and the

Cyrenaics', in P. Vander Waerdt (ed.), *The Socratic Movement* (Ithaca, NY/ London), 367–91.

MCPHERRAN, M. (1987). 'Skeptical Homeopathy and Self-Refutation', *Phronesis*, 32: 290–328.

—— (1989). '*Ataraxia* and *Eudaimonia* in Ancient Pyrrhonism: Is the Skeptic Really Happy?', *Proceedings of the Boston Area Colloquium in Ancient Philosophy*, 5: 135–71.

—— (1990). 'Pyrrhonism's Arguments Against Value', *Philosophical Studies*, 60: 127–42.

MAJNO, G. (1991). *The Healing Hand: Man and Wound in the Ancient World* (Cambridge, Mass.). Originally published 1975.

MANSFELD, J. (1986). 'Diogenes Laertius on Stoic Philosophy', *Elenchos*, 7: 295–382.

—— (1989). 'Stoic Definitions of the Good (Diog. Laert. VII 94)', *Mnemosyne*, 42: 487–91.

MARTINI (1901). 'Demetrios 87', *Paulys Realencyclopädie der Classischen Altertumswissenschaft* (Stuttgart), IV: 2841–2.

MATES, B. (1953). *Stoic Logic*, University of California Publications in Philosophy 26. Reprinted 1961 (Berkeley/Los Angeles).

MIGNUCCI, M. (1988). 'The Stoic Notion of Relatives', in J. Barnes and M. Mignucci (eds.), *Matter and Metaphysics* (Naples), 131–217.

MITSIS, P. (1993). 'Seneca on Reason, Rules and Moral Development', in J. Brunschwig and M. Nussbaum (eds.), *Passions and Perceptions: Studies in Hellenistic Philosophy of Mind* (Cambridge), 285–312.

MORAUX, P. (1973). *Der Aristotelismus bei den Griechen*, vol. I (Berlin/New York).

MORRISON, D. (1990). 'The Ancient Sceptic's Way of Life', *Metaphilosophy*, 21: 204–22.

MUELLER, I. (1982). 'Geometry and Scepticism', in J. Barnes, J. Brunschwig, M. Burnyeat, and M. Schofield (eds.), *Science and Speculation: Studies in Hellenistic Theory and Practice* (Cambridge), 69–95.

NEHAMAS, A. (1985). 'Meno's Paradox and Socrates as a Teacher', *Oxford Studies in Ancient Philosophy*, 3: 1–30.

NUSSBAUM, M. (1994). *The Therapy of Desire* (Princeton).

OWEN, G. (1957). 'A Proof in the *Peri Ideōn*', *Journal of Hellenic Studies*, 77: 103–11. Reprinted in G. Owen, *Logic, Science and Dialectic: Collected Papers in Greek Philosophy*, ed. M. Nussbaum (Ithaca, NY, 1986), 165–79.

PAPPENHEIM, E. (1881). *Erläuterungen zu des Sextus Empiricus Pyrrhoneischen Grundzügen* (Leipzig).

POHLENZ, M. (1972). *Die Stoa: Geschichte einer geistigen Bewegung*, 4th edn. (Göttingen).

POPKIN, R. (1979). *The History of Scepticism from Erasmus to Spinoza*, 3rd edn. (Berkeley/Los Angeles/London).

Porro, P. (1994). 'Il *Sextus Latinus* e l'immagine dello scetticismo antico nel medioevo', *Elenchos*, 15: 229–53.

Reale, G. (1981). 'Ipotesi per una rilettura della filosofia di Pirrone di Elide', in G. Giannantoni (ed.), *Lo Scetticismo Antico* (Naples), 243–336.

Reesor, M. (1983). 'On the Stoic Goods in Stobaeus, *Eclogae* 2', in W. Fortenbaugh (ed.), *On Stoic and Peripatetic Ethics: The Work of Arius Didymus*, Rutgers University Studies in Classical Humanities, 1 (New Brunswick, NJ), 75–84.

Rist, J. (1969). *Stoic Philosophy* (Cambridge).

Sandbach, F. (1971). 'Ennoia and Prolēpsis in the Stoic Theory of Knowledge', in A. Long (ed.), *Problems in Stoicism* (London), 22–37.

Schmidt, E. (1970). 'Archedemos 5) & 6)', in *Paulys Realencyclopädie der Classischen Altertumswissenschaft* (Stuttgart), suppl. vol. XII: 1356–92.

Schmitt, C. (1983). 'The Rediscovery of Ancient Skepticism', in M. Burnyeat (ed.), *The Skeptical Tradition* (Berkeley/Los Angeles/London), 225–51.

Schofield, M. (1980). 'Preconception, Argument and God', in M. Schofield, M. Burnyeat, and J. Barnes (eds.), *Doubt and Dogmatism: Studies in Hellenistic Epistemology* (Oxford), 283–308.

—— (1984). 'Ariston of Chios and the Unity of Virtue', *Ancient Philosophy*, 4: 83–96.

—— (1991). *The Stoic Idea of the City* (Cambridge).

Sedley, D. (1973). 'Epicurus, *On Nature* book XXVIII', *Cronache Ercolanesi*, 3: 5–83.

—— (1983). 'The Motivation of Greek Skepticism', in M. Burnyeat (ed.), *The Skeptical Tradition* (Berkeley/Los Angeles/London), 9–29.

Stopper, M. R. (1983). 'Schizzi Pirroniani', *Phronesis*, 28: 265–97.

Striker, G. (1974). '*Kritērion tēs alētheias*', *Nachrichten der Akademie der Wissenschaften in Göttingen*, Phil.-hist. Kl., no. 2: 51–110.

—— (1983). 'The Ten Tropes of Aenesidemus', in M. Burnyeat (ed.), *The Skeptical Tradition* (Berkeley/Los Angeles/London), 95–115.

—— (1990a). '*Ataraxia*: Happiness as Tranquillity', *Monist*, 73: 97–110.

—— (1990b). 'The Problem of the Criterion', in S. Everson (ed.), *Companions to Ancient Thought 1: Epistemology* (Cambridge), 143–60.

—— (1991). 'Following Nature: A Study in Stoic Ethics', *Oxford Studies in Ancient Philosophy*, 9: 1–73.

—— (1994). 'Plato's Socrates and the Stoics', in P. Vander Waerdt (ed.), *The Socratic Movement* (Ithaca, NY/London), 241–51.

Tarrant, H. (1994). 'The *Hippias Major* and Socratic Theories of Pleasure', in P. Vander Waerdt (ed.), *The Socratic Movement* (Ithaca, NY/London), 107–26.

Todd, R. (1973a). 'Chrysippus on Infinite Divisibility (Diogenes Laertius VII.150)', *Apeiron*, 7: 21–9.

—— (1973b). 'The Stoic Common Notions: A Reexamination and Reinterpretation', *Symbolae Osloenses*, 48: 47–75.

TSEKOURAKIS, D. (1974). *Studies in the Terminology of Early Stoic Ethics*, Hermes Einzelschriften 32 (Wiesbaden).

VANDER WAERDT, P. (1994). 'Zeno's *Republic* and the Origins of Natural Law', in P. Vander Waerdt (ed.), *The Socratic Movement* (Ithaca, NY/London), 272–308.

VLASTOS, G. (1990). 'Is the "Socratic Fallacy" Socratic?', *Ancient Philosophy*, 10: 1–16.

VOELKE, A.-J. (1990). 'Soigner par le Logos: La Thérapeutique de Sextus Empiricus', in A.-J. Voelke (ed.), *Le Scepticisme antique: perspectives historiques et systématiques*, Cahiers de la Revue de Théologie et de Philosophie, 15: 181–94. Reprinted in A.-J. Voelke, *La Philosophie comme thérapie de l'âme* (Fribourg/Paris, 1993), 106–26.

WILAMOWITZ-MOELLENDORFF, U. VON (1886). *Isyllos von Epidauros, Philologische Untersuchungen*, ed. A. Kiessling and U. von Wilamowitz-Moellendorff, vol. 9 (Berlin).

WILLIAMS, B. (1985). *Ethics and the Limits of Philosophy* (Cambridge, Mass.).

WOODRUFF, P. (1988). 'Aporetic Pyrrhonism', *Oxford Studies in Ancient Philosophy*, 6: 139–68.

INDEX NOMINUM

INDEX LOCORUM

Long and Sedley (LS)
Note: The list below contains those citations of LS which refer partly or wholly to ancient texts; citations of LS which refer purely to Long and Sedley's commentary are listed in the Index of Names, under both 'Long' and 'Sedley'.

SUBJECT INDEX